MW01244196

BILLY THE KID'S

PRETENDERS

BRUSHY BILL
AND
JOHN MILLER

BY
GALE COOPER

GELCOUR
BOOKS

SECOND PRINTING: 2012

ISBN: 978-0-9845054-0-1
LIBRARY OF CONGRESS CONTROL NUMBER: 2010902741

GELCOUR BOOKS
13170 Central Avenue SE # 289
Albuquerque, NM 87123-5588

ORDERING
Amazon.com, BarnesandNoble.com, bookstores

**OTHER BILLY THE KID BOOKS
BY AUTHOR:**

JOY OF THE BIRDS: A NOVEL
*MEGAHOAX: THE STRANGE PLOT TO EXHUME BILLY THE KID
AND BECOME PRESIDENT*
BILLY THE KID'S WRITINGS, WORDS, AND WIT

Printed in the United States of America

This book is printed on acid-free paper.

For William H. Bonney,
the real Billy the Kid

"Acting is a nice childish profession - pretending you're someone else and, at the same time, selling yourself."

Katharine Hepburn (actress; 1907-2003)

"If you are a dreamer, a wisher, a liar, a hoper, a prayer, a magic-bean buyer; if you are a pretender, come sit by my fire, for we have some flax-golden tales to spin. Come in! Come in!

Shel Silverstein (writer/poet; 1930-1999)

"A clown's make-up and character, that's all he has to sell. He loves and believes in that character."

Emmett Kelly (professional clown; 1898-1979)

CONTENTS

DEBUNKING OLIVER "BRUSHY BILL" ROBERTS

DEBUNKING JOHN MILLER

DRAWING CONCLUSIONS

APPENDIX

SOURCES

FORWARD

Howdy. I'm putting in my two cents for this here author, cause she's gotten in the habit of starting her Billy the Kid books with my two cents. Not that I'm not clumsy with words as a foundered stud struggling to do his duty.

But with me being a fictional character - the old-timer who started out in her novel about Billy called *Joy of the Birds* - I got plenty of leeway for saying what I choose, cause I ain't in no position where nobody can touch me; if you get my drift.

So here's my two cents about this here book: meaning my two cents about those varmints who pretended to be Billy, years after lawman, Pat Garrett, sent him to the eternal range. They was just airing their lungs. And them that believes their hogwash, could as likely listen to a pack mule.

You see, my family knew Billy. And he was as different from those old liars as a silver dollar to a plugged nickel. Those fellers weren't fit to shoot at, for unloading your gun. And them that writ their gabbing into books, you'd be a fool to sleep aside them ifen you snore open-mouthed and got gold teeth.

Well, Missy, the author here, took on them fakers, showing that the closest those clowns got to Billy was eyeing his tintype. I say: it was about time somebody called their bluff.

One more thing: Missy'd already done a book on a passel of modern varmints trying to hijack Billy's history by digging him up so's to get on TV. So she threw in pieces of that book here, cause those new varmints was using the yarns of those old varmints for their jawing against the truth.

Here's the point. Nobody matches up with real Billy Bonney aka Billy the Kid. And when it comes to messing with him, Missy'd fight a rattler, and give him the first bite. So she was bound to give his imposters and hoaxers a rough ride.

Vern Blanton Johnson, Jr.
Lincoln, Lincoln County,
New Mexico
February, 2012

PREFACE

Billy the Kid's Pretenders is, in part, excerpted from my book: *MegaHoax: The Strange Plot to Exhume Billy the Kid and Become President.* The latter is an exposé of a Billy the Kid hoax, starting in 2003 and still ongoing, and known as the Lincoln County Billy the Kid Case.

Arguably the most elaborate historic-forensic hoax ever perpetrated, its fabricated, publicity-grabbing contention was that Sheriff Pat Garrett had not killed Billy the Kid; but was a conniving murderer of an innocent victim to permit Billy's escape.

That modern Billy the Kid Case hoax drew on pretender hoaxes of the mid-1900's. A given for those old-timers alleging to be Billy was that they (as him) had survived Pat Garrett's historically famous shooting on July 14, 1881. The best known pretenders, because they acquired authors, were Oliver "Brushy Bill" Roberts and John Miller.

Invading the graves of these two pretenders became an intrinsic part of the modern Billy the Kid Case hoax; with the purported purpose of forensically determining whether they were truly Billy. (The modern hoaxers blithely ignored and concealed that they lacked true DNA of Billy the Kid for identity determination of anyone.)

Part of my hoaxbusting for *MegaHoax* necessitated debunking those old time pretenders, Oliver "Brushy Bill" Roberts and John Miller, since their own tall-tales alone removed need for "identity determining" exhumations - as well as any reason to take them seriously.

Worse for the modern hoaxers, the death scene/survival concoctions of "Brushy Bill" Roberts and John Miller were completely different from their own death scene/survival concoctions - also removing the need to exhume those pretenders.

Nevertheless, the pretenders are interesting characters in their own right. Though not the real Billy Bonney aka Billy the Kid, their lives bridged the period from actual frontier days to mythologized Old West legends.

In a sense, by identifying with Billy, the most iconic figure of that period, the imposters paid eccentric homage to his fame.

But since that reflected glory is underserved by them, and since "Brushy Bill," at least, still has conspiracy theory true-believers, the pretenders merit a disconnect from real Billy's coattails. That is the purpose of this book.

This book also resulted from my earlier docufiction novel on Billy Bonney titled *Joy of the Birds*. Ten years in the writing, utilizing 40,000 pages of archival documents and books, it is my dramatizing of the unsung, lost, multi-cultural, freedom fight of the Lincoln County War; in which Billy was both a participant and a precipitant in that inspiring and tragic rebellion against the corrupt political machine known as the Santa Fe Ring. Against that political backdrop is Billy Bonney's true and star-crossed romance with young Paulita Maxwell, one of the richest heiresses in New Mexico Territory.

My later non-fiction book, *Billy the Kid's Writings, Words, and Wit*, further sealed proof of Billy Bonney's brilliance, literacy, and brave rebellion.

So the magnificence of Billy's history, really lived, and my admiration for him, inspired my zeal in opposing the modern Billy the Kid Case hoaxers and the past pretenders - all so lackluster in comparison to actual Billy's identity and life path. My goal is reclaiming and protecting that real history for our day and for future generations.

Gale Cooper
Sandia Park, New Mexico
February, 2012

INTRODUCTION

PRETENDER PREREQUISITES

In the real world, Sheriff Pat Garrett fatally shot William Bonney aka Billy the Kid on July 14, 1881.

In the imaginary world of Billy the Kid pretenders and modern Billy the Kid history hoaxers, Pat Garrett did not; and Billy the Kid survived to old age.

Those old-timer pretenders claimed (obviously) not to have been shot on that dangerous night; and that Sheriff Pat Garrett killed an innocent victim as Billy's grave filler.

Modern hoaxers added poison icing to that pretender cake: that Pat Garrett, before purposefully murdering that innocent victim, was the Kid's accomplice in his jailbreak killing of his two deputy guards!

That means, from the get-go, buying into pretender and hoaxer tales makes world-famous lawman Pat Garrett a world-class criminal; who garnered fame, but deserved infamy.

Other antique pretender and modern hoaxer prerequisites followed from their concoctions. The historically certain killing of Billy the Kid - as certain and as verified by direct and profuse witnesses as was President Abraham Lincoln's assassination - had to be ignored. New non-historical stories had to be invented for the new non-historical death scenes. And the old-time imposters and modern hoaxers needed motivation for their effort. Madness, money, and media circuses sufficed.

But nothing that procession of players could do could conceal from scrutiny that they were nothing but clowns.

DECIDING IF YOU ARE VERY FAMOUS

Certainty about your being very famous sometimes comes only after your death. If you are in the highest echelon of celebrity - a person garnering universal fascination - you may not "really die." Unfortunately, this does not benefit your corpse.

But it will benefit your fans, who disliked reality's chosen end for you. So becoming one of the living dead is a good measure of fame.

You join, for example, King Arthur, still elusively roaming England's hills; and post death-day appearances by Elvis Presley, Princess Diana, and Adolph Hitler (infamy having its own potency).

A drawback to this immortality is that you may not like it, since it means that your dying - a big step taken by you - was not taken seriously. But having attained that glorious stage, you are irrelevant. You have transcended into pure fame.

You also - for better or for worse - become the founder of a secondary industry: pretenders - people who step forward to be you and to bask in your glory. You - as them - can also bask in the adulation of a strange, starry-eyed, and squishy-minded audience of conspiracy theorists.

Not only will conspiracy theorists believe you survived death; but they will have reality-defying explanations of just how you did it, and why those who know you died - no matter their numbers - made that up.

This death-defying opportunity also gives pretenders - who might otherwise be insultingly considered insane - a measure of self-esteem, and a way of spending their otherwise inane lives as someone famous.

One pretender example arose from assassination of Russia's last Tsar, Nicholas II, killed with his wife, daughters, and son, by Bolsheviks, in Ekaterinburg, on July 17, 1918. Nevertheless, the Tsar's lovely, bullet-riddled, youngest daughter, Grand Duchess Anastasia, got the chance to wander for a borrowed lifetime as "Anna Anderson." And, despite eventual DNA evidence to the contrary, and being identified as a mentally disturbed, Polish factory worker named

Franziska Schanzkowska, "Anna" - having joined actual Anastasia in the great beyond in 1984 - still has loyal believers.

So, with the dark and bizarre humor of past "Saturday Night Live" writer and member, Jack Handy, one can capture the creepy irony of these crazy clowning pretenders and hoaxers by his quote: "To me clowns aren't funny. In fact, they're kind of scary. I've wondered where this started and I think it does back to the circus, and a clown killed my dad."

BILLY THE KID TAKES THE CAKE

William Henry Bonney or Billy Bonney, with an aka of Billy the Kid - and with earlier last names of McCarty and Antrim - takes the cake with profiteering pretenders seeking to "kill" his history. He died on July 14, 1881, compliments of a bullet in his heart provided by New Mexico Territory's Lincoln County Sheriff Pat Garrett.

Billy, only 21 at the time, and, by the next day, six feet under in Fort Sumner, nevertheless had the opportunity to "live on" for about 70 more years, as several old men who said they were him; and were unperturbed by joining a crowd of like claimants. And modern hoaxers tried to resurrect them.

The two luckiest of these imposters got authors to spread their word beyond their bemused families and bamboozled neighbors. They are Oliver "Brushy Bill" Roberts and John Miller. The former got the most mileage; even being featured in the 1990 movie, "Young Guns II," as the "real" Billy the Kid.

But John Miller, one could say, beat "Brushy Bill" by actually getting exhumed as "Billy the Kid," on May 19, 2005, as part of a Billy the Kid hoax so big, that both old pretenders were just segments of a planned frenzy of made-for-TV disinterments - though "Brushy" was its intended punch line.

Starting in 2003, and continuing to this day, that hoax was named, by its promulgators, the "Billy the Kid Case;" and was conducted as a real, New Mexico, sheriff's department, murder investigation against dead Pat Garrett. So it got the special distinction of having taxpayers pay for being tricked.

Tossing Off Billy's Coattail Riders

Given the longevity and preposterousness of the scams of Oliver "Brushy Bill" Roberts, John Miller, and the Billy the Kid Case hoaxers, the true Billy the Kid deserves their debunking.

Billy also deserves their disconnect from his actual grand and still unsung history: a history of his role in the Lincoln County War freedom fight, and his Romeo and Juliet-style star-crossed romance with young New Mexico Territory heiress, Paulita Maxwell - all unknown to the old imposters, and ignored by the modern hoaxers.

And, for Old West lawman fanciers, that debunking removes the unnecessary cloud of doubt which the pretenders and the Billy the Kid Case hoaxers placed over Sheriff Pat Garrett.

So, at stake in the debunking, is famous and iconic Old West history; and a good laugh at its coat-tail riders, who got taken too seriously for too long by too many.

As Stephen Sondheim, the creator of 1973's musical "A Little Night Music," said in a 2008 interview about his lyrics for "Send in the Clowns": "The song could have been called 'Send in the Fools" ... Well, a synonym for fools is clowns."

So here come the clowns.

Real

Billy Bonney

History_____

Billy the Kid, the Lincoln County War, and the Rest of that History

HOAXBUST: One needs to know real history of Billy Bonney to debunk his pretenders and the Billy the Kid Case hoaxers, who used those pretenders as fodder for their own fake claims. And, when reading that real history, one should not forget the obvious: real Billy would have known it!

BILLY THE KID'S BIG PROBLEMS

Billy the Kid's biggest problem was that he had no luck (unless you consider becoming internationally famous after being murdered at 21 as lucky). First (not counting his hard childhood), Billy's side (the good guys) in the 1878 the Lincoln County War lost the fight. So the victors, the land-grabbing, corrupt, Santa Fe Ring, political machine (the bad guys), wrote their own version (false) of the original history.

Their lying version nastily portrayed Billy as a maniacal killer-rustler-counterfeiter, who was short with little hands.

Next, Billy was promised a pardon for war-time killings by the Territory's governor; and that fellow reneged. So Billy got sentenced to hang for a murder he probably did not commit.

Then Billy escaped jail before that hanging, but decided to hide out in a town where he thought everyone was his friend. He was wrong. His sweetheart's rich brother set up his ambush by Pat Garrett right there in the family mansion. It succeeded.

Billy's second biggest problem was that the details of his actual history are known. That part was good. The bad part was that, by the time legitimate historians sorted it out, Billy's false history had gotten a foothold. Worse, and strangely, the public absorbed practically none of that history's details, true or false. So it was unclear why Billy was even famous.

But generalized ignorance, plus high name-recognition, was the perfect set-up for Billy's next piece of ill luck: spawning of decrepit pretenders, a half-century after his death. That was unlucky, not just because they were not him, but because they were an embarrassing caricature of the old Santa Fe Ring propaganda slamming him.

Then things got worse. Mercenary law enforcement hoaxers in 21st century New Mexico - over a half century after Billy's discredited imposters were maggot meat - decided to cash in on his fame by fabricating their own version of his history with a fabricated "CSI forensic murder investigation," called by them the "Billy the Kid Case." But it really relied on pretender assertions of Pat Garrett's not having killed Billy.

In fact, the only New Mexico, historical farce that Billy Bonney has, so far, avoided, is being linked up with the crash-landing of space aliens in Roswell.

BILLY THE KID'S REAL HISTORY

Ground zero for debunking the historical fakers, is Billy Bonney's real history. It is complex, colorful, traumatic, and amazing that he fit so much in his 21 years. Most of it was unknown to Billy's pretenders. All of it was a problem to the modern Billy the Kid Case hoaxers.

This is what actually happened in the life and death of William Henry McCarty Antrim Bonney aka Kid and Billy the Kid.

******

In heat of a New Mexico Territory full-mooned night as bright as day, the 21 year old, homeless youth, Billy Bonney, in trusting stockinged feet, approached the Fort Sumner white-porticoed mansion of the Maxwell family, at about a quarter to mid-night.

That day, July 14, 1881, was the third anniversary of the Lincoln County War's start, which had ultimately left him the most hunted outlaw in the country; though, to himself, he was a soldier: the last of the Regulators; and the only War participant, out of 200, to be tried and sentenced.

Only his enemies called him Billy the Kid.

Now, that July night, Billy planned to cut a dinner steak from the side of beef hanging on the mansion's north porch; but first to stop at its south porch, at its south-east corner bedroom, to check with the town's owner, Peter Maxwell.

Asleep in that mansion was Billy's secret lover, Maxwell's sister, Paulita, seventeen, and just pregnant with his child.

In the mansion also was a never-emancipated Navajo slave, Deluvina, purchased, as a child, by Peter's and Paulita's fabulously wealthy, deceased father, Lucien Bonaparte Maxwell, when the family still lived in Cimarron, one of the towns Lucien built on his almost two million acre land grant, encompassing northern New Mexico Territory, and southern Colorado; and known as the Maxwell Land Grant.

That was before Lucien Maxwell had been cheated out of it by Santa Fe law partners, Thomas Benton Catron and Stephen Benton Elkins, founders of the Santa Fe Ring.

As Billy was aware when he walked to death, that corrupt collusion of politicians, attorneys, law enforcement officers, and big money still had a stranglehold on New Mexico Territory. The failed Lincoln County War of 1878 had been a grass roots fight against that Santa Fe Ring; as had been the Colfax County War, a year before, in the northern part of the Territory. Even Grant County, to the west, had threatened secession from the Territory in 1876, to escape Ring clutches.

Billy also knew that a month had passed since his scheduled hanging date of May 13th; evaded by his jail break on April 28th. Pursuit was inevitable by Lincoln County Sheriff Pat Garrett, who had captured him on December 22, 1880, at Stinking Springs, for his hanging trial; and whose Lincoln jail Billy had escaped after killing his two deputies - and who would shoot him on sight.

When first tracking him, Pat Garrett had even killed Billy's closest friends, Tom O'Folliard and Charlie Bowdre - missing Billy only by chance.

To be near Paulita Maxwell, Billy had made this reckless choice to return to Fort Sumner, instead of fleeing to Mexico. But he was confident of Paulita's family's protection; as well as of the townspeople's - known by him since late 1877.

Billy was a second son, born illegitimately in New York City as William Henry McCarty, on November 23, 1859. Raised in Indianapolis, he became "Henry Antrim" after his mother's New Mexico Territory marriage to William Henry Harrison Antrim in 1873. The family, including him and his older brother, Josie, settled in the mining town of Silver City.

Smart, and able to write well-spelled Spencerian-style script, Billy probably became bi-lingual in this period, and thereafter amicably bridged Anglo and Hispanic sub-cultures in those racist times.

His mother's tuberculosis death, a year and a half later, in 1874, left him a homeless victim of his stepfather's avarice, and relying on thievery, as well as butcher shop and hotel work; until, the following year, he was arrested for laundry and revolver theft by Silver City's sheriff, Harvey Whitehill. Billy faced ten years hard labor, the law making no provision for juveniles. His first desperate and dramatic escape - through the jail chimney - yielded necessary relocation to Bonita, in Arizona Territory.

In Arizona, as Henry Antrim, Billy again combined work - cooking at a small hotel - with illegality: stealing blankets, saddles, and horses. In 1876, jailed with his accomplice, John Mackie, he escaped the local fort's guardhouse by wriggling through a ventilation space under the roof.

But he stayed in Bonita, the rustling charges having been dropped through a technicality.

Billy's life changed again on August 17, 1877, when his heated argument, at Bonita's Atkin's Cantina, with a bullying blacksmith named Frank "Windy" Cahill, escalated to his fatally shooting that unarmed man. Billy escaped on a stolen horse. The Coroner's Jury declared him - as Henry Antrim - guilty of unjustified homicide, though in absentia.

Billy saved himself by return to New Mexico Territory, with an alias: William Henry Bonney - Billy Bonney. Then 17½, by the next month – September of 1877 - he joined the Santa Fe Ring-affiliated gang of rustler, Jessie Evans.

Only weeks later, by October of 1877, he abandoned outlawry and became a Lincoln County ranch hand for wealthy Englishmen, John Henry Tunstall, a Ring competitor. Soon Billy was affectionately nick-named "Kid" by the older workers.

Billy became locally popular by virtue of his charismatic combination of high spirits, intelligence, sharp shooting skills, singing, and dancing. In partnership with one of the employees, a half-Chickasaw named Fred Waite, Billy was given, by John Tunstall, a Peñasco River ranch under the Homestead Act - probably one of his proudest moments.

The February 18, 1878, Ring murder/mutilation of John Tunstall, again changed everything for Billy, who was at the ambush. The slide began into that July's Lincoln County War.

By then, the Civil War had already ruined the life of Patrick "Pat" Floyd Garrett. Born to an Alabama plantation family; relocated to Claiborne Parrish, Louisiana, when nine and a half - and Billy was just born - Garrett was even willed a slave by his grandfather. His family lost everything in the War; and Garrett became a westward wanderer, ending up in Texas. There, he may have abandoned a common-law wife and child, as well as possibly murdering a black man, before becoming a buffalo hunter from 1876 to 1878, with two partners, and, initially, with a kid named Joe Briscoe. Garrett shot that kid point-blank, one irritable day in camp, but claimed self-defense. On the range, Garrett never met fellow buffalo hunter, John William Poe. Later Garrett's, Poe's, and Billy's histories would merge on that July 14th night.

By early 1878, Garrett, tall at 6'4", had settled in New Mexico Territory's town of Fort Sumner, and had met there the transient youth named Billy Bonney, as both gambled at Hargrove's or Beaver Smith's Saloons. Of different generations, their only bond was mutual recognition, and townspeople's nicknames: "Big Casino" and "Little Casino," for their poker playing and height discrepancies.

The original fort, yielding that town's name, was built by the U.S. government in 1865 on desert flatlands east of the Pecos River for soldiers guarding a concentration camp named Bosque Redondo, holding 3,500 Navajos and 400 Apaches. Their starvation became an embarrassment; and, in 1868, the Navajos were sent back to their homeland; the Apaches already having escaped.

In 1870, that military property, with fort and surrounding thousands of acres, was purchased by Lucien Bonaparte Maxwell, by then one of the Territory's richest men. There he moved his wife, Luz Beaubien; daughters, including Paulita; and son, Peter; having turned the military buildings around the original parade ground into residences and businesses; and making its refurbished officers' quarters his mansion.

Retained was the half acre military cemetery for his family. It eventually received Billy's body, to lie beside Pat Garrett's earlier victims: Billy's Regulator pals, Tom O'Folliard and Charlie Bowdre.

Lucien Maxwell planted a peach orchard and crops; and ranched primarily sheep. He died in 1875, leaving his town to the care of his wife and his son, Peter, who would be the family's ruin through financial mismanagement. But when Pat Garrett and Billy gambled there, it was still thriving.

Before buying Fort Sumner, Lucien Maxwell's wealth arose first from his almost 2 million acre Maxwell Land Grant, then by his selling it; though he was probably cheated out of its full profit by its negotiating attorneys, Thomas Benton Catron and Steven Elkins, who resold it for twice the amount.

That Catron-Elkins profit and technique was used to start the Santa Fe Ring, their ongoing land grab scheme to disenfranchise Hispanic land grant owners. Recruited, by favor or fear, was the Territorial Governor, Samuel Beach Axtell, many other public officials and law enforcement officers, and the local military.

Those robber barons, Catron and Elkins, profited immensely, in land, railroads, banks, and mines. Catron would own six million acres - more than any man in United States history. And, during the Lincoln County War period, he held the Territory's highest legal post: U.S. Attorney.

By 1878, Pat Garrett and Billy Bonney had separate lives, though connected to Fort Sumner's Gutierrez sisters: Juanita, Apolinaria, and Celsa. Billy befriended Celsa, married to her cousin, Saval Gutierrez, a Maxwell sheep herder.

Pat Garrett married Juanita, who died shortly of a possible miscarriage. Two years later, Garrett married Apolinaria, with whom he would father eight children. It was a double marriage with his Fort Sumner, best friend, Maxwell's foreman, Barney Mason, later a spy assisting his capture of Billy.

In 1878, Garrett still lacked financial security. Initially, for Peter Maxwell, he drove a wagon. Then he worked with a local hog raiser, Thomas "Kip" McKinney. A bartending job in Hargrove's Saloon was little improvement.

Then came 1880 and the opportunity of his life. Lincoln County - the largest county in America; almost a quarter of the Territory, and big enough to fit Massachusetts, Connecticut, Vermont, Rhode Island, and Delaware - needed a new sheriff for its November election, one compatible with Santa Fe Ring interests. To qualify, Garrett moved with his wife, Apolinaria, to that county's town of Roswell; adding, as a boarder, an unemployed journalist named Ashmun "Ash" Upson.

By 1880, Lincoln County was finally emerging from its 1878 war, about which Garrett knew little. Its town of Lincoln had been the epicenter of Santa Fe Ring abuses, where the House, a giant two-story store run by its local bosses, Lawrence Murphy and James Dolan, bled cash-poor Mexicans and white homesteaders with exorbitant credit on goods.

Redress was impossible; Ring thuggery maintained the stranglehold. In 1875, when a rancher, named Robert Casey, won an election against James Dolan, he was shot down the same day. And the opposing Mexican community leader, Juan Patrón, was likewise shot by Dolan's partner, John Riley; though he survived.

The future Lincoln County uprising began in late 1876 with the arrival in the town of Lincoln of sweet-tempered, wealthy, English merchant, John Henry Tunstall; persuaded to settle there by a local attorney, Alexander McSween, a Ring opponent, but once legal counsel to Murphy and Dolan.

By 1877, John Tunstall built, just a quarter mile east of the Murphy-Dolan House, a large store with bank; and he purchased land for two cattle ranches; all constituting direct competition with the Santa Fe Ring. He also hoped to wrest from the House its beef and flour traderships to the local fort, Stanton, and to the Mescalaro Indian Reservation; and even exposed, in a local newspaper, Lincoln County Sheriff William Brady's abuse of tax money to pay for Ring cattle.

So John Tunstall became next for elimination on the Ring's list; Alexander McSween being a close second.

The Ringmen preferred to kill with guise of legality. So they entangled Tunstall in a fabricated web. Its thread began with Tunstall's friend, Attorney Alexander McSween, who had retained an important House connection: representation of the estate of its founding partner, Emil Fritz, who had died intestate in 1874, and had two siblings in the Territory.

The Ring chose, as a hook for legal harassment, that $10,000, Fritz, life insurance policy, which McSween was attempting to collect from its dishonestly evasive, New York City company. That collection was eventually achieved by McSween's hired New York law firm, which subtracted about $3,000 for their effort.

Alexander McSween, knowing that the Murphy-Dolan House - on the verge of bankruptcy from Tunstall competition - would wrangle that Fritz money from the local heirs, dug in strategically. He did not turn over the remaining $7,000, claiming that additional possible heirs in Germany delayed settlement of Emil Fritz's estate.

Then he left on business to St. Louis with his wife and with John Tunstall's business associate, the cattle king, John Chisum, then also president of the bank in Tunstall's store.

The Ring pounced, declaring McSween an absconding embezzler of the Fritz insurance money. Ring head, U.S. Attorney Thomas Benton Catron, prepared warrants to arrest Alexander McSween before he left the Territory.

McSween, transported to the town of Mesilla to be indicted by Ring judge, Warren Bristol (later Billy's hanging judge), avoided possible assassination if incarcerated in Lincoln's underground pit jail by intervention of an honest deputy sheriff from his arrest site in Las Vegas, New Mexico - Adolph Barrier - who kept him in personal custody.

But Judge Bristol had set a trap. When he indicted McSween, he did two things. First, he set his bail at $8,000; but granted its approval only to Ringman, District Attorney William Rynerson, who refused all bondsmen. That meant McSween could be taken into possibly fatal custody at any time by Ring loyalist, Lincoln County Sheriff William Brady.

The second stipulation was the clincher. Bristol attached McSween's personal property to the sum of $10,000 - deemed as the amount of embezzled money - to satisfy any judgment against McSween at the April Grand Jury trial.

The catch was that Judge Bristol falsely declared that John Tunstall was in partnership with McSween, and attached his property also against the sum of $10,000. And Sheriff Brady and his deputies would do the attaching.

Hoped for was a violent response from John Tunstall and his employees - including hot-headed Billy Bonney - to these provocations, to achieve his "justifiable" killing in a fight.

But noble Tunstall merely said one man's life was worth more than all he owned. Nevertheless, he protectively transferred his fine horses, which were immune to attachment.

That stock movement, from his ranch back to Lincoln, was, nevertheless, used by Sheriff Brady, on February 14, 1878, to send his posse (illegally including outlaw, Jessie Evans, and his boys) to pursue Tunstall and his ranch hands, including Billy.

In the posse's attack, Tunstall, becoming separated from his fleeing men, was murdered; his body and slain horse mutilated.

This martyrdom, and its aftermath, triggered the Lincoln County War through escalating Santa Fe Ring outrages.

First, Sheriff Brady blocked service of the Tunstall killers' murder warrants - which included ones for James Dolan and Jessie Evans, along with other possemen. Those warrants, legally issued by Lincoln Justice of the Peace John "Squire" Wilson, had been given, for service, to Tunstall employees, Billy and Fred Waite, whom Wilson had appointed as deputy constables under Lincoln's Town Constable Atanacio Martinez.

But illegally, Sheriff Brady briefly jailed those three in Lincoln's pit jail to prevent their arrests of Dolan and others; and he confiscated Billy's Winchester '73 carbine.

Justice of the Peace Wilson next deputized Tunstall's foreman, Dick Brewer, who appointed Tunstall's men, including Billy, as his posse to serve those murder warrants.

Meanwhile, recognizing his extreme risk from the murderous Santa Fe Ring, Attorney McSween, with Deputy Sheriff Barrier, went into hiding.

By March, Brewer's posse had captured Tunstall murder possemen, William "Buck" Morton and Frank Baker, who were shot attempting escape. Billy was in the firing group.

At that point, including "Windy" Cahill, Billy was now involved in three murders.

Then the Ring acted again. Governor Samuel Beach Axtell, by official proclamation, illegally removed "Squire" Wilson's Justice of the Peace title, outlawed Dick Brewer's posse, and declared Sheriff William Brady Lincoln County's only law enforcer.

Enraged, Tunstall's men named themselves "Regulators" after Revolutionary War vigilantes. Those Regulators included Billy; Fred Waite; John Middleton; Jim "Frenchie" French; cousins, George and Frank Coe; Charlie Bowdre; and a John Chisum cattle detective, Frank MacNab. Dick Brewer was named their leader.

The next crisis was the April 1, 1878, anticipated return of Alexander McSween for his Lincoln, Grand Jury embezzlement trial. To prevent his assassination by Sheriff Brady, five Regulators - four with carbines, and Billy with only a revolver - ambushed him and his three deputies from behind an adobe wall fronting the southeast side of the Tunstall store's corral.

Sheriff William Brady and Deputy George Hindman died.

Recklessly, Billy, with Jim "Frenchie" French, ran out to the street to retrieve his confiscated, Winchester carbine from Brady's body; and both youths got leg wounds from firing, surviving Deputy Jacob Basil "Billy" Matthews.

Three days later, occurred a Regulator debacle as Dick Brewer, in search of stolen Tunstall horses, led Billy, Tom Middleton, Fred Waite, Frank Coe, George Coe, and Charlie Bowdre to privately owned Blazer's Mill, surrounded by the Mescalaro Indian Reservation. There they encountered bounty-hunter and Tunstall murder posseman, Andrew "Buckshot" Roberts, for whom they had an arrest warrant.

Encountering resistance, Bowdre shot "Buckshot" Roberts in the belly; but Roberts pumped Winchester carbine bullets, one hitting Bowdre's belt buckle. That ricocheting bullet struck George Coe's extended revolver, mutilating his trigger finger. Middleton, shot in the chest, survived. Roberts next killed Brewer, and later died himself. Billy had not fired a shot.

But Billy's murder involvement now totaled six men; though only Frank "Windy" Cahill was demonstrably by his own hand.

Attorney Alexander McSween's exoneration at the April, 1878 Grand Jury, energized his attacks on the Ring. Knowing that murder of a foreign citizen could elicit a Washington investigation, he informed the British ambassador and President Rutherford B. Hayes of John Tunstall's murder.

In response, investigating attorney, Frank Warner Angel, was sent by the Washington D.C. Departments of the Interior and Justice. In New Mexico Territory, Attorney Angel obtained over a hundred depositions, among them Billy's.

And Lincoln's public optimism of Santa Fe Ring overthrow further grew when their County Commissioners' appointed a McSween side-sympathizing sheriff: John Copeland.

Optimism was short-lived. The new Regulator leader, Frank MacNab, was killed by Dolan men on April 28th.

By May 28th, because Sheriff John Copeland had forgotten a technicality of posting a tax collecting bond, Governor Samuel Beach Axtell, by another proclamation, removed him; the replacement being George Peppin, a Ring partisan and former Sheriff Brady deputy - present in the fatal April ambush.

Alexander McSween was unaware that Santa Fe Ring influence extended to Washington, D.C.; but Attorney Frank Warner Angel, after documenting the violations of Governor Axtell, U.S. Attorney Catron, and Sheriff Brady's posse, concluded his October 4, 1878 report falsely, possibly under duress, that no U.S. officials had been involved in Tunstall's murder.

But Thomas Benton Catron did resign as U.S. Attorney; and Governor Axtell was removed. He was replaced by Civil War General Lew Wallace on October 1, 1878.

Alexander McSween did not live to see those Regulator achievements. Months earlier, war fervor had built, with Tunstall men and Lincoln area Mexicans calling themselves "McSweens." Billy's affiliation with local, firebrand youth, Yginio Salazar, and Billy's closeness to Hispanic residents of nearby San Patricio and Picacho, arguably forged the bond that brought the Mexicans into their alliance.

By April 30th of 1878, McSweens were skirmishing with Ring partisans, known as "Murphy-Dolans," though Lawrence Murphy was, by then, dying of alcoholism. Of necessity, McSween hid, often in the town of San Patricio.

A retaliatory massacre of San Patricio's inhabitants occurred on July 8th, by Lincoln County Sheriff George Peppin, who outrageously brought in John Kinney's rustler gang from Mesilla as his posse.

Six days later, on July 14th, the Lincoln County War began. McSween, with about sixty men - Regulators and Hispanic residents of San Patricio and Picacho - rode into Lincoln to take a stand.

Reflecting McSween's optimism at a peaceful victory, in his big double-winged house had remained his wife; her sister, with her five young children; and that sister's attorney husband's law intern, Harvey Morris.

McSween's men took strategic positions in houses throughout the town, most of whose inhabitants had fled.

When Seven Rivers and John Kinney's men joined James Dolan and Sheriff Peppin, Billy; his friends, Yginio Salazar and Tom O'Folliard; and San Patricio men - José Chávez y Chávez, Ignacio Gonzales, Florencio Chávez, Francisco Zamora, and Vincente Romero - went to McSween's house, where Jim French had been stationed alone.

Though the Dolan-Peppin men attained the foothills south of the town, they were kept at bay for five days by McSweens.

But Alexander McSween was unaware that nearby Fort Stanton's new commander, Colonel Nathan Augustus Monroe Dudley, was a Ring partisan. Further reassuring McSween, was that, the month before, the Posse Comitatus Act had been enacted, baring military intervention in civilian disputes.

But, in the days of mutual gunfire, a fort soldier, cavalryman, Private Berry Robinson, sent to Lincoln by Commander Dudley for fact-finding, had almost been hit. Without basis, McSween was blamed. And, by July 18th, Dolan informed Commander Dudley that women and children were at risk at the home of Ring partisan resident, Saturnino Baca.

The next day, the 19th, risking Posse Comitatus Act violation, Dudley marched on Lincoln with a 60 troops - white infantry, black 9th Cavalry, and white officers - two ambulances; a mountain howitzer cannon; and a Gatling gun: a machine gun and that time's most awesome weapon of war.

Panicked by the might, the McSween men - except for those in his besieged house - fled north across the nearby Bonito River. Colonel Dudley personally informed McSween that, if any of his soldiers was shot, he would raze his house with his cannon and Gatling gun. Furthermore, Dudley left three soldiers at the McSween property, and allowed three more to stay with Sheriff Peppin, though they did not participate in shooting. In addition, Dudley forced Justice of the Peace "Squire" Wilson to write out arrest warrants for Alexander McSween and his men as Private Berry Robinson's assailants.

With those inhibitory advantages, on July 19th, Sheriff George Peppin's men soon took strategic positions and set fire to the west wing of the McSween house; while Commander Dudley cautiously kept his non-participating soldiers in the east side of town. Evacuated from the house were only McSween's wife, Susan, her sister, and her sister's children.

By nightfall, the McSween house conflagration - worsened by an exploding gunpowder keg inside - left the desperate men marooned in the east wing. At about 9 PM, escape was made into the fire-lit shooting adversaries. In Billy's group was law intern, Harvey Morris, whom he saw killed.

And, before Billy and others crossed the Bonito River, and were rescued by waiting fellow Regulators, Billy witnessed Commander Dudley's secret and illegal intervention: three of his white soldiers had been among the burning building's assailants, and had fired at least one volley at Billy and his escaping fellows from the rear corner of Tunstall's adjacent property.

Shot dead at the house were Alexander McSween, Francisco Zamora, and Vincente Romero. Yginio Salazar survived, but with two bullets in his back. The war was lost.

Symbolizing Billy's trauma, that night the house's starving, yard chickens consumed the eyeballs of McSween's corpse. Again was murder and mutilation in Lincoln County.

Though most Regulators fled the Territory, Billy stayed. With fellow Regulators, Tom O'Folliard and Charlie Bowdre - who had relocated to Fort Sumner with his wife Manuela - Billy made guerilla attacks of cattle rustling on Catron's brother-in-law, Edgar Walz, and the man he most blamed:

John Chisum, who had refused make-or-break aid of his 80 cowboys to Tunstall or McSween; and had also reneged on his promise to pay Tunstall's men for their services.

For his stolen stock, Billy used non-Ring outlets: Pat Coghlan in the western part of the Territory; and Dan Dedrick, a counterfeiter and rustler at Bosque Grande, a Pecos River ranch 12 miles south of Fort Sumner. Dedrick, with his two brothers, also owned a livery stable receiving stock in White Oaks, about 45 miles northwest of Lincoln.

Billy also sold rustled horses in Tascosa, Texas, where he wrote a subsequently famous, bill of sale to a Henry Hoyt for an expensive sorrel. Billy also gambled to get additional money.

Lincoln County citizens' next hope was Governor Lew Wallace; son of an Indiana governor; a Civil War Major General; an attorney; an author of a best selling novel, *The Fair God*; and then writing *Ben-Hur*. Wallace had desired an ambassadorship to exotic Turkey, not the backwater he got.

To deal with "the Lincoln County troubles," Lew Wallace merely posted, a month after his October 1878 arrival, an Amnesty Proclamation, excluding those already indicted. Billy had been indicted for the murders of Sheriff William Brady, Deputy George Hindman, and Andrew "Buckshot" Roberts.

Another source of local hope was an attorney named Huston Chapman, whom McSween's widow, Susan, brought to Lincoln to charge Commander N.A.M. Dudley with murder of her husband and arson of her house.

In that atmosphere of scrutiny, James Dolan made peace overtures, first to McSween's widow, then, demonstrating Billy's importance in Ring resistance, to him. Billy's bi-lingual closeness to the Hispanic population had arguably brought men into the War - and could do so again in another uprising.

The Billy-Dolan peace meeting was fatefully scheduled on February 18, 1879, the anniversary of Tunstall's murder. It ended in calamity.

As Dolan; Billy; Jessie Evans and Jessie's gang member, Billy Campbell; and Billy's friends, Tom O'Folliard and Josiah "Doc" Scurlock, walked Lincoln's dark street afterwards, they encountered Attorney Huston Chapman. Dolan and Campbell fired at close range, killing him, and igniting his clothing. Again was murder and mutilation in Lincoln County.

Huston Chapman's killing forced Lew Wallace to finally come to Lincoln. There, his quixotic plan was quelling unrest by elimination of outlaws and rustlers.

Someone accused Billy as an outlaw, an indication of Ring vengeance. Informed about the astronomical reward of $1000 on his head, Billy wrote his subsequently famous letter to Governor Wallace, offering his testimony against Huston Chapman's murderers in exchange for a pardon for his Lincoln County War indictments. It was a calculated risk for negating Ring power over himself.

That masterfully articulate letter led to the March 17, 1879, nighttime meeting of Billy and Lew Wallace in Justice of the Peace "Squire" Wilson's Lincoln house.

Billy requested arrest as cover from assassination before his April Grand Jury testimony. For that sham, he was kept in the home of Juan Patrón, the town jailer and a McSween sympathizer. Billy wore shackles for effect.

By then, Alexander McSween's intrepid widow had retained Attorney Huston Chapman's associate, Attorney Ira Leonard, to continue her case against Commander Dudley.

Aware of his legal risks, Dudley had obtained defamatory affidavits stating that she was a woman of low repute, thus, lacking courtroom credibility. Dudley also requested a Court of Inquiry into his conduct that fateful day of July 19, 1878, knowing that being cleared by the military would cast a favorable light in a later civilian court trial.

Vindication was inevitable, though he already had two prior Court Martials. For one, a year before the Lincoln County War, he had been represented by Thomas Benton Catron himself.

For the Court of Inquiry, Catron's friend and famous trial lawyer, Henry Waldo, took his case. And the Presiding Judge would be Dudley's good friend: Colonel Galusha Pennypacker.

But, annoyingly, Governor Lew Wallace planned to testify against Dudley, ignoring or ignorant of Ring machinations.

Though testifying in that Dudley Court of Inquiry was not part of his Wallace pardon deal, Billy volunteered; doing so on May 28th and 29th of 1879, during his Patrón incarceration.

In his precise presentation, unfazed by Attorney Henry Waldo's bullying, Billy devastatingly stated that he had seen three white soldiers fire a volley - that meant officers; that meant under orders; that meant Colonel Dudley was guilty of treason (firing on citizens in violation of the Posse Comitatus Act). Billy was now fighting the Ring in his own way.

And Billy was successful in the Grand Jury, his testimony yielding James Dolan's and Billy Campbell's indictments for Chapman's murder, and accessory to murder for Jessie Evans.

Billy had fulfilled his pardon pact in spades. And, had the Dudley Court of Inquiry been fair, Dudley would have progressed to Court Martial based on Billy's testimony alone.

The Ring took action to protect their endangered members; and Billy was an important focus for elimination. His lack of a pardon from hypocritical Governor Wallace left him vulnerable to a hanging trial.

Ring partisans, District Attorney William Rynerson and Judge Warren Bristol, set Billy's trial in Doña Ana County's Mesilla for his murder indictments for Andrew "Buckshot" Roberts, Sheriff William Brady, and Deputy George Hindman; to eliminate him before he could testify in any future murder trials against Dolan, Campbell, and Evans.

Billy, at that point, had achieved two things: Ring enmity at the highest level; and friendship with Susan McSween's attorney, Ira Leonard, who continued to press Lew Wallace for Billy's pardon, and also initially represented him in his 1881 hanging trial.

And while Billy was still in Patrón's Lincoln jail, he would have heard, that, in town, on April 25, 1879, an assassination attempt on Ira Leonard had occurred by a shooting in Lincoln, to stop his legal pursuit of Colonel N.A.M. Dudley - just as Huston Chapman had been stopped.

In mid-June, Billy simply departed Juan Patrón's fake house arrest to avoid his inevitable hanging trial; though that feigned "escape" yielded a myth of his "slipping" wrist shackles by having double-jointed thumbs or very small hands.

When Billy was loose, he would have heard about Colonel Dudley's ominous Court of Inquiry exoneration on July 5th. But Billy still refused to leave New Mexico Territory. The Ring had one option for that gadfly: hang or shoot him.

Meanwhile, Billy had gained a "reputation" as a gunman. On January 3, 1880, when he was leaving Hargrove's Saloon in Fort Sumner, a Texan stranger, Joe Grant, attempted to shoot him in the back. Grant's gun misfired; and Billy retaliated fatally. Obvious self-defense, it was not legally pursued.

Billy was now involved with the murders of seven men.

By then, Billy may have heard the first mythological whispers of his killing a man for every year of his life. The Santa Fe Ring was setting its trap for him.

In addition to murderer and rustler, Billy would be declared a counterfeiter. That brought in the Secret Service, a branch of the Treasury Department, with federal funds for pursuit. James Dolan initiated that process by reporting receipt of a counterfeit $100 bill in his Lincoln store.

By September 11, 1880, Secret Service Special Operative Azariah Wild was on his way to Lincoln. Dolan's counterfeit bill payment was linked to Billy, though it actually came from two youths who worked with the real counterfeiter, Dan Dedrick; but who also occasionally rustled with Billy and his regulars: Tom O'Folliard, Charlie Bowdre, and a "Dirty Dave" Rudabaugh.

Wild, astoundingly, was led to believe, by Dolan and other Ringmen, first that Billy was part of the largest counterfeiting and rustling gang in the country; then, that he was its leader.

In late December, the *New York Sun* ran a story about Billy as: "Outlaws of New Mexico. The Exploits of a band headed by a New York Youth. The Mountain Fastness of the

Kid and his Followers - War Against a Gang of Cattle Thieves, Murderers, and Counterfeiters." Billy was alias "the Kid." And his national fame was starting.

The Santa Fe Ring plan, however, almost backfired because of Attorney Ira Leonard, whom Azariah Wild had interviewed.

Leonard assured Wild that Billy would testify against the actual counterfeiters. Wild wrote in his daily report to his Chief, James Brooks, on October 8th, that he would arrange Billy's pardon in exchange for that testimony.

But Wild told James Dolan his plan, resulting in Dolan's convincing him that Billy was the *gang leader*!

In his October 14, 1880 report, Wild wrote that he would arrest Billy in their upcoming meeting with Attorney Leonard about the testimony.

By then, Billy was cautious. He held up the stagecoach with Operative Wild's mail, read that report, and avoided apprehension by avoiding that meeting.

The Santa Fe Ring needed a sheriff to arrest Billy. George Peppin, having quit, had been replaced by a McSween-side sympathizer, George Kimbrell.

The Ring chose Pat Garrett.

Secretly, Azariah Wild worked with Garrett and James Dolan to create a dragnet to capture Billy and his "gang;" while, for the upcoming election, Garrett was advertised as a law-and-order man to Lincoln County's new gold-rush settlers in White Oaks, unaware of Lincoln County War issues, but a third of the county's population and voting block.

In the November 2, 1880 sheriff's election, Garrett got 358 votes to Kimbrell's 141. Azariah Wild, convinced that Kimbrell was shielding the "Kid gang," gave Garrett Territorial power for capture by making him a Deputy U.S. Marshall.

Billy, unaware, would have believed Pat Garrett's authority did not extend to Fort Sumner's San Miguel County.

Also, unaware that his "outlawry" was so publicized, Billy continued to bring stolen horses to the Dedrick brothers' livery in White Oaks.

On November 22nd, a White Oaks posse ambushed Billy, Tom O'Folliard, Billy Wilson, Tom Pickett, and "Dirty" Dave Rudabaugh at nearby Coyote Spring, killing two of their horses before they all escaped.

Five days later, that posse surrounded them at the way station ranch of "Whiskey" Jim Greathouse, 45 miles northeast of White Oaks; killing one of their own, Jim Carlyle, in friendly fire; but blaming it on Billy.

That accusation prompted another of Billy's ultimately famous Wallace letters. On December 12th, he wrote, denying his outlawry and the Carlyle murder. Wallace never responded.

On December 22nd, Lew Wallace placed a notice in the *Las Vegas Daily Gazette* saying, "Billy the Kid: $500 Reward."

Wallace would repeat it in the *Daily New Mexican* in May of 1881, when Garrett was tracking escaped Billy to his July death. The Wallace betrayal was complete.

Dreadful days were about to begin for Billy, unaware that Garrett had assembled posses to ride after him - using mostly Texans, since New Mexicans refused.

The first Garrett ambush was December 19th, when Billy, Tom O'Folliard, Charlie Bowdre, Billy Wilson, Tom Pickett, and Dave Rudabaugh rode into Fort Sumner on its snowy night. O'Folliard was killed; the rest escaped.

Billy and the others, trying to flee the Territory in a snowstorm, stopped, on December 21st, at the rock-walled line cabin at Stinking Springs, east of Fort Sumner.

There Pat Garrett ambushed them the next morning, killing Bowdre, mistaken for Billy by wearing his sombrero. The survivors surrendered. That was Garrett's greatest moment - before killing Billy seven months later.

Garrett transported his prisoners by train, via Las Vegas, to the Santa Fe jail. Billy remained there from December 27, 1880 to late March of 1881, awaiting completion of the railroad to Mesilla - so fearful was the Santa Fe Ring of his rescue - a measure of the boy's following as a freedom fighter hero.

In fact, Billy nearly escaped the Santa Fe jail by tunneling out with fellow prisoners.

From his Santa Fe jail cell, Billy wrote four unanswered letters to Governor Lew Wallace, pleading and cajoling for his pardon; on March 4, 1881, saying, "I have done everything that I promised you I would, and you have done nothing that you promised me."

Billy's Mesilla murder trial, under Ringman judge, Warren Bristol, began on March 30, 1881.

Billy was represented by Attorney Ira Leonard for Case Number 411, the United States versus Charles Bowdre, Josiah Scurlock, Henry Brown, William Bonney alias Henry Antrim alias the Kid, John Middleton, Frederick Waite, Jim French, and George Coe for the murder of Andrew Roberts.

Surprising everyone, Ira Leonard got the indictment quashed based on a technicality that the federal government - listed as the plaintiff - had no jurisdiction over Blazer's Mill, the murder site, since private property, like it, was under *Territorial jurisdiction*. The fact that the property was surrounded by the federally controlled Mescalaro Reservation was irrelevant. That argument was correct. Judge Bristol was forced to quash the indictment.

It seemed possible that Billy could win. Left only were the Brady and Hindman indictments, and, not only had Billy been firing in a group, he had only a revolver, arguably lacking accurate range. But, suddenly, Ira Leonard withdrew, possibly after a Ring threat. That was a major and traumatic set-back.

Billy received a court appointed attorney, Albert Jennings Fountain, who, though not a Ringman, believed Billy to be an outlaw.

On April 8th and 9th, was Billy's trial for the Brady murder. His Spanish-speaking jury, without a translator, heard only witnesses against him, including James Dolan.

After instructions by Judge Bristol (with translator), making Billy's mere presence the same as killing, the jury found him guilty of first degree murder, its sole punishment being hanging.

On April 13th, Bristol set the hanging date for May 13th, insuring insufficient time for an appeal.

Ironically, the new Lincoln jail, in which Billy was incarcerated under Sheriff Pat Garrett to await hanging, was in the past House. James Dolan had repositioned himself, first mortgaging the House to Thomas Benton Catron, then buying the vacated Tunstall store for himself.

Catron, in turn, sold the building to the county, which converted it into a new courthouse, with a second floor jail.

Billy arrived to Sheriff Garrett's custody on April 21, 1881. For Billy's 24 hour guard, Garrett deputized a White Oaks man, James Bell, and a Seven Rivers man, Robert Olinger; as well as shackling Billy at wrists and ankles, and securing him to a ring in the plank floor - all to guarantee his hanging death.

But on April 27th, Pat Garrett left for three days to collect White Oaks taxes. The next day, Billy escaped.

An unknown accomplice either left him a revolver in the outdoor privy, or he wrested away Deputy Bell's weapon while being guarded.

A likely suspect for the scenario of providing a gun was the building's caretaker: Gottfried Gauss. He had been John Tunstall's loyal cook; and was even present when Tunstall and his men rode from the Feliz River ranch to the fatal ambush - three years before Billy's courthouse-jail escape. And Billy had access to the outdoor privy for a gun's possible plant.

So, with a revolver, Billy shot Deputy James Bell, as the man fled down the second-story jail's stairway. The weapon was never found.

Deputy Robert Olinger, across the street at the Wortley Hotel, taking lunch with other jail prisoners, either heard the shot, or was told.

Olinger ran back, and Billy, waiting at an eastward-facing, jail window, shot him with his own Whitney double-barrel shotgun.

Billy then broke his leg chain with a miner's pick provided by Gottfried Gauss. Taking more weapons from the building's armory, he escaped on a pony, also from Gauss.

Billy had now been involved in the murder of nine men, James Bell and Robert Olinger, adding to Frank "Windy" Cahill and Joe Grant, as his only provable killings.

Of the dead, Billy would have said he was a posseman with William "Buck" Morton and Frank Baker, would have denied shooting at Andrew "Buckshot" Roberts, would have called Cahill and Grant self-defense, and would have seen Bell's death as necessary to save himself.

Only Robert Olinger, hated as possibly present in each confrontation - from the Tunstall murder posse to the Frank MacNab ambush, to the war in Lincoln - would have been killed vengefully. Billy's rage was so great, that after the shooting, he smashed apart the man's shotgun, delaying his escape.

That count of nine killed men - with only four certain - remained as Billy's final tally.

Billy's escape route was across the east to west, Capitan Mountains, en route to the Las Tablas home of his friend, Yginio Salazar.

From there, he returned to Fort Sumner and Paulita Maxwell, remaining hidden in outlying sheep camps.

Though speculation, the elopement of Billy and Paulita was possible. Paulita's oldest sister, Virginia, had chosen that option in Cimarron, leaving for New York with the local Indian Agent, Captain A.S.B. Keyes, in 1870, the year their father sold the Maxwell Land Grant.

By July 14, 1881, though he was unaware, Billy had traitors in Fort Sumner. Barney Mason, Pat Garrett's friend and Secret Service Operative Azariah Wild's informant, though no longer Peter Maxwell's foreman, himself had spies, evidenced by his knowing that Billy was in the town.

Garrett's two deputies for that final pursuit, John William Poe and Thomas "Kip" McKinney, did not know Billy. Poe, a buffalo hunter, a past Deputy U.S. Marshall in Texas, a cattle detective, and a recent White Oaks settler, had met Garrett during the Azariah Wild-assisted, tracking of the "Kid gang." McKinney knew Garrett from their hog farming days.

That final plans for ambushing Billy were uncertain, is indicated by dissent between Garrett and John William Poe. Garrett was pessimistic about Billy's being in Fort Sumner. Poe tipped the balance to staying.

As a stranger, Poe did recognizance in Fort Sumner during the day of July 14th; Garrett and "Kip" McKinney remaining a few miles away. Poe also checked with the nearby postmaster, Milnor Rudolph, in Sunnyside, seven miles to the north.

When Poe met Garrett and McKinney that night, he believed Billy was near; and the ambush was planned.

And, the location being Peter Maxwell's bedroom, necessitated both Maxwell's involvement, and concealment of that treachery (given Billy's popularity in the town).

While Poe and McKinney went to the vicinity of the Maxwell mansion, Garrett checked the peach orchard. There he saw distant shadowed figures - possibly Billy with Paulita - before he went to Maxwell's bedroom to await the ambush.

Poe and McKinney remained outside, presumably to prevent Billy's escape.

Billy began his near-midnight death walk across Fort Sumner's 300 yard square parade ground, around which the town formed a perimeter.

He exited the converted barracks house of Celsa and Saval Gutierrez, carrying their butcher knife to cut his dinner steak.

The moon was unusual. Rising at about 10 PM to the southeast, almost full, through the night it skimmed the horizon, looking giant and mimicking daylight.

Approaching the mansion, occupying much of the west side, Billy went first to Maxwell's curtained darkened bedroom, a task presumably assigned by an additional Fort Sumner traitor. Maxwell was in bed as a decoy. Beside it, Pat Garrett hid with his blued, Colt .44, single action revolver, with a 7½ inch barrel and serial number 55093.

Though strangers in town were common, Billy, as the most hunted man in the country, reacted with caution to John William Poe, asking in Spanish - presumably as a disguise - who he was, and drawing his gun. Poe supposed him to be a Maxwell worker or guest. Then Billy entered Maxwell's darkened bedroom.

Almost immediately sensing someone in shadows, Billy asked, in Spanish, who it was.

Pat Garrett recognized his voice.

In seconds, Poe, McKinney, and townspeople heard the first shot. Another was then fired wild. But Billy was already dead.

As Peter Maxwell ran out, John William Poe, thinking he was Billy escaping, almost shot him. Then Garrett exited.

Uncertainty that Billy was dead, led to Maxwell's sending in family servant, Deluvina. Placing her candle, she would have been the first to see the deceased boy, 21 years old. Then Pat Garrett checked.

Shocked townspeople were allowed to take Billy's body across the parade ground to the town's carpenter's shop for a candlelit vigil; he being laid out on the workbench.

The following morning, the Coroner's Jury of six men met. Their foreman, Sunnyside postmaster Milnor Rudolph, no fancier of Billy, had a son, Charlie, who had ridden on one of Garrett's posses; and had himself been a Ringman politician.

The jurymen identified the body, interviewed the eye-witness, Peter Maxwell, and declared the killing by Pat Garrett to be justifiable homicide. The case was closed.

Billy's body was buried in the northwest corner of the Maxwell cemetery, beside Charlie Bowdre and Tom O'Folliard. Among the participants was Billy's local friend, Paco Anaya, who later wrote a memoir: *I Buried Billy.*

Modern old-timers and old photographs confirm Billy's gravesite as a weed-strewn plot, not at the current, more central location in the cemetery's half acre.

That memorial for tourists, dating to the 1950's, is protected against souvenir-seekers by a brown concrete slab (with three mounds - for Billy and his murdered friends), inside a protective barred cage, within which is a granite headstone, proclaiming "Pals" and their names. A small foot-stone at Billy's place, declares that he killed a man for each of his 21 years. Mythology was, thus, his marker.

Pat Garrett had blasted himself to fickle fame of disappointing sales of his book, *The Authentic Life of Billy the Kid The Noted Desperado of the Southwest, Whose Deeds of Daring and Blood Made His Name a Terror in New Mexico, Arizona, and Northern Mexico.* - ghostwritten by his Roswell boarder, journalist "Ash" Upson. But he attained a lifetime of acclaim for killing "outlaw" Billy the Kid.

Garrett himself died in 1908, ambushed by his goat herder, tenant, Wayne Brazel, (declared innocent by a jury), or by political intriguers unrelated to his homicide of Billy Bonney.

By 1937, Garrett's *Authentic Life of Billy the Kid* was reprinted because of Billy's expanding fame, as glory and profit-seekers emerged with sufficient "Billy owned firearms" for an arsenal; enough Garrett possemen for an army; and even nubile relatives claiming unsubstantiated motherhood of Billy's alleged children.

The Maxwell family, despite having lost ownership of Fort Sumner by 1884, even claimed, almost fifty years after the fact, to possess Billy's corpse's carpenter's bench.

And Billy was sighted for years after his demise - as he had been seen sighted all around the country, when alive and really in Fort Sumner, after his great escape.

And with the early movie industry making Billy the Kid big business, dozens of old-timers began to proclaim themselves as him by having survived Pat Garrett's shooting.

In the mid-1900's, Billy's mother, Catherine Antrim, also rode his tsunami of popularity. Two hundred sixty miles southwest of Billy's grave, in Silver City's Memory Lane Cemetery, her granite gravestone was placed for tourists, in 1947, seventy-three years after her demise, and in the cemetery's new part!

She had first been buried, in 1874, in a different and downtown Silver City cemetery, purchased in 1881 by a rich, eccentric local, for building his residence. He reburied all remains, without scrutiny, outside the town in Memory Lane.

Rumor is that Catherine Antrim's marker was once in Memory Lane's old section. That makes three graves, all impossible to verify, for Billy's mother.

Real Billy Speaks For Himself

It Was Not Easy To Be Billy

HOAXBUST: The real Billy Bonney was charismatic, brilliant, and literate; and he left a big paper trail proving all that. His imposters, Oliver "Brushy Bill" Roberts and John Miller, were left with an unattainable standard to mimic. And the modern Billy the Kid Case hoaxers were stuck with backing those old pretenders by their own misbegotten attempts to add credence to claiming that Sheriff Pat Garrett had killed an innocent victim to allow Billy to escape and live to old age as either of these unintelligent, inarticulate, and illiterate fellows.

Oliver "Brushy Bill" Roberts and John Miller had moxie as well as madness, given their day's incomplete history for miming Billy. Their authors sold them with empty hype consisting of: (1) their man knew details *only the real Billy the Kid* would know; and (2) their man's photos looked just like him. But authors meant books; and the books demonstrate neither first-person historical knowledge nor photo-identity.

Pretender ignorance is embarrassing. If someone claimed to be you, but were younger than you by two decades, or older by a decade; could not speak Spanish, in which you were fluent; did not know where you were born; did not know that you had a brother, or had a mother who died of tuberculosis, or a had mean step-father; did not know that you were jailed as a boy for theft and escaped to Arizona; did not know that your committing murder there forced escape back to New Mexico Territory; were unaware that your boss gifted you a ranch on a river, or that you gave a deposition about his murder to a presidential investigator; did not know that you fought a political ring in a grass-roots war, in which they were ignorant of its preliminary massacre of Hispanics, its weaponry, its participants, or its locations; had minimal knowledge about your attempted governor's pardon; did not know that you had a devoted attorney trying to protect you, who almost was assassinated; did not know your pursuit was backed by the Secret Service; did not know the details of your capture or hanging trial; did not know why your jail escape led you to Fort Sumner, or even about your true-love there; called themselves outlaws, when you considered yourself a soldier; and did not look like you, would you find it hard to argue against their claims of being you? That sums up the pretenders' problems.

Besides lacking facts, the pretenders' tales also lacked Billy's emotions, motivations, or traumas: the stuff of identity.

The pretenders and modern Billy the Kid Case hoaxers relied on Mark Twain's observation: "The most outrageous lies that can be invented will find believers if a man only tells them with all his might."

THE REAL WILLIAM BONNEY

Real Billy Bonney might have become the maniacal killer of legend, if facing the pretenders' mediocrity insulting his intelligence. And he left considerable proof of his smarts.

From 1878 to 1881, he wrote letters and a bill of sale in excellent Spencerian penmanship. He gave a deposition, on June 8, 1878, about John Tunstall's murder to Investigator Frank Warner Angel; and testified on May 28th and 29th of 1879, in a Court of Inquiry for Commander N.A.M. Dudley's potential Court Martial. And his testimony in the Lincoln Grand Jury of April, 1879 - for his Governor Lew Wallace pardon deal - yielded successful indictments.

As to his appearance, Billy's full-length tintype photograph, taken when he was about 20, has impeccable provenance of Dan Dedrick, to whom he gave it; and who left it to a family member by marriage: Elizabeth Upham, who, in turn, willed it to her two sons.

WRITINGS AND WORDS OF BILLY BONNEY

Billy's most famous letter sets the hoaxbusting stage. Written about March 13, 1879, to Governor Lew Wallace, it was the first of many. His articulateness and ability to spell even "indicted," contrast the pretenders' illiteracy (though he did not capitalize sentence starts). Billy wrote:

To his Excellency the Governor
General Lew Wallace
  Dear Sir I have heard that You will give one thousand $ dollars for my body which as I can understand it means alive as a witness. I know it is as a witness against those that murdered Mr Chapman. if it was so as that I could appear at Court, I could give the desired information. but I have indictments against me for things that happened in the late Lincoln County War and am afraid to give up because my Enimies [sic] would Kill me. the day Mr. Chapman was murderded [sic] I was in Lincoln; at the request of good Citizens to meet Mr. J. J. Dolan to meet as Friends, so as to be able to lay aside our arms and go to Work. I was present when Mr Chapman was murderded [sic] and know who did it and if it was not for these indictments I would have made it clear before now if it is in your power to Annully [sic] those indictments I hope you will do so so a[s] to give me a chance to explain. please send me an annser [sic] telling me what you can do You can send annser [sic] by bearer

 I have no wish to fight any more indeed I have not raised an arm since Your proclamation. as to my Character I refer to any of the Citizens, for the majority of them are my friends and have been helping me all they could. I am called Kid Antrim but Antrim is my stepfathers name.

  Waiting for an annser [sic] I remain
Your Obedient Servant
   W.H. Bonney

Billy wrote again to Lew Wallace on March 20, 1879 to arrange his feigned arrest for their pardon deal. From his safe haven of the Hispanic town of San Patricio, it reflects his courage in the face of risk, as well as his literary skill.

This is the letter:

Thursday 20th 1879

General Lew Wallace:

*Sir. I will keep the appointment I made; but be Sure and have men come that You can depend on **I am not afraid to die like a man fighting but I would not like to be killed like a dog unarmed.*** [author's boldface] *tell Kimbal* [Sheriff Kimbrell] *to let his men be placed around the house and for him to come in alone: and he can arrest us. all I am afraid of is that in the Fort We might be poisoned or killed through a Window at night. but You can arrange that all right. tell the Commanding Officer to watch Lt. Goodwin he would not hesitate to do anything there Will be danger on the road of Somebody waylaying us to kill us on the road to the Fort. You will never catch those fellows on the road. Watch Fritzes, Captain Bacas ranch and the Brewery they Will either go to Seven Rivers or to Jicarillo Mountains they will stay around close until the scouting parties come in. give a spy a pair of glasses and let him get on the mountain back of Fritzes and watch and if they are there there will be provisions carried to them. it is not my place to advise you; but I am anxious to have them caught, and perhaps know how men hide from Soldiers better than you. please excuse me for having so much to Say and I still remain Yours Truly,*

W H. Bonney

P.S.
I have changed my mind. Send Kimbal to Gutiereses just below San Patricio one mile, because Sanger and Ballard are or were great friends of Camels [sic - Campbell's] *Ballard told me ~~today~~ yesterday to leave for you were doing everything to catch me. it was a blind to get me to leave. tell Kimbal not to come before 3 oclock for I may not be there before*

Billy also knew proper legalize, as seen in his October 24, 1878 Bill of Sale for a horse to Dr. Henry Hoyt. It began: *"Know all persons by these presents that I do hereby sell and deliver to Henry F. Hoyt one sorrel ..."*

It ends with Billy's most famous signature: *"W HBonney,"* artistically linking the H and B.

DEPOSITION OF WILLIAM BONNEY

In a deposition given to Presidential Investigator Attorney Frank Warner Angel, Billy Bonney, then 18, described, in his characteristic meticulous and articulate detail, the murder of his boss, John Henry Tunstall. He also identified himself as having a ranch on the Peñasco River along with another Tunstall employee, Fred Waite.

Lacking that still-undiscovered deposition, pretenders had to invent a Tunstall's murder scenario. And Billy's Peñasco ranch was unknown to them.

The transcriptionist recorded Billy's words as follows:

Territory of New Mexico)
County of Lincoln)
)

William H. Bonney was duly sworn, deposand says that he is a resident of said county, that on the 11th day of February A.D. 1878 he in company with Robt. A. Widenmann and Fred T. Waite went to the ranch of J. H. Tunstall on the Rio Feliz, that he and said Fred T. Waite at the time intended to go to the Rio Peñasco to take up a ranch for the purpose of farming. That the cattle on the ranch of said J. H. Tunstall were throughout the County of Lincoln, known to be the property of said Tunstall; that on the 13th of February A.D. 1878 one J.B. Matthews claiming to be Deputy Sheriff came to the ranch of said J.H. Tunstall in company with Jesse Evans, Frank Baker, Tom Hill and [sic- blank space] Rivers, known outlaws who had been confined to the Lincoln County jail and had succeeded in making their escape, John Hurley, George

42

Hinman, [sic- blank space] *Roberts and an Indian aka Poncearo the latter said to be the murderer of Benaito Cruz, for the arrest of murderers of whom (Benaito Cruz) the Governor of this Territory offers a reward of $500. Before the arrival of said J.B. Matthews, deputy Sheriff, and his posse, having been informed that said deputy sheriff and posse were going to round up all the cattle and drive them off and kill the persons at the ranch, the persons at the ranch cut portholes into the walls of the house and filled sacks with earth, so that they, the persons at the ranch, should they be attacked or their murder attempted, could defend themselves, this course being thought necessary as the sheriffs posse was composed of murderers, outlaws, and desperate characters none of whom has any interest at stake in the County, nor being residents of said County. That said Matthews when within about 50 yards of the house was called to stop and advance alone and state his business, that said Matthews after arriving at the ranch said that he had come to attach the cattle and property of A.A. McSween, that said Matthews was informed that A.A. McSween had no cattle or property there, but that if he had he, said Matthews could take it. That said Matthews said that he thought some of the cattle belonging to R.M. Brewer, whose cattle were also at the ranch of J.H. Tunstall, belonged to A.A. McSween, that said Matthews was told by said Brewer that he Matthews could round up the cattle and that he, Brewer, would help him. That said Matthews said that he would go back to Lincoln to get new instructions and if he came back to the ranch he would come back with one man. That said Matthews and his posse were then invited by R.M. Brewer to come to the house to get something to eat.*

Deponent further states that Robert A. Widenmann told R.M. Brewer and the others at the ranch, that he was going to arrest Frank Baker, Jesse Evans and Tom Hill said Widenmann having warrants for them. That said Widenmann was told by Brewer and the others at the ranch that the arrest could not be made because if it was made they, all the persons at the ranch would be killed and murdered by J.J. Dolan and their party. That said Evans advanced upon said Widenmann, said Evans swinging it his gun and catching it cocked and pointed directly at said Widenmann. That said Jesse Evans asked said Widenmann whether he, Widenmann, was hunting for him, Evans, to which Widenmann answered that if he was looking for him, he, Evans, would find it out. Evans also asked Widenmann whether he had a warrant for him; Widenmann answered that it was his (Widenmann's) business. Evans told Widenmann, that if he ever came to arrest him (Evans) he, Evans would pick Widenmann as the first man to shoot at, to which Widenmann answered that that was all right, that two could play at that game. That during the talking Frank Baker stood near said Widenmann, swinging his pistol on his finger, catching it full cocked pointed at said Widenmann. The persons at the ranch were R.M. Brewer, John Middleton, G. Gauss [sic - Gottfried Gauss], M. Martz, R.A. Widenmann, Henry Brown, F.T. Waite, Wm McClosky and this deponent. J.B. Matthews after eating started for Lincoln with John Hurley and Poncearo the rest of the party or posse saying they were going to the Rio Peñasco. Deponent started to Lincoln with Robert A. Widenmann and F.T. Waite and arrived at Lincoln the same evening and again left Lincoln on the next day, February the 14th in company with the above named persons, having heard that said Matthews was going back to the ranch of said J.H. Tunstall with a large party of men to take the cattle and deponent and Widenmann and Waite arrived at said ranch the same day. Deponent states that on the road to Lincoln he heard said Matthews ask said Widenmann whether any resistance would be offered if he Matthews returned to take the cattle, to which said Widenmann answered that no resistance would be offered if the cattle were left at the ranch but if an attempt was made to drive the cattle to the Indian Agency and kill them for beef as he, said Matthews had been heard to say would be done, he, said Widenmann, would do all in his power to prevent this.

Deponent further says that on the night of the 17th of February A.D. 1878 J.H. Tunstall arrived at the ranch and informed all persons there that reliable information had reached him that J.B. Matthews was gathering a large party of outlaws and desperados as a posse and that said *posse was coming to the ranch, the Mexicans in the party to gather up the cattle and the balance of the party to kill the persons at the ranch. It was thereupon decided that all persons at the ranch excepting G. Gauss, were to leave and Wm Mcclosky was that night sent to the Rio Peñasco to inform the posse who were camped there, that they could come over and round up the cattle, count them and leave a man there to take care of them and that Mr. Tunstall would also leave a man there to help round up and count the cattle and help take care of them, and said Mcclosky was also ordered to go to Martin Martz, who had left Tunstall's ranch when deponent, Widenmann and Waite returned to the town of Lincoln on the 13th of February and ask him said Martz to come to the ranch of said Tunstall and aid the sheriffs posse in rounding up and counting the cattle and to stay at the ranch and take care of the cattle.*

Deponent left the ranch of said Tunstall in company with J.H. Tunstall, R.A. Widenmann, R.M. Brewer, John Middleton, F.T. Waite, said Tunstall, Widenmann, Brewer, Middleton and deponent driving the loose horses, Waite driving the wagon. Said Waite took the road for Lincoln with the wagon, the rest of the party taking the trail with the horses. Deponent says that all the horses which he and the party were driving, excepting 3 had been released by sheriff Brady at Lincoln that one of these 3 horses belonged to R.M. Brewer, and the other was traded by Brewer to Tunstall for one of the released horses.

Deponent further says, that when he and the party had traveled to within about 3 miles from the Rio Ruidoso he and John Middleton were in drag in the rear of the balance of the party as just upon reaching the brow of a hill they saw a large party of men coming towards them from the rear at full speed and that he and Middleton at once rode forward to inform the balance of the party of the fact. Deponent had not more than barely reached Brewer and Widenmann who were some 200 or 300 yards to the left of the trail when the attacking party cleared the brow of the hill and commenced firing at him, Widenmann and Brewer. Deponent, Widenmann and Brewer rode over a hill towards a another which was covered with large rocks and trees in order to defend themselves and make a stand.

But the attacking party, undoubtedly seeing Tunstall, left off pursuing deponent and the two with him and turned back at the caño in which the trail was. Shortly afterwards we heard two or three separate and distinct shots and the remark was then made by Middleton that they, the attacking party must have killed Tunstall. Middleton had in the meantime joined deponent and Widenmann and Brewer. Deponent then made the rest of his way to Lincoln in company with Robt. A. Widenmann, Brewer, Waite and Middleton stopping on the Rio Ruidoso in order to get men to look for the body of J.H. Tunstall.

Deponent further says that neither he nor any of the party fired off either rifle or pistol and that neither he nor the parties with him fired a shot.

William H. Bonney

Sworn and subscribed before me this eighth day of June A.D. 1878.

John B. Wilson
Justice of the Peace

COURT TESTIMONY OF WILLIAM BONNEY

Billy's two day, 1879 testimony in the Fort Stanton Court of Inquiry for potential Court Martial of its past Commander Nathan Augustus Monroe Dudley also reveals his precise mind.

It concerns the July 19, 1878 turning point in the Lincoln County War, when Dudley, violating the Posse Comitatus Act, brought his soldiers, a howitzer cannon, and a Gatling gun to aid Lincoln County's Ring-partisan sheriff, George Peppin.

Noteworthy is that Alexander McSween, during his house's besiegement, gave Billy letters, *to read.* ("Brushy Bill" claimed illiteracy; and John Miller appeared so.) Demonstrated also is Billy's personal freedom fight, since his pardon deal included *only* testifying about the murder of Attorney Huston Chapman. Yet he risked his life to oppose this local commander, who was responsible for their defeat in the Lincoln County War.

In the transcript below, the "Recorder" is the military prosecutor. He was being assisted by Attorney Ira Leonard, who was also in the court. (So Leonard would have seen Billy's testimony - possibly cementing his loyalty to the brave and brilliant boy.) "By Col. Dudley" refers to Dudley's defense attorney, Henry Waldo, the Territory's best trial lawyer.

In his first day of testimony, on May 28, 1879, Billy responded as follows:

Q. by Recorder. Where were you on the 19ᵗʰ day of July last and what, if anything, did you see of the movements and actions of the troops in that city, state fully?

Answer. I was in the McSween house in Lincoln, and I saw soldiers come from the post with sheriff's party, that is the sheriff's posse joined them a short distance below there, the McSween house. Soldiers passed on by and the men dropped off and surrounded the house, the sheriff's party. Shortly after the soldiers came back with Peppin, passed the house twice afterwards. Three soldiers came and stood in front of the house, in front of the windows. Mr. McSween wrote a note to the officer in charge asking what the soldiers were placed there for. He replied saying that they had business there, that if a shot was fired over his camp, or at Peppin, or at any of his men, that he had no objection to blowing up, if he wanted, his own house. I read the note myself, he handed it to me to read. I saw nothing further of the soldiers until night. I was in the back part of the house. When I escaped from the house three soldiers fired at me from the Tunstall store, outside corner of the store. That's all I know in regards to it ...

Q. By Col. Dudley. In addition to the names you have given, are you also known as the "Kid?"

Answer. I have already answered that question, Yes Sir, I am, but not "Billy Kid" that I know of ...

[AUTHOR'S NOTE: Billy does not use the name: "Billy the Kid" for himself.]

Q. By Col. Dudley. Whose name was signed to the note received by McSween in reply to the one previously sent by him to Col. Dudley?

Answer. Signed N.A.M. Dudley, did not say what rank, he received two notes, one had no name signed to it.

[AUTHOR'S NOTE: Another confirmation that Billy could read.]

Q. By Col. Dudley. Are you as certain of everything else you have sworn to as you are to what you have sworn to in answer to the last proceeding question?

Answer. Yes Sir.

Q. By Col. Dudley. From which direction did Peppin come the first time the soldiers passed with him?

Answer. Passed up from the direction of where the soldiers camped, the first time I saw him.

Q. By Col. Dudley. What direction did he come from the second time?

Answer. From the direction of the [Wortley] *hotel from the McSween house.*

Q. By Col. Dudley. In what direction did you go upon your escape from the McSween house?

Answer. Ran towards the Tunstall store, was fired at, and there turned towards the river.

Q. By Col. Dudley. From what part of the McSween house did you make your escape?

48

Answer. The Northeast corner of the house.

Q. By Col. Dudley. How many soldiers fired at you?

Answer. Three.

Q. By Col. Dudley. How many soldiers were with Peppin when he passed the McSween house each time, as you say?

Answer. Three.

Q. By Col. Dudley. The soldiers appeared to go in company of threes that day, did they not?

Answer. All that I ever saw appeared to be three in a crowd at a time after they passed the first time.

[AUTHOR'S NOTE: Billy, only 19, cannot be shaken by bullying Attorney Henry Waldo.]

Q. By Col. Dudley. Who was killed first that day, Bob Beckwith or McSween men?

Answer. Harvey Morris, McSween man, was killed first.

Q. By Col. Dudley. How far is the Tunstall building from the McSween house?

Answer. I could not say how far, I never measured the distance. I should judge it to be 40 yards, between 30 and 40 yards.

Q. By Col. Dudley. How many shots did those soldiers fire, that you say shot from the Tunstall building?

Answer. I could not swear to that on account of firing on all sides, I could not hear. I seen them fire one volley.

[AUTHOR'S NOTE: Illustrated are Billy's precision in answering, and his observation of a "volley" - meaning firing in unison, under orders.]

Q. By Col. Dudley. What did they fire at?
Answer. Myself and Jose Chavez ...

Billy resumed his Court testimony the following day: May 29, 1879; and further identified the shooting soldiers. In a fair trial, a Court Martial could have resulted from this testimony alone.

Q. by Court. Were the soldiers which you say fired at you as you escaped from the McSween house on the evening of July 19ᵗʰ last, colored or white?

Answer. White troops.

Q. by Court. Was it light enough so you could distinctly see the soldiers when they fired?

Answer. The house was burning. Made it almost light as day for a short distance all around.

LOST TESTIMONY OF WILLIAM BONNEY

Billy fulfilled his part of the Lew Wallace pardon deal by testifying against the murderers of Attorney Chapman - James Dolan, Billy Campbell, and Jessie Evans - in the April 1879 Lincoln County Grand Jury.

By doing that, he was also implicating the Santa Fe Ring and risking his life. And his testimony achieved those men's murder indictments (James Dolan and Billy Campbell for murder; Jessie Evans for accessory to murder).

That court record is missing. A compelling guess is that it fell victim to what appears to have been systematic Santa Fe Ring expurgations of records incriminating to its partisans.

Nevertheless, a letter to Governor Lew Wallace by Attorney Ira Leonard confirms not only that Billy gave the testimony, but that, while giving it, he endured harassment by Ringman District Attorney William Rynerson. As in the Dudley Court of Inquiry, however, Billy could not be thrown off course by intimidation of authority figures. And his course was zealous opposition of the Santa Fe Ring.

A LEGEND IN HIS TIME

Billy Bonney generated his mythology when still alive. Examples are his fabricated pre-death sightings and even fabricated deeds after his great escape from the Lincoln County courthouse-jail on April 28, 1881.

In reality, in this period before his killing 2 ½ months later, Billy was hiding out in Fort Sumner and its sheep camps, and presumably secretly making whoopee with Paulita Maxwell. But those fabricated and attention-seeking sightings heralded his equally false, "post-death sightings" and recounted "deeds."

The following examples appeared in the *Santa Fe Daily New Mexican* in May of 1881, the month following his escape:

On May 5, 1881: "There was a report on the streets last night that the Kid was then in Albuquerque, and was bound for Santa Fe. It was also said that he had killed another man there, but the rumor thus far lacks confirmation."

On May 13, 1881: "The latest news in regard to the whereabouts of Billy the Kid ... was received yesterday. It came through a private letter to General Atkinson, written from Chloride City [southwestern part of the Territory - Grant County], under the date of the 9th inst. The writer says, 'I slept with the Kid last night, and did not know who he was. I see him across the street now' ... So the Kid was in Chloride City four days ago."

On May 19, 1881: "The Kid is believed to be in the Black Range [western part of the Territory], but that is about all that is known in regard to him."

On May 20, 1881: "Billy the Kid was seen in Lincoln County, a man who knows him well having talked with him a few days ago. The Kid says he is among friends and is all right. His friends keep him provided with newspapers and he seems satisfied in his present quarters ... This report, if true, effectively contradicts the rumor of the Kid's presence in the Black Range where everybody believed him to be."

So on the lam, or eventually six feet under, Billy the Kid - in the mind of his eager audience - kept up his appearances; unrestricted even by being two places (or more) at once.

That eager audience would be granted further performances of Billy the Kid by old pretenders and modern hoaxers, relying on that audience's ignorance about real Billy Bonney, and themselves eager to cash in on that ignorance's bliss.

BILLY THE KID CASE

HOAX HISTORY ___

HISTORY OF THE BILLY THE KID
CASE HOAX

HOAXBUST: The elaborate historic-forensic hoax, called by its perpetrators the "Billy the Kid Case," is a real murder investigation filed against Pat Garrett in 2003. It is debunked in my book: MegaHoax: The Strange Plot to Exhume Billy the Kid and Become President. Its extensive bibliography is included herein to justify my allegations of its fakery. That hoax belongs in this book debunking Billy Bonney's pretenders - Oliver "Brushy Bill" Roberts and John Miller - since it used their "survival stories" for "suspicion" that Garrett had shot an innocent victim instead of Billy on July 14, 1881. Also, it appears that the Billy the Kid Case hoax planned ultimately, by using false forensics, to "prove" "Brushy" as the real Billy the Kid. Though my exposés of it managed to stop that historical catastrophe, the Billy the Kid Case hoax succeeded in elevating those imposters to mainstream TV documentaries. The unintended positive contribution of the hoaxers, however, was justifying modern debunking of those old pretenders.

Historical hoaxes have real history: their own. And the Billy the Kid Case hoax was a whopper for its convoluted lies and ability to reinvent itself when trapped by truths.

It was devised in 2003 by New Mexico's then governor, Bill Richardson; one of his major political donors; colluding sheriffs and deputy sheriffs; and a university professor, appointed as its "official historian."

The Billy the Kid Case was an eccentric publicity stunt for Bill Richardson's upcoming presidential run in 2008; as well as the pot of gold at rainbow's end for the other participants.

It grabbed national media attention by claiming that Sheriff Pat Garrett had not shot Billy the Kid; but, in collusion with him, shot an innocent youth to enable Bonney's escape.

Governor Richardson's law enforcement compatriots, thus, in 2003, opened a real murder investigation against Pat Garrett, filed in two, New Mexico, sheriffs' departments.

Filed in Lincoln County as Case No. 2003-274, with a Probable Cause Statement [APPENDIX: 1] of doubletalk and fakery, it attested that Garrett was a justifiable suspect.

The fact that the Billy the Kid Case hoaxers had no evidence - historical or physical - for their murder accusation; the fact that the historical evidence to the contrary was conclusive; the fact that Garrett was dead and could not be prosecuted; the fact that their "investigation" - to the present - uncovered *no* evidence supporting their accusation; and the fact that their claim required a conspiracy of concealment of corpse identity by Garrett, by Fort Sumner townspeople viewing the body, by the coroner's jurymen at Billy Bonney's inquest, and by all historians, were ignored by the hoaxers and their press.

The Billy the Kid Case hoax billed itself as solving the murder by "high-tech CSI forensics." DNA from Billy's only known kin, his mother, buried in Silver City, would be compared with that of remains in his Fort Sumner grave. Omitted was that both sites were merely tourist markers, and that the New Mexico Office of the Medical Investigator had refused them exhumation permits based on any remains from uncertain graves being invalid for DNA for matchings. Also, the hoaxers' exhumation petitions for Billy and his mother were blocked in district courts in the gravesites' counties.

Undaunted, the hoaxers reworked their hoax, claiming to have found the carpenter's bench on which Billy the Kid had been laid out. From it they claimed to get his "blood DNA." And with that "DNA," they hoped to prove a pretender as real.

Lastly, those future DNA matchings were linked with a future Bill Richardson gubernatorial pardon for "Billy the Kid," by claiming that as, "Brushy Bill," Billy would deserve it for having led a "long and law-abiding life!"

The undeniably shared goal of Billy the Kid's pretenders and hoaxers was a media circus for themselves, understood best by an actual circus impresario, P.T. Barnum, who said, "Without promotion something terrible happens: Nothing!"

SPLASHING IN THE PRESS

The Billy the Kid Case hoax entered the world big time: on the front page of the *New York Times* of June 5, 2003, in an article by a reporter named Michael Janofsky, titled "122 Years Later, The Lawmen Are Still Chasing Billy the Kid."

It gave the whole shebang: the hoaxers' names, their fake forensic plans, and the ludicrous claim that "Brushy Bill" Roberts should be taken seriously - confirmed by none other than one of his most fervent, conspiracy theory believers. Missing was input from any legitimate historians.

Michael Janofsky wrote:

LINCOLN, NEW MEXICO – For more than 120 years, Pat Garrett has enjoyed legendary status in the American West, a lawman on a par with Wyatt Earp, Bat Masterson, even Matt Dillon. As sheriff here in Lincoln County in 1881, Garrett is credited with shooting to death the notorious outlaw known as Billy the Kid, a killing that made Garrett a hero. For years, a patch bearing his likeness has adorned uniforms worn by sheriff''s deputies here.

But now, modern science is about to interrupt Garrett's fame in a way that some say could expose him as a liar who covered up a murder to save his own skin and reputation.

Officials in New Mexico and Texas are working out plans to exhume and conduct genetic tests on the bodies of a woman buried in New Mexico who was believed to be the Kid's mother and a Texas man known as Brushy Bill Roberts, who claimed to be the Kid and died in 1950 at the age of 90. If test results suggest that the two were related, it would add new evidence to a long-held alternative theory that Garrett shot someone other than the Kid and led a conspiracy to cover up his crime. [author's boldface]

Such skepticism is hardly uncommon. Disputes over major events in the Old West have engaged historians almost since they happened. The debate over Billy the Kid is one of the longest-running.

Beyond renewing interest in the Kid saga, the possibility that testing could enlarge Garrett's reputation or destroy it has even caught the fancy of Gov. Bill Richardson of New Mexico, who has offered state aid for the investigation and a possible pardon that an earlier New Mexico governor had once promised the Kid for a murder he committed.

"The problem is, there's so much fairy tale with this story that it's hard to nail down the facts," said Steve Sederwall, the mayor of Capitan, N.M., who is working with Lincoln County's current sheriff, Tom Sullivan, to resolve the matter. "All we want is the truth, whatever it is. If the guy Garrett killed was Billy the Kid, that makes him a hero. If it wasn't, Garrett was a murderer, and we have egg on our face, big time."

No matter what the genetic testing may show - and it might not show much of anything – it is hard to overstate the prominence of Garrett and the Kid in Western lore, especially here in southeastern New Mexico where their lives converged during and after the gun battles for financial control of the region that were known as the Lincoln County War. The Kid's notoriety grew after he and friends on one side of the conflict killed several men in an ambush, including Garrett's predecessor, Sheriff William Brady. For that, the Kid was hunted down, captured by Garrett, found guilty of murder and taken to the Lincoln jail, where he was placed in shackles to await hanging. He was only 21.

Today the tiny town of Lincoln, population 38, is a memorial to what happened next. More than a dozen buildings, including one that housed the jail, have been preserved as a state monument that attracts as many as 35,000 visitors a year.

Historians generally agree that the Kid, born Henry McCarty and known at times as William H. Bonney, escaped after it became apparent that Gov. Lew Wallace had reneged on a promise to pardon him in exchange for information about another killing in the county war. On April 28, 1881, the Kid managed to get his hands on a gun, kill the two deputies assigned to watch him and leave the area on horseback.

But then the stories diverge, providing fuel for two major theories of where, when, and how the Kid's life ended.

The version embraced here and supported by numerous books and Garrett relatives is that the Kid made his way to a friend's ranch in Fort Sumner, about 100 miles northeast of Lincoln. The ranch owner, Pete Maxwell, was also a friend of Garrett and somehow got word to Garrett that the Kid was in the area. After arriving, Garrett posted two deputies at the door.

As the Kid approached on the night of July 13 [sic], he spoke a few words in Spanish to the deputies, who did not recognize him. But Garrett, waiting inside, knew the voice. When the Kid walked in, Garrett turned and shot him in the heart.

William F. Garrett of Alamogordo, N.M., who is Garrett's grand-nephew, said years of research, including conversations with his cousin Jarvis, the last of Garrett's eight children, convinced him there is "no question about it" that his great-uncle killed Billy the Kid at Maxwell's. Jarvis died in 1991 at the age of 86.

"He was hired to get the Kid, and he got the Kid," Mr. Garrett said in an interview. "uncle Pat was a person of integrity who did his job. He was a law abider, not a law breaker."

But just as the story of Garrett as hero has flourished over the years, so have others, including the tale of Brushy Bill of Hico, Tex. His trip to New Mexico in 1950 to seek the pardon he said he was denied nearly 70 years before gave new life to an alternative possibility, that Garrett had not killed the Kid at all, but a drifter friend of the Kid's named Billy Barlow.

This story holds that Garrett and the Kid may have been in cahoots for some reason and that Garrett had stashed a gun at the outhouse at the jail that the Kid used to kill the deputies and escape. Even if only part of that is true, it would strongly suggest that Garrett killed the wrong man.

[AUTHOR'S COMMENT: So, from the start, "Brushy Bill" was key in the hoax.]

Speaking with the same person as Garrett's great-nephew, Jannay P. Valdez, curator of the Billy the Kid Museum in Canton, Tex., said he had no doubt that Garrett killed someone else and that Brushy Bill was the Kid. "I'm absolutely convinced," he said here on Monday after meeting with Mr. Sederwall to discuss theories and how to begin the kind of genetic testing that has been used to ascertain lineage of other historical figures like Thomas Jefferson and Jessie James. "I'd bank everything I have on it."

[AUTHOR'S COMMENT: Jannay Valdez is a fervent "Brushy Bill" believer.]

As longtime friends, Mr. Sederwall and Sheriff Sullivan decided they wanted to settle the matter once and for all but could do so only through scientific analysis. To justify the effort that would require much of their time and, perhaps at some point, taxpayer money,

[AUTHOR'S COMMENT: At the start, the hoaxers admitted to taxpayer money. Later, under investigation, and having used it, that was denied.]

They needed an official reason. So in April, they opened the first-ever investigation into the murders of the two deputies shot in the Kid's escape, James W. Bell and Robert Olinger, to examine what happened at the jail and Maxwell's ranch.

[AUTHOR'S COMMENT: Janofsky is parroting hoax double-talk.]

As Mr. Sederwall said, "There's no statute of limitations on murder."

[AUTHOR'S COMMENT: This article announces the taxpayer funded, real murder investigation; though it misrepresents the statute of limitations issue, which, through a state law technicality, did not apply to this New Mexico case.]

The goal now, he said, is to compare genetic evidence of Catherine Antrim, believed to be the Kid's mother, who died of tuberculosis in 1874 and is buried in Silver City, N.M., and of Brushy Bill, who lived out his life in Texas. A Dallas firm [sic Houston] has agreed to help, and a spokesman for governor Richardson said the state would assist by clearing legal hurdles to gain access to the mother's body.

[AUTHOR'S COMMENT: Note state aid.]

The Kid was buried at Fort Sumner, N.M., although the whereabouts of the grave are uncertain;

[AUTHOR'S COMMENT: This uncertain grave location, though true, was later denied by the hoaxers, when trying to exhume it.]

He has no known living relatives. Mr. Valdez said he had already secured permission to exhume the body of Brushy Bill,

[AUTHOR'S COMMENT: This is untrue. And permission was never obtained.]

who is buried 20 miles from Hico in Hamilton, Texas.

But solving the mystery might not be so simple. For one thing, Mr. Valdez said he was certain that the woman buried in Silver City was but "a half aunt." And even if tests disqualify Brushy Bill as Billy the Kid, other "Kids" have emerged over the years, including a man named John Miller, who died in 1937 and is buried in Prescott, Ariz. Mr. Sederwall said that efforts would be made to exhume his body as well.

The investigators conceded that much is riding on their quest. Sheriff Sullivan, a tall, strapping man who carries a turquoise-handled .357 magnum on his right hip, said he, like so many others in the West, revered Garrett for gunning down the Kid. The uniform patch with Garrett's likeness was his design. Now, the legend is threatened.

[AUTHOR'S COMMENT: Only Sheriff Sullivan, and his fellow hoaxers, are threatening Pat Garrett's reputation!]

"I just want to get to the bottom of it," said Sheriff Sullivan, who is retiring next year. "My integrity's at stake. So's my department's. So's what we believe in and even New Mexico history. If Garrett shot someone other than the Kid, that makes him a murderer and he covered it up. He wouldn't be such a role model, then, and we'd have to take the patches off the uniforms."

A HOAX GROWS IN NEW MEXICO

To fancy-up the path worn by the old-timer pretenders, the Billy the Kid Case hoaxers had made their claim of using "modern, high-tech, CSI-style DNA forensics" to investigate Pat Garrett's murder of the innocent victim.

A statement by Guy Laliberte, CEO of "Cirque de Soliel," is apropos: "We didn't reinvent the circus. We repackaged it in a much more modern way."

That repackaging also needed a murder motive for Sheriff Pat Garrett. So manufactured was a "friendship" with Billy Bonney - side-stepping that a "friendship" causing wanton murder and risk of his own hanging to save the Kid put Garrett in a man-to-man love story rivaling "Brokeback Mountain!" Omitted too was that Pat and Billy were merely acquaintances.

But to spice up that fake "friendship," the hoaxers added that Garrett also assisted Billy in his Lincoln jailbreak by giving him the gun; thus, being the accomplice to the boy's killing of his deputy guards, 2 ½ months prior to allowing Billy to escape again - permanently as "Brushy" or John Miller.

So, according to the hoaxers, Garrett was the Old West's most heinous lawman, and Billy was a lucky son-of-a-gun.

Also, the Billy the Kid Case hoax's "modern, high-tech, CSI-style, DNA forensics" repackaging had a big problem: there existed no valid DNA pertaining to Billy the Kid anywhere on the planet to use for it. However, since they planned to fake DNA results anyway, that was not their worry.

The last part of the repackaging was that the Billy the Kid Case hoaxers had to say *something* - in a probable cause statement for their murder case, in court documents for exhumations, in press interviews, and in TV documentaries - but they had not an iota of evidence. So they did the obvious: hoaxing. I named their techniques: "alien invasion illogic," "fuzzy factoids," "confabulation," and just plain lying.

ALIEN INVASION ILLOGIC

History is hoaxer heaven: vulnerable to "how do you know *for sure?*" Obviously, if one ignores all historical, legal, and scientific evidence, anything goes.

The hoaxers settled on fake logic to conceal lack of *any* evidence. It was like the ancient Greek theater ploy of *deus ex machina*: a mechanical god dropping to the stage to solve a plot impasse. To modernize that, I dropped in outer-space aliens, and called the hoaxers' ploy "alien invasion illogic." "What ifs" based on unfounded "suspicion," were dropped to make any desired conclusion - as if real evidence had been provided.

This is how the silly technique it works to deny Abraham Lincoln's assassination (here using aliens with the ifs):

HOAXER: (*Feigning dead seriousness*) It seems suspicious that Abraham Lincoln went to Ford's Theater the night he was killed - because it provided *so many witnesses!*

What if alien beings knew Lincoln risked assassination and made a rescue plan, *in collusion with Lincoln*, since they collect unusual people for their planet? What if those aliens then did mind-control for murder on John Wilkes Booth - after giving him a derringer with a blank bullet? What if they also made the whole audience think Lincoln was shot dead? What if they superimposed a Lincoln hologram on someone they actually shot for the White House lying-in-state?

That makes me conclude that Lincoln is not in his grave, and needs me to check by digging him up for a TV program.

Here goes for spoofing the Billy the Kid Case hoax with alien invasion illogic:

BILLY THE KID CASE HOAXERS: (*Feigning dead seriousness, and in chorus*) It seems suspicious that old men claimed to be Billy the Kid, fifty years after he was supposedly (*pause slyly*) shot dead by Sheriff Pat Garrett.

What if aliens landed in Roswell, New Mexico, and gave Garrett a revolver, and used mind-control to make him give Billy that revolver for his jail escape? What if the aliens then took the Kid away on their space ship (to join Abraham Lincoln)? What if - to cover-up that disappearance of the boy, and to collect the reward money for eliminating him - Garrett killed someone else to fill Billy's grave?

So we need to check Billy the Kid's grave - in a "media circus" - to see who is really there.

(*Gleeful chuckling*) Then, in conclusion - even though we'll be hiding the fact that we got no real DNA findings - we'll crown a Billy of our choosing, and - in an even bigger "media circus" - the governor will pardon *him*!

HOAXBUSTER: (*Laughing*) The only historical facts are Old West names, and Billy's grave. The rest is "alien invasion illogic" - and any conclusion the hoaxers choose to make.

FUZZY FACTOIDS

The sole Billy the Kid Case hoax "evidence" ever presented by the hoaxers was what I called "fuzzy factoids": documents of obvious hearsay or lying - that legitimate historians dismiss.

Thus, after-death sightings of Billy - anywhere in the country - became "proof" that he had not been killed.

Omitted, however, was that Billy's *pre-death* sightings all over the country were as profuse after his Lincoln jail escape, when he was actually hiding-out in Fort Sumner!

And the pretenders, Oliver "Brushy Bill" Roberts and John Miller, and their authors, had, more than a half century before these modern hoaxers, presented the same "fuzzy factoid" evidence for their own self-justifications as being Billy the Kid.

Coming full circle, the modern hoaxers also recycled those old fellows' "fuzzy factoid" yarns for their own "fuzzy factoid" yarns.

CONFABULATION

Used by the pretenders, and by the modern hoaxers in the form of old-timer affidavits attesting to Billy's survival, confabulation is a mental condition yielding made-up stories.

Not purposeful lying, it usually arises from brain pathology, and can follow chronic alcoholism.

As defined by Harold Kaplan's and Benjamin Sadock's *Synopsis of Psychiatry*, it is "unconscious filling of gaps in memory by imagined or untrue experiences that a person believes but have no basis in fact."

Characteristic are over-embellished details around any claim, thus mimicking a portrayal real experience.

The hoaxers hoped that insanity was unnoticeable in their claimants, as had the promoters of the old time pretenders.

LYING

Most frequently, the Billy the Kid Case hoaxers simply lied. And they lied about everything. After all, their murder case was a hoax. So they made up forensic findings, historical events, and their own validations of the pretenders - omitting those old guys' own transparent lies.

HOAX SEEKS PRETENDERS UNDERGROUND

Legally stopped from exhuming Billy and his mother for DNA from gravesites that were not verifiably theirs, the hoaxers persisted by becoming more reckless and silly; proving that Governor Bill Richardson possessed the tenacity to be a president, though lacking other needed machinery, like a moral compass.

After all, Richardson was on a mission to become America's first governor willing to destroy his state's iconic history and tourist industry for a self-serving publicity stunt. And he was poised to give that history to either John Miller's Arizona or, preferably, to "Brushy Bill's" Texas.

Apparently, Fort Sumner's roadside sign - "We've Got The Kid" - was to be replaced by an arrow pointing to either state saying, "Billy the Kid Ended Up Thataway."

But the hoaxers needed a way to continue the media circus. So, in 2004, they wheeled in forensic expert, Dr. Henry Lee - notorious for his questionable forensic defense testimony in O.J. Simpson's murder case. Lee's task was to get the hoaxers "DNA of Billy the Kid." The fact that none was verifiable on the planet fazed none in that group.

But they had gotten their hands on an old carpenter's workbench, first surfacing about fifty years after Billy the Kid's killing, when a Maxwell family descendant put it in her private museum as the one on which Billy had been laid out.

So the merry coalition of hoaxers claimed, without basis or any definitive testing, that, after 123 years, that bench still had Billy's "blood!" So Dr. Henry Lee scraped and swabbed it to get "Billy's blood" specimens to send to his participating Texas laboratory, Orchid Cellmark - which was implicated, later that same year, in faking DNA computer data in another case.

The switcheroo the hoaxers hoped their audience missed was their *victim!* To use the bench for "Billy's blood," they had to change their hoax story: *Billy himself* had to be shot.

But that scenario created a bigger problem. Dead Billy was conventional history, not attention-grabbing news. Their "bleeding-Billy-on-the-bench-version" required his survival as "Brushy" or John Miller. So they preposterously claimed that shot Billy merely "played dead and bled."

That claim was also needed for their sham of "Pat Garrett as the suspect" in their filed murder investigation, so they could still use law enforcement titles and taxpayer facilitation.

So, in their hoaxland, after "playing-dead-Billy" left the bench (painfully), Garrett tossed on his "innocent victim," in front of the grieving townspeople, who noticed nothing amiss!

And though neither "Brushy Bill" nor John Miller claimed that bizarre carpenter's bench scenario, they still remained in the hoaxers' sights for Billy's "identity" and "pardon."

By 2005, a new Lincoln County Sheriff, Rick Virden, was elected. Joining the hoax - in which he had participated as Undersheriff since 2003 - he immediately deputized his predecessor Sheriff, Tom Sullivan, and his predecessor's deputy, Steve Sederwall, to continue murder Case No. 2003-274 against dastardly dead lawman: Pat Garrett.

Immediately, all these hoaxing law enforcement clowns claimed, of course, that Dr. Henry Lee, via Orchid Cellmark Laboratory, had isolated the actual, honest-to-goodness, bloody DNA of Billy the Kid from that old carpenter's workbench.

The hoaxers were now in the exhumation business; ready to compare "Billy's bloody DNA" with DNA of any exhumed pretender to determine if *he* was Garrett-shot-playing-dead-bleeding-Billy. Cleverly, they were still within the parameters of their murder case when using pretender exhumations, since, if they declared a "match" of pretender DNA with fake Billy bench DNA, they could extrapolate that Garrett *had* killed the innocent victim for the Fort Sumner grave, since their old-timer claimant was Billy the Kid who survived to old age.

Omitted for the public was: 1) the bench was unprovable as related to Billy's shooting, 2) no blood was definitively proven on it, and 3) any DNA isolated was impossible to prove as Billy's since there exists no certain Billy DNA for comparison. So the hoaxers approached grave-digging with no Billy the Kid DNA at all!

That did not stop the hoaxers' planned digging rampage. Alleging dozens of Billy the Kid identity claimants, they could have kept on exhuming through two Bill Richardson presidency terms - if things had worked out as planned.

But the hoaxers hid a great irony. Their "high-tech CSI investigation" now stood, not on the shoulders of forensic DNA giants, but the shoulders of two crazy old men - "Brushy Bill" Roberts and John Miller - and their odd-ball authors.

Their Billy the Kid Case had become a throwback to 1950's historical ignorance and pretenders' tall tales. "Modern forensics" was overkill. Plain old history was enough to blow their scheme out of the water. "Brushy Bill" canceled out as twenty years too young: "Billy the Tot." John Miller bit the dust as nine years too old: "Billy the Codger."

Nevertheless, as undaunted by reality as had been those demented old men, the hoaxers merely concealed that the pretenders' death-scenes had no playing-dead-on-the-bench escape ploy; and that nothing else in those old-timers' fabrications indicated, to any rational and knowledgeable person, that they were Billy the Kid.

The Billy the Kid Case hoaxers' backhoe headed first to Prescott, Arizona, and pretender John Miller, simply because Governor Bill Richardson was friends with Arizona's then governor, Janet Napolitano, in whose state-owned cemetery that fellow had been laid to rest in 1937. And her morals reputedly matched Bill Richardson's. So she allegedly gave permission for the meaningless exhumation/desecration.

John Miller's rest ended on May 19, 2005, when the hoaxers ravaged his grave and coffin, removing bones for comparison with their fake Billy-bench-DNA.

Unfortunately for John Miller's underground neighbor, a man named William Hudspeth, the hoaxers dug him up too, since both graves were unmarked and they felt above the law under Richardson's big umbrella. So, the Director of Orchid Cellmark Laboratory, Dr. Rick Staub - on hand for a cameo in their TV documentary being filmed - for good measure took poor Hudspeth's bones back with him to Texas too.

Ultimately, and embarrassingly, Orchid Cellmark only got DNA from random man William Hudspeth; and irrationally matched *him* to Dr. Henry Lee's fake bench-DNA!

Nevertheless, to Governor Janet Napolitano, the hoaxers declared a DNA match - of sorts! It was actually 80%, which meant no match – a match being 100%, meaning identical.

Soon, however, the Billy the Kid Case hoaxers repented of that close call of giving Billy the Kid to Arizona, even stating publicly that John Miller could not be Billy since he had no carpenter's bench death scene (leaving out that "Brushy lacked one also); and they headed after bigger game in Hamilton Texas: the gravesite location of Oliver "Brushy Bill" Roberts.

Unfortunately for the hoaxers, Bill Richardson, it appeared, lacked an adequately corrupt, high-level friend there; because the Hamilton mayor, with his town council, kicked the clowning pack right out of "Brushy's" realm.

So the hoaxers were then left with concealing their concocted DNA documents (carpenter's bench, John Miller, William Hudspeth, and DNA matchings) from my open records act investigations, and continuing their path to fame and fortune by seeking media circuses in newspapers, TV, and film.

That gambit started with their 2004 History Channel program "Investigating History: Billy the Kid;" and was continued by a French-made film about the "mystery of Billy's murder," shown in the 2006 Cannes Film Festival. And they have continued to the present with a website and more TV documentaries. Thus, the hoaxers proved for real that faking Billy was good business.

But they had made a Faustian bargain. Without "high-tech forensics," they were forced to keep alive the old pretenders' tall tales, even more ridiculous in the 21st century than the 20th, because so much more actual history is now known.

And with that real history as armament, the pretenders and the modern hoaxers could be blasted by the weapon most dangerous to their existence: truth.

ATTACK BY
REAL HISTORY_____

HISTORICAL ATTACK WEAPONRY

HOAXBUST: Key to pretender and Billy the Kid Case hoax debunking is the armamentarium of historical information contradicting their survival premise. It is certain that Pat Garrett killed Billy the Kid. That, and other facts, come from Billy Bonney's contemporaries and top-notch historians.

Real Billy and real Pat Garrett possess an arsenal of documentation, which blasts away fabrications of pretenders and Billy the Kid Case hoaxers. The Lincoln County War period was a hot-bed of letter-writing, petitions, trials, investigations with depositions, a military court of inquiry, Secret Service reports, photographs, and later autobiographies.

BIG GUNS: HISTORIANS

Historians have dealt blows to pretenders in two ways. First, the paucity of their publications in the pretenders' day, gave slim pickings for impostorship research. Second, when the history books appeared, they proved the pretenders' tales false.

The modern Billy the Kid Case hoaxers, and modern pretender believers, simply ignored that onslaught of truth.

Readily available in the time of "Brushy Bill" Roberts and John Miller, was only Walter Noble Burns's groundbreaking but limited research, presented in his 1926 book, *The Saga of Billy the Kid.* From it, imposters gleaned historical names - with some connected history.

Robert N. Mullin and Maurice Garland Fulton were also early researcher/writers, but no salvation for pretenders.

The rest of the historical writings came too late for them. William Keleher's 1957 *Violence in Lincoln County 1869-1881*, contained a photocopy of the Coroner's Jury Report on Garrett's shooting of Billy, which Keleher re-discovered (and which the modern hoaxers and pretender followers conceal).

The historical renaissance had, as unsurpassed master, Frederick Nolan, with his *The Life and Death of John Henry Tunstall* in 1965; *The Lincoln County War: A Documentary History* in 1992; and *The West of Billy the Kid* in 1998, (filled with period photographs).

Billy's adolescence in Silver City, New Mexico, and Bonita, Arizona, was first elucidated by Jerry Weddle's 1993 *Antrim is My Stepfather's Name: The Boyhood of Billy the Kid.*

Pat Garrett himself also acquired a top-level historian: Leon Metz. His *Pat Garrett: The Story of a Western Lawman* came out in 1974.

Other modern historians were Joel Jacobson in 1994 with *Such Men as Billy the Kid. The Lincoln County War Reconsidered*; Phillip Rash with his 1995 *Trailing Billy the Kid*; and the excellent popularizer, Robert Utley, with his 1989 *Billy the Kid: A Short and Violent Life.*

Other Lincoln County War period participants got their own authors. In 1965, A.M. Gibson recorded *The Life and Death of Colonel Albert Jennings Fountain.* Grady E. McCright and James H. Powell wrote *Jessie Evans: Lincoln County Badman*, in 1983. E. Donald Kayne came out, in 2007, with *Nathan Augustus Monroe Dudley, 1825-1910: Rogue, Hero, or Both?*

GOING NUCLEAR: BILLY HIMSELF

As discussed earlier, Billy Bonney himself represented annihilation to pretenders. He appears in his own letters, in his own deposition on John Tunstall's murder, in his own court testimony against Commander N.A.M. Dudley, in his own tintype photograph, and in biographies of his contemporaries; all putting lies to pretenders' presentations.

LETTERS

Billy's spectacular letters – nine known - have seven to Governor Lew Wallace concerning his pardon (March 13, 1879, March 20, 1879, December 12, 1880, January 1, 1881, March 2, 1881, March 4, 1881, and March 27, 1881).

On March 18, 1879, Billy wrote to Lincoln County Justice of the Peace John "Squire" Wilson to facilitate his pardon meeting with Lew Wallace. And Billy's April 15, 1881 letter to Attorney Edgar Caypless, who was pursuing a replevin case for the theft of Billy's bay mare by one of Garrett's possemen at the Stinking Springs capture, shows Billy's pride in his Spencerian handwriting; since he apologizes for its bad quality, attributing it to his wearing handcuffs!

BILL OF SALE

Billy's "Bill of Sale," written in Tascosa, Texas, on October 24, 1878, for an expensive horse, to a Henry Hoyt, uses correct legalize, as well as Billy's characteristically fine penmanship.

LEW WALLACE'S INTERVIEW NOTES

Governor Lew Wallace took notes on his March 23, 1879 interview meeting with Billy, while the boy was in the sham Juan Patrón house arrest. They demonstrate the boy's depth of knowledge of Territorial outlaws, and the geography of their hide-outs and rustling trails (all unknown to the pretenders).

NEWSPAPER INTERVIEWS

Billy's many known newspaper interviews reflect, not only his denial of his alleged outlawry, but his lively humor.

For example, in a December 28, 1880 interview with "Lute" Wilcox of the *Las Vegas Gazette*, right after his Stinking Springs capture and facing hanging, Billy said, "What's the use of looking on the gloomy side of everything. The laugh's on me this time."

At a Las Cruces train station, on March 28, 1881, Billy teased the *Newman's Semi-Weekly* reporter, asking for Billy the Kid, by pointing to his balding attorney, Ira Leonard, and saying, "This is the man."

On the same day, Billy was quoted by the *Daily New Mexican*, jesting that two hundred men died in the Lincoln County War period, and he had not killed all of them!

HISTORICAL DOCUMENTS

As to other important documents on Billy, there exists the marriage record of his mother and step-father by Reverend David F. McFarland, in his Santa Fe, First Presbyterian Church's entry of March 1, 1873 listed in the *"Ledger: Session Records 1867-1874. Marriages in Santa Fe New Mexico. Mr. William H. Antrim and Mrs. Catherine McCarty."* Being unpublished, it was unknown to the pretenders. So they were unaware of Billy's brother Josie, listed in it!

Also, there exists Billy's Coroner's Jury Report, showing him undeniably dead and legally identified, and written in Spanish on July 15, 1881. It is photo-reproduced in William Kelleher's *Violence in Lincoln County, 1869-1881*, published in 1957. Of all the weapons of mass destruction against the old pretenders and the modern hoaxers, it is that document.

TINTYPE

Billy appears in the flesh, at about age 20, in a full-length tintype photograph; forcing any imposter to match-up physically, and yielding *sine qua non* failure by mismatch - and hilarious pretender attempts to mimic it because of their ignorance that tintypes were right-to-left reversed.

MORE BULL'S-EYE STRIKES: CONTEMPORARY PARTICIPANTS

Adding to imposter problems were massive, contemporary, official reports, containing depositions, court transcripts, and daily notes. Most emerged after the pretenders' day; all contradicted them.

ATTORNEY FRANK WARNER ANGEL: The Angel reports on the Lincoln County troubles and corruption were discovered in 1956 by historian Frederick Nolan.

Attorney Angel, sent in May of 1878 by President Rutherford B. Hayes, and via the Departments of Justice and the Interior, to investigate the February 18, 1878 murder of John Henry Tunstall, as well as other possible wrong-doings in the Territory, was an energetic and observant chronicler.

Frank Warner Angel produced a prodigious amount of first-hand documentation by taking depositions, among which was Billy Bonney's.

So, left for posterity, are Angel's October 4, 1878 *In the Matter of the Examination of the Causes and Circumstances of the Death of John H. Tunstall a British Subject,* and *In the Matter of the Lincoln County Troubles.* Dated October 3, 1878, was Angel's *In the Matter of the Investigation of the Charges Against S. B. Axtell Governor of New Mexico.* And Angel's October 2, 1878 report was: *Examination of Charges against F. C. Godfroy, Indian Agent, Mescalero, N. M.*

Attorney Angel also provided incoming Territorial Governor Lew Wallace with a notebook listing significant people and their Santa Fe Ring affiliations; information which Billy also would have known - and pretenders did not.

Added bonus came from Frank Warner Angel's letters to Secretary of the Interior Carl Schurz, documenting attempted Santa Fe Ring interference with his investigation.

ATTORNEY IRA LEONARD: Probably Billy's best friend in a high place, Leonard, was widow Susan McSween's attorney against past Commander N.A.M. Dudley.

Leonard met Billy in March of 1879, and was at Dudley's Fort Stanton Court of Inquiry when Billy testified. Billy would have known about the Ring assassination attempt on Leonard in April of 1879. Leonard also continued attempts to get Billy his pardon, and represented him in his 1881 hanging trial.

Attorney Leonard even empathized with Billy's pressure, during the boy's pardon-deal testimony, in the April 1879 Grand Jury, against the Ringmen murderers of Chapman. In his letter to Lew Wallace on April 20, 1879, Leonard stated:

I will tell you Gov. that the prosecuting officer of this Dist. [William Rynerson] *is no friend to the enforcement of the law. He is bent on going for the Kid & ... is proposed to destroy his testimony & influence. He is bent on pushing him to the wall. He is a Dolan man and is defending him by his conduct all he can.*

About Billy Bonney's critical and heart-felt relationship with Attorney Ira Leonard, the pretenders knew zero.

COLONEL NATHAN AUGUSTUS MONROE DUDLEY: Comparable in magnitude to the Angel reports, is the Court of Inquiry for possible Court Martial for Fort Stanton's Commander Nathan Augustus Monroe Dudley. It has over a hundred testimonies of the people involved in the Lincoln County War, including Billy's own, given on May 28th and 29th of 1879. Others speaking through time include the plaintiff herself, Alexander McSween's widow Susan McSween, whose pivotal and courageous role in the post-war Lincoln County struggle was unknown to the pretenders. She would have seemed a heroine to Billy Bonney; and his testimony in the Dudley Court of Inquiry was on her behalf.

SECRET SERVICE OPERATIVE AZARIAH WILD: Azariah F. Wild, by Secret Service guidelines, wrote daily activity reports on pre-printed forms like the following:

𝔘.𝔖. 𝔗reasury 𝔇epartment
SECRET-SERVICE DIVISION

New Orleans District

James J. Brooks,
    Chief U.S. Secret Service

Sir: I have the honor to submit the following, my report as _Chief_ Operative of this District for _Monday_ the _29th_ day of _December,_ 18 _79,_ written at _New Orleans, Louisiana,_ and completed at _9_ o'clock A M on the _30th_ day of _December,_ 18 _79_

In 1880, those daily records documented Wild's being assigned to track down an alleged counterfeiting gang in New Mexico Territory. There he was duped by Ringmen to believe that Billy Bonney headed both that gang and a rustling operation. As a consequence, Wild assisted Pat Garrett in becoming both a sheriff of Lincoln County and a Deputy U.S. Marshal to track Billy down. Billy, having stolen some of Wild's mailed reports, discovered the operative's plot to arrest him; and was forced to abandon his plan to testify against the real counterfeiters in exchange for finalizing of his Wallace pardon.

The pretenders, however, were entirely unaware of the Secret Service role, of Azariah Wild, and of how close Billy actually came to getting his pardon. Obviously, Billy himself knew all that.

THE SECRET SERVICE PARDON

In 1880, Azariah Wild could have actualized Billy's Wallace pardon promise of 1879. That possibility appears in Wild's October 8, 1880 report to his Chief (boldfaced below). Billy, via Attorney Ira Leonard, knew about it. The pretenders did not. The report stated:

I left Fort Stanton at 7 o'clock A.M. on the stage and reached Lincoln the County seat at 8:30 A.M. ... The object of my visit to Lincoln was to see Judge Ira Leonard ... In my report of October 5th ... I spoke of an outlaw whose name was Antrom alias Billy Bonney. During the Lincoln Co. War he killed men on the Indian Reservation for which he has been indicted in the territorial and the United States Court. Gov. Wallace has issued a proclamation granting immunity to those not indicted but as Antrom has been indicted the proclamation did not cover his (Antrom's) case and he (Antrom) has been in the mountains as an outlaw ever since a space of about two years time.

Governor Wallace has since written Antrom's attorney on the subject saying he should be let go but has failed to put it on shape that satisfied Judge Leonard Antrom's attorney.

It is believed and in fact is almost known that he (Antrom) is one of the leading members of this gang.

Antrom has recently written a letter to Judge Leonard which has been shown to me in confidence that leads me to believe that we can use Antrom in these cases provided Gov. Wallace will make good his written promises and the **U.S. Attorney will allow the case pending in the U.S. Court to slumber and give him (Antrom) one more chance to reform.** [author's boldface]

I have promised nothing and will not except to receive and propositions he Leonard and his client see fit to make and submit them to U.S. Attorney Barnes.

Judge Leonard has written Antrom to meet him (Leonard) at once for consultation.

The chances are that the conversation will take place within the next week I will report fully to you and submit whatever propositions they see fit to make to US. Attorney Barnes for such action as he deems proper to take.

MORE BARRAGE: OTHER LEGAL DOCUMENTS

The pretenders' floated tall tales were also sunk by the very complex, Emil Fritz, life insurance policy case: a Ring-instigated legal entanglement to arrest Attorney Alexander McSween as an embezzler, and to illegally seize John Henry Tunstall's property. It led to Tunstall's murder, and the Lincoln County War, and would have been the talk of Lincoln town and of Tunstall's men, including Billy. But the pretenders are unaware of its details or implications.

LINCOLN COUNTY SHERIFF WILLIAM BRADY: Lincoln County Sheriff William Brady was the Ring enforcer for the Fritz insurance policy case's embezzlement charge. Its documents still exist: the Action of Assumpsit to permit seizure of McSween's possessions, the Writ of Attachment for that deed (which falsely claims a partnership of McSween with Tunstall, making Tunstall's possessions sizeable also), and the inventory of items Sheriff Brady attached.

Billy, and the other Regulators would have been aware of these machinations - and outraged. Again, the pretenders were unaware of any specifics of the injustice, or of their larger Santa Fe Ring implications.

EMIL FRITZ SIBLINGS: Documents of the siblings of Emil Fritz (Charles Fritz and Emilie Scholand) pertaining to that Emil Fritz life insurance policy and alleged McSween embezzlement case are likewise still in existence.

COUP DE GRÂCE: WRITINGS OF
BILLY'S CONTEMPORARIES

Many other contemporaries were recorders of events: events of which the pretenders are ignorant; and which the modern Billy the Kid Case hoaxers were forced to distort or conceal to continue their caper.

PAT GARRETT: The main victim of pretender and hoaxer lies, is Pat Garrett: the man they disgracefully and unjustly accuse of violation of his lawman code, being an accomplice to murder of his two deputies, and murder of an innocent victim to assist the escape of his condemned prisoner, Billy Bonney.

Available to both pretenders and hoaxers was Garrett's 1882, ghost-written, book: *The Authentic Life of Billy the Kid The Noted Desperado of the Southwest, Whose Deeds of Daring and Blood Made His Name a Terror in New Mexico, Arizona, and Northern Mexico.*

Though written like a dime novel of that time for its commercial goal, it clearly states that he killed Billy the Kid.

And it demonstrates no "friendship with Billy;" though the modern hoaxers claimed that as Garrett's criminal motive (there being no other motive for their outlandish "murder").

GOTTFRIED GAUSS: As the caretaker of the courthouse-jail, Gauss was present on April 28, 1881 when Billy made his great escape. He provided first-hand information about it, including Billy's killings of his guards: Deputies James Bell and Robert Olinger.

JOHN WILLIAM POE: As Pat Garrett's deputy, present at his killing of Billy, Poe gets raked over the coals by the modern hoaxers because of his additional confirmation of Billy's murder.

The pretenders, however, do not use the historical killing scene; so they omit him. Poe's book, *The Death of Billy the Kid*, with introduction by Maurice Garland Fulton, was published in 1933. Poe had originally written "The Killing of Billy the Kid" as a personal letter to Charles Goodnight, dated July 10, 1917.

And Poe's wife's posthumous biography of him, *Buckboard Days*, was printed in 1964. The modern hoaxers grasped at Poe's initial uncertainty that Billy was the victim. But not knowing him, Poe just recounted his surprise. The body was then profusely identified; Poe was not needed for that.

JOHN HENRY TUNSTALL: A prolific letter writer, with a family who retained them, Tunstall was also a recorder of events. Those letters, discovered by Frederick Nolan in the 1960's, were too late for the pretenders to build their houses of cards. Many of the letters appear in Nolan's *The Life and Death of John Henry Tunstall*.

OTHER BILLY BONNEY CONTEMPORARIES: Billy's 20th century fame yielded books by those who had known him.

George and Frank Coe, cousins, farmers, and Billy's fellow Regulators, knew him from his first arrival at Lincoln County, when he was not yet 18. They praised the boy, who Frank called "a wonder," and who bore no resemblance to the boorish pretenders.

George Coe, in 1934, published *Frontier Fighter, The Autobiography of George Coe Who Fought and Rode With Billy the Kid*. He gave vivid images of Billy's charisma, intelligence, and talent in singing and dancing. George wrote:

"Billy came down to the Dick Brewer Ranch on the Ruidoso. He was the center of interest everywhere he went, and though heavily armed, he seemed as gentlemanly as a college-bred youth. He quickly became acquainted with everybody, and because of his humorous and pleasing personality grew to be a community favorite. In fact, Billy was so popular there wasn't enough of him to go around. He had a beautiful voice and sang like a bird. One of our special amusements was to get together every

few nights and have singing. The thrill of those happy
evenings still lingers – a pleasant memory – and tonight I
would give a lot to live through one again. Frank Coe and
I played the fiddles, and all of us danced, and here Billy,
too, was in demand."

Frank Coe's impression of Billy was found by Frederick
Nolan in an unpublished letter to a William Steele Dean, dated
August 3, 1926. Frank emphasized Billy's multi-culturalism
and above average height (5'6" was average). Frank wrote:

[He was] 5 ft 8 in, weight 138 lb stood straight as an Indian,
fine looking a lad as I ever met. He was a lady's man, the
Mex girls were all crazy about him. He spoke their
language well. He was a fine dancer, could go all their
gaits and was one of them. He was a wonder, you would
have been proud to know him."

Henry Hoyt, who wisely kept Billy's October 24, 1878
bill of sale for a horse, got a book out of that: his 1929
A Frontier Doctor. Hoyt, like the Coe cousins, admired Billy's
intelligence and emphasized his fluency in Spanish. He wrote:

After learning his history directly from himself and
recognizing his many superior natural qualifications,
I often urged him, while he was free and the going was
good, to leave the country, settle in Mexico or South
America, and begin all over again. He spoke Spanish like a
native and although only a beardless boy was nevertheless
a natural leader of men. With his poise, iron nerve, and
all-around efficiency properly applied, he could have made
a success anywhere.

"Teddy Blue" Abbott, having merely heard of Billy,
published, in 1955, his *We Pointed Them North, Recollections
of a Cowpuncher*. Abbott's small mention of Billy, however, was
important. Like George Coe, he recorded the boy's atypical
multi-culturalism - unknown to the pretenders. Abbott stated:

The Lincoln County troubles was still going on, and you had to be either for Billy the Kid or against him. It wasn't my fight ... it was the Mexicans that made a hero of him.

Paco Anaya was a Fort Sumner friend of Billy's. His 1991, posthumously printed memoir held poignant truth in his title: *I Buried Billy.*

The Maxwell family, illustrious in its own right, has given rise to many history books. The Maxwells were also Billy's most important family connection in the Lincoln County War period and after.

But the pretenders were unaware of all that. In addition, the pretenders were unaware of the lay-out of Fort Sumner or of the Maxwell house, though the town was the closest place to a home that homeless Billy possessed.

CRUSHING THE BATTLEFIELD: HISTORICAL ELEPHANTS

The pretenders, laid low by historical information in general, were flattened by two elephants tromping through that history. Without those two behemoths, the events of Billy Bonney's life made no sense. They represented extreme danger and extreme love.

THE SANTA FE RING:

Missed by the pretenders is the Santa Fe Ring: the cause of the Lincoln County War, the cause of years of turmoil in New Mexico Territory, and the ultimate cause of real Billy's death.

Anyone really present in Lincoln County's revolutionary political foment of 1878, would have known the specifics, as well as the lead-up to the final crisis of war.

In 1876, the eastern county of Grant (in which was Silver City), had written a "Declaration of Independence," in attempt to escape the Ring stranglehold by annexing to Arizona.

By 1877, northern New Mexico Territory, had endured a Santa Fe Ring struggle resulting in about 200 deaths in the Colfax County War. Its culminating murder of one of their leaders, Methodist minister, Reverend Franklin J. Tolby, and the Ring-partisan military intervention from Fort Union eerily mirrored the Lincoln County War's murders and Fort Stanton troop involvement the following year.

Multiple contemporary documents confirm the existence of the Santa Fe Ring. In addition, Attorney Frank Warner Angel had prepared a 1878 notebook for incoming Governor Lew Wallace to educate him on its players.

Furthermore, Angel's exposé of Ring-partisan Governor Samuel Beach Axtell's illegalities against the McSween side led to his mid-term removal and replacement by Lew Wallace.

And the name Thomas Benton Catron would have loomed gigantic to Territorial residents as head of the Santa Fe Ring - though it was unknown to the pretenders.

Furthermore, Attorney Ira Leonard, an associate of Governor Wallace's, and eventually Billy's attorney, wrote to the governor on May 20, 1879 that *"the Santa Fe ring ... has been so long an incubus on the government of this territory."*

A modern Ring documenter was a descendant of one of the Ring-fighting families from the Colfax County War. He was Norman Cleaveland of the Morley family.

The Santa Fe Ring is also described in D.W. Meinig's 1998 *The Shaping of America. A Geographical Perspective on 500 Years of History, Volume 3: Transcontinental America 1850 - 1915.* Meinig wrote:

> In the 1870's anticipation of railroad connections to the East began to alter the prospects [in New Mexico] for profits and position. Slowly forming over the years, the "Santa Fe Ring" now emerged into full notoriety: "it was essentially a set of lawyers, politicians, and businessmen who united to run the territory and to make money of this particular region. Although located on the frontier, the ring reflected the corporative, monopolistic, and multiple enterprise tendencies of all American business after the Civil War. Its uniqueness lay in the fact that, rather than dealing with some manufactured item, they regarded land as their first medium of currency." "Land" meant litigation, and "down the trail from the states came ... an

amazing number of lawyers" who, "still stumbling over their Spanish, would build their own political and economic empire out of the tangled heritage of land grants." And so, somewhat belatedly, a general repetition of the California situation got under way, and with the same general results: "eventually over 80 per cent of the Spanish grants went to American lawyers and settlers." Important differences were the presence in New Mexico of a much greater number of Hispanic peasants and communities well rooted on the land, the considerable resistance and violence generated by this American assault, and the sullen resentment created in an increasingly constricted and impoverished people who felt they had been cheated out of much of their lands. In contrast to common representations it was not a case of vigorous, expanding society moving upon "a static culture," for "the Hispanos were still settling and conquering New Mexico, ever-extending their control" when the Anglos arrived. Here even more starkly than in California the conflict arose not just out of simple imperial position and crass chicanery but out of the clash of two fundamentally different sets of values, perceptions, and motivations. For ordinary Hispanos land was simply basic to a comfortable existence: "enough land to farm, enough pasture for stock, enough game to hunt, enough wood to burn, and enough material to build," all "to help one live as one ought to live" - including the continuity of such life generation after generation. Although operating to a great extent on tradition and custom, this was not the simple, "primitive" society most Anglos took it to be; it had its own laws relating to land and water, its own complexities of status, politics, and factions. To the Anglos land was a commodity to buy and sell, to exploit as quickly as possible, a means of profit and propellant of one's personal progress. Furthermore, "American land policy featured precise measurement and documentation, assumed individual ownership, and came out of a tradition that expected western land to be open for settlement." And it came out of eastern lands - out of the humid woodlands of Europe and America - and its assumptions about settlement and family farms, its rigid uniform rectangular survey system, its laws relating to water, cultivation, and seasonal use were incongruous with the needs and practices of Hispano farming and stock raising in the arid southwest. The most vulnerable parts of the Hispano system were the common lands, essential to the grazing economy, but often used without title, or held by a patrón who ultimately sold or lost his title, or by a community grant that was readily challenged under American law and likely to be declared by the courts to be public land subject to routine survey and sale. This process of Anglo encroachment went through several phases over several decades but reached an important victory in an early court approval of the Maxwell Grant, an infamous case wherein the original 97,000 acres was inflated to nearly 2 million covering a huge county-sized area of prime piedmont lands. Well before the owner had certain title to this baronial tract he sold it to London speculators, and once the country that had "seemed worthless to Kearny's soldiers" became "an item in the stock exchange and a topic of interest in a dozen investment houses in Europe," the invasion of New Mexico had taken on a new momentum.

Unaware of the Santa Fe Ring, the pretenders missed real Billy's world - with its rebellion of those downtrodden.

BILLY'S ROMANCE:

Missed also by the pretenders is the love story of Billy and Paulita Maxwell, arguably the American Romeo and Juliet. To join his young lover was the tragic reason for Billy's return to Fort Sumner - and almost certain death - rather than escape to Old Mexico.

That love story was confirmed in an unpublished letter by historian, Walter Noble Burns. On June 3, 1926, he wrote to Jim East, one of Pat Garrett's Stinking Springs possemen:

I also know that the Kid and Paulita were sweethearts - at least I heard that story on most good authority many times. But I was unable to write it frankly because my publishers were afraid any such statement might lay them open to a libel suit.

ESCAPING HISTORY

For the old pretenders and modern Billy the Kid Case hoaxers, the means of escape from being crushed by the mountain of historical facts was public ignorance.

Unknown still is that the Lincoln County War was a freedom fight of poor Anglo farmers and disenfranchised Hispanic people against the oppressive and brutal Santa Fe Ring. Unknown was Billy's role in bridging those two impacted sub-cultures and bringing Mexicans into that War. Unknown was Billy's future risk to the Ring as a potential leader of another uprising (along with equally zealous Hispanics, like his friend, Yginio Salazar). Unknown too was Billy's more immediate risk to the Ring by testifying against its murderer members - unless he was eliminated first. Certainly unknown, except by name, were almost all the other historical participants.

So, Billy the Kid's massive popularity plus massive ignorance about him, added up to an ideally non-critical but receptive audience for old imposters and modern hoaxers.

RECLAIMING HISTORY

To tell Billy Bonney's real story, I wrote the historical novel, *Joy of the Birds* and the non-fiction *Billy the Kid's Writings, Words, and Wit.* And I wrote *MegaHoax* to expose and to stop the Billy the Kid Case hoaxers.

And this book, focusing on the pretenders, continues the goal of reclaiming true history, and undoing its past and present misinformation - paraded by a circus-full of clowns.

DEBUNKING OLIVER "BRUSHY BILL" ROBERTS

OLIVER "BRUSHY BILL" ROBERTS AND HIS FIRST AUTHORS

HOAXBUST: The only "identity" between Oliver P. Roberts and Billy Bonney was the name "Bill," which Roberts used for his moniker: "Brushy Bill." The rest of Roberts's bid is built on known historical names, and confabulated pseudo-history built around them; plus his authors' fakery. Although "Brushy Bill" was used by the modern Billy the Kid Case hoaxers for "survival suspicion;" he lacked their Garrett-friendship-playing-dead-on-bench-scenario death scene, thus, removing need for his DNA to match their carpenter's bench DNA of "playing-dead-Billy" (though they ignored that). And "Brushy Bill's" other total mismatches to real Billy and his history did not faze "Brushy's" later conspiracy theory authors.

GETTING BACKERS

OLIVER P. "BRUSHY BILL" ROBERTS'S transformation into Billy the Kid arose from alliance of three eccentrics, each now dead. Their 1955 book, *Alias Billy the Kid*, became "Brushy Bill's" later followers' bible.

The first strange person was "Brushy Bill" himself: a creative confabulator with at least 12 aliases and life stories, all of famous period characters - Billy the Kid being merely one. "Brushy" claimed also to be a member of the Jesse James gang and of Roosevelt's Rough Riders, a participant in Buffalo

Bill Cody's Wild West Show, a Pinkerton Detective, a bronco rider, a friend of Bell Starr, a Deputy U.S. Marshall, a rancher in Mexico, and an associate of Pancho Villa.

The second participant was Charles Leland Sonnichsen, an historian listed as *Alias Billy the Kid*'s first author, but later - allegedly to dissociate from the book's subsequent derision - claiming to have been only its proof-reader.

Lastly, was William V. Morrison, an amateur historian and the second author, who called himself an attorney, but was not; said he was a descendant of Lucien Maxwell's oldest brother, Ferdinand, but was unsubstantiated; and is idolized by "Brushy's" conspiracy theory followers as a hero. I consider him a hoaxer and huckster, as revealed by his evident coaching of mentally disturbed "Brushy," and his sensationalist seeking of a 1950 governor's pardon for him as Billy the Kid.

William V. Morrison's "Brushy" hoax took work. He even included his sources as footnotes, apparently hoping they seemed corroborating, instead of cribbing for his creation of "Brushy" as Billy.

That "research" included Billy's famous letters to Governor Lew Wallace and Attorney Edgar Caypless - which give "Brushy" near-verbatim quotes - 70 years post-alleged penning (and, even worse, with a claimed "friend" as their writer)!

Used also were Pat Garrett's *Authentic Life of Billy the Kid*, Walter Noble Burns's *The Saga of Billy the Kid*; works by historians Robert N. Mullin and Maurice Garland Fulton, and others by Billy's published contemporaries: Charlie Siringo, Jim East, and George Coe.

Added were archival documents - like a page of Billy's Court of Inquiry testimony (not the informative ones above).

Also, in 1949, William Morrison interviewed residents in Lincoln County for period "memories;" and, in 1950, he toured "Brushy," through its historic town of Lincoln.

Lastly, were "Brushy's" taped words and scribblings of this coaching, rife with his own confabulatory errors - which Morrison cannily edited out for *Alias Billy the Kid*. There, "Brushy" is called illiterate, to remove suspicion of studying-up.

Tellingly, when historical sources ran out, so did "Brushy's" "memory" - or his confabulations took over.

THE PITTMON PROBLEM

By December 16, 1987, "Brushy Bill's" niece, Geneva Pittmon, became his nemesis. Morrison and "Brushy" had added 20 years to his life. But she knew her uncle, called him emotionally unstable, and refuted his claim with the family Bible. On that date, she sent Joe Bowlin, co-founder of the Billy the Kid Outlaw Gang, a letter and a copy of the family Bible's genealogy page. She concluded: "*My uncle was Not Billy the Kid ... He was born Aug 26, 1879.*"

In response, "Brushy's" later believers craftily replaced his Hamilton, Texas, tombstone to give a birth date of December 31, 1859 – instead of 1879! But no explanation was offered for Geneva Pittmon's "conspiracy" to discredit the man!

LOSING A PARDON, GAINING A BOOK

Morrison's and Sonnichsen's *Alias Billy the Kid* unravels when facts are interpolated and errors are highlighted. It reads like a "Through the Looking Glass" story, with historical names and basic events drifting in topsy-turvy chaos of "Brushy's" compensatory confabulatory creations - all wrong.

With 90 pages of text and 8 pages of photographs, it begins with introductory comments; the rest is "Brushy's" "own words," with Morrison's narration. There are appendices of 40 pages, mixing real Billy's documents with "Brushy's" fakery.

The "Publisher's Forward" pronounces the book's foundation "suspicion": "Was Billy the Kid really shot to death by Sheriff Pat Garrett on that July night in 1881, or was someone else the victim?"

Emphasized is Morrison's mantra: "Brushy" knew things "never printed." The Publisher states as that come-on: "It was generally believed, for example, that there was a federal charge outstanding against Billy the Kid. Brushy Bill said the case 'was thrown out of court.' Legal records, when found, proved Brushy Bill's statement."

But this "never printed" information is, in fact, lifted from Billy's available letter to one of his attorneys: Edgar Caypless.

The "Prologue" then gives the gambit's punch line purpose: "Brushy Bill" wanted the "Billy the Kid" governor's pardon.

MORRISON INTRODUCES HIS MAN

The "Prologue" is also William V. Morrison's generalized sell of "Brushy Bill" Roberts as Billy the Kid.

First meeting "Brushy" in Texas in 1949 (when Roberts was 70), Morrison says he "was amazed to see a man 90 years old in excellent physical condition."

Morrison's hoaxing begins with physical likeness relying on the famous Billy the Kid tintype photograph. So Morrison claims "Brushy Bill's" "*left ear*" [author's italics] protruded "noticeably farther from the head than the right ear." In the tintype, Billy's hat is rakishly tilted to the *right*, so its brim pushes out his *right* ear. But Morrison, unaware of a tintype's right-to-left reversal, puts a "funny" ear on his man's left.

Saying "Brushy" was toothless, avoids Billy's protruding front teeth; and pre-edentulous, young "Brushy's" photos in the book appear to lack that oddity.

When "Brushy" speaks, things only get worse. Morrison quotes him: "I done wrong like everyone else in those days." That illiterate crudeness was compatible with 1950's readers' expectations of Billy the Kid; but incompatible with real Billy.

IMPOSSIBLE ERRORS FROM THE GET-GO

Alias Billy the Kid has a predicament. It alleges to be a first-person account, but lacks information for that. Gamely, "Brushy Bill" fills in the historical blanks - with mistakes.

For starters and "physical identity," "Brushy" shows Morrison a scar on his hip, and says in his inimitable way: "That scar was from the time I run into the street in Lincoln to take the guns off the body of Sheriff Bill Brady. Billy Matthews ran behind an adobe wall and fired. His shot went through the flesh of this hip and then hit Wayte [sic]."

The incident and names are famous, but garbled; and the specifics are all wrong.

It was Billy and the Regulators who ambushed Brady *from behind an adobe wall*. Jacob Basil "Billy" Matthews, a Deputy Sheriff, next fired at them from *inside the Cisneros house*.

The shot friend was Jim "Frenchie" French, not Fred Waite (another known Regulator). And the *single* firearm recovered by Billy was his *Winchester '73 carbine* (confiscated after John Tunstall's murder by Brady in a brief arrest of Billy); though "Brushy" says they were *pearl-gripped .44 revolvers.*

"Brushy" throws in, apparently from viewing movie Westerns of his day, "I wore my pistols in the scabbard with the butts toward the back. I fanned the hammer at times." Double-holstered guns and fanning would not have been used by real Billy.

A false Billy myth, from his prison escapes, involved slipping from wrist shackles. That became a pretender prerequisite; so "Brushy" flexes his thumbs to "slip through handcuffs." Added are "Brushy's small hands": another myth belied by real Billy's muscular ones seen in his tintype.

Ambidextrousness, a known Billy trait, is claimed, but ruined by "Brushy's" favoring the left, repeating his tintype reversal error, where Billy's *right* hand is cocked beside his Colt revolver's butt - showing he favored the right!

Next fails Morrison's "he-knew-things-never-printed" trick - supplying details appearing first-hand and relying on reader ignorance of the truth. So "Brushy" "remembers" that, in his Mesilla murder trial, the witnesses lacked subpoenas. First, as the jailed defendant, he would not have known. And, in fact, the subpoena of witness, Isaac Ellis, still exists.

For the Garrett posse chase-down, Morrison has "Brushy" say: "I was never afraid to die like a man fighting, but I did not want to be shot down like a dog without a chance to fight back."

The actual and literate quote - "I am not afraid to die like a man fighting but I would not like to be killed like a dog unarmed" - comes from Billy's available, March 20, 1879 letter to Governor Lew Wallace, presented earlier in this book.

All this effort seems preparation for "Brushy's" pardon plea as "Billy" to New Mexico's governor, Thomas Jewett Mabry. Pardon was the defining goal of the story that "Brushy Bill" and William V. Morrison were constructing. Years later, it would be repeated in the modern Billy the Kid Case hoax.

LITERARY LIFE AFTER THE FLUBBED PARDON

Impressively, "Brushy Bill" and William V. Morrison got Governor Thomas Jewett Mabry's ear. But they failed.

Governor Mabry concluded: "I am taking no action, now or ever, on this application for a Pardon for Billy the Kid because I do not believe this man is Billy the Kid."

That should have ended the game. But Morrison simply changed direction. First was an excuse: "Brushy" had been intimidated by the audience with kin of Pat Garrett, "Kip" McKinney, and William Brady; as well as historians.

Then "Brushy Bill" did Morrison a big favor. He died.

William Morrison kept his foot in the door of real Billy's fame. He had accumulated "Brushy's" tape recordings, notes, and jottings. So Morrison wrote in weird third person: "He was convinced that Roberts was really what he claimed to be and made up his mind that this man should have a hearing even if it had to be posthumous." In other words, freed of the old coot's limitations, Morrison could now make up a better version.

First, William Morrison needed fancy validation. So, for an historian named C.L. Sonnichsen, Morrison did a "he-knew-things-never-printed" trick, telling him "Brushy" had claimed that "negro soldiers from Fort Stanton took positions on the hillside and joined in the firing that day when the Murphy men burned down McSween's house."

This interaction proves two things: Morrison was more persuasive than "Brushy;" and neither Morrison nor Sonnichsen (and, of course, "Brushy") knew the real history.

The Lincoln County War, from July 14, 1878 to July 19, 1878 - the day Morrison is referring to - had multiple eye-witnesses. It is known that Commander Nathan Augustus Monroe Dudley's *all-black 9th cavalry were not on the south foothills, and never fired.* All troops were encamped at the east part of town. A few non-shooting soldiers were left near the McSween house and were with Sheriff George Peppin.

On the high south hills of Lincoln were only shooting *possemen* of Sheriff George Peppin; all were white.

But soldiers did fire. Unknown to Morrison, "Brushy," and Sonnichsen, Commander Dudley had also marched into Lincoln with white infantry and officers. When real Billy testified in the Dudley Court of Inquiry, he stated he saw three *white* soldiers fire a volley at himself and others as they fled the burning McSween house. Being white, they were either Dudley's infantrymen or officers - not the black cavalrymen.

But duped C.L. Sonnichsen came on board. Morrison was in the book-writing business.

I AM "BILLY THE KID," HEAR ME ROAR IN PRINT

In *Alias Billy the Kid*, "Brushy" was on the firing line with direct quotes for 44 pages in "Brushy Bill's Story." But back in the 1950's, real Billy's known history started in 1877 (when he was 17-18). So a beginning was needed. "Brushy" jumped in: "I was born at Buffalo Gap [Texas] on December 31, 1859." Why not Billy's birthday, November 23rd, or birthplace, New York? Morrison says "Brushy," as Billy, had made up those details, because "that's what bad men did in those days!"

Sixteen long blank years remained for the dynamic duo. Not till 1993, would Billy Bonney's early adolescence be known from Jerry Weddle's *Antrim was my Stepfather's Name*. It presented Billy's Silver City and Arizona years. So necessity mothered invention.

"Brushy" confabulated a Kathleen Bonney, kin to his "real" mother, who died when he was "three," to take him to Silver City. (Morrison/"Brushy" were unaware of the historical mother's name of "Catherine McCarty Antrim;" or that she died when Billy was 14½; or that "Bonney" was merely Billy's alias from 1877 onward.)

Ignorance also omits Billy's major, early life crises: his 1875 Silver City escape from Sheriff Harvey Whitehill's jail through its chimney after incarceration for stealing clothing and revolvers from a Chinese laundry; and his subsequent life in Arizona, with imprisonment for horse theft, and escape.

Instead, "Brushy" placidly leaves Silver City "to see his people" in Texas, where, as a "cowboy," he adventures in Indian Territory; Dodge City, Kansas; and even Chihuahua, Mexico!

Morrison then jumps to 1877, and real Billy's known return to New Mexico Territory - but wrongly "from Mexico." Used next is Billy's known crossing of the Guadalupe Mountains to reach Pecos River settlements. Missed, however, is *why* Billy returned: his first murder! On August 17, 1877, in Bonita, Arizona, he shot blacksmith, Frank "Windy" Cahill, and escaped, on a stolen horse, back to New Mexico Territory.

When finally "at the Pecos," "Brushy" lacks all real Billy knowledge. He states: "Jim and John Jones were working for Chisum, so I went to work for them - I think up at Bosque Grande. Frank McNab [sic - MacNab] was foreman."

Only the names are historical; everything else is made up. The Jones boys did work for Chisum prior to 1877, but, in late 1877, were making a Roswell store with their father, Heiskell. MacNab was a cattle detective with consortium Hunter and Evans, which had bought John Chisum's huge herd. Bosque Grande, Chisum's original ranch, south of Fort Sumner, was not connected to Billy until 1879 or 1880, when Billy sold rustled stock to its new owner, Dan Dedrick (to whom he gave the famous tintype). By then, John Chisum was living near Roswell at his South Spring River Ranch. And Billy never worked for the Joneses. By September of 1877, he had joined the outlaw, Jessie Evans, and his boys.

But "Brushy" says: "I went to work with them [the Joneses] at Murphy's Seven Rivers camp that winter."

Actually, that Murphy-Dolan cow camp was far south of Seven Rivers; and Billy never worked there. By October of 1877, Billy was hired as a ranch hand by John Tunstall in Lincoln, and worked for Tunstall's ranches on the Feliz and Peñasco Rivers.

However, available sources let "Brushy" name a few Tunstall employees, when he belatedly gets to his Tunstall job.

But he gets wrong the McSween-Tunstall attachment order from the Fritz life insurance case, attributing it to "trouble about McSween's law fee," instead of the Santa Fe Ring's concocted accusation of McSween's embezzlement - known to real Billy (but reflecting "Brushy's" day's ignorance of the Ring's existence or of its role in Lincoln County War history).

John Tunstall's murder is threadbare and errorful, since it lacked Frank Warner Angel's Report with specifics - coming from Billy's own deposition. Found in 1954 by historian Frederick Nolan, and cited in 1956 in his article "Sidelight on the Tunstall Murder," it was too late for "Brushy," dead by 1950; or for William Morrison's 1955 *Alias Billy the Kid*.

Conventional history follows, until the Sheriff Brady ambush murder, where, again, a wall is hit. "Brushy" pulls a "pearl-handled .44 off his body" (forgetting his earlier claim of *two* .44's) - when the gun was really a Winchester '73 carbine.

Unaware that the impending Lincoln County War was a freedom fight against the Santa Fe Ring, and sticking to the Billy-as-outlaw myth, "Brushy" was forced to fabricate a murder motive for that ambush, and stated: "Sheriff Brady was gunning for me with warrants for cattle stealing."

"Brushy" is dead wrong. Sheriff Brady's April 1, 1878 murder was only a month and a half after he headed the Tunstall murder posse. (Real Billy's rustling started late in 1878, after the Lincoln County War was lost.) Brady was ambushed by the Regulators, including Billy, to prevent his likely murder of Attorney Alexander McSween, returning to Lincoln, that day, for his Grand Jury trial for his fake embezzlement charge, concocted by the Santa Fe Ring.

Also massacred by misinformation, the Lincoln County War, gets a big Morrison pitch. He states: "The three-day battle in Lincoln, July 17, 18, and 19, 1878, was the end of the struggle for the McSween faction. It was a bloody business, and Brushy Bill Roberts described it as if every detail had been burned into his memory with a branding iron."

This was empty promotion. First of all, the War began on the 14th - so it was six days long. Then, "every detail" presented are just known superficialities - plus black shooting soldiers. Even Commander N.A.M. Dudley's awe-inspiring Gatling gun and howitzer cannon - that caused retreat of all the McSween men, except those in his besieged house - are missed!

But Morrison's single Dudley Court of Inquiry page crib sheet does list people escaping from McSween's burning house; so "Brushy" gets some right!

Lew Wallace enters next to replace the past governor. Using the real Billy letter of March 13, 1879 to Wallace, quoted earlier, "Brushy"/Morrison cover the Attorney Huston Chapman murder along with the offer to testify.

Next comes the Wallace-Billy meeting. With the "he-knew-things-never-printed" trick, Morrison adds a fake elaboration of a "Brushy" quote: "We didn't meet like they say we did in the daytime at Patron's."

All that is false. First of all, it has never been claimed that the initial Wallace-Billy meeting was at Juan Patrón's Lincoln house, or in the daytime. The meeting was on March 17, 1879, at night, and at the Lincoln house of Justice of the Peace John "Squire" Wilson.

Then trouble strikes again: no records. Help is delayed all the way to the end of the next year with the December 12, 1880 real Billy letter to Lew Wallace about the killing of Jim Carlyle at the Greathouse Ranch ambush; a murder of which Billy was accused, though he wrote that Carlyle was mistakenly shot by his fellow possemen. "Brushy," not unexpectedly, gets that claim right. Morrison even refers to the letter!

But the location of the Greathouse Ranch was unknown until the 1980's. So "Brushy" *completely forgets* where in New Mexico the darn place was. He also "forgets" the Coyote Spring ambush by the same White Oaks posse that immediately preceded that ambush at "Whiskey Jim" Greathouse's place.

Known history gets the dynamic "Morrison/"Brushy" duo through Pat Garrett's sheriff election and his capture of Billy. But an embarrassing gaffe comes because neither know why Billy was being pursued by Garrett. They guess the Carlyle murder; when it was for murders of Sheriff William Brady, Deputy George Hindman, and Andrew "Buckshot" Roberts.

Billy's Mesilla hanging trial, however, gets color from Billy's known April 15, 1881 letter to Attorney Edgar Caypless, "remembered" by "Brushy" as: "In April I pleaded to the federal indictment and it was thrown out of court."

Real Billy had written: "My United States case was thrown out of court and I was rushed to trial on my Territorial charge."

A story about Billy's famous bay mare is then mutilated by ignorance. In reality, Garrett's posseman, Frank Stewart, had stolen her from Billy at the Stinking Springs capture. Billy wanted to sell her to pay for a new attorney after Ira Leonard's withdrawal from his case - as Billy described in the letter to Caypless. Billy had also made a replevin (retrieval) case for the mare against Frank Stewart with Attorney Caypless.

But "Brushy"/Morrison fill in their blanks of ignorance by saying the mare ended up at a Scott Moore's, because "Brushy" (as Billy) "owed him money for board."

In truth, Scott Moore was the person to whom Frank Stewart illegally sold the mare. He was the rich owner of the luxurious Moore's Hotsprings Hotel in Las Vegas, New Mexico.

Historically, after Billy's hanging trial in Mesilla, the next big historical event was his famous escape from the Lincoln County courthouse-jail in the town of Lincoln.

Morrison notes that he took "Brushy" to Lincoln in August of 1950 - in obvious preparation for miming that important episode. Nevertheless, the escape story "Brushy" and Morrison present is only the bare-bones conventional one. And it leaves "Brushy" unable to "remember" his escape route; so he claims "everything had changed."

In truth, that rural area is still almost identical to Billy's day. The problem is that *no one knows* Billy's route, so "Brushy"/Morrison again ran out of script.

But they knew Billy had crossed the Capitan Mountains to his friend Yginio Salazar; except it is spelled "Higinio," a mistake Yginio's bi-lingual, literate friend, real Billy, would not make.

But spewing historically familiar names, "Brushy" finally gets himself to Fort Sumner, where information totally ceases.

He says disastrously, "I knew Celsa and Pat's wife, who were sisters to Saval Gutierrez."

Wrong! They *were* sisters, but Celsa Gutierrez was *married* to Saval, her cousin. Since "Brushy" and his author are ignorant of this relationship - clearly known by real Billy, who even began his death-walk from the couple's house - they also have Celsa wanting to run off to Old Mexico with "Brushy Bill!"

This "sisters to Saval" error by "Brushy"-Morrison, nicely reveals hoax underpinnings. It arose from the known fact that Saval Gutierrez *was* Garrett's *"brother-in-law."* But "Brushy" and Morrison are unaware that it was *by marriage,* so they created Saval as a "brother-in-law" by virtue of being a *brother* to Celsa and to her sister, Apolinaria, Garrett's wife.

Next, "Brushy" claims he hid out at the Yerby Ranch; that name coming from the December 12, 1880 Billy letter to Governor Wallace. But that location is unlikely. Thomas Yerby held some of Billy's rustled stock, since Charlie Bowdre, Billy's friend, worked there; but Yerby was not Billy's friend.

THE ODD DEATH SCENE

Then comes the Fort Sumner death scene: not at all that of the Billy the Kid Case hoaxers: with a Garrett-shot Billy bleeding while playing dead laid on the carpenter's workbench. There is just an "innocent victim" mistaken for "Brushy" (as Billy the Kid), and accidentally shot because of resemblance.

That victim is "Brushy's" claimed partner, Billy Barlow, who, oddly, is killed *on the back porch* of the Maxwell house.

No attempt is made by William Morrison to reconcile the famous, Old West, death scene in Peter Maxwell's bedroom. But "Brushy" embellishes his own scene with his inimitable garrulous confabulation, claiming himself shot in the jaw and shoulder (though not by whom).

And Celsa Gutierrez aids "Brushy's" escape, while "they were passing off his [Barlow's] body as mine."

No "Billy Barlow" has been historically found; though *he* would be the modern Billy the Kid Case hoaxers' laid-out-Billy-carpenter's bench-blood-DNA source!

"BRUSHY" HEADS OFF INTO THE SUNSET

After that death scene, a hoaxbuster is grateful, since the book's story becomes Oliver P. Roberts's own life, is irrelevant, and the task of reading his silly, clowning tale ends.

A PICTURE IS WORTH A THOUSAND WORDS

Since Oliver "Brushy Bill" Roberts was not Billy the Kid, William Morrison's photo section in *Alias Billy the Kid* lacks reality, but is made more ludicrous by Morrison's selections.

For example, for Katherine Ann [sic] Bonney, is a picture commonly used for real Billy's mother. But, unknown to Morrison, it was fake.

To quote from Frederick Nolan's *The West of Billy the Kid:* "The original was owned by the George Griggs family, who exhibited it at their Billy the Kid Museum. It was called the Kid's mother sometime in the late 1930's, when Eugene Cunningham, author of the book, *Triggernometry*, identified it as such to photographic collector Noah H. Rose in order to obtain from Rose another photograph ... he eventually confessed that he had no idea who the woman was."

Other photographs are a randomly meaningless mélange: Lincoln County War participants, an illustration of the Billy tintype, a revolver of "Brushy's," a revolver claimed taken from Billy "when he surrendered to Garrett," the towns of Lincoln and Fort Sumner, the Lincoln courthouse, the Maxwell mansion, and Fort Sumner's barracks.

Then come photographs of "Brushy Bill" himself; the first, six months before his death in 1950. He looks in his seventies - which he was (though claiming to be 90). Another shows him at "about age 30" on a horse, proving he sat straight in the saddle.

Lastly, is a bizarre collage "comparing ears." John Jones - cut from his historical, group picture with other Seven Rivers boys - appears inscrutably as "Billy at seventeen." Jones's small ears, of course, are unlike "Brushy's" big flappy ones with rolled rims - such ears also being present in "Brushy's" photos at ages fourteen, twenty-seven, fifty-five, and eighty-five (in "new tombstone" years).

When one enlarges the tintype picture of real Billy, one sees an average-sized ear, without rolled rim. And a 1989 professional analysis denied photo-match of "Brushy Bill" and real Billy. After William Morrison's day, attacking that photo-match problem would be the task of later "Brushy" believers.

APPENDICES AND UNDERPINNINGS

Alias Billy the Kid "Appendices" reveal William V. Morrison's "tools of the trade": archival William Bonney documents that he and coached "Brushy Bill" used to create the hoax, but presented in an apparent attempt to make the book appear as scholarly research.

Thrown in as more "identity proofs" of "Brushy" as Billy are "fuzzy factoid" affidavits by historically unknown individuals attesting that "Brushy Bill" Roberts *is* Billy the Kid; or that Billy was seen somewhere after his death date.

As a reader bonus, *Alias Billy the Kid* concludes with more of Oliver P. Roberts's quotations, all misinformation.

"Brushy" says, "Jesse [sic - Jessie] Evans knew that Garrett didn't kill the Kid." [AUTHOR'S NOTE: Oops! Shouldn't "Brushy" have said "*me?*"]

In fact, the outlaw, Jessie Evans, would have known nothing of the sort. In 1881, he was in jail in Huntsville, Texas; and absent from New Mexico Territory since his March, 1879 escape from his Fort Stanton incarceration for the Huston Chapman murder.

"Brushy" also says: "Jim East, I knew him too. He was a friend of mine."

This is laughable. Jim East was a Pat Garrett posseman, hunting down Billy, and present at Billy's Stinking Springs capture; *definitely* not real Billy's friend!

About Governor Lew Wallace, "Brushy Bill" Roberts concludes: "I done everything I promised him to do."

Their real Billy prompt-letter of March 4, 1881 to Wallace said beautifully: "I have done everything that I promised you I would, and you have done nothing that you promised me."

In the end, the Morrison-Sonnichsen-"Brushy Bill" book only proves a pig's ear cannot make a silk purse.

"Brushy Bill" Gets More Authors

Forty years after William V. Morrison's hoaxed book, *Alias Billy the Kid*, "Brushy" and he got true-believer authors.

In 1997, a W.C. Jameson and a Frederic Bean, conspiracy theorists, published *The Return of the Outlaw Billy the Kid*, a hefty 256 pages.

As W.C. Jameson admits in its beginning, "This amazing story captivated me such that for the next twenty-eight years I investigated it at every opportunity."

Jameson and Bean had a mission. Converted by the "he-knew-things-never-printed" trick - and apparently avoiding like the plague the mass of history books on Billy written since William Morrison's day - they would let "Brushy" talk through Morrison's original transcripts to convince people.

Adding "forensic science" - here, photo-comparisons - "Brushy's" identity as Billy the Kid would be clinched.

The plan was disastrous. By revealing atrocious "Brushy Bill" Roberts errors - which sly Morrison had edited out - W.C. Jameson and Frederick Bean expose more of Morrison's original hoaxing and "Brushy's" breath-taking confabulating.

THE MODERN HOAXERS JOIN JAMESON

Frederick Bean is dead, but W.C. Jameson, a country music singer, was listed amusingly by the Billy the Kid Case hoaxers as one of their "historians."

And in the Billy the Kid Case promulgators' 2004 History Channel program plugging their own hoax (as real history), W.C. Jameson appears on-screen to plug "Brushy" as Billy.

The year before, in November of 2003, Billy the Kid Case hoax-promoting, glossy, *True West* magazine had showcased W.C. Jameson in a "debate" titled "Was Brushy Bill Really Billy the Kid? Experts face off over new evidence."

They used Leon Metz, Pat Garrett's biographer, against Jameson, who spewed Morrisonisms, as follows:

> On one side, passionate supporters of the historical status quo assert Roberts was a fraud, yet to date they have provided no logical, definitive proof ...
>
> Roberts was an illiterate man, yet he was astonishingly intimate with the people, geography, architecture and events of Lincoln County, New Mexico, in the late 1870s-early 1880s – an intimacy that could have come only from being present and involved ...
>
> After Roberts' image was compared to the only known photograph of Billy the Kid, one researcher concluded that William Henry Roberts was, in all likelihood, Billy the Kid, and as such, history needed to be rewritten ...

W.C. Jameson's *True West* interview, like his *The Return of the Outlaw Billy the* Kid, resembles a bull charging again and again; like he and Bean had struck again and again at Morrison's obstacles: "Brushy's" wrong age, Billy's missing Silver City years, Billy's literacy, the strange death scene, and the failed photo-likeness. It was all sound and fury signifying nothing.

HISTORICAL IGNORANCE IS BLISS

Pervasive historical ignorance of W.C. Jameson and Frederick Bean, that left them prey to William Morrison's hoaxing, is evident in *The Return of the Outlaw Billy the Kid's* initial historical overview, apparently from Morrison's records. One example, all errors, is as follows:

> At one point, Murphy retained lawyer McSween to collect on a $10,000 life insurance policy on partner Fritz, who died while on a trip to Germany. McSween collected the money but refused to hand it over to Murphy. Under orders from Murphy, Sheriff Brady attempted to seize some of Tunstall's cattle as partial payment.
>
> Tunstall decided he needed to confer with Brady and arrange an appointment with him in Lincoln. On 18 February 1878 John Tunstall, riding a buckboard and accompanied by several of his hired gunmen, including Billy the Kid, headed for Lincoln. As they approached the

town of Ruidoso, the gunmen spotted a flock of turkeys and set off in pursuit. Seconds later, a group of men led by Jesse [sic] Evans rode up to Tunstall in the wagon and shot him dead.

Tunstall's hired hands, led by Dick Brewer, vowed vengeance and organized themselves into a vigilante group they called the Regulators.

Here are the mistakes - which real Billy would not make:

1) **Murphy did not hire McSween**. McSween was hired to represent the interests of the Emil Fritz estate by Emil Fritz's siblings and that estate's Administrators: Charles Fritz and Emilie Fritz Scholand.

2) **McSween only collected part of the money**, the rest was retained by the New York City law firm, Donnell and Lawson, as fee for their collection services from the company.

3) **McSween refused to hand over the money to Dolan, not Murphy**. By 1878, Murphy was dying of alcoholism and had retired. The money was for Fritz's heirs; not Dolan. Dolan made a legal claim to it; but was rejected by Probate Court Judge Florencio Gonzales in San Patricio.

4) **Sheriff Brady did not attempt to seize Tunstall cattle as partial payment**. The mistake is "payment." The insurance money became part of the fake embezzlement case again McSween, with Tunstall added falsely as "his business partner." That criminal complaint was filed February 4, 1878. The Grand Jury was not until that April. To guarantee the $10,000 until the trial's outcome, a Writ of Attachment (meaning appraisal) of both men's property was made. Tunstall's cattle were for Writ appraisal, not payment.

5) **Tunstall did not head to Lincoln on February 18, 1878 to confer with Sheriff Brady**. Tunstall knew the attachment would be done that day on the 600 cattle at his Feliz Ranch, 50 miles south of Lincoln. Believing his horses were exempted, and to avoid a violent clash with Brady's

possemen, he headed back to Lincoln with his men herding that stock. On that trip, Tunstall was murdered.

6) **Tunstall did not ride on a buckboard**. Tunstall was on horseback with his men. Fred Waite was sent with the buckboard on another road. Tunstall's horse was killed with him. Billy himself said this in his Angel deposition!

7) **Tunstall's men were not gunmen per say.** They were his ranch hands at his Feliz and Peñasco River properties. At this stage, there was no overt fighting.

8) **They were not approaching the town of Ruidoso.** It did not exist then. They were less than an hour from the Ruidoso *River* homestead ranch of Tunstall's foreman, Dick Brewer where they could have kept the horses overnight.

9) **The murder did not occur at a wagon.** (see 6).

10) **The Regulators were originally not an outlaw vigilante group**. After John Tunstall's murder, his men were a legal group, deputized to arrest his murderers by Lincoln County Justice of the Peace John "Squire" Wilson. After they were illegally named "outlaws" by Governor Axtell, in his March 9, 1878 Proclamation, they continued with their legal mission to make arrests, calling themselves Regulators.

"Brushy's" total erroneousness continues unabated, and is incompatible with real Billy's knowledge.

Sheriff Brady's murder is described as for "vengeance," rather than to protect McSween from assassination by Brady.

The Blazer's Mill murder of Andrew "Buckshot" Roberts by the Regulators is described as when they "sought sanctuary" there; when, in fact, it was a Murphy-Dolan stronghold, no "sanctuary;" and they were there seeking stolen Tunstall stock.

The dramatic final day of the Lincoln County War is reduced to a single, Sheriff Peppin' deputy setting fire to the McSween house. And no Gatling gun is in sight! And Billy is called head of the Regulators; though he never was.

The Huston Chapman killing - to which Billy was witness - lists Jessie Evans as the murderer, but Jessie was only an accessory by presence. (The shots were fired by James Dolan and Billy Campbell - to which real Billy himself testified and got them indicted for murder; with Jessie only as an accessory.)

Dates and events are also utterly jumbled by "Brushy" and Morrison, as revealed by naïve Jameson and Bean.

Incidents recorded in Billy's letters to Lew Wallace in 1879 and 1881 get mixed up. Real Billy's "escape" from the Patrón house arrest (Billy's departure occurred on June 17, 1879), is called "a short time later" to his "January 10, 1880" killing of Joe Grant (which was actually on January 3, 1880).

And that Joe Grant killing is attributed to "an argument;" when it was really an unprovoked gunslinger attempt by the stranger, "Texas Joe" Grant, to shoot Billy in the back.

Pat Garrett's 1880 election as sheriff leads to "Brushy's" confabulated version of Garrett's tracking of Billy - even falsely adding Garrett to the Jim Carlyle murder's White Oaks posse.

The Stinking Springs capture misses Charlie Bowdre's dramatic killing when mistaken for Billy by the posse.

Skimmed over is the Mesilla hanging trial, Billy's courthouse escape, and his destination of Fort Sumner. There, a funny fabrication has Peter Maxwell betray "Billy" to Garrett because of "the outlaw's affections for his servant girls!"

Then Jameson and Bean embarrassingly mix up "Brushy's" and Morrison's back porch, murder scene with the conventional bedroom one with real, dead, identified Billy!

CONSPIRACY OF HISTORIANS

Jameson's and Bean's "great conspiracy" of historians is the core of their book. Conspiracy is the only explanation for such true-believers. They state: "There exists a confederacy of Billy the Kid researchers and writers, an informal alliance composed of a number of adherents to the prevailing and accepted theories regarding the death of the outlaw ... The alliance dismissed Roberts ... The truth is, however, their efforts were never supported by valid scientific and historical research."

But Jameson's and Bean's assaults against this "conspiracy" are like attacks of butterflies. Historians, they say, "repeat themselves" - referring merely to reusing accepted documentation. They conclude that historians want to maintain the *status quo*; refuse to admit being wrong for so long; and, thus, perpetuate "myth and misinformation."

CONSPIRACY OF GARRETT

Since W.C. Jameson and Frederick Bean have absolute belief that "Brushy Bill" Roberts as Billy survived the Fort Sumner murder, it follows, for them, that *someone* made up existing history to the contrary. Maybe it was Pat Garrett?

Offered is that Garrett was "an aspiring political figure." That is both untrue and unfathomable as to motivation.

Adding as little, are swipes that Garrett was "overrated," "never succeeded in anything," and Billy was "a thousand times braver." From that, Jameson and Bean somehow conclude that Garrett "was a man of questionable veracity and integrity."

Or, maybe, they postulate, he wanted the reward money. For that foray, they say Pat Garrett "was denied his territorial reward for killing the Kid by the territorial legislature" because of an unidentified corpse.

This is false. That $500 reward was Wallace's personal one, and paid belatedly because he had left the Territory to be Ambassador to Turkey. And the corpse was profusely identified as Billy's - including by the official coroner's jury. And this claim of "unidentified corpse" may be an example of lying by Jameson and Bean, instead of their usual Morrison parroting.

Another focus for a "Garrett conspiracy" is the Jameson Bean contemplation of Garrett's and Poe's lying about how they knew Billy was in Fort Sumner.

Though irrelevant to the identity of real Billy as the victim, that lying is probably historically true, and likely done to conceal Peter Maxwell's possible, traitorous assistance in Billy's fatal ambush in a town populated by his protective adherents.

Then Jameson and Bean use Poe's quote about his initial concern that Garrett had killed the wrong man. It is irrelevant, since Poe could not recognize Billy; and immediately accepted the body's multiple identifications.

Against Pat Garrett are also used hearsay "fuzzy factoid" quotes, from William Morrison, and by people unrelated to the historical events, who claim, for example, that "Kip" McKinney's grandson told Morrison that Garrett had said "the Kid got away;" or that someone in a Texas saloon had made a telephone call (note the modern timing) to a business to say he had overheard McKinney tell Garrett the same thing!

CONSPIRACY OF CORONER'S JURYMEN

W.C. Jameson's and Frederick Bean's conspiracy ruminations next focus on the Coroner's Jury Report. Its clear-cut identification of Billy is any pretender's biggest headache. So Jameson and Bean contrive irregularities, which they call "suspicious."

The storage of the report receives obsessing.

They say: "For reasons never completely explained, this coroner's jury report never made it to the official records of San Miguel County. In fact, Justice of the Peace Segura never made an entry regarding the report in his own books."

So another of their possible "conspirators" is Segura.

But, as Justice of the Peace, Alejandro Segura would have stored the Report in his courthouse office or in his home. Records like those, years later, were taken to Santa Fe, and, at times, temporarily or permanently lost.

The former happened to Billy's Coroner's Jury Report, which, as the authors acknowledge, was found in a storage box in the 1930's. So nothing untoward happened.

As to Segura's record keeping, the implication is only that he was careless; or that some of his other records got lost.

Next, "suspicions" escalate. W.C. Jameson and Frederick Bean say: "Like the shooting, the inquest has also been shrouded in confusion and mystery."

What "confusion and mystery?" They say "the inquest was handled quickly." Why not? It was hot July; the body would rot.

They offer: "The body was not put on public display." For whom would a decaying corpse be displayed in rural New Mexico Territory? And they omit the townspeople's nighttime vigil "display" in their town's carpenter's shop.

Jameson and Bean also want photos of dead Billy; forgetting people, back then, did not own cameras.

Their "clincher" is an allegation of *two* Coroner's Reports prepared at different times. "Evidence" is a non-referenced newspaper interview with an A.P. Anaya. But he is the same "Paco" Anaya, whose own book is named *I Buried Billy*. Jameson and Bean are garbling Anaya's tale with the fact that there was a Spanish version of the Report.

They then misstate: "To date no one has ever seen a copy of the document." But in their own bibliography, is the book containing its photocopy: *Violence in Lincoln County*! They even quote its author, historian, William Keleher, relating how that Spanish version was found in the 1930's. Slyly, they note that Keleher gives Billy's famous "quién es?" quote in English, when they are merely seeing Keleher's 1957 translation of the original Coroner's Jury Report.

Jameson's and Bean's fretting follows about misspelling of signers' names; or that Garrett forged it.

All this misinformation yields a non-sequitor leap to their conclusion: "There is, in fact, *no legal proof of the death of Billy the Kid*" [their italics]. Thus, they contend, a conspiracy of coroner's jurymen must have concealed the corpse's identity.

CONSPIRACY OF BURIAL

Next up for conspiracy is the burial; beginning falsely with W.C. Jameson and Frederick Bean claiming few witnesses.

Then they provide a false one, stating that a *Grant County Herald* "reporter," S.M. Ashenfelter [sic - owner, Singleton M. Ashenfelter], wrote, on July of 1881, that the corpse was dark-skinned and bearded. Since Grant County would have put Ashenfelter about 250 miles from the almost immediate, Fort Sumner burial, after a sudden ambush killing, Ashenfelter apparently fantasized his "outlaw" description for his public.

But Jameson and Bean solemnly, and with what they later call "scientific style," cite a book on sexual maturity (with "SMR's - Sexual Maturity Ratings") to compare Ashenfelter's corpse to fair beardless Billy, to show the impossibility of his transformation (while forgetting that Billy Barlow, *their* purported victim, "looked like" their *fair* "Roberts-Billy")!

"Fuzzy factoid" survival tales follow. A Morrison quote says a man in 1914 said Garrett did not shoot Billy. Another, from 1980, recalls "his uncle" (an unsubstantiated participant) dug the grave, and an "armed guard" (historically unknown) prevented anyone looking in the casket.

W.C. Jameson's and Frederick Bean's foregone conclusion is: "The facts stated above cause grave doubts about the identity of the body in the casket."

MOTHERS OF ALL CONSPIRACY THEORIES

By the book's end, Jameson and Bean launch conspiracy theories that knock the breath from you. Here they are.

1) **All Fort Sumner people were in a conspiracy.** They tricked Garrett into thinking he had killed Billy, since they were "friendly and sympathetic to the Kid." They perpetuated "the masquerade well into the twentieth century because they knew the Kid was still alive." This scenario is "Brushy's" own, since Jameson and Bean state: "According to Roberts, the two (Jesus Silva and Deluvina) decided to perpetuate a deception, perhaps allowing Garrett to believe the victim was, in fact, the wanted outlaw." More than absurdity ruins this; it needs Garrett unable to recognize Billy. But Garrett knew Billy; captured Billy at Stinking Springs; and transported Billy by train to Las Vegas, then Santa Fe, for jail. And, as sheriff, Garrett imprisoned Billy, awaiting hanging.

2) **All of New Mexico is in a conspiracy.** The reason given is "tourism." If Billy was a Texan, the loss would be "millions of dollars each year." So, Governor Thomas Mabry had been in cahoots with the assembled historians and descendants to call "Brushy" an imposter for economic reasons.

3) **The Lincoln County Heritage Trust was in a conspiracy.** The reason given is that their 1989 photo-analysis (discussed below) refuted "Brushy Bill" as Billy the Kid. Again, it was tourism dollars that made the director, Bob Hart, lie to protect his job; and the Trust was a big business.

4) **Historical conferences and a television program on "Prime Time Live"** (date not given) **were conspiracies.** The reason given is that historians denied "Brushy" was Billy; and TV presenter, Sam Donaldson, was "a resident of Lincoln County." (Apparently, that came back to tourism dollars.)

A FAMILY TREE GROWS FOR "BRUSHY"

If conspiracy is heart of W.C. Jameson's and Frederick Bean's *The Return of the Outlaw Billy the Kid*, "Brushy Bill" himself is its meat. To flesh him out, these authors soldiered into nonsense not dared by William V. Morrison.

Dealing with "Brushy's" being under two years old at Billy's death - the Geneva Pittmon-knowledgeable-niece-Bible problem - reveals. Jameson and Bean to be as creative as they are unacademic. They simply dispense with Pittmon by calling *her* "Brushy Bill" relative - Oliver P. Roberts - not *the actual* "Brushy Bill" - meaning two old coots had that same moniker!
Their "Brushy Bill," from a *different family*, is Oliver *L.* Roberts! Anyway, *his really real* name was William Henry.
How did they prove all this? They do not say; but like William Morrison's "P," "L" was born in Buffalo Gap, Texas! They add that since Billy could ride and shoot, he could not have been from New York anyway!
And "L's" new family came with a family tree.
He even had *another family Bible* from a Martha Vada Roberts Heath and "genealogical papers" from a Eulaine Emerson Haws of Tyler, Texas.
This tree has a "Cherokee wife" with two marriages. Her first was to a "Bonney," to produce "Catherine Bonney." Her second, to a "William Dunn," yielded Mary Adeline Dunn, whose son, "William Henry Roberts" (their "Brushy Bill"), came from marrying a James Henry Roberts. In case the

reader missed the point, beside this Dunn-Roberts son is added "aka Billy the Kid."

What happened to the new name: "Oliver *L.* Roberts?" It is abandoned. "Brushy" will be called "William Henry" for their *The Return of the Outlaw Billy the Kid* book.

Jameson and Bean do admit that this new family tree for "Brushy Bill" is "reconstructed" - leaving contemplation of "how reconstructed by them," when their Catherine Bonney has, as husbands, a "Michael" McCarty (also called "Edgar" elsewhere by them), and then a William Antrim. (Note that the names "McCarty" and "William Antrim" have been added from real Billy's mother's relationships elucidated after Morrison's day; but this "Catherine" on the new family tree is not the mother of their "Roberts-Billy;" as real Catherine Antrim was of real Billy.)

Remaining mysterious, is "Brushy's" new tombstone, birth date of December 31, 1859, *since no dates are given for anyone in the new family tree* - the point of family Bible notations!

Later, W.C. Jameson and Frederick Bean make the confused claim that by using the name Bonney for Billy's mother, "Brushy" solved the mystery of where the name arose; thus, forgetting their own claim that their Oliver L. William Henry "Brushy Bill" Roberts's" mother was the "Dunn" daughter," not the "Bonney" one! So he was a Billy Dunn!

LITERATE ILLITERATE "BRUSHY"

"Brushy" is called "semi-literate" by W.C. Jameson and Frederick Bean to encompass his jottings. Then Jameson and Bean head off a cliff by trying to stick with illiteracy.

"Brushy" says about the first famous Billy letter (cited earlier): "I had a friend who spelled it out in a letter for me, what I wanted from Governor Wallace."

Big mistake. Billy, with his distinctively modified Spencerian penmanship, wrote his letters in different locations from 1879 through 1881; including solitary confinement inside the Santa Fe jail! So that "friend" had to be "Brushy's" shadow!

Score zero for that Jameson and Bean try; touchdown for disproving their man as Billy.

LETTING "BRUSHY" STUFF HIS FOOT INTO HIS MOUTH

Probably the most calamitous decision of W.C. Jameson and Frederick Bean was to turn "Brushy" loose. William Morrison had wisely edited out his biggest gaffes.

"History," right from "Brushy Bill's" mouth, lays bare his utter ignorance about causality of events, dates, and participants. Worse, it demonstrates how he confabulated his tales around known historical kernels.

In addition, Jameson and Bean, though apparently averse to legitimate history books, do narrate in a few, new, real, historical facts - whose omission by Morrison was too glaring.

From Jameson and Bean comes "Brushy's" new childhood. There is a fabricated "New York Children's Aid Society" caring for him. (What happened to Billy the Kid's being from Buffalo Gap, and not being from New York, where people cannot shoot?). There is the Dunn mother death; and "Brushy's" being taken in by her half-sister, "Catherine Ann Bonney," who relocates him to Colorado and "several other locations" (unnamed).

Catherine Ann Bonney then marries a William Antrim in New Mexico (real historical fact of his name and marriage place). Humorously, child Billy then meets, in Silver City (real historical place for young adolescent Billy), child Jesse [sic - Jessie] Evans: the Ring thug gunslinger of the Lincoln County War (whose youth was actually in Kansas).

Their "Billy" then wanders the West, meeting every famous outlaw, including Bell Starr and the James brothers.

With seeming Jameson-Bean fix, "Brushy" bounces back to Arizona in 1877 to murder a "Windy" Cahill (a plucked historical name), but is incorrectly described as arrested.

Finally back in New Mexico Territory, "Brushy" calls himself "Billy the Kid" - which real Billy never did. The moniker was from his Santa Fe Ring enemies.

But "Brushy Bill" quotations, gratuitously provided, yield an unintended window into the chaos of "Brushy's" mad mind. For Lincoln County War history, he ruinously states:

I remember how it all started ... Lawyer McSween had been hired by the Murphy bunch to prosecute some of the Chisum cowboys for rustling cattle, but when he found out the Chisum boys were only taking back Chisum cows that were stolen by Murphy's men, [McSween] switched sides and joined up with John Tunstall. The Murphy-Dolan Ring operated a store where they sold supplies to the ranches, and then John Tunstall came along and opened his own store. That's where the trouble really started, between the two stores. McSween formed a partnership with Tunstall when he worked the case for Emil Fritz.

Everything is wrong.

- Emil Fritz was dead. McSween represented his estate.

- McSween had no partnership with Tunstall.

- McSween had been a Murphy-Dolan lawyer, but for their mercantile business.

- The "Murphy bunch" were themselves stealing Chisum's cattle for their beef contracts with the Mescalaro Indian reservation and Fort Stanton.

- McSween was not working for Murphy and Dolan in late 1876 when Tunstall came; having quit earlier because of distaste for their corruption.

- The Fritz life insurance money case had nothing to do with Tunstall. It was being done by McSween before his arrival. It became the embezzlement case precipitating Tunstall's murder and the Lincoln County War.

Next mauled by "Brushy" is that complex, Emil Fritz, life insurance money, embezzlement case. Lawrence Murphy is portrayed as initiating the attachment of property; though it was done, via Judge Warren Bristol, by the Fritz siblings, goaded by James Dolan. Murphy was then dying of alcoholism.

For John Henry Tunstall's murder scene, the errors place him incorrectly in a wagon, have Roberts-Billy falsely as a witness of the murder itself, and mistakenly have James Dolan present in the on-site attacking posse.

In the post-murder period, when the Regulators pursued Tunstall's assassins, "Brushy's" lack of knowledge has the Regulators - after their capture of William "Buck" Morton and Frank Baker - head west to Lincoln, from the distant Pecos River location, by "the north road, over the mountains."

Perhaps "Brushy" got this misconception on his 1950, sight-seeing trip to Lincoln, courtesy of William Morrison. But he is wrong.

The east to west Capitan Mountains may have *looked to him like a barrier* to the town, but the road to Lincoln used by the Regulators was a military one, skirting the mountains' eastern terminus, and over flatlands (where, unbeknownst to "Brushy," Morton and Baker were killed by the Regulators).

The Sheriff Brady murder scene repeats the Morrison book's errors; as does the murder scene of "Buckshot" Roberts, in Blazer's Mill. "Forgotten" by "Brushy," were "Buckshot's" not inconsequential carnage of killing Regulator leader, Dick Brewer, by one shot through the head; mangling George Coe's hand; and blasting John Middleton's chest.

For the Lincoln County War, "Brushy" is unaware of which buildings McSween's men occupied in Lincoln town. Nor does he know who were their assailants. "Brushy" guesses Sheriff Peppin "accompanied by several deputies." In actuality, there were almost 50 men from Seven Rivers and Mesilla in Peppin's posse.

Most dramatically, missing, as in Morrison's book, is the most horrifying event of the War: when Commander Dudley brought into Lincoln, with his troops, a howitzer cannon and a Gatling gun. And Dudley personally told McSween that those weapons might be used to bring down his house. All inside, including Billy, would have heard that threat.

Unaware of real military specifics, "Brushy" just has shooting, black soldiers running rampant for effect!

"Brushy" states, for the burning McSween house escape: "We opened the back door and looked out just as Bob Beckwith and some of them niggers started to come in."

The mistakes are glaring. Bob Beckwith, deputized to serve McSween's arrest warrant, entered the east back yard after Billy and others had fled the scene. Beckwith was accompanied only by Sheriff Peppin's white possemen.

Commander Dudley had exercised caution in his questionable military intervention by keeping his white infantrymen, black cavalrymen, and white officers in an encampment at the northeast end of town.

The three white soldiers firing a volley, seen by Billy in his escape, were hiding behind the Tunstall store. No other soldiers fired all day.

And, for Billy's burning building escape route, "Brushy" misstates that the men crossed Peñasco River - 100 miles to the south of the *Bonito River*, which they did cross!

"BRUSHY" WACKS GOVERNOR LEW WALLACE AND OTHER PEOPLE

Next "Brushy" demolishes the Lew Wallace period in the life of real Billy Bonney.

Attorney Huston Chapman's murder comes first, with "Brushy's" bad grammar, as in: "Me and Tom were standing right there and saw the whole thing."

But what "Brushy" "saw" is wrong: Chapman with Alexander McSween's widow, Susan. In fact, Chapman was alone; though Susan McSween had hired him for her murder and arson case against Commander N.A.M. Dudley.

"Brushy's" version of the Billy-Wallace-pardon-meeting reveals William Morrison's hoaxing, thanks to Jameson's and Bean's providing "Brushy's" flubbed coaching.

Billy's real letter (cited above) stated that Lew Wallace had *offered a $1000 reward for his capture*; and Billy offered to testify about the Chapman murder in exchange for a pardon annulling his Lincoln County War murder indictments.

But via Jameson-Bean narration, poor "Brushy" babbles: "Wallace had offered a thousand dollars *to the outlaw* if he would turn himself in and testify about the illegal activities of the Dolan faction."

"Brushy" continues, "He also wanted me to testify against Colonel Dudley in his court-martial at Stanton."

All wrong! Stanton testimony was *not* part of the pardon deal, and real Billy - who did testify - knew it was not a Court Martial, but a Court of Inquiry for *possible* Court Martial.

"Brushy's" Lew Wallace fabrications spiral downward from there. Jameson and Bean say for him: "Before leaving, Wallace promised to pardon the Kid if Billy would agree to stand trial for the killing of Sheriff Brady. He even promised to have his own personal lawyer, Ira E. Leonard, represent the young outlaw."

These thirty-seven words should constitute: give-up-already-"Brushy." Everything is wrong:

1) **Wallace wanted "Billy" to stand trial for the Brady murder**. No. The pardon was to *avoid* standing trial for that murder. More subtly, Wallace and Billy would have known, that a trial, with the courts controlled by the Santa Fe Ring, would only have ended in his hanging.

2) **The "exchange" for the pardon.** The actual "exchange" was Wallace's pardon for Billy's testifying as an eye-witness to the Huston Chapman murder.

3) **Ira Leonard was *not* Wallace's "personal attorney."** Leonard was widow Susan McSween's attorney, replacing her murdered attorney: Huston Chapman. Later, Leonard was Billy's first attorney in his Mesilla hanging trial.

"Brushy Bill's" total confusion about names and events then reigns. He names Albert Jennings Fountain as Billy's attorney for the 1879, Lew Wallace, pardon-related legalities; when Fountain was actually Billy's April, 1881, court-appointed attorney for Billy's Mesilla hanging trial (after Attorney Ira Leonard withdrew).

Billy's June, 1879 feigned "escape" from sham arrest in Juan Patrón's house-jail, gets mixed up with the November 28, 1880 Jim Carlyle murder at the Greathouse ranch. So "Brushy" has the latter's White Oaks posse absurdly tracking Billy after that Patrón house sham "escape" - which lacked any tracking.

The Mesilla murder trial has "Brushy" say about the Sheriff Brady murder: "They pinned the whole affair on me."

In fact, Billy Bonney had many co-defendants - John Middleton, Henry Brown, Frank MacNab, Fred Waite, and Jim French - but they had already fled the Territory by 1881.

Ignorant of the disastrous wake of glaring and discrediting mistakes they were leaving, Jameson and Bean sailed on.

GARRETT GETS THE "BRUSHY" TREATMENT

"Enter Garrett" - as the authors say - and then let "Brushy" get everything wrong.

"Brushy" claims Pat Garrett knew Billy from Texas, though Garrett had left the buffalo range there in early 1878 to move to Fort Sumner; and real Billy had only brief rustling trips to Texas in late 1878, and possibly through 1880.

"Brushy" also says that Garrett worked at Fort Sumner's Beaver Smith's Saloon, when it was at Hargrove's Saloon.

And "Brushy's" erroneous guess, that Garrett tracked down Billy because of the Jim Carlyle killing, is repeated.

For Garrett's murder of Billy's friend, Tom O'Folliard, "Brushy" falsely includes, in the tracking posse, a Tip [sic] McKinney. Tossed in is that McKinney was O'Folliard's cousin.

Nothing is true. McKinney was not related to Tom O'Folliard; his nick-name was "Kip;" and he was on no Garrett posses. He was one of Pat Garrett's two deputies present at Billy's killing.

Garrett's Stinking Springs capture of Billy also fares terribly, with "Brushy" calling Billy's fellow captives Regulators, when that group had disbanded two years earlier. Except for past-member, Charlie Bowdre, the other captives were just petty criminals: "Dirty" Dave Rudabaugh, Billy Wilson, and Tom Pickett.

DEATH SCENES GALORE

W.C. Jameson's and Frederick Bean's foray into presenting "Brushy's" discrepant death scene, unintentionally indicates why William Morrison was circumspect in quoting his man. "Brushy," it appears, elaborated his errors to absurdity - and without reconciliation to the historical scene. But Jameson and Bean provide all versions! A saving grace is their placement throughout the text, so a reader with a memory disorder might not notice.

If one does remember, one receives: (1) a victim in the bedroom shot accidentally by Garrett, and concealed by Garrett's staying "locked in the murder room" with Poe and McKinney as "guards;" (2) a bedroom victim, rumored in town as "not Billy the Kid;" (3) a shooting of Billy Barlow, *near* Maxwell's bedroom *and* the hanging beef, by someone unidentified, while "Brushy," running out, is wounded in the jaw, back, and scalp; (4) a vertiginously confusing rendition with Garrett and Poe quoting the bedroom shooting and the carpenter shop vigil over the body; accompanied by "Brushy's" contradictory quotes of dead Billy Barlow on the back porch with unclear murderer; (5) a Jameson-Bean version with a Maxwell bedroom murder by Garrett, and Peter Maxwell and Deluvina viewing the body, but with nit-picking of Garrett's and Poe's reporting; and (6) a rumor-anecdote of a 1944 interview with Attorney Albert Jennings Fountain's son, who says Garrett told him a different story - but confirming that Garrett shot the Kid!

Besides no credible refutation of the historical version, or of the multiple body identifications (including the Coroner's Jury), or use of unhistorical Barlow, "Brushy's" own errors in his long verbatim transcripts are his undoing, as follows:

1) Unaware of the actual, bright, almost full moon on July 14, 1881, "Brushy" confabulates: "It was dark that night, but there was enough moonlight to make shadows." That **"dark" night** [author's boldface] would later be a clue to "Brushy's" believers, who would repeat his devastating error.

2) The barrage of gunfire which injures "Brushy," goes oddly unnoticed in the small town (and, ever-after, by history).

3) "Brushy" does not know the configuration of the Maxwell house, or the location of its hanging side of beef. (It was at the north porch: the opposite side of the mansion from Peter Maxwell's bedroom, at the south porch.) So, in death scene version (3), "Brushy" wrongly calls the beef "hanging near Maxwell's bedroom;" and in version (4) puts the hanging beef wrongly at the back (west) porch, which "Brushy" calls the "trap" - ignoring the actual Peter Maxwell bedroom trap.

4) "Brushy" also has no idea of the Maxwell property's lay-out. Thus, after hearing "pistol shots," he runs "from Silva's [the foreman] into Maxwell's backyard" to shoot. In fact, that long journey around that converted officers' quarters, would have put "Brushy" nowhere near Maxwell's bedroom or the hanging beef - though he says he encountered assailants there.

Next, apparently unaware that the town lay around the perimeter of an open parade ground, he flees "into the gallery of a nearby adobe house," when, in fact, there was no "nearby" house: flight would require crossing, from the west perimeter of the parade ground, occupied by the mansion, over the exposed 300 yard square, to the residential quarters along its east or south sides.

Though, inadvertently having discredited Brushy' Bill's" renditions by his own mistakes, W.C. Jameson and Frederick Bean proclaim: "None of the so-called facts relating to the death of Billy the Kid at the hands of Sheriff Pat Garrett have ever been supported by concrete, or even competent, evidence."

RESEARCHING LIFE AFTER DEATH

Calling themselves "researchers," W.C. Jameson and Frederick Bean check up on "Brushy's" claims about his post-July 14, 1881 life. That "life" included his rollickingly funny repertoire of being personally involved with every famous name he could come up with, as previously mentioned here.

So, dead serious, Jameson and Bean seek evidence of his having been a Buffalo Bill Cody performer, a Pinkerton detective, a bronco rider, a U.S. Deputy Marshal; recognized by the Dalton Gang as Billy the Kid (who had no way of recognizing Billy), a Rough Rider with Teddy Roosevelt; or having gone to Mexico, where its President in 1899 seized his ranch in a gunfight; or having come back to the United States to make his own wild west show; or having returned to Mexico to fight in the Mexican Revolution and ride with Pancho Villa.

Predictably, Jameson and Bean discovered nothing. But they surmise that "Brushy" used aliases - though avoiding Billy the Kid was enough! And he could have stuck with good ol' Oliver P. (or L.) Roberts for anonymity.

JAMESON AND BEAN AND SHERLOCK HOLMES

Jameson-Bean "research" continues with "Evidence For and Against William Henry Roberts as Billy the Kid;" though it begins with its predictable conclusion: "There exists a great deal of evidence that leads to a conclusion for some that William Henry Roberts was, in fact, Billy the Kid."

Their investigation will involve: (1) physical similarities, (2) "Brushy's" revelations, (3) anecdotal evidence, and (4) identification affidavits.

"Physical similarities" parrot William Morrison's book, but preview Jameson's and Bean's own photo-analysis to come.

"Revelations" are the "he-knew-things-never-printed" trick. Added will be Lincoln town itself, from "Brushy's" 1950 field-trip there with Morrison; as well as miscellaneous (already debunked herein) claims, like "shooting black soldiers," and the federal versus territorial indictment for the Mesilla trial.

LINCOLN TRIP REVELATIONS

Lincoln "revelations" concern only two sites in town: the old Lincoln County courthouse-jail and the McSween house. Unrecognized by Jameson and Bean, "Brushy's" errors abound, even after his 1950 "educational tour" by William Morrison.

As to the courthouse, Jameson and Bean extol "Brushy's" statements about the commonly known, later addition of outside stairs to the second story balcony. And the south-side armory, from which Billy stole escape weapons, is incorrectly placed in the north-side room where other prisoners were held.

The McSween house fares no better, though Jameson and Bean inscrutably state, "Roberts' intimacy with the layout of the McSween house and yard could only have come from personal experience." (Having been burned down, its lot is bare and its floor plan is unknown.)

"Brushy's" "intimacy" yields only that the kitchen had a window, the corral had a fence, and there was a woodpile. For filler, he concocts events of its Lincoln County War siege; but gets them wrong. He has "Murphy men ... just across the river" - where no attackers were.

Missing are any intimate specifics of July 19, 1878: a holocaust in which that McSween house was burned around Billy, his fellows, and the McSween and Shield families; while the fire ignited a demolishing explosion of a gunpowder keg - while they were trapped inside. All is unknown to "Brushy."

MISCELLANEOUS REVELATIONS

W.C. Jameson and Frederick Bean worsen William Morrison's "revelation" of "shooting black troopers" by adding, as "revelations," more of "Brushy's" confused contributions::

1) They state, "Roberts told Morrison that, following the killing of Tunstall, he, and several of the Regulators, escorted Alexander McSween to his house in Lincoln. After fighting off the sheriff's posse, most of the Regulators took refuge in McSween's house while the remainder sought shelter at Tunstall's store."

Everything is wrong. Fused are the Tunstall murder day of February 18, 1878 and the first War day of July 14, 1878. On the War day, a minority of Regulators, including Billy, joined McSween, already in his house. A few other Regulators were at Tunstall's store. The rest of McSween's approximately 60 followers entered the José Montaño building, the Juan Patrón house, and the Isaac Ellis building.

And the McSweens did not take "refuge;" they were strategically placed from west to east to hold the town peacefully - before fighting began with influx of Seven Rivers and John Kinney's men to assist Sheriff George Peppin.

2) A "revelation" of the escape from the courthouse-jail is a freebie for "Brushy," since no one knows how Billy did it. So "Brushy" claims his thumb trick for slipping out of handcuffs. (Noteworthy for foiling the Billy the Kid Case hoaxers use of "Brushy" as their potential "Billy," is that "Brushy" *does not* claim Pat Garrett as friend or accomplice.)

3) The Jim Carlyle murder "revelation" is lifted from the Billy to Wallace December 12, 1880 letter already discussed.

4) A "revelation" incident after the Stinking Springs capture - historically related by Garrett posseman, Jim East - portrays Billy's farewell to the Maxwell family.

"Brushy's" telling, weaves that known information with his own elaborations. He has "an Indian servant girl" fetch him to the meeting, and, oddly, at that moment, give him her scarf; for which he gifts her with the famous tintype! This concoction draws on Walter Noble Burns's book, *The Saga of Billy the Kid*, where the Maxwell family servant, Deluvina, had knit Billy a scarf - another indication that Roberts could study-up.

But real Billy would have used her name; the tintype had already been given to Dan Dedrick; and the actual punch line of the Jim East scene was Billy's farewell to truelove, Paulita.

As to the "revelation" of their story, Jameson and Bean say the East letter, from which it came, was unknown until 1949.

That is wrong. In 1920, Charles Siringo, another Garrett posseman from Texas, reproduced it in his book, *The History of Billy the Kid*.

5) Tiny tales make next "revelations."

a) In one tale, a Severo Gallegos, in old age, claims to have helped Billy catch the horse for his courthouse-jail escape, and tie a rope to the saddle - unaware that it was a *blanket* tied to the saddle so Billy's severed ankle chains would not frighten the animal.

b) Another anecdote has a Mrs. Bernardo Salazar, say that Yginio's cousin cut off of Billy's leg irons after the escape.

These tiny tales expose a William Morrison' hoaxing technique. In 1949, he conducted interviews in Lincoln. The Gallegos and Salazar anecdotes, collected then (as he himself cites in his *Alias Billy the Kid* book), clearly became "coaching."

ANECDOTAL EVIDENCE

After W.C. Jameson's and Frederick Bean's "revelations," comes "anecdotal evidence," which would be polite to call silly.

1) One learns that, once, on a Texas street, a mother called to her child, "Billy!" And Roberts turned. (The authors forgot that *they and he* claimed his name was both "Brushy *Bill*" and "William"!)

2) Another story is that, in 1990, the grandson of a one-time Pinkerton detective, said, in 1945, his grandfather cried out to Roberts, "Bonnie [sic] ... you're under arrest." (This proves that in 1945 there were at least two Texas eccentrics.)

3) And, in 1983, a Texan wrote a letter saying that Garrett's blind daughter told him Pat did not shoot Billy (shades of more "fuzzy factoid" hearsay by another unknown).

4) Similarly, in 1948, someone told someone in Las Cruces, New Mexico, that Billy was not shot by Garrett, because he saw him in Mexico in 1914. He knew Billy, he said, when they lived in Silver City from 1868 to 1871. (Real Billy lived there from 1873 to 1875.)

5) Yginio Salazar is cited as believing Billy was not killed. That is true. But Yginio had no first-hand knowledge, living 150 miles from Fort Sumner, in Las Tablas. His belief rested on a visit he got in old age from a teacher from Mexico - not "Brushy." That pretender, with forgotten name, disappeared. By then, Yginio was an unreliable morphine addict, from pain of the two, Lincoln County War bullets, still in his back.

AFFIDAVITS

Five identification affidavits follow in *The Return of the Outlaw Billy the Kid*, proving merely, like William Morrison did in his *Alias Billy the Kid* book, that you could get random people to swear that "Brushy" was Billy.

CONCLUDING EVIDENCE

Jameson and Bean end chivalrously with "Evidence Against William Henry Roberts as Billy the Kid;" and announce that the "only available evidence" is "Garrett's word" that he had killed Billy.

They conclude: the case "for Roberts being Billy the Kid is considerably stronger than the case against."

PIECE DE RESISTANCE: PHOTO-COMPARISON

W.C. Jameson's and Frederick Bean's 1990 "Photo-Comparison Study," as their so-called "scientific research," yielded Jameson's 2003 *True West* magazine boast that "history needed to be rewritten."

"Photo-Comparison" meant that "Brushy's" image would be compared to the famous Billy tintype. Recall that Morrison's book had pictures of young Oliver Roberts. Yet Jameson and Bean gave their photo-expert "Brushy's" death-year picture.

Precautions were unnecessary. They had found their own version of the Billy the Kid Case hoaxers' forensic expert, Dr. Henry Lee. That man was Dr. Scott T. Acton, at the Department of Electrical and Computer Engineering and the Laboratory for Vision Systems and Advanced Graphic Laboratory at the University of Texas.

But there was a starting-gate problem.

A year before their photometric analysis by Dr. Scott Acton, one had been done by a Thomas G. Kyle for the Lincoln County Heritage Trust: the Lincoln, New Mexico, museum which, at that time, housed the Billy the Kid tintype. And Thomas Kyle had concluded that "Brushy" was not Billy based on eye position, nose, chin, and ears – namely everything on his head!

To Jameson and Bean, as cited earlier, Kyle's finding mismatch meant conspiracy: "economic," or for historical "status quo." Now they question Thomas Kyle's equipment and statistical methods. And they get mean: saying that, for him, the whole thing had been "more like a hobby." Finally, they declare that ears should not have been used!

Then comes their "good guy" in "The Acton Study."

Jameson and Bean enthuse about Dr. Scott Acton's "state of the art facilities," and inventory his equipment. Revealed, thus, is a shockingly old computer system from 1972 and 1976, and unimpressive 92% success rate ("success" not being defined).

Helping ridicule, Jameson and Bean give Acton's data and his quote that "the similarity between the facial structure of Roberts and the man in the ... tintype is indeed amazing."

Amazing is that conclusion.

The clowning starts with "mouths." Old "Brushy's" photo has a fish-tail mustache, whose blunt-cut length *covers his mouth.* Yet, in Acton's "mouth breadth" measurements, tintype Billy gets an "80" to "Brushy's" "82." And tintype Billy's "mouth" is as unreal as "Brushy's." Acton used the severely deteriorated tintype in which dark spots are on the mouth.

It gets worse. Acton created - and the authors dutifully reproduce - a "restoration of the Dedrick-Upham photograph of Billy the Kid." Instead of *correcting* the mouth mars, Acton uses the spots to elongate real Billy's small mouth. And "Brushy's" "restoration" uses his mustache shadow for a long straight mouth. These fixed mouths yield Acton's "80 to 82!"

Wisely, Acton follows the Jameson-Bean "law," and omits Roberts's ears, unlike Billy's; though in Billy's Acton-restored picture, generously added by Acton is real Billy's missing left ear and rolled rims on both - emulating "Brushy's!"

This leaves one with an opinion of Dr. Acton, identical to Jameson's and Bean's opinion of Thomas Kyle. And Morrison's book's photos of Roberts at 27 and 14, look nothing like Billy.

Jameson and Bean finish unexpectedly subdued, saying only that the two pictures are "a very close match."

Amusingly, pretender John Miller's author also "proved" *he* was Billy by *her* photo-analysis with recreated busts!

In short, at the end of the Jameson and Bean game, the score was still "Brushy" zero.

"Brushy Bill" Gets Hollywood

When gauging good story, one has to admit that "Brushy Bill's" fantasy tale hits an archetypal nerve: defying death after living a life of daring-do; then continuing a life of daring-do.

But it took Hollywood 40 years to notice that; so dead "Brushy Bill" and dead William Morrison saw not a penny.

The resulting movie, "Young Guns II" was created by screenwriter, John Fusco; and came out in 1990.

Not by co-incidence was John Fusco interviewed for glossy *True West* magazine's August/September 2003 edition by staff writer, Janna Bommersbach. She, and the magazine's editor-in-chief were promoting the Billy the Kid Case hoax in a series of stories. John Fusco, therefore, ended up in her article titled "Digging up Billy. If Pat Garrett didn't kill the Kid, who's buried in his grave?"

The answer was supposed to be "a stranger" - or even Billy Barlow - and John Fusco was apparently brought on scene to pitch "Brushy Bill" Roberts's "survival" for hoax help.

Instead, apparently satiated by 44 million dollars in profit, Fusco was frustratingly honest, saying that he did not believe "Brushy" was Billy; but his movie had made a lot of money!

So William Morrison had been right all along. There really was gold in them thar gray matter hills of "Brushy's" brain.

John Fusco, though believing actual Billy the Kid history, as a good screenwriter had run with the show-biz option of making up whatever he wanted - even out-Brushying "Brushy."

So "Young Guns II" has an old "Brushy Bill" narrating his story to a young historian. Emilio Estevez stars as Billy, a leader of an outlaw gang, known as the Regulators. Cattle king John Chisum pays Pat Garrett to kill Billy. As Billy's friend, Garrett only pretends to do the deed. And Billy rides off into life as "Brushy." And the public thought that Fusco fantasy was real history.

The modern Billy the Kid Case hoaxers, neither adverse to public duping nor to garnering gold, knew the formula of "Pat did not kill Billy" had already proven itself a bonanza. They were ready for its encore.

"BRUSHY BILL" AND MODERN HOAXERS

Oliver "Brushy Bill" Roberts came closest to becoming Billy the Kid through the chicanery of the Billy the Kid Case hoaxers. He certainly, though long dead, got a new lease on life.

The Billy the Kid Case hoaxers' goal was hinted at from their, already cited, first announcement on the June 5, 2003 front page of the *New York Times*, with headline declaring "122 Years Later, The Lawman Are Still Chasing Billy the Kid."

Based on a press release from Governor Bill Richardson, and featuring the participating sheriff and deputy, their murder case against Pat Garrett was presented to the world. And Richardson promised state support for this vital pursuit.

Most eye-popping, however, was their "expert" as to Garrett's guilt. Lacking any legitimate historians on their side, they provided Jannay Valdez, owner of "The Billy the Kid Museum" of Canton, Texas - *his* museum for "Brushy Bill" Roberts. Valdez was quoted: "I'm absolutely convinced that Garrett killed someone else and that Brushy Bill was the Kid."

But there remained coyness. Did the hoaxers *actually* plan to "prove" that "Brushy" was Billy?

There was never a definitive public claim. Rather than open the sluices to a level of ridicule that William Morrison's daughter was rumored to believe brought her father to an early grave, the Billy the Kid Case hoaxers merely extended teasers. So, somehow, "Brushy's" name kept on coming up in their court papers, press, and TV documentaries - to the present.

"BRUSHY BILL" GETS HIS DAY IN COURT

In my *MegaHoax* exposé, I long hypothesized that "Brushy" was the centerpiece of the Billy the Kid Case hoax; and that only his past embarrassing trouncing by historical authorities necessitated secrecy about that fact.

In *MegaHoax*, I argued that the "Brushy"-as-Billy motive might have been an outlandish pay-to-play from then Governor Bill Richardson to his largest political donor, Texas attorney, Bill Robbins III: an active hoax participant who gave tantalizing hints of being a "Brushy Bill" believer.

And it was Attorney Bill Robins's district court exhumation petition that put "Brushy" in black and white and in court as he argued, in Fort Sumner and Silver City, for the exhumations of Billy and his mother for DNA comparisons to prove Pat Garrett murdered the innocent victim.

On February 26, 2004, Attorney Robins, with Attorneys David Sandoval and Mark Acuña (to provide New Mexico law licenses which he lacked, being from Texas), filed the "Tenth Judicial Court of De Baca County Case No. CV-2004-00005, Petition for the Exhumation of Billy the Kid's Remains." "Brushy Bill" Roberts makes his grand entrance under its "IV. Historical Background."

In retrospect, this document holds all the clues needed to infer that "Brushy" was being floated by the Billy the Kid Case hoaxers as Billy the Kid.

Bill Robins repeats "Brushy's" "dark night" error for the murder scene in Fort Sumner; and he ruminates about "whether the Kid went on to live a long and peace-abiding life elsewhere." (Hint, hint!).

In this Billy the Kid exhumation petition, Robins also uses the hoaxer style of undermining established history merely by sly and fake innuendo like: "This was also a time whose history was not accurately nor completely written." Who says *that* besides conspiracy theorists and the hoaxers themselves?

Or Robins states: "For generations now, the life of Billy the Kid has been the subject of historical debate. Perhaps the most significant lingering question involves whether Billy the Kid was indeed shot by Sheriff Pat Garrett in an ambush." Who says *that* besides conspiracy theorists and hoaxers?

And Attorney Robins would be the only person - including William Morrison and W.C. Jameson to tenderly call Oliver "Brushy Bill" Roberts "Ollie!"

But at the early 2004 date of this exhumation petition, I could not conceive the full horror that the crazy clown, "Brushy Bill" Roberts, was being resurrected. Though now, he was getting real attorney Robins, not pretend lawyer, William Morrison; and a veritable army including New Mexico's Governor, law enforcement officers, a forensic expert and lab, an "official historian" professor, and limitless taxpayer funding!

This is the Attorney Bill Robins III "Petition for the Exhumation of Billy the Kid's Remains" with its embedded secret agenda:

COME NOW, Co-Petitioners, and respectfully request that this Court order that the body of William H. Bonney, aka "Billy the Kid" be exhumed, and in support of the Petition state:

I. The Petitioners

1. The Co-Petitioners are Gary Graves, Sheriff of De Baca County, Tom Sullivan, (Sheriff) and Steve Sederwall (Deputy Sheriff) of Lincoln County, New Mexico. (hereinafter the "Sheriff-Petitioners").

2. Co-Petitioner Billy the Kid is one of the subjects of an investigation being conducted by the Sheriff-Petitioners. Bill Robins III and David Sandoval have been appointed by the Honorable Bill Richardson, Governor of the State of New Mexico, to represent the interests of Billy the Kid in the investigation.

II. Jurisdiction and Venue

3. Jurisdiction is proper with this Court on the basis of 1978 NMSA Statute 30-12-12.
4. Venue is proper in this County on the basis that the remains that are the subject of this exhumation are located in deBaca [sic] County.

III. Procedural Background

5. The Sheriff-Petitioners initiated investigation in their respective counties to set the historical record straight as to the guilt or innocence of the legendary Sheriff Pat Garrett in the death of Billy the Kid. The investigative files bear the numbers 03-06-136-01 (*deBaca* [sic] *County*) and 2003-274 (*Lincoln County*).

134

[AUTHOR'S NOTE: Under open records act investigation from 2007 to the present, its law enforcement officers would lie, claiming the Billy the Kid Case was merely their "hobby," and/or that the case was just the investigation of the deputy murders by Billy the Kid - falsely omitting their Garrett murder case.]

6. The remains of Billy the Kid's mother, Catherine Antrim, currently lie in a marked grave located in Silver City, New Mexico. The Sheriff-Petitioners previously filed a Petition to Exhume the remains of Catherine Antrim (hereinafter the "Antrim Petition") which is currently pending before the Honorable District Court Judge Quintero in the Sixth Judicial District. Counsel for Billy the Kid filed a Petition to Intervene in support of that exhumation.

[AUTHOR'S NOTE: Robins's client is dead Billy!]

7. The purpose of the Antrim Petition is to disinter her remains to extract vital mitochondrial DNA to then be used to compare with the DNA sought to be extracted from the purported remains of Billy the Kid. Those purported remains of Billy the Kid lie in a cemetery in Ft. Sumner, New Mexico. A hearing on the merits of the Antrim exhumation is scheduled for August 16-18, 2004.

8. Exhumations, DNA extractions and comparisons have become an increasingly common and accepted investigatory method and tool in forensic criminology and historical investigation ...

IV. Historical Background

[AUTHOR'S NOTE: For years, from the February 2004 filing of this petition, I believed this section on "Historical Background" marked "Brushy's" Billy the Kid Case entry, along with his pseudo-history. That was wrong. On March 23, 2010, I obtained Robins's January 5, 2004 Silver City "Billy the Kid's Pre-Hearing Brief" - APPENDIX: 2 - and received, spelled out, the hoaxers' entire plot for "Brushy" as Billy as pardonworthy.]

9. Billy the Kid is New Mexico's best known Old West figure. He has even been called the best known New Mexican ever. The Kid is no doubt the stuff of legend, myth, and continuing popular attention.

10. The Kid lived during a complex and violent time in New Mexico history which included the "Lincoln County War." It was a time when the distinction between "outlaw" and "lawman" was blurred due to rival political factions having deputized their respective supporters. Billy the Kid himself was deputized during these times.

11. This was also a time whose history was not accurately nor completely written.

[AUTHOR'S NOTE: This vague statement is hoaxer-style fake "suspicion," which, early-on in my *MegaHoax* exposé, I believed to be the only reason for citing pretenders: for "survival suspicion" to justify accusing Pat Garrett of a murder of an innocent victim instead of Billy the Kid.]

For generations now, the life of Billy the Kid has been the subject of historical debate. Perhaps the most significant lingering question involves whether Billy the Kid was indeed shot by Sheriff Pat Garrett in an ambush **one dark night** [author's boldface] in Ft. Sumner **or whether the Kid went on to live a long and peace-abiding life elsewhere.** [author's boldface]

[AUTHOR'S NOTE: Robins, faking that "historical debate" exists, is quoting "Brushy's" confabulation about the "dark night," ignorant of the full moon. His purpose is to validate intended pretender exhumations.]

12. The debate has been sparked at various times in the past by at least two individuals who laid claim to his identity. **Ollie** "Brushy Bill" Roberts [author's boldface] resided in Hico, Texas and claimed to be Billy the Kid. John Miller, in Arizona also died still claiming he was Billy the Kid. Co-Petitioners are in the initial phases of pursuing exhumations of these individuals as well.

[AUTHOR'S NOTE: Amusingly and revealingly, Robins affectionately and familiarly calls Roberts "Ollie."]

13. The Sheriff-Petitioners' investigation has certainly fueled debate as to whether or not Pat Garrett's version of events surrounding his claimed killing of Billy the Kid is in fact historically accurate. The investigation has renewed questions as to whether Billy the Kid lies buried at the fabled grave-site in Ft. Sumner. Allowing the exhumation of the remains at Ft. Sumner grave site for extraction of DNA to be compared with that of Ms. Antrim's will likely finally provide definitive answers to this historical quandary.

[AUTHOR'S NOTE: As discussed, these DNA claims are fake, and were the basis of the Office of the Medical Investigator's refusal of exhumation permits.]

IV. Claim for Relief, *Exhumation of Remains*

14. Co-Petitioners repeat and re-allege the foregoing paragraphs 1-13 as if fully set herein.

15. Section 30-12-12 of the New Mexico Statutes grants district courts power and discretion to order the exhumation of remains at a grave site.

16. This Court's power and discretion should be exercised and the exhumation be allowed to proceed for purposes of examining the purported remains of Billy the Kid. And for the extraction of DNA samples from the same.

WHEREFORE, Petitioners request that this Court issue an order allowing the exhumation of William H. Bonney, and all such further relief as the Court deems just and proper.

Respectfully submitted this 24th day of February, 2004.

Heard, Robins, Cloud, Lubel & Greenwood L.L.P.
Bill Robins III, David Sandoval
Attorneys for Co-Petitioner BILLY the KID

[AUTHOR'S NOTE: Do not miss that Bill Robins's *client* is the dead Billy the Kid - requesting his own exhumation! After all, this was a hoax done by people who felt above the law.]

"BRUSHY" HIDES IN THE BILLY THE KID CASE

More evidence that "Brushy Bill" was to be crowned ultimately as "Billy the Kid" by the Billy the Kid Case hoaxers, came from discoveries yielded by my 2007 to the present, open records violation case against the Lincoln County Sheriff, to obtain the concealed forensic DNA documents of his Lincoln County Sheriff's Department Case No. 2003-274. This long legal struggle is presented in my *MegaHoax* book.

As part of that open records case, on September 3, 2008, the sheriff handed over his carefully expurgated murder file - lacking all the requested forensic documents!

Nevertheless, that file contained revealing papers. About one third of that murder investigation on suspect Pat Garrett, constituted articles about "Brushy Bill" Roberts!"

Even more telling, was the presence of a document which the hoaxers had kept secret from the 2003 inception of their Case No. 2003-274.

That document, probably created around April of 2003, is a draft of the lawmen's never-used Probable Cause Statement for Pat Garrett as the murder suspect. (Their actual Probable Cause Statement for Case No. 2003-274 was signed and dated December 31, 2003. [APPENDIX: 1])

Dramatically, in this preliminary and abandoned version, "Brushy's" "survival" is presented as *key* "evidence" for Pat Garrett's not having killed Billy - meaning, according to the hoaxers, "Brushy Bill's" tall tales were credible as a law enforcement case's probable cause to prosecute Garrett for murder of an innocent victim!

In that scenario, "Brushy Bill's" creation, Billy Barlow, takes the innocent victim role. So, according to the fledgling Billy the Kid Case hoax, non-historical Billy Barlow would be their corpse in Billy's Fort Sumner grave - and recipient of their hoax's "high-tech, modern, CSI, DNA forensics."

It was shades of ol' "Brushy" meets "Young Guns II;" meets the Lincoln County Sheriff's Department; meets a media circus; meets the strangest ploy ever for a potential presidential candidate; meets duped New Mexico taxpayers being taken for a ride in arguably the weirdest political pay-to-play ever.

That secret "Brushy" document was titled: "Lincoln County Sheriff's Office, Lincoln County New Mexico, Case: William H. Bonney, a.k.a. William Antrim, a.k.a. The Kid, a.k.a. Billy the Kid: An Investigation into the events of April 28, 1881 through July 14, 1881 - seventy-seven days of doubt."

I nick-named it the "Seventy-Seven Days of Doubt Document." Abandoned, it had no date. The typed-in signers were to be the Sheriff and his deputy who opened the departmental case; though the actual author is unclear.

This "Seventy-Seven Days of Doubt" document bears no resemblance to the final Probable Cause Statement for Case No. 2003-274. That document is debunked in *MegaHoax* (and here in APPENDIX: 1) as pseudo-historical, with only "alien invasion illogic" of "ifs" and fake "suspicion" claim that Pat Garrett had not killed Billy. It resembles the "Seventy-Seven Days of Doubt" document only by maligning Garrett.

Most dramatic, is that it reveals what is absent in the final Probable Cause Statement: neither "Brushy Bill" Roberts nor John Miller are even whispered. A naive reader could not guess that hidden pretender goal.

A segue into the "Seventy-Seven Days of Doubt" version, however, takes one, from mimicked solid ground of history and law enforcement, down a rabbit hole into Conspiracy Theory Wonderland. There "Brushy" is king. John Miller, scampering by as the white rabbit, disappears as a fleeting denizen of that imaginary land.

Though it was never signed, and the typed in names are of the 2003 sheriff and his participating deputy, I hypothesized in *MegaHoax* is hypothesized that the mystery author was Attorney Bill Robins III. The are words of a "Brushy" believer, which I guessed him to be. Valuable are long passages of "Brushy's" own words - convincing only to those as historically ignorant and enamored as are "Brushy's" followers.

So Lincoln County Sheriff's Department Case 2003-274 - the Billy the Kid Case — from the starting-block, was to prove Oliver P. Roberts as "Billy the Kid!"

Then something must have spooked the hoaxers into concealment. But here follows that entire damning document.

LINCOLN COUNTY SHERIFF'S OFFICE
LINCOLN COUNTY, NEW MEXICO

Case: *William H. Bonney, a.k.a.* **William Antrim,**
a.k.a. **The Kid,** *a.k.a.* **Billy the Kid**

An Investigation into the events of April 28, 1881 through July 14, 1881 - seventy-seven days of doubt.

Just minutes after twelve, noon, on April 28, 1881, two lawmen lay dead, in the yard of the courthouse in Lincoln, New Mexico, from gunshot wounds. In less time then [sic] it took the New Mexico breeze to clear the gunsmoke, history was clouded with the myth of the shooting and escape of William H. Bonney, a.k.a. Billy the Kid from the make-shift jail, where he awaited a date with the hangman.

The following is a thumbnail sketch of the most widely excepted [sic] account of the events of the escape, capture and shooting death of William H. Bonney a.k.a. Billy the Kid.

The Last Days of William H. Bonney

On August 17, 1877, in George Atkin's cantina near Camp Grant, Arizona, William H. Bonney, who answered to "The Kid" found himself in an altercation with Francis P. "Windy" Cahill over cards or Cahill's woman, no one is quite sure as newspapers report both. It's reported that Windy Cahill called The Kid a "pimp", and in response The Kid dubbed Cahill a "sonofabitch". Infuriated, Cahill reportedly grabbed the Kid and The Kid shoved his pistol into Cahill's stomach, sending a hot round into his belly. With Cahill on the floor, The Kid fled on a stolen horse. Cahill died the next day. A coroner's jury headed by Miles Wood found the shooting by The Kid to be *"criminal and unjustifiable"*. The Kid now being a bona fide outlaw drifted across the line into New Mexico's Lincoln County where he signed on as a cowboy working for London born rancher John Tunstall.

Tunstall and his lawyer friend Alexander McSween had decided to challenge the chock-hold [sic] monopoly L.G. Murphy & Company had on Lincoln County. Murphy and his associates, with the backing of the "Santa Fe Ring" ran Lincoln County as they pleased and verticality [sic] unchecked until Tunstall's challenge. The Santa Fe Ring, with their powerful political and financial backing and through Murphy controlled the sheriff, maintained a buddy-buddy relationship with the military and appropriated by means both legal and illegal most of the government money out of the Mescalaro Apache Indian Agency near Fort Stanton. When Tunstall wouldn't back down and his challenge became to [sic] powerful for the Murphy faction to turn their heads to, Tunstall was killed. His death on February 18, 1878 fanned the spark that raged into the white-hot flame that became the famed and bloody Lincoln County War.

As history goes Bonney was insignificant as a man, but there exist [sic] no better example of how legends of the west are born and continue to grow. By participating in a number of bloody shootouts, included [sic] the assassination of Lincoln County Sheriff William Brady and one of his deputies, on April 1, 1878, Bonney was catapulted from his status of an unknown drifter to the undisputed leader of the Tunstall-McSween faction and into history becoming bigger the [sic] life.

[AUTHOR'S NOTE: Though beginning when Bonney was 17 ½ (not his last days!), this flaunting of "historical knowledge" its false. Bonney was never the leader of the Tunstall-McSween faction. The writer attempts to blur history and "legend," to falsely assert that actual history was merely legend. Beyond that, everything is irrelevant to any probable cause statement.]

After newly elected Lincoln County Sheriff Pat Garrett captured Bonney at Stinking Springs, east of Fort Sumner, just before Christmas 1880, Bonney was held in the jail in Santa Fe for several months and then taken to La Mesilla, New Mexico for trial.

The Dona Ana County, District Court records reveal on April 13, 1881, William H. Bonney was convicted of the April 1, 1878 murder of Lincoln County Sheriff William Brady. United States District Judge, Warren Henry Bristol, of the Third Judicial District, sentenced Bonney to be confined in Lincoln County until Friday, May 13, 1881. Looking down from the bench, the judge proclaimed, *"between 9 a.m. and 3 p.m., William Bonney, alias Kid, alias William Antrim, be taken from such prison to some suitable and convenient place of execution within said county of Lincoln, by Sheriff of such county and that then and there, on that day and between the aforesaid hours thereof, by the sheriff of said county of Lincoln, he, the said William Bonney, alias Kid, alias William Antrim, be hanged by the neck until his body be dead."*

On April 21, 1881, Bonney was transported back to Lincoln under heavy guard. Because Lincoln had no adequate jail Bonney was incarcerated in the upstairs of the old Murphy-Dolan store, recently bought by the county to be used as the courthouse. A staircase led up to a hallway that ran north to south across the middle section of the building. The room ahead and to the left of the hallway was being used as the sheriff''s office. Off the sheriff''s office, with access only through the sheriff''s office was the room where Bonney was confined.

With no bars on the windows of this room, Sheriff Garrett had special leg shackles made, and Bonney was chained to the hardwood floor at all times. In addition, Garrett assigned Lincoln County Sheriffs Deputy J.W. Bell and Deputy United States Marshall [sic] Bob Olinger, to guard the prisoner twenty-four hours a day. On the floor Bonney's guards drew a chalk line across the center of the room, a line which Bonney was forbidden to cross or he would be shot by the guards.

On Wednesday, April 27, 1881 Sheriff Pat Garrett left Lincoln on a tax-collecting mission to White Oaks, New Mexico. Just after twelve, noon, the next day, Thursday, April 28, Deputy United States Marshall [sic] Olinger escorted all the prisoners with the exception of Bonney to the Wortley Hotel, across the street from the courthouse, for their midday meal, leaving Deputy Sheriff Bell in charge of Bonney.

No eye witness record can be found of the escape of Bonney with the exception of the following statement made by the courthouse caretaker Gottfried Gauss, published in the *Lincoln County Leader* on January 15, 1890, nearly a decade later.

I was crossing the yard behind the courthouse, when I heard a shot fired then a tussle upstairs in the courthouse, somebody hurrying downstairs, and deputy sheriff Bell emerging from the door running toward me. He ran right into my arms, expired the same moment, and I laid him down, dead. That I was in a hurry to secure assistance, or perhaps to save myself, everybody will believe.

When I arrived at the garden gate leading to the street, in front of the courthouse, I saw the other deputy sheriff Olinger, coming out of the hotel opposite, with the four or five other county prisoners, where they had taken their dinner. I called to him to come quick. He did so, leaving his prisoners in front of the hotel. When he had come up close to me, and while I was standing not a yard apart, I told him that I was just after laying Bell dead on the ground in the yard behind. Before he could reply, he was struck by a well-directed shot fired from a window above us, and fell dead at my feet. I ran for my life to reach my room and safety, when Billy the Kid called to me: "Don't run, I wouldn't hurt you – I am alone, and master not only of the courthouse, but also of the town, for I will allow nobody to come near us." "You go," he said, "and saddle one of Judge (Ira) Leonard's horses, and I will clear out as soon as I have the shackles loosened from my legs." With a little prospecting pick I had thrown to him through the window he was working for at least an hour, and could not accomplish more than to free one leg. He came to the conclusion to wait a better chance, tie one shackle to his waistbelt, and start out. Meanwhile I had saddled a small skittish pony belonging to Billy Burt (the county clerk), as there was no other horse available, and had also, by Billy's command, tied a pair of red blankets behind the saddle ...

When Billy went down the stairs at last, on passing the body of Bell he said, "I'm sorry I had to kill him but I couldn't help it." On passing the body of Olinger he gave him a tip with his boot, saying, "You are not going to round me up again." And so Billy the Kid started out that evening, after he had shaken hands with everybody around and after having a little difficulty in mounting on account of the shackle on his leg, he went on his way rejoicing.

There are numerous theories about the killing of Deputy J.W. Bell. One is that he was coming up the stairs when shot. Another theory is Bell was running down the stairs and was at the bottom of the stairs and heading to the doorway when Bonney shot him. Garrett's testimony seems to be the most solid. Garrett says, *"Bell was hit under the right arm, the bullet passing through his body and coming out under the left arm. The ball had hit the wall on Bell's right, caromed passed through his body, and buried itself in an adobe (wall) on the left. There was no other proof besides the marks on the walls."*

Garrett later said of Olinger, that he was *"hit in the right shoulder, breast and side. He was literally riddled by thirty-six buckshot."* Each pellet weighed four grams - nearly a quarter pound of lead in all hit Olinger.

It's hard to determine how many shots were fired at Bell from Bonney's pistol. In the 1920's Maurice G. Fulton saw the building and states there were *"any number of bullet holes"*. Fulton had a photograph taken in the 1930's prior to the restoration, which shows three.

With only two people on the stairway that day numerous versions of what happened have been brought forth, and debated. One theory in the Kid's escape is that he slipped his irons, which were double the usual weight, over his small wrists and hands. He turned on Bell striking the deputy over the head with the irons and grabbing the deputy's pistol. This theory could have come from the following article.

In the *Grant County Herald's*, May 14, 1881 edition an article appeared quoting an "anonymous bystander" as testifying about the Kid's escape. *He had at his command eight revolvers and six guns. He stood on the upper porch in front of the building and talked with the people who were in Wortley's, but he would not let anyone come towards him. He told the people that he did not want to kill Bell but, as he had to. He said he grabbed Bell's revolver and told him to hold up his hands and surrender; that Bell decided to run and he had to kill him. He declared he was "standing pat" against the world; and while he did not wish to kill anybody, if anybody interfered with his attempt to escape, he would kill him.*

In this statement the "anonymous bystander" claims Bonney says he took Bell's pistol from him and used it to kill the deputy. In Garrett's book *The Authentic Life of Billy the Kid*, Garrett writes this about the escape:

From circumstances, indications, information from Geiss (also spelled Gauss – the courthouse caretaker) and the Kid's admissions, the popular conclusion is that:
At the Kid's request, Bell accompanied him down stairs and to the back corral. As they returned, Bell allowed the Kid to get considerably in advance. As the Kid turned on the landing of the

stairs, he was hidden from Bell. He was light and active, and with a few noiseless bounds, reached the head of the stairs, turned to his right, put his shoulder to the door of the room used as an armory (thought locked, this door was well known to open by a firm push), entered, seized a six-shooter, returned to the head of the stairs just as Bell faced him on the landing of the stair-case, some twelve steps beneath, and fired. Bell turned, ran out into the corral and towards the little gate. He fell dead before reaching it. The Kid ran to the window at the south end of the hall, saw Bell fall, then slipped his handcuffs over his hands, threw them at the body, and said: "Here, damn you, take these, too."

Garrett's account seems to have to [sic] many holes to be taken as truth in this matter. At the beginning of Chapter XXII, where this account is found Garrett begins, *On the evening of April 28, 1881, Olinger took all the other prisoners across the street to supper, leaving Bell in charge of the Kid in the guard room.* It is a known fact that the escape did not happen in the evening as Garrett writes but just after noon.

Frederick Nolan, in his commentary notes at the side of the page in this book, points out the following: *The "popular" conclusion set forth here - that Bell would have allowed the Kid latitude and time he needed to perform these maneuvers - has already been examined. That he could have moved "noiselessly" when wearing manacles and leg irons defies belief. And would Billy have waited until after killing Bell before he "slipped his handcuffs over his hands?" Either the Kid struck Bell over the head with his handcuffs, grabbed Bell's gun and killed him with it, or, far more plausibly, someone hid a pistol in the outhouse privy, which Billy retrieved and, when they got inside, killed Bell with it.*

When Garrett describes The Kid shooting Olinger he says that ... *Olinger appeared at the gate leading into the yard, as Geiss appeared at the little corral gate and said, "Bob, The Kid has killed Bell." At the same instant the Kid's voice was heard above: "Hello, old boy," said he. "Yes, and he's killed me too," exclaimed Olinger, and fell dead with eighteen buckshot in his right shoulder and breast and side.*

It is doubtful that Olinger would have time to say the words that Garrett contributes [sic] to him before the Kid cut him down, making Garrett's account difficult to be taken as true accounting of the events.

[AUTHOR'S NOTE: Though lacking sly finesse of the final Probable Cause Statement, this author likewise uses Garrett's ghostwritten, dime-novel-style book to discredit him. But it is irrelevant to Garrett as a murderer.]

Garrett also says about The Kid in his account – *He took deliberate aim and fired the other barrel, the charge taking effect in nearly the same place as the first; then breaking the gun across the railway of the balcony, he threw the pieces at Olinger, saying: "Take it, damn you, you won't follow me any more with that gun."*
This doubtful this happened. [sic] The account of The Kid breaking Olinger's shotgun on the balcony is not found elsewhere. Added to the fact that Olinger's shotgun was a Whitney, serial number SN903, and is now on loan to the *Texas Ranger Hall of Fame* in Waco, Texas from the James H. Earl [sic - Earle] Collection; the shotgun is in tact [sic].

[AUTHOR'S NOTE: Error. The Deputy Olinger, Whitney, double-barrel shotgun is broken at its waist, and repaired, at some unknown time, by a wrapping of copper wire. Its curator at the Texas Ranger Museum, attesting to the description, is Don Agler. This is another irrelevant attempt to discredit Garrett.]

The version which seems the more popular, is that Bonney, retrieved a pistol that had been hidden in the outhouse by a "friend." History has theories but no firm answers to the identity of the "friend" who put the pistol in the outhouse.

[AUTHOR'S NOTE: Error. This seems to be a confusion of the Bell killing with Olinger's, for which the Whitney was used.]

After the Kid shot and killed both of his guards he gather [sic] weapons, and left Lincoln about 3 p.m. on a stolen horse. The Kid's whereabouts from the date of his escape until just before his death, as nearly every aspect of the case, is still debated. The Kid later showed up in Ft. Sumner, New Mexico. Pete Maxwell's teenage daughter, Paulita,

[AUTHOR'S NOTE: Error. Paulita was Peter Maxwell's sister. Also, using Paulita contradicts the "love tales" of "Brushy Bill" (Celsa) and John Miller (Isadora), and eliminates them as Billy contenders!.]

was supposedly in love with the Kid and he with her, which seems to be the most likely motive for him to return to Ft. Sumner.

On the night of July 14, 1881, after searching the area around Ft. Sumner Lincoln County Sheriff Pat Garrett and his deputies John Poe and Thomas C. "Kip" McKinney were about to ride back to Lincoln. Before leaving they thought it a good idea to check with Pete Maxwell. In Garrett's account of this he takes credit for wanting to check with Maxwell before giving up the chase, Deputy Poe differs with Garrett. In Deputy Poe's account written in 1919 we see the events through his eyes.

Garrett seemed to have but little confidence in our being able to accomplish the object of our trip, but said that he knew the location of a certain house occupied by a woman in Fort Sumner which the Kid had formerly frequented, and that if he was in or about Fort Sumner, he would most likely be found entering or leaving this house some time during the night. Garrett proposed that we go to a grove of trees near the town, conceal our horses, then station ourselves in the peach orchard at the rear of the house, and keep watch on who might come or go. This course was agreed upon, and we entered the peach orchard about nine o'clock that night, stationing ourselves in the gloom or shadow of the peach trees, as the moon was shining very brightly. We kept up a fruitless watch here until some time after eleven o'clock, when Garrett stated that he believed we were on a cold trail; that he had very little faith in our being able to accomplish anything when we started on the trip. He proposed that we leave the town without letting anyone know that we had been there in search of the Kid.

I then proposed that, before leaving we should go to the residence of Peter Maxwell, a man who up to that time I had never seen, but who, by reason of his being a leading citizen and having a large property interest should, according to my reasoning, be glad to furnish such information as he might have aid us [sic] in ridding the country of a man who was looked on as a scourge and curse by all law-abiding people.

Garrett agreed to this, and there-upon led us from the orchard by circuitous by-paths to Maxwell's residence, which was a building formerly used as officers' quarters during the days when a garrison of troops had been maintained at the fort. Upon our arriving at the *residence (a very long, one-story adobe, standing end to the flush with the street, having a porch on the south side, which was the direction from which we approached, the premises all being enclosed by a paling fence, one side of which ran parallel to and along the edge of the street up to and across the end of the porch to the corner of the building).\, Garrett said to me, "This is Maxwell's room through the open door (left open on account of the extremely warm weather), while McKinney and myself stopped on the outside. McKinney squatted on the outside of the fence, and I sat on the porch.*

It should be here that up to this moment I had never seen Billy the Kid, nor Maxwell, which fact in view of the events transpiring immediately afterward, placed me at an extreme disadvantage.

It was probably not more than thirty seconds after Garrett had entered Maxwell's room, when my attention was attracted, from where I sat at the little gateway, to a man approaching me on the inside of and along the fence, some forty or fifty steps away. I observed that he was only partially dressed and was both bareheaded and barefooted, or rather had only socks on his feet, and it seemed to me that he was fastening his trousers as he came toward me at a very brisk walk.

As Maxwell's was the one place in Fort Sumner that had considered above suspicion of harboring the Kid, I was entirely off my guard, the thought coming to my mind that the man approaching was either Maxwell or some guest of his who might be staying there. He came on until he was almost within arm's length of where I sat, before he saw me, as I was partially concealed from his view by the post of the gate.

Upon seeing me, he covered me with his six-shooter as quick as lightening, sprang onto the porch, calling out in Spanish "Quien es" (Who is it?) - at the same time backing away from me toward the door through which Garrett only a few seconds before had passed, repeating his query, "Who is it?" in Spanish several times.

At this I stood up and advanced toward him, telling him not to be alarmed, that he should not be hurt; and still without the least suspicion that this was the very man we were looking for. As I moved toward him to reassure him, he backed up into the doorway of Maxwell's room, where he halted for a moment, his body concealed by the thick adobe wall at the side of the doorway, form [sic] whence he put his head and asked in Spanish for the fourth time who I was. I was within a few feet of him when he disappeared into the room.

After this, and until after the shooting, I was unable to see what took place on account of the darkness of the room, but plainly heard what was said on the inside. An instant after the man left the door, I heard a voice inquire in a sharp tone, "Pete, who are those fellows on the outside?" An instant later a shot was fired in the room, followed immediately by what anyone within hearing distance thought were two shots. However, there were only two shots fired, the third report, as we learned afterward, being caused by the rebound of the second bullet, which had struck the adobe wall and rebounded against the headboard of a wooden bedstead.

I heard a groan and one or two gasps from where I stood in the doorway, as of someone dying in the room. An instant later, Garrett came out, brushing against me as he passed. He stood by me close to the wall at the side of the door and said to me, "That was the Kid that came in there onto me, and I think I got him". I said, "Pat, the Kid would not come to this place; you have shot the wrong man".

Upon saying this, Garrett seemed to be in doubt himself as to whom he had shot, but quickly spoke up and said, "I am sure it was him, for I know his voice to [sic] well to be mistaken". This remark of Garrett's relieved me of considerable apprehension, as I had felt almost certain that someone whom we did not want had been killed.

The next day Billy the Kid was buried in Fort Sumner. Or was it the Kid in the grave?

[AUTHOR'S NOTE: Poe's initial, and natural, uncertainty about the identity of Billy, appears the only indication that this hoax writer uses to cast doubt on the identity of the victim. Missing are all witnesses and the Coroner's Jury. Missing too is the Garrett friendship plot that characterized the mature hoax and its final Probable Cause Statement.]

What Happen [sic] to William H. Bonney a.k.a. Billy the Kid?

Soon after the shooting in Maxwell's home on July 14, 1881, the rumor took life that Garrett shot the wrong man and that he knew he shot the wrong man but covered it up.

[AUTHOR'S NOTE: This Seventy-Seven Days document is transparently tailored to fit the pretenders.]

Some even say that Garrett had an empty coffin buried the next day in Fort Sumner. Some say Garrett wrote the book *The Authentic Life of Billy the Kid*, in which he demonizing [sic] Billy the Kid, to prop up his waning popularity that was being eroded by the rumor that he killed The Kid in less than a fair fight or that he did not kill The Kid at all.

[AUTHOR'S NOTE: These contentions, without sources, appear made up.]

To this day the rumor still has life that Billy the Kid never died that night.

[AUTHOR'S NOTE: Nothing has been presented to support that "rumor."]

Most everything we know about William H. Bonney a.k.a. Billy the Kid is what is know [sic] about him in during the last three years of his life. The date and place of his birth, who his father was, where he lived, as a child is still a mystery. Most of what we do know and what we call history is flawed by myth. Even where he is buried is the subject of controversy these 122 years later.

[AUTHOR'S NOTE: This illogic tries to make Bonney's death uncertain, by manufacturing "uncertainties" in his earlier history.]

In England is a grave with the name William H. Bonney on the headstone, where is it said [sic] Billy the Kid is buried. The story is that the Tunstall family, in apparition [sic] of his help and loyalty to John Tunstall, brought the Kid back to England where he lived a long life dying of old age.

[AUTHOR'S NOTE: This is so bizarre, it seems a delirium, rather than an argument. It does indicate the author lacks ability to sort fact from fiction.]

[AUTHOR'S NOTE: The case for Garrett's murder of an innocent ceases here without having established its probable cause or any truth proof; and the segue is to establishing the pretenders – "Brushy Bill" Roberts in particular.]

John Miller

[AUTHOR'S NOTE: At this preliminary stage - years before the hoaxers needed John Miller's exhumation to keep their hoax afloat - he was of minimal interest; their goal being "Brushy." This disinterest is reflected in the following cursory text.]

In 1993 Helen Airy published a book by Sunstone Press entitled *What* [sic- Whatever] *Happened to Billy the Kid*. In this book the claim is made that a John Miller who died on November 7, 1937, at six-thirty in the evening, in the Pioneer [sic] Home in Prescott, Arizona and was buried in the Prescott Pioneer [sic] home cemetery, was Billy the Kid. In Airy's book Miller is quoted as saying, *"there was a Mexican shot and buried in the coffin that is supposed to be the Kid."*

In her book *What* [sic- Whatever] *Happened to Billy the Kid* these accounts are found:

Page 162 paragraph 2 - *Ann Storrer of Belen writes: "My father, Charlie Walker, grew up around Fort Sumner during the early 1900's. A Mexican he used to work for told him that he saw Billy the Kid at the bullfights in Mexico long after he was supposed to be dead. The rumor around Fort Sumner was that Pat Garrett and Bill [sic] the Kid were good friends and Garrett tried to stop everyone from killing Billy. My father believed there was never a body in the grave.*

Page 162 paragraph 3 and 4 - *Arleigh Nation of Albuquerque supplied the Following story; "A man by the name of Trujillo, who died in 1935 at the age of ninety-five told Nation he worked for Pete Maxwell at the time Billy the kid was supposed to have been killed. He said the day before the shoot-out they dressed up an Indian, who had died the night before, to look like the Kid. The Indian was buried in the grave that was said to have been the Kid's.*

Nation, who is a Billy the kid Buff, also said a neighbor of his who lived in Lincoln, Mrs. Syd Boykin, told him that the kid stayed as [sic] her home in Lincoln many times after he was supposed to have been dead.

Airy states that a John Collins claimed to have been a friend of Billy the Kid. Collins says that he helped bury the corpse of the man Garrett killed on July 14, 1881, and it was not Billy the kid.

Arley Sanches interviewed Nadine Brady, of Adelino, New Mexico, and whose grandfather was Sheriff William Brady, who was shot by the Kid, for a story, which appeared in the *Albuquerque*

Journal on September 8, 1990. Nadine says one old timer told her Garrett didn't shoot Bonney. He told her Garrett and Bonney were friends and Garrett invented a story to help his friend escape. A wanderer was killed and buried, and Garrett told everyone he had shot Billy the Kid.

Airy says Frank Coe, a friend of Billy the Kid during the Lincoln County War, believed to the day of his death that Billy was still alive, and spent a great deal of time tracing reports that he had been seen.

The El Paso Herald Post, June 29, 1926 reported a story that a "government official" re[ported that "Billy the Kid and Garrett framed an escape" from Lincoln, New Mexico. The government official claimed the Kid was still alive in this article.

The El Paso Times, July 26, 1964, reported that retired Immigration and Naturalization Service Inspector, Leslie Traylor of San Antonio, Texas claimed Billy the Kid was a man named Henry Street Smith. Traylor said he traced Smith and believes him to be buried under the name of John Miller who died in 1935 in Prescott, Arizona.

[AUTHOR'S NOTE: Airy's John Miller hoax is debunked later in this book. The writer here, however, does not appear to argue for Miller as Billy. And no death scene is presented, that being the purpose of a probable cause statement for a murder case!]

William Henry Roberts a.k.a. Brushy Bill Roberts

[AUTHOR'S NOTE: Now comes the hoaxers' apparent heir to Billy's identity. But the effusions that follow here, were concealed in the ensuing Billy the Kid Case, seemingly to be replaced by the fake forensics "do the proving." And the subsequent problem of "Brushy's" non-bench death scene - presented below in unabashed detail - was not anticipated, since the hoaxers expected the exhumations to be slam dunks.]

Before Sheriff Pat Garrett could clean his pistol the bogus Billy the Kid's began to crop up everywhere. Some were too ridiculous to take notice of and some convinced a few people but were forgotten with the passage of time. Out of all the men to come forward to claim they are Billy the Kid the one that caused the most stir and gained national and even worldwide attention was Brushy Bill Roberts.

152

To this day Roberts' claim is being taken seriously by many. In Hamilton, Texas, where William Roberts is buried there stands a sign that proclaims that his grave is "The Authentic Grave Site of Billy the Kid." A plaque states that he spent the last part of his life attempting to get a "promised pardon" from the New Mexico Governor. Just weeks before Roberts death he and his attorney [sic - William Morrison, not an attorney] approached the Governor of New Mexico and asked for a pardon for the Kid, who Roberts claimed to be. Dubious of Roberts claims the Governor granted no pardon.

[AUTHOR'S NOTE: This "Brushy" pardon focus adds credence to the otherwise non sequitor quest for the pardon in the Billy the Kid Case hoax. For that, the Garrett murder "investigation" is irrelevant. But gaining the pardon was the "Brushy"-Morrison goal – and the secret goal of the modern hoax.]

The story goes that in 1948, William V. Morrison was working as an investigator for a law firm. Morrison was a graduate attorney [sic - Morrison was not an attorney] and it was said that he had a "good nose for evidence". He was a member of the Missouri Historical Society and a descendant of Ferdinand Maxwell, the brother of Lucien Bonaparte Maxwell and uncle of Pete Maxwell. [AUTHOR'S NOTE: Allegedly this lacks evidence.] Because of this, Morrison possessed a keen interest in New Mexico history.

During this time Morrison was sent to Florida to investigate an inheritance claimant by the name of Joe Hines. Hines' brother, in North Dakota, had passed away and Hines claimed to be the sole inheritor of some property. As Morrison interviewed the old man the story did not match with the facts Morrison possessed. After more questions Joe Hines told Morrison his name, Hines, was an alias. Hines claimed his real name was Jesse [sic] Evans and he was a survivor of the Lincoln County War.

[AUTHOR'S NOTE: Important Error: This would not be made by someone in the "Brushy Bill" inner circle. Hines claimed to be a Jimmy McDonald, not Jessie Evans. And the contact person for "Brushy" was J. Frank Dalton, whom "Brushy's" conspiracy theorist believers consider to have been Jesse James!. This would, however not cancel out Attorney Bill Robins III.]

Morrison being proud of his ancestral connection to New Mexico history mentioned to Hines (Evans) that Billy the Kid worked for the Maxwells at one time

[AUTHOR'S NOTE: Error: Billy did not work for the Maxwells.]

and added that the Kid was shot and killed in Maxwell's house on July 14, 1881. To that Hines replied, "Garrett did not kill the Kid on July 14, 1881, or any other time." Hines went on to say, "In fact Billy was still living in Texas last year. The reason that I know is that a friend of mine, now living in California stops over to visit with me here every summer. He and Billy and me are the only warriors left of the old Lincoln County bunch.

[AUTHOR'S NOTE: Besides the fact that everything here is non-historical, real Jessie Evans would not have called himself a Lincoln County War "warrior."]

Later that year Morrison became acquainted with another man in Missouri who said he knew who all the parties were and gave Morrison an address of a man named O.L. Roberts who lived in Hamilton, Texas. In June of 1948 Morrison drove to Hamilton, Texas and met Roberts. On their first meeting Roberts told Morrison that the Kid was his half brother and was still alive in Old Mexico. The next day Morrison came back to Roberts home and Roberts sent his wife to a neighbor's house saying he and Morrison had business to discuss.

After Mrs. Roberts left the house Morrison claims Roberts pointed his finger at him and said, "Well, you've got your man. You don't need to look any farther. I'm Billy the Kid. But don't tell anyone. My wife doesn't know who I am. She thinks my half brother is Billy the Kid, but he died in Kentucky many years ago. I want a pardon before saying anything about this matter. I don't want to kill anyone anymore, but I'm not going to hang." Morrison goes on to write that Roberts told his story and tears coursed down his cheeks, as he said, "I done wrong like everyone else did in those days. I want to die a free man. I do not want to die like Garrett and the rest of them, by the gun. I have been hiding so long and they have been telling so many lies about me that I want to get everything straightened out before I die. I can do it with some help. The good Lord left me here for a purpose and I know why He did. Now will you help me out of this mess."

154

Morrison wanted proof that Roberts claims were true and knew the scars the Kid would have on his body. Morrison had Roberts strip and from the scars on Roberts' body Morrison was convinced that he was talking to the true William H. Bonney.

Roberts tells Morrison in detail how he escaped death at the hands of Sheriff Pat Garrett the night of July 14, 1881. In a statement Roberts records the following:

[AUTHOR'S NOTE: The following is an excellent example of "Brushy's" confabulatory style. This text can be found in pages 105-117 of W.C. Jameson's and Frederick Bean's 1997 *The Return of the Outlaw Billy the Kid*. They claimed to have gotten the transcript from *Alias Billy the Kid* author, William Morrison's, step-grandson, Bill Allison.]

[AUTHOR'S NOTE: Do not miss the dramatic validation of "Brushy" that this document represents. His own words are being used in *a real law enforcement case* to show probable cause that Garrett was a murderer.]

I rode into Fort Sumner from Yerby's a few days before Garrett and his posse rode in. When they rode in that day, I had spent the day with Garrett's brother-in-law, Saval Gutierrez. Nearly all the people in this country were my friends and they helped me. None of them likes Garrett. It was dark that night, but there was enough moonlight to make shadows. Me and my partner Billy Barlow, rode up to Jesus Silva's house when we reached Fort Sumner. We had been staying at the Yerby Ranch laying low for a while. Word was all around that Pat Garrett and a posse were after me. Pat's wife was a sister to my friend Saval Gutierrez, and Saval told me that Pat was after me, that he heard it from his sister.

Things were mighty hot in Lincoln County for me right about then, but I wasn't running from it. I meant to have a talk with Pt Garrett and set things straight between us if I could. We used to be friends ... We hid our horses in the barn and walked up to Jesus' back door. Barlow was nervous about being in Fort Sumner with me and I couldn't blame him much. Jesus came to the back door when I tapped on it with the barrel of my six-shooter. When he saw that it was me, he grinned and let us in. I told Jesus we were hungry. We'd been out in the hills all day, scouting around fort Sumner for any sign of

*Garrett and his posse. "I have nothing but cold frijoles, compadre,"
Jesus whispered as he closed the door. Barlow made a sour face. "I
want some meat," he said, "we have been living on beans and
tortillas all week. Ain't you got any beef?*

According to Roberts statement Jesus Silva told Barlow that Pete
Maxwell had some meat hanging on his porch. Barlow wanted to get
the beef to cook but Roberts told him it was too dangerous and they
should not move from the house. Barlow would not listen. According
to Roberts statement Barlow took a butcher knife and left the house to
head to Maxwell's to get the beefsteak. While Roberts and Jesus were
lighting the wood stove they hear [sic] gunfire in the direction of Pete
Maxwell's place. Roberts' statement goes on to describe the
following events:

*I pulled one of my .44's and ran through the door, trying to see in
the dark. Two more shots came from a shadow beside the Maxwell
house. I couldn't find a target to shoot at. It was too dark to see. I ran
toward Maxwell's back porch. I heard another gunshot and felt
something hit me in the jaw. I stumbled and kept on running with a
broken tooth rolling around my tongue. I tasted blood and spit the
mess out of my mouth as I started emptying my six-shooter at the
shadow where I saw the muzzleflash. From the corner of my eye I saw
a body lying on the back porch ... I knew it had to be Barlow.
My partner had walked right into a trap, and the trap had likely
been set for me. I pulled my other .44 and ran toward the porch to
check on Barlow, but I ran into a wall of gunfire. I knew I wasn't
going to make it to my partner. Too many guns were shooting at me. I
didn't have a chance. I turned for a fence across the back of
Maxwell's yard and dove for it when a bullet caught me in the left
shoulder. I jumped over the fence and landed hard on the far side,
with the echo of gunshots all around me, ringing in my ears. I
staggered into an alley that ran behind the house, firing my .44 over
my shoulder until it clicked empty. My mouth and shoulder were
bleeding and I lost track of where I was, but I knew I had to get away
from Maxwell's before they killed me. I heard a shout and another
gunshot. Something passed across my forehead like a hot branding
iron. I was stunned. I lost footing and fell on my face in the darkness.
I knew I was hurt bad and wondered if I would make it out of this
scrape alive.*

I forced myself up again, wiping the blood from my eyes with my shirtsleeve as I stumbled headlong down the ally. I didn't know how bad the head wound was, only that it was bleeding and I couldn't see. It wouldn't matter if the found me in the alley just then, they were bent on killing me, to be sure. If I fell again I knew they'd find me and finish the job, so I kept running down the ally as hard as I could, barely able to see where I was going. I heard them shouting to each other behind me, arguing over something, but I was too woozy to think about what they were saying and too frightened to care. The gunshot to my head had knocked me senseless. I kept on staggering and running down the alley, trying to get away. Blood was pouring into my eyes; I couldn't see a thing. I ran past a little adobe shack down the alley from Pete Maxwell's. I supposed all the shooting woke everybody up, because a door opened just a crack when I ran behind the adobe and I could see a lantern light spilling from the doorway across the alley.

I stumbled toward the light not knowing what else to do. I needed help and the open door was the only place I could find, hurt like I was. A Mexican woman pulled me inside. She saw the blood on my face and threw her hands over her mouth. She closed the door quickly and helped me to a chair. I sleeved the blood from my eyes, watching her, loading my Colts.

In Roberts' statement he identifies the woman as Celsa Cutierriz [sic - if the writer is referring to Celsa Gutierrez] who he had known previously. Ms. Cutierriz [sic] helped Roberts and kept him at her home that night. Roberts says that later Ms. Cutierriz [sic] had Frank Lobato saddle his horse and bring it around in the alley so he can [sic] escape. Before Roberts was able to leave Ms. Cutierriz [sic] told him it was rumored about Fort Sumner that Sheriff Garrett was telling everyone he had killed the Kid.

Roberts says, *I started puzzling over what Celsa told me. Garrett was trying to pass off Barlow's body as that of Billy the Kid. I wondered how he figured to get away with it. Garrett knew by now that he'd killed the wrong man in the dark. Billy Barlow looked a lot like me, the same general description, with blue eyes like mine. But in the daylight, a lot of folks who knew me would know they had the wrong body. I couldn't figure it, unless Garrett realized his mistake and was making a try at collection [sic] the reward money that was out on me anyway ...*

Roberts says it was 3 a.m. when Celsa brought his horse up to the house. He says he left with Frank Lobato. Roberts stayed in a camp south of Fort Sumner until his wounds healed and the first of August he rode to El Paso, Texas.

[AUTHOR'S NOTE: Debunking of this error-filled "Brushy" hoaxing appears in this book, though this expansive dialogue demonstrates excellently the relentless floridness of his confabulations and imagination. Noteworthy for the Billy the Kid Case hoaxers, however, is that this choice of death scene with back-porch-Barlow points to an early phase of their own faking, where they were not yet concealing the major discrepancies between "Brushy's" tale and their own.]

Questions About the Case

There seems [sic] to be problems with every account of the escape of Billy the Kid from the make shift [sic] jail in Lincoln and the shooting at Fort Sumner by Pat Garrett. In every account there remain questions as to what really happened.

[AUTHOR'S NOTE: The above uses the hoaxers' technique of "vague, though unfounded, suspicions" instead of actual evidence - which they lacked. What follows is "alien invasion illogic" of "ifs" to attain hoaxed conclusions – here listed as "Questions." It represents the writer's last chance to fake a link of Garrett to a "probable cause" of murder.]

[AUTHOR'S NOTE: It is all "alien invasion illogic." For clarity, the illogical transitions are put in boldface. The breath-taking leap of the scam is seen when the "ifs" of the outhouse version, lead to a fake, implied accusation that Garrett presented the armory version to conceal that *he* was the pistol-giving "friend." Missing only is the "what if" of Roswell aliens giving Garrett that gun for placing!]

1. In the historical account of the escape of Billy the Kid, from the courthouse in Lincoln, **it's believed** that a "friend" placed a pistol in the outhouse for Billy to use in his escape. The identity of the "friend" who placed the pistol in the outhouse has gone nearly unasked. **If this** version is true, and a "friend" left a pistol in the outhouse to aid in Bonney's escape that "friend" is a coconspirator to the murder of Bell and Olinger. This "friend" also should have been charged with two

counts of homicide but remained at large. **Why** didn't Sheriff Garrett pursue the question of the idenety [sic] of the "friend" who hid the pistol? Garrett says the Kid took the pistol from the armory. **If** the story of the pistol in the outhouse is true did Garrett have a reason to say it was from the armory?

2. **If** Roberts account and claim about the night of July 14, 1881, is to be believed then Lincoln County Sheriff Pat Garrett was not the hero that history portrays him as. Instead, he becomes a murderer who killed Billy Barlow and covered up that killing and passed off Barlow's body as that of Billy the Kid. With the sign in at [sic] Brushy Bill's grave site claiming to the [sic] grave site of Billy the Kid they are in short saying Pat Garrett lied. Did Garrett lie?

[AUTHOR'S NOTE: This earliest version of the Billy the Kid Case hoax relies heavily on Roberts; later he would be concealed by the hoaxers. Here, confidence of victory without scrutiny apparently yielded a devil-may-care revealing attitude.]

[AUTHOR'S NOTE: This earliest version of the hoax also is unabashedly vicious in accusing Garrett of heinous crimes. Later, under scrutiny, the hoaxers would claim the case was to protect Garrett's honor against "others" who had accused him!]

3. **If** Roberts claims are believed, it beings up other questions? [sic] He claims in his statement when talking about Pat Garrett, *"we use* [sic] *to be friend"* [sic]. **If** Garrett and Roberts were friends did Garrett and Garrett [sic] allowed The Kid out of friendship to escape from Fort Sumner, *did he also* arrange his escape from Lincoln? Did Garrett question why **his friend, the Kid**, with all the others involved in all the killing was the only one to be convicted and sentenced to hang? The Kid **mentions this** in an interview that was published in the *Mesilla News* on April 15, 1881 when he said, *Think it hard that I should be the only one to suffer the extreme penalties of the law."*

[AUTHOR'S NOTE: Here, long-discredited "Brushy" appears as an authority. "If-ing" with him runs rampant. And the "if-ings" of "alien invasion illogic" that falsely make Garrett both Billy's "friend" and "accomplice." In addition, there is a switcheroo, by misusing the words "mentions this" (boldfaced above), when the Kid's words are only referring to his own sense of injustice, not a friendship with Garrett.]

4. **Did** Garrett arrange having the pistol put in the outhouse by the "friend" **and is this** why he did not search for the coconspirator to the murder of the two lawmen? **If this is the case then** Garrett is also a coconspirator in the murder of those two lawmen.

[AUTHOR'S NOTE: More "alien invasion illogic."]

5. In the Lincoln County Courthouse Caretaker Gauss' statement he quotes Bonney as saying about Bell, *"I'm sorry I had to kill him but couldn't help it."* This statement must raise the question did Bonney, when he produced the pistol he retrieved from the outhouse

[AUTHOR'S NOTE: Note the switcheroo from the "ifs," now using the outhouse as a fact.]

order Bell to surrender? Did Bell panic and instead of throwing up his hands, turn and run causing Bonney to shoot him?

[AUTHOR'S NOTE: Irrelevant question, but possibly inserted to promote the outhouse option to falsely build a Garrett case.]

6. Other questions come to mind in this investigation, some about Gauss. It should be noted that Gauss had worked with Tunstall, so had Bonney. Gauss and Bonney shared the same table as they took meals, slept on the same floor and spent a great deal of time together when Bonney was in the courthouse under guard. It goes to reason that Gauss was sympathetic towards Bonney. With that in mind it could be pointed out that there were a number of things missing from Gauss's account. Gauss made no reference to how Bell was killed, and leaves out the fact that Bonney used Olinger's own shotgun to kill him. If Bonney retrieved a pistol from the outhouse it had to be prearranged with Bonney and the "friend" as to what date and where to place the pistol in order for Bonney to find it. Since Gauss spent so much time with Bonney would he not have heard something about the plot?

[AUTHOR'S NOTE: The writer here appears less adroit at conning than the author of the final Probable Cause Statement. Inadvertently, he is building a case for Gauss as the gun-placing "friend," negating the argument for Garrett as the colluding accomplice - the purpose of a Probable Cause Statement!]

7. Since the caretaker Gauss worked outside it is not outside the realm of possibility that he saw who put the pistol in the outhouse?

> [AUTHOR'S NOTE: This argument was not used for the later version of the Billy the Kid Case hoax.]

8. It is known that Bonney ate his meals at the courthouse and the only time he was allowed to leave was to use the outhouse. Bell and Olinger took turns escorting the prisoners to the hotel for lunch, leaving the other in charge of Bonney. Bonney as well as the others would have known that Olinger would be escorting the prisoners to lunch that day. Bonney was aware that out of the two guards Bell was the one to make his escape move on since Bell was easy going and seemed to get along with him. Bonney also knew that Olinger had killed men in the past and had threatened to kill him. **Had Garrett and the Kid discussed this and chose Bell** as the deputy for Bonney to make his move thinking Bell would just give up giving the Kid an hour to escape while Olinger was eating?

> [AUTHOR'S NOTE: "Alien invasion illogic," with highlighted absurd jump.]

9. **If** Garrett was part of the plot for the Kid's escape **is that why** he rode to White Oaks on a "tax collecting" trip, to give himself an alibi?

> [AUTHOR'S NOTE: Good example of "alien invasion illogic."]

10. **If Garrett were part of the plot to allow the Kid to escape he would have reason to chase the Kid. He could not afford for the Kid to tell of his involvement in the two killings of the lawmen. Garrett also has a weak link in the plot, that being the "friend" who put the pistol in the outhouse. If Roberts' story is true, is Billy Barlow the one who put the pistol in the outhouse under orders of Garrett? In Roberts' accounting he shows up at Fort Sumner with no one but Barlow. Did he meet Barlow after he rode out of Lincoln and move on [sic] to Fort Sumner?** [author's boldface]

> [AUTHOR'S NOTE: All highlighted – the prize for most absurd "alien invasion illogic," missing only little green men themselves!]

11. If Garrett shot Billy Barlow in the dark, by mistake, on July 14, 1881, and Barlow was the only one who could tell the story of Garrett's involvement other than the Kid, would Garrett not know the Kid would run to keep from hanging?

[AUTHOR'S NOTE: This incoherent reverie, appears to contradict the Pat-Billy friendship on which the hoax is based.]

12. In Deputy John W. Poe's statement as he lays out the shooting in Maxwell's house on July 14, 1881, he says "... Garrett came out, brushing against me as he passed. He stood by me close to the wall at the side of the door and said to me, That was the Kid that came in there onto me, and I think I got him.' I said, "Pat, the Kid would not come to this place; you have shot the wrong man.' Upon my saying this, Garrett seemed to be in doubt himself as to whom he had shot ..." Did Garrett kill the wrong man by mistake and cover it up?

[AUTHOR'S NOTE: The writer forgot that backing "Brushy" means no bedroom murder scene – but a Barlow-on-back-porch one. He also forgets "Brushy" had enough ambient gunfire to rival the Alamo.]

[AUTHOR'S NOTE: Similar to the final Probable Cause Statement, this "question" omits the multiple identifications of Bonney, following this moment of doubt in a darkened room.]

13. Most researchers and historians have accepted without much question, the statement that Billy the Kid was born Henry McCarty, in New York on November 23, 1859. It should be noted that the first time this information comes to light is in Pat Garrett's book *The Authentic Life of Billy the Kid.*

[AUTHOR'S NOTE: Error. This information came out during Billy's lifetime, and while he was being tracked down by Garrett and Secret Service Agent Azariah Wild. Its bibliographic reference is: No Author. "Outlaws of New Mexico. The Exploits of a Band Headed by a New York Youth. The Mountain Fastness of the Kid and His Followers - War Against a Gang of Cattle Thieves and Murderers." December 27, 1880. *The Sun.* New York. Vol. XLVIII, No. 118, Page 3, Columns 1-2.]

In the book the evidence for this claim is sited [sic] to have come from a birth announcement that appeared in the New York Times on November 25, 1859. In 1950 William Morrison the attorney [AUTHOR'S NOTE: Morrison was not an attorney] for William (Brushy Bill) Roberts claims he asked the *New York Times* about the announcement and the Times replied that no information about birth announcements appeared in that issue. A ghostwriter by the name of Marshall Asmon [sic - Ashmun] Upson is credited with writing Garrett's book. It might also be worth mentioning the date November 23, is the birth date of Marshall Asmon [sic - Ashmun] Upson. Is it by chance that Upson and the Kid have the same birthday or by design?

[AUTHOR'S NOTE: Irrelevant, but a clumsy and fake "everything seems suspicious" ploy used as pseudo-evidence.]

14. As stated above most believe Billy the Kid was born in New York. This information also appeared for the first time in Garrett's book. [AUTHOR'S NOTE: See *New York Sun* 1880 article reference above.] It is also believed that Billy the Kid was shot and killed in 1881 at the age of 21. However, according to the United States Bureau of Census, 1880 census, Fort Sumner, San Miguel County, William Bonney says differently. Between June 17 and 19, 1880, while taking census records at the Fort, Lorenzo Labadie, a former Indian Agent, noted the vital statistics of one William Bonney, who was living next to Charlie Bowdre and his wife Manuela, leaving us to believe this to be the William Bonney of Lincoln County fame. What is interesting about the entry is that he gave his age as twenty-five, and his place of birth not New York but Missouri.

[AUTHOR'S NOTE: Irrelevant, but a clumsy attempt at the "suspiciousness" ploy. Also, it is thought that Manuela Bowdre gave the interview and incorrect information.]

The attorney Morrison asked Roberts why Garrett would say he was born in New York. Roberts told him that is what the told the "Coe boys" when he first came to New Mexico. Roberts went on to say he never saw New York until he was a grown man.

[AUTHOR'S NOTE: Morrison was not an attorney.]

[AUTHOR'S NOTE: Irrelevant paragraph since "Brushy" was not Billy Bonney.]

Conclusion

If history is correct and William H. Bonney a.k.a. Billy the Kid was shot and killed by Lincoln County Sheriff Pat Garrett on July 14, 1881, at the house of Pete Maxwell in Fort Sumner, and was buried the next day in Fort Sumner, then Brushy Bill Roberts is a fake and nothing more than a story teller of the first order.

[AUTHOR'S NOTE: Again, this early document points to "Brushy" as Billy; that direction later became more covert.]

However, if it is not the body of William H. Bonney buried in Fort Sumner then Lincoln County Sheriff Pat Garrett killed the wrong man on July 14, 1881. He covered up that killing with help from others such as Pete Maxwell. If it is not Bonney buried at Fort Sumner then Garrett is a murderer and Maxwell is a knowing coconspirator to that homicide.

[AUTHOR'S NOTE: This is the first, Billy the Kid Case hoax attempt at constructing a conspiracy theory. And the Garrett "friendship" appears abandoned for "Brushy's" "accident" version. Maxwell is added without giving motive or evidence - since neither exist.]

If Brushy Bill Roberts were William H. Bonney then one would have to assume that the body in the grave is that of Billy Barlow as Robert's claims. If that is true Sheriff Garrett could quite possibly be a coconspirator of the double murder of two lawmen that occurred during the Kid's escape from Lincoln.

[AUTHOR'S NOTE: This illogical jump even leaves "Brushy" behind, since he never claimed a collusive jail escape plot with Garrett, or that a "friendship" with Garrett related to the escape.]

The Lincoln County Sheriff's Department believes, with the unanswered question as to who is buried in Fort Sumner

[AUTHOR'S NOTE: This is fakery. The victim is not doubted.]

there remains serious doubt as to what involvement Sheriff Pat Garrett played in the escape of Billy the Kid from Lincoln that resulted I the deaths of two lawmen.

[AUTHOR'S NOTE: This is fakery. There has been no evidence that Garrett assisted the jail escape of Bonney.]

If the body of William H. Bonney is buried in Fort Sumner the claims of William Roberts'' and others alleging to have been Billy the Kid are unfounded and the name of Pat Garrett is cleared of any wrong doing in this incident. It is the duty of the Lincoln County Sheriff''s Office to clear this mystery and possible crime off the books of history in a professional manner and to allow the guilt to fall where it belongs.

[AUTHOR'S NOTE: The pretenders are easily debunked without exhumations. And no one is accusing Garrett, except pretenders and hoaxers – and without basis.]

Billy the Kid's mother is buried in Silver City, New Mexico. To exhume her body could provide the DNA to solve this 122-year-old mystery. Her DNA would hold the key to the true answer as to where William Bonney is buried and if Pat Garrett was a murderer or a Sheriff doing his duty.

If those in Hamilton, Texas believe Roberts is in fact Roberts [sic] this DNA should prove their claim. If he is not the town of Hamilton, Texas needs to take down the signs that the grave of Roberts is "The Authentic Grave Site of Billy the Kid." However, if Roberts is William Bonney then history should be rewritten showing what really happened in Lincoln County and Fort Sumner.

If Bonney is buried in Fort Sumner the History stands and the name of Sheriff Pat Garrett would be cleared and he did not kill some incendet [sic] person in Fort Sumner and would appear he had no hand in the escape of William Bonney from Lincoln and the death of Olinger and Bell.

Lincoln County Sheriff, Tom Sullivan and the Lincoln County Sheriff''s Office believe it our duty to put this mystery to rest after 122 years of doubt. Since these questions continue to nag at our conscience, and since there is no statute of limitations on Murder we feel this investigation should answer the question of "is Pat Garrett a murderer?" or a Sheriff doing his duty and wrongly accused of a crime?

[AUTHOR'S NOTE: No probable cause has been established to implicate Garrett as a murder suspect.]

In Pat Garrett's book *The Authentic Life of Billy the Kid* he pens these words - "*Again I say that the Kid's body lies undisturbed in the grave - and I speak of what I know.*"
It is the intention of the Lincoln County Sheriff's Office to prove one way or the other if these words are true.

_____

Tom Sullivan: Sheriff
Lincoln County Sheriff's Office

_____

Steven M. Sederwall: Deputy Sheriff
Lincoln County Sheriff's Office

_____

Date

* * * * * * * * * * * * * *

THE MODERN HOAX RE-RUNS A PARDON FOR "BRUSHY BILL" AS BILLY THE KID

Throughout the Billy the Kid Case, its hoaxing promulgators repeated an apparently nonsensical mantra: "We have to dig up Billy the Kid so that Governor Bill Richardson can decide on whether to pardon him."
What could exhuming anyone have to do with granting them a posthumous pardon for having committing murder?
Though the Billy the Kid Case hoax was rife with absurdity, this claim took the cake. But I had rationalized it as a two phase publicity stunt: shovel and get press; pardon and get more press. I was wrong.

The truth was more terrible than I could fathom during my years of hoax-fighting. The truth was that New Mexico Governor Bill Richardson and Attorney Bill Robins III were not *ever* planning on pardoning the *actual* Billy Bonney! All along, the pardon was to be for Oliver "Brushy Bill" Roberts: Robins's dear "Ollie."

That revelation of mine finally cracked the hoax in March of 2010. That "Brushy" pardon appeared to be Richardson's reward for Robins's political donations. That "Brushy" pardon was the bowl of porridge, filled with political publicity, that Richardson would trade for New Mexico's historical birthright.

Long past was the 1950's political climate when honest New Mexico Governor Thomas Jewett Mabry refused "Brushy" a pardon as Billy the Kid with the words: "I am taking no action, now or ever, on this application for a Pardon for Billy the Kid because I do not believe this man is Billy the Kid."

The sentiment was replaced by Bill Richardson's: "Pay me, then play."

So, apparently, big campaign donor Bill Robins III's "play" was to "buy" "Brushy Bill" a "governor's pardon."

That gubernatorial seal of approval, coupled with Billy the Kid Case's fake DNA forensics declaring "Brushy" as Billy, would have doomed the historical truth forever. And cuckoo bird "Brushy," laid and hatched in the famous history's nest, would become its inheritor. The Billy the Kid Case hoax *was intended all along* to make "Brushy" Billy the Kid.

I became convinced of that plot thanks to Attorney Bill Robins III's own words. In March of 2010, preparing depositions for my next courtroom round against the hoaxers' concealing their fake forensic records from my open records act inspection, I obtained a legal paper from an obscure, Silver City hearing that took place in our 2004 fight to protect Catherine Antrim's remains from the Billy the Kid Case's exhumation petitions in Judge Henry Quintero's court.

Dated January 5, 2004, and by Attorney Bill Robins III, it was titled "Billy the Kid's Pre-Hearing Brief" [APPENDIX: 2] and was 15 pages of legal double-talk and misrepresented "precedent cases." But it linked exhumations and the pardon!

Possibly "Brushy's" madness was contagious. Because, in his brief, Attorney Robins actually claimed that *he himself* was channeling (or had become) Billy the Kid! And, as such, he was able to convey to the Court dead Billy's wishes!

What did "spirit Billy" want? Of course, Billy wanted his mother dug up. Billy said (and Robins dutifully wrote it down in his brief for the judge) that digging up Mom for DNA would help his "legacy" by demonstrating that, as "Brushy," he had led a "long and peaceful and crime-free" life. Consequently, he - as "Brushy Bill" - deserved the governor's pardon.

What did Mom - Catherine Antrim - feel about all that? Like a loving spirit mom, she channeled to Attorney Robins. Of course, she wanted the best for her son, so she backed the shoveling - and refused, obviously, to talk to the mean Silver City Mayor standing in opposition to her exhumation.

And what did the judge hearing this insanity think? That judge was Henry Quintero; a lawyer whose ambition for judgeship had been fulfilled by Governor Bill Richardson's appointment on February 8, 2003 - eleven months earlier. So, "strangely" Henry Quintero did not notice that dead Billy was speaking in his Court via an attorney who was a channeler with no client other than cadaverous Billy the Kid himself.

But contemplate this: Bill Robins's "Billy" was *not* Billy Bonney. There were really two shades present in Judge Henry Quintero's Court: "Ollie" Roberts himself was there too as the "Billy the Kid" for whom Attorney Robins was speaking.

But in January 5, 2004, the day "Brushy"-as-Billy-as-Bill Robins spoke in Grant County District Court, the hoaxers were unaware of the opposition I had organized against them. They felt untouchable, and, thus, spelled out their whole crazy diabolical truth in Robins's "Billy the Kid's Pre-Hearing Brief."

So one can say that, by January 5, 2004, "Brushy Bill" Roberts was just four plotting people and one enabling judge removed from winning real Billy's identity. The group was: Governor Bill Richardson; Attorney Bill Robins III; Lincoln County Sheriff Tom Sullivan; his deputy, Steve Sederwall; and Judge Henry Quintero.

Then my opposition caught up; their Billy and mother exhumation petitions failed, and the hoaxers became more

168

cautious in their claims. Nevertheless, "Brushy's" cameos continued in their TV programs and press - apparently waiting digging him up for the crown of fake Billy-DNA on his skull.

But "Billy the Kid's Pre-Hearing Brief" is one of the Billy the Kid Case hoax's high points of audacity. Presented here are some quotes. The entire document is debunked in APPENDIX: 2. But it *cracked the hoax* by linking exhumations and a and pardon! (See page 171 below for Attorney Robins's quote.)

SOME PREPOSTEROUS QUOTES FROM "BILLY THE KID'S PRE-HEARING BRIEF"

(1) COME NOW, Bill Robins, III and David Sandoval, of the law firm of Heard, Robins, Cloud, Lubel & Greenwood, LLC, and on the behalf of the **estate** [author's boldface] of William H. Bonney, aka "Billy the Kid."

> [AUTHOR'S COMMENT: In this introductory statement the claim is for Billy's "estate." First of all, Billy had no estate - meaning posthumous property for probate court. Secondly, property has nothing to do with exhuming his mother. Thirdly, this cover of something that sounds real - like an estate - will next be switched to Billy talking all by himself. Note that Attorney Sandoval was present to provide the New Mexico law license which Robins lacked.]

(2) This is an interesting proceeding in that the relief sought here is not exclusively **judicial** [author's boldface]. "[N]ormally a district court would not become involved in such matters unless a protesting relative or interested party files an injunction or takes some other legal action to halt the autopsy or disinterment,"

> [AUTHOR'S COMMENT: Robins's brief is not "judicial" at all. It is an unsupported amateur historical rambling, misstating history, and introducing the irrelevant idea of a pardon as its fake justification. And its legal citations are all irrelevant filler.]

(3) Petitioners [Lincoln County Sheriff and his deputy] should thus be commended for bringing this Court into the picture and in doing so, **offering** the town of Silver City, **a relative of another descendent buried in the cemetery, and the legal interests of Billy the Kid, an opportunity to participate in the process.** [author's boldface]

> [AUTHOR'S COMMENT: Robins is beginning the switcheroo into speaking as Billy and his mother, themselves requesting exhumation. Here "they" are getting the "opportunity to participate in the process."]

(4) As will be shown clearly, Billy the Kid's **interests** [author's boldface] are real, legitimate, proper for consideration, and we respectively ask the Court to recognize them as such.

> [AUTHOR'S COMMENT: Segueing into speaking for Billy, Robins switches from "estate" to "interests." But a dead person has no "real, legitimate" interests - being dead, meaning non-existent.]

(5) To the extent that the Court remains concerned with **the presence of Billy the Kid in this litigation** [author's boldface], it is a matter that can be more properly addressed pursuant to legal requirements of standing and intervention, which the discussion below shows the Kid satisfies.

> [AUTHOR'S COMMENT: This is the switcheroo point: now Billy himself enters the courtroom. Robins even claims that Billy has "standing," meaning the legal right to be present in court.]

(6) The governor has the "power to grant reprieves and pardons." Undersigned counsel intends on seeking a pardon for Billy the Kid. Certainly Governor Richardson is within his inherent appointment power to hire counsel to advise him on the merits of such a pardon.

> [AUTHOR'S COMMENT: Tricky Robins omits that pardon advising gives no legal justification to be appointed to this court seeking the exhumation of

Catherine Antrim. Robins is just functioning as an amateur historian.]

(7) Counsel's appointment here is in the nature of an appointment as a **public defender** [author's boldface].

[AUTHOR'S COMMENT: Robins claims appointment by Richardson to "defend Billy." But only the judge can legally appoint an attorney for an indigent client in court - and, obviously the client has to be alive.]

(8) Billy the Kid's **interest here is his legacy** [author's boldface]. As noted in previous briefing the very question of his life and death will be impacted by the results of the Petitioners' investigation.

[AUTHOR'S COMMENT: Here Billy, the sentient corpse, has let Robins know he cares about "his legacy." Besides being preposterous, that is not the meaning of "interest," which has legal justification for a case, not sentimentality of an historical nature.]

B. *The Planned Request For Pardon Confers Standing Here*

(9) Undersigned counsel intends to ask Governor Richardson that he **pardon** Billy the kid for the murder conviction of Sheriff Brady **on several known bases** [author's boldface] including the fact that then Territorial Governor Lew Wallace reneged on his promise to pardon the Kid.

[AUTHOR'S COMMENT: The pardon issue, though irrelevant to exhuming Catherine Antrim, is here segueing into "Brushy Bill" territory with "several known bases" that will apply to him and not to Billy Bonney.]

(10) There were at least two individuals that laid claim to Billy the Kid's identity years after his alleged shooting by Garrett. **Both of them apparently led long and peaceful and crime-free lives.** [author's boldface]

[AUTHOR'S COMMENT: Here is the jump to "Brushy." And the "several known bases" for pardon are his long, peaceful, and crime-free life. The second pretender, John Miller, seemed to be thrown in by the hoaxers to diffuse their focus on "Brushy." And John Miller, unlike "Brushy," did not claim a crime-free, post Garrett shooting period. He admitted to murdering his Mexican ranch hand, and having 12 bullet wounds from other fights.]

(11) The reasons that the exhumation is sought is to disinter the remains of Billy the Kid's mother for the extraction of Mitochondrial DNA. As such, Ms. Antrim presents the only source of such DNA. Should the exhumation be denied, **Billy the Kid will be forever denied the opportunity to make use of modern technology to shed light on his life and death** [author's boldface].

[AUTHOR'S COMMENT: Now Billy is right in Court, pleading for modern technology to help him. But do not miss the more subtle absurdity: this is a pretender argument by channeled "Brushy," wanting *his* life and death vouched for as Billy the Kid. Real Billy - if he could talk - would require no "proof" of his historical events of life and death.]

(12) **Should the DNA extracted from Ms. Antrim confirm that one of the potential Kids was in fact Billy the Kid, undersigned counsel will be able to make an even stronger argument for pardon by citing to the long years of law abiding life** [author's boldface].

[AUTHOR'S COMMENT: **HERE IS THE SENTENCE THAT CRACKED THE BILLY THE KID CASE HOAX.** And here is the almost full-blown hoax plot: prove a pretender by faking DNA, then pardon him - "Oliver "Brushy Bill" Roberts - as THE Billy the Kid. Omitted is that "Brushy's" and John Miller's histories alone demonstrated them as pretenders. No exhumations were necessary to prove the obvious - unless one intended to fake the DNA results.]

(13) This Court has allowed the intervention of the Town of Silver City in this matter. The municipal politicians there have apparently authorized the Town's Mayor to oppose the exhumation. **Billy the Kid acknowledges the existence of case law** [author's boldface] that accords standing to the owners of the cemetery concerned in such proceedings.

> [AUTHOR'S COMMENT: Do not miss that speaking, channeled dead Billy even has legal expertise on "case law" about court standing! Apparently Heaven has law school!]

(14) What is of interest here, is that such standing is often given to the cemetery owner because it may be the only entity that can represent the wishes of the deceased, an element typically considered in whether to order an exhumation ...

As expected, the Mayor here opposes the exhumation and is positioned to present evidence in support of its objection. Whether or not that truly represents the interests of Ms. Antrim can never be known. Given the identity of the decedent and the time that has passes since her death, the Mayor cannot possibly have any direct evidence of Ms. Antrim's wishes. As such, the evidence that is presented by the Mayor can be viewed as best, supposition, or at worst, utterly unreliable.

> [AUTHOR'S COMMENT: Do not miss the bizarreness of this argument. The Mayor, whose duty is to protect the remains in the cemetery under his authority, according to Robins, needs to mind-read corpse Catherine to find out if she really really wants to be dug up. But do not loose hope; Attorney Robins the channeler is about to come to the rescue!]

(15) One is left to question why such a party with such a remote interest and lack of express knowledge about the decedent's wishes is conferred standing while the interests of Billy the Kid go unheard if this Court denier him standing. **Allowing such a party to appear and present evidence while denying the same opportunity to a party that has been appointed to represent the interests of**

the decedent's son does not seem prudent nor fair [author's boldface].

> [AUTHOR'S COMMENT: This argument is so crazy that a reader might be tempted to rationalize that it cannot be as crazy as it sounds. Attorney Robins is saying that dead Billy has more credibility to let his wishes be known than the live Mayor whose obligation it is to protect the cemetery. And by the way, Robins can tell the exact wishes of the dead, unlike the more limited Mayor. And also, by the way, this adds up to corpse Billy having court standing - better standing than the Mayor.]

(16) 1st Factor Public Interest, Billy the Kid's name is forever tied to New Mexico and to that of another legendary figure of the Old West, Sheriff Pat Garrett. A commonly held version of history paints a picture of an ambush in which Garrett killed the Kid in Ft. Sumner where most believe the Kid still lies at rest. **This version has been questioned. It is the investigation into whether Garrett killed the Kid that has prompted these investigators to seek exhumation**. [author's boldface]

> [AUTHOR'S COMMENT: This is again the land of "Brushy Bill." Only his believers question the reality of known history in their fervor to make him Billy. So Robins here is spouting pure hoaxer illogic. The only ones to "question" history are the hoaxers themselves for their stunt. There is no "public interest," meaning public value. There are only the self-serving motives of the hoaxers.]

(17) 2nd Factor, the Decedents wishes. In spite of Silver City's position to the contrary, we simply do not know what the decedent's wishes would be. Given the present circumstances, however, where her remains could possibly provide critical evidence to be used by modern day advocates to clear her son's name, one might easily surmise that Silver City's dogged **attempt to resist exhumation would not be appreciated by Ms. Antrim** [author's boldface].

[AUTHOR'S COMMENT: Here is Robins channeling Billy's mom enough to know that Silver City's blocking her exhumation would "not be appreciated" by her! She is apparently a "Brushy" believer too!]

(18) 3rd Factor, Surviving Relatives Wishes. There are no relatives of Ms. Antrim currently before the Court ... **The closest party currently before the Court is in fact Billy the Kid as represented by the undersigned counsel** [author's boldface]. As is apparent from the arguments set forth in this brief, the kid's [sic] interests would be furthered by the exhumation.

[AUTHOR'S COMMENT: Here is Robins channeling dead Billy to say that HE wants his mom dug up!]

(19) Billy the Kid believes [author's boldface] that the evidence adduced at the exhumation hearing will certainly support an order of exhumation here.

[AUTHOR'S COMMENT: Robins has crossed entirely into the "Exorcist" movie's territory. He has "disappeared" as an entity; only dead Billy is talking now. The creepy thought is that Robins might not be faking. He may think he IS "Brushy Bill" incarnate.]

(20) The foregoing has established that the undersigned counsel may legally and properly appear in these proceedings on behalf of, and to represent the interests of Billy the Kid.

[AUTHOR'S COMMENT: Only in his fevered and delusional "Brushy Bill" dreams, has Robins established anything at all "legal" to justify being in Court and channeling dead Billy.]

(21) Respectfully submitted this 5th day of January, 2004. Heard, Robins, Cloud, Lubel & Greenwood, L.L.P.

Bill Robins III
David Sandoval
Address and Telephone Numbers
ATTORNEYS FOR BILLY THE KID

HOW "BRUSHY" ALMOST WON IN THE BILLY THE KID CASE HOAX BY ALMOST BEING DUG UP

By May of 2007, I had blocked the Billy the Kid Case hoaxers' exhumations of Billy and his mother, but had failed to get Arizona criminal convictions for their May 2005 exhumations of John Miller and William Hudspeth.

Governor Bill Richardson's protection provided invulnerability. Their Arizona criminal investigation for grave robbing ended in 2006 by the prosecutor's simply ignoring that, for no reason, they had dug up John Miller and random William Hudspeth. She closed the case for "lack of evidence": evidence that her morals matched the hoaxers'.

So, by that May of 2007, the Billy the Kid Case hoaxers' clowning path had finally led them to the "big top": the Hamilton, Texas, grave of "Brushy Bill" Roberts.

But they did have another hurdle to jump, compliments of me. Through 2006, I pursued an American Academy of Forensic Sciences Ethics Complaint against Dr. Henry Lee for his preposterous claims about getting the bloody DNA of Billy the Kid from the old carpenter's workbench.

Though wily Henry Lee got off the ethics hook by denying, as his, all statements attributed to him by his fellow Billy the Kid Case participants, he apparently blocked the hoaxer's future use of his name in connection with their carpenter's bench DNA.

Thus, with the gall that was their defining feature, the hoaxers headed after "Brushy" with *no DNA at all claim* for comparison with his remains.

By then, the new Lincoln County Sheriff, Rick Virden, who, in 2005, had continued the Garrett murder case - still filed as Case No. 2003-274 - had deputized its past promulgating sheriff and deputy to continue it.

So, in 2007, Sheriff Virden wrote, on his official Lincoln County Sheriff's Office stationery, to Hamilton's mayor, Roy Rumsey, misspelling his name, but providing his law enforcement seal of credibility to get the job done:

Hamilton Texas
Mayor Roy Ramsey

Mayor Ramsey,

This letter will inform you that Tom Sullivan and
Steve Sederwall are both commissioned deputies with the
Lincoln County New Mexico Sheriff's Department.

They have been investigating case # 2003-274. Their
investigation has been funded by them personally and has
been conducted on their own time.

Mr. Mayor, should you have any questions please do
not hesitate to contact me.

R.E. Virden
Lincoln County Sheriff

Virden stressed "funded by them personally," because of
my years of open records exposure of the hoaxers' taxpayer
money spent; and they were defensive.

So Sheriff Virden was actually communicating to
Mayor Roy Rumsey that he was sending his deputies for his
New Mexico murder case - which was really a hobby - but
those deputies had his permission to dig up "Brushy,"
though his jurisdiction was Lincoln County, New Mexico;
and certainly not Texas!

Mayor Rumsey did not have to decipher that craziness
on his own, since I had already informed him that the circus
was coming to town. Deputy Steve Sederwall met with him.
Rumsey told me that he told Sederwall: "If 'Brushy Bill' is
Billy the Kid, I'm Pancho Villa."

Rumsey added for the press in a May 5, 2007
Houston Chronicle article titled "DNA could solve the
mystery of Billy the Kid":

"Roberts was 'just a big windbag who went around
telling stories. Few people, if anybody, believed him."

Texas was not proving easy for the modern hoaxers.

But, ever creative, Deputy Sederwall put his spin on the situation. The Stephenville, Texas, press, in "Billy the Kid exhumation a possibility," quoted:

Sederwall said if DNA is allowed to be obtained from Roberts, investigators will pursue exhuming the body of Catherine McCarty Antrim, who researchers have confirmed was Billy the Kid's mother.

Sederwall just happened to leave out for the Stephenville reporter that the Antrim exhumation had been dead in the water since 2004 - and no return to Silver City was possible.

On May 4th, New Mexico's hoax-backing *Albuquerque Journal* printed "Manhunt for Real Billy the Kid Goes On: Deputy hopes DNA will finally reveal outlaw's true identity." Steve Sederwall again blew smoke.

"Those (Hamilton City) people want to know, they are not afraid ... You talk to Fort Sumner and they want to pull pistols on us. You talk to Hamilton City and they're like, 'Sure, we'd like to know.' "

On May 10, 2007, Hamilton's Town Council, with Texas's own "Brushy Bill" fanatic, Jannay Valdez, present and pitching, unanimously opposed exhumation.

It was over for Oliver "Brushy Bill" Roberts.

But what would the hoaxers have done if they had gotten "Brushy's bones?

Who knows; but I would bet they would have located a new "forensic DNA expert," and found more "Billy the Kid DNA" ("Didn't Gramps say that Billy the Kid had vomited on his saddle?"). And trusty Orchid Cellmark could have "matched" Billy-vomit-DNA to "Brushy"-bones-DNA. Then the hoaxers' "official" Richardson-appointed University of New Mexico historian could have made a TV documentary on the "truth" about the mystery of Billy the Kid's death.

And Attorney Bill Robins III could finally have gone to bed a happy man, dreaming about his man's certain pardon.

"Brushy Bill" Gets a History Channel Plug

In the real world of greedy profit - rather than in the esoteric world of my anti-hoax victories, "Brushy Bill" Roberts continued to do well in the new millennium. He got a big plug on television in 2004.

That was when the Billy the Kid Case hoaxers presented their most complete hoax creation to date: a History Channel program titled "Investigating History: Billy the Kid."

Their hoaxing history professor from the University of New Mexico, appointed by Governor Richardson as the Billy the Kid Case's "official historian," wrote and co-produced that program.

Oddly, however, despite his obvious role, when questioned, that professor denied *any* involvement in the Billy the Kid Case! His tangled tales are untangled in my *MegaHoax* book.

EXPOSÉ OF BILLY THE KID CASE HOAXERS' HISTORY CHANNEL PROGRAM

HOAXBUST: Debunked in detail in the MegaHoax book, the Billy the Kid Case hoaxers' 2004, History Channel program, "Investigating History: Billy the Kid," is a major hoax production; and it disseminated hoax damage to a national level. It has also been continuously reshown to the present. Though that program utilized the Billy the Kid Case hoax's attention-grabbing premise of Garrett not killing Billy, it featured then a new hoax spin: the Billy the Kid Case was being done to determine a governor's pardon for Billy. And, unbeknownst to the public, the varied selection of talking heads - the professor, the Lincoln County lawmen, Attorney Bill Robins III, the editor-in-chief of True West magazine, and Governor Bill Richardson himself, were all colluding hoaxers. And on behalf of "Brushy," promoted as a credible contender for Billy, appeared none other than author-believer W.C. Jameson!

OVERVIEW:

For their television program, "Investigating History: Billy the Kid," the Billy the Kid Case hoaxers joined forces on-screen and presented, their hoax tenets: Garrett's victim was probably not Billy; the body was not identified; there existed no coroner's jury report; good friend Garrett helped Billy escape; and tourist interests prevented their truth-seeking exhumations for DNA.

Added was a new twist: their "homicide investigation" (here shape-shifted from Garrett's killing the innocent victim, to Billy's killings during the Lincoln County War) was to assist Governor Richardson's decision as to pardoning Billy.

This switcheroo of the murder definition left an unresolved problem for the scammers: they still needed Pat Garrett as the killer of "the innocent victim" to justify more TV programs on pretender exhumations.

But their writer-producer, "official historian" professor apparently chose to delay that preposterous murder claim, along with its fake forensics, since the carpenter's bench goes unmentioned as a Billy the Kid DNA source.

But the professor added the pardon spin. Billy became the "good guy;" Pat Garrett the "bad guy." So the professor states incorrectly, to beef up injustice for Billy, that he was the "only one" blamed for the Sheriff Brady killing. And the hoax-participating Lincoln County sheriff adds, on screen: "I'm not sure the Kid was all that bad." Maligning Garrett, the professor alleges that he tracked Billy only "for the reward."

Something else is striking. The error-filled pronouncements and reenactments are very familiar: many appear lifted from the writings of William Morrison, W.C. Jameson, and Frederick Bean! And Jameson himself appears as an historical expert!

One can, thus, guess from this program that, for the projected pardon, Richardson was set, not to undo Governor Lew Wallace's injustice to real Billy Bonney; but to undo what true-believers felt was Governor Thomas Jewett Mabry's "injustice" to "Brushy Bill" Roberts.

THE PROGRAM:

The TV program begins with its transparent purpose: fabricate doubt about the death scene; fabricate doubt about Garrett's veracity; and fabricate doubt about legitimate historians of the subject.

Shadow Billy approaches the dark Maxwell house. The narrator (the professor as writer) supplies the first quote: "This is one of the most controversial moments in the history of the Old West: history's version of the last seconds of Billy the Kid."

With that hoax lie, one can almost hear the professor scornful hissing of "hissstory," since what will follow is his error-filled presentation, and apparent avoidance of hissstory books.

He continues: "Pat Garrett fires into the darkness ... Billy the Kid is dead when he hits the floor - or is he?"

The answer you will get from the professor is entirely hoax-speak "suspicion."

So, on screen, he says, after doubting a successful shot in a dark room: "The story is almost too good. The idea that the Kid ... would come strolling into this room unarmed and right into the hands of the law enforcement official ... is just too bizarre."

What is bizarre, is that, in front of a national audience, the professor had the gall to make all that up.

But to complete Garrett's character assassination, the professor fabricates that Garrett lied about Billy's being armed, because "Garrett took a lot of heat for killing the Kid without giving him a chance." (What "heat?" Was the professor hoping for a duel; for the OK Corral?)

He lies that history is "Garrett's version;" says that the only murder eye-witness was Pete Maxwell, "who was never interviewed" (omitting Maxwell's Coroner's Jury statement, and the townspeople eye-witnesses), and says Deputy Poe "contradicted" Garrett's statement (Poe was merely initially unsure that Garrett had shot Billy, whom he could not recognize.)

One can postulate that this presentation was to set the stage for an ongoing hoaxer series for "Investigating History," in which a "bad Garrett" was needed to allow a "good Billy's escape," so that pretenders would appear credible objects for their greedy shovels.

Indeed, the John Miller exhumation was filmed by the same production company as filmed this program. That Billy the Kid Case hoax "Part Two," however, remained (so far) in the can after the Arizona criminal charges for illegal exhumations were made against the law enforcement hoaxers as diggers.

The professor's ongoing errors of apparent ignorance rely for success on viewer unawareness.

For example, as to early years, he says Billy's mother died when he was 12 (actually 14 ½); and calls Jessie Evans Billy's "old side-kick" (Billy rode with Jessie one month: September, 1877).

As to errors in the lead-up to the Lincoln County War, the professor, like "Brushy Bill" and his authors, thinks Tunstall and McSween were in partnership in the Lincoln store (actually the Ring's frame-up lie); and says the House filed a civil case against Tunstall (the case was against McSween; was filed by the Fritz heirs; was both a civil breech of contract and a criminal embezzlement; and Tunstall's property was attached by falsely alleging partnership, making it McSween's property).

After Tunstall's murder, the professor, still in line with "Brushy," says Brady was shot in revenge (when he was ambushed to protect McSween, returning to town that day); says "only" Billy was charged with Brady's shooting (when the murder defendants included all the shooting Regulators).

For the Lincoln County War, the professor thinks the McSweens lost because of being "divided up" throughout the town (when they were strategically placed in both the east and west sides, held the town for five days, and lost only because of military intervention - omitted as a scene, or as the reason).

As to Lew Wallace, his Amnesty Proclamation is called by the professor "for everyone;" when the remainder of Billy's tragic fate depended on the fact that it excluded those already indicted, like him.

As to Billy's potential Wallace pardon, the professor claims Billy's testimony in the 1879 Grand Jury failed to indict Dolan for the Huston Chapman murder because the district attorney was Dolan's friend. (This is a *big error* by the professor, who misses the impact of the injustice of Billy's not getting the pardon - what this program is supposedly about! In fact, Billy's testimony succeeded in indicting Dolan and Billy Campbell for the murder, and Jessie Evans as an accessory - thus, fulfilling the pardon agreement. And the Grand Jury *indicts*; the D.A. merely *cross-examined witnesses*, even though that district attorney, William Rynerson, was a Ring partisan.)

As to Pat Garrett's election, the professor says he was chosen for sheriff by Lew Wallace (when Garrett was elected by the citizens; though "favored" by the Ring faction and Secret Service Operative Azariah Wild); and says - in good "Brushy" tradition - that Garrett wanted to be sheriff to get the $500 reward (when he simply wanted a job with self-esteem; and the Wallace reward was not offered until about two months after Garrett won the election).

About Garrett's capture of Billy, the professor wrongly thinks it was the day after the first ambush (which killed Tom O'Folliard). It was days later.

As to Billy's post-capture, the professor says Billy wrote his famous prison letters to Wallace from the Lincoln County courthouse- jail, when it was from the Santa Fe jail, where he was kept for months.

Of course, the escape is skewed to implicate Garrett (without any evidence). **But "evidence" is manufactured by this "official" Billy the Kid Case historian. It is a re-enactment scene with Garrett putting the gun in the outhouse!** [author's boldface - to emphasize the hoax heart of this TV production]

Ongoing errors of simple ignorance abound in the rest of the re-enactment scenes.

For example, after Brady is shot, Billy runs out to steal *Brady's* Winchester carbine (a silly reason to risk one's life), when he was retrieving *his own Winchester*, illegally, maliciously, and enrageingly confiscated earlier by Brady.

Blatant hoax-jive appears throughout. But the take-home message appears to be: everything is "suspicious;" "Brushy" may be Billy.

Here are some examples:

- HOAXING MURDER SUSPICIONS: The professor omits actual evidence to show that Billy's killing was well documented, and that the corpse's identifications were profuse. Instead, he opts for: "The line between fact and legend is elusive." He continues with misleading falsities: [This is] "the beginning of a mystery that still haunts the West today." "No one could believe Billy the Kid was shot ... Poe said, 'Pat you shot the wrong man.' " "This is Pat Garrett's version ... but questions linger." "The only other eye witness, Pete Maxwell, never gave his version of the story." "Was it really the Kid shot ... the story seems unlikely." "The Kid's reputation was so fearsome that no one wanted to go inside to identify the body."

- HOAXING DEATH ESCAPE: The professor, on screen, proclaims: "Some suggested that it was more likely that Pat Garrett, Billy's friend, let him go ... burying someone else in his place." (The professor is hoax-talking both the fake friendship and "innocent victim.") Doing backup, a fellow hoax promoter and editor-in-chief of *True West* magazine, comes on-screen to state snidely that: "Friends of Pat Garrett conducted what they called an autopsy. But there were no photographs." He adds that those "friends" said in the report that Garrett deserved the reward. (The Coroner's jurymen were not Garrett's friends; that misstated report said

Garrett was deserving of "reward," not *the Wallace* reward; and it was a legal coroner's jury report, not an "autopsy" report.) The editor also claims that Garrett did the killing in "secrecy," and buried the body the next day. (This misinformation conceals the Coroners Jury Report, wants a camera when they were unavailable in those days; and implies that burying a rotting corpse a day after death was peculiar.) Do not miss that these concoctions echo W. C. Jameson's and Frederick Bean's in their "Brushy Bill" book: *Return of the Outlaw Billy the Kid.*

- HOAXING GARRETT FRIENDSHIP: This necessary part of the hoax (though irrelevant to the pardon) rests on no supporting evidence given by the professor. He falsely claims friendship, and presents the fake re-enactment. While it plays, the professor says: "Pat Garrett put the gun in the privy because he and the Kid were old friends and he wanted to help him escape." If this program was a livestock fair, and if each hoax statement by the professor was a 4H sheep, this one would get the blue ribbon.

- "BRUSHY BILL" PLUG: At last, one gets to the hoaxers' "hero." The screen fills with a picture of the cover of "Brushy Bill's" first book: *Alias Billy the Kid*, accompanied the professor's narration: "Over the years that story has gained some credence." Then W.C. Jameson gets his moment, appearing to say, untruthfully, that the "Coroner's Jury Report was never found;" and that there was "no evidence jurymen saw the body." Then comes the hoax-participating deputy sheriff to say: "If "Brushy Bill" is Billy the Kid, it comes down to this ... Garrett had to have let him escape in Fort Sumner."

- PARDON: Billy's pardon ("Brushy's" prize) is falsely entangled with the Billy the Kid Case Garrett murder accusation. Governor Richardson appears and declares: "I might pardon him." But he wants to find out the truth "through science" (though no "science" pertains to the pardon - except by faking DNA for "Brushy."). Attorney Bill Robins is next as "an attorney seeking pardon evidence," and saying Billy "should never have been charged." Hidden is exhumation-Robins, declaring for his Billy dig-up petition on February 26, 2004: "Perhaps the most significant lingering question involves whether Billy the Kid was indeed shot by Sheriff Pat Garrett." (And do not forget Robins's "dark night" for "Ollie's" Billy Barlow murder scene.)

So Attorney Bill Robins III, for his TV script about the "mystery" of whether Pat Garrett had shot Billy the Kid, was nearly reciting his personal agenda.

In his first entry into public awareness in connection with the Billy the Kid Case, and brought to the forefront because the local Silver City attorney seemed unprepared to counter the legal opposition being mounted, Robins was not circumspect.

On November 19, 2003, in an internet reporter from Silver City was quoted as follows:

> Robins says he's excited to represent the Kid. His first duty as Billy's lawyer will be to intervene in the Silver City case to exhume the body of Billy's mother, Catherine Antrim. DNA testing is supposed to show whether Antrim was related to Ollie "Brushy Bill" Roberts. If Antrim is related to Roberts, that would mean Billy the Kid is buried in Hico [sic - Hamilton], Texas - not Fort Sumner.

As Bill Richardson's big political donor, Bill Robins III was backing him for president in 2008. If "Brushy" as Billy the Kid was to be Robins's pay-to-play prize, contemplate this: Mad "Brushy" may have risen to a king-maker - or president-maker!

"Brushy Bill" Goes to the Cannes Film Festival

Of the Billy the Kid Case hoax's many hooked dupes, the biggest fish was French film maker Anne Feinsilber.

Inspired by the hoaxers', already cited, 2003, *New York Times* article, with its quote of "Brushy" believer, Jannay Valdez, ("I'm absolutely convinced that Garrett killed someone else and that Brushy Bill was the Kid"), Feinsilber created a nearly million dollar film, "Requiem for Billy the Kid," about "the mystery of the murder of Billy."

And "Brushy Bill" Roberts hovered like its omnipresent ghost, representing "Billy as a murder scene escapee."

Feinsilber's film went on to be screened at the 2006 Cannes Film Festival, then spread virally.

"REQUIEM" SPELLS REQUIEM

Anne Feinsilber's "Requiem for Billy the Kid" got wide publicity; and it gave the Billy the Kid Case hoaxers the chance to disseminate self-serving misinformation about their own endeavor.

On May 21st, from *Variety* magazine, came the review of "Requiem for Billy the Kid" by a Todd McCarthy. He said:

> With Sam Peckinpah's Billy, Kris Kristofferson re-enlisted to portray the Kid delivering his account of what happened between him and Pat Garrett in 1881, pic goes on a photogenic search for the "truth" about the young killer. Seems there has always been a rumor that Billy escaped and lived to a ripe old age, and Tom Sullivan, who was sheriff of Lincoln County when pic was shot in the fall of 2004, describes his efforts to exhume the body of Billy's mother for DNA, efforts shot down by a judge whose motives Sullivan describes as baldly financial.

A May 25th review by Dave McCoy of MSN Movies, as "L 'Ouest Américain," wrote: "Feinsilber follows up on a rumor that Pat Garrett shot the wrong man and Billy the Kid actually isn't buried where it's said he is."

Feinsilber's damage was further evidenced on a May 6, 2006 Internet version of *The Hollywood Reporter* in reviewer, Ray Bennett's, "Bottom line: A story well told." He wrote:

> History has it that Sheriff Pat Garrett, a reformed villain, gunned down William Bonney, also known as Billy the Kid, at Fort Sumner, where his grave has a much-visited marker. Some say, however, that the friendship between Garrett and Bonney led the lawman to let the outlaw go and another man's body lies beneath his headstone. Could Billy the Kid have lived to see two world wars and driven a car? Feinsilber sets out to discover the truth and she finds several people in New Mexico whose grandparents were said to have known Bonney. Competing factions would like to exhume the bodies of Billy and his mother Catherine, who died of tuberculosis when Billy was 14, in order to prove once and for all when he died. Such myths fuel tourism, however, and the mystery has remained unsolved.

With this hoax victory, Pat Garrett became a "reformed villain," the friendship between Garrett and Billy was real, a stranger's body likely lay in Billy's grave, the exhumation would have solved the questions, but the "mystery" was being left unsolved to "fuel tourism."

Anne Feinsilber's contagion of disinformation continued. New Mexico reporter, Julie Carter, enthused on June 9, 2006 for *RuidosoNews.com* under "The cowboys are back in town, film in six months," announced the American showing of the film, along with release to PBS and sales of DVD's.

It seemed only a matter of time for Texas to receive New Mexico's iconic history of "Billy the Kid." And if it did not get that outright, the consolation was that "Brushy" the old clown was back in the running.

What's It All About, "Brushy?"

Oliver "Brushy Bill" Roberts's unbelievable media success proves that pretending does pay; though imposters might need life-extension to see the fruits of their labors.

At least "Brushy" confirms a comment by Italian actor/comedian Roberto Benigni: "I remember in the circus learning that the clown was the prince, the high prince."

A prince to his believers, "Brushy" was still just a clown posing as Billy Bonney, while juggling historical names in his three ring circus of smoke and mirrors errors. Some of their multitude are summarized below:

"BRUSHY" BOTCHES BILLY

DEBUNKING OLIVER "BRUSHY BILL" ROBERTS

- Birth Date: August 26, 1879 .... [Billy's Birthdate: November 23, 1859. "Brushy" fabricated a birthdate of December 31, 1859 for himself]

- Birthplace: Buffalo Gap, Texas .... [Billy's Birthplace: New York City, New York]

- Claims mother, named Mary Adeline Dunn-Roberts, died when he was three .... [Billy's mother, Catherine McCarty Antrim, died when he was 14 ½]

- Claims mother's half-sister, Kathleen Bonney, raised him .... [Unrelated to real Billy's history]

- Named Oliver P. Roberts; self-named "Brushy Bill;" claimed names William Henry Bonney and Billy the Kid .... [Billy's names: William Henry McCarty, Henry Antrim, William Henry "Billy" Bonney, nickname "Kid." Never used "Billy the Kid"]

- Unaware of Billy's brother .... [Billy's brother was Joseph, "Josie"]

- Favored left hand .... [Billy was ambidextrous and favored the right]

- Near illiterate; claiming a "friend" wrote for him .... [Billy was highly literate]

- No claim of bi-lingual skill .... [Billy spoke fluent Spanish]

- Unaware of life incidents in Silver City .... [Example: Unaware of Billy's imprisonment for theft and escape from jail chimney]

- Unaware of Billy's Arizona period from ages 15 1/2 to 17 1/2, incarceration for theft, or killing of "Windy" Cahill .... [Fabricates that Billy visited family in Texas; went to Oklahoma Indian Territory; Dodge City, Kansas; and Mexico]

- Called self an "outlaw" and bad man" .... [Billy considered himself a soldier, deputy constable, and posseman]

- Unaware of the chronology or specifics of Billy's return to New Mexico Territory in 1877 .... [Example: Thinks Billy worked for the Jones family]

- Unaware of the Santa Fe Ring .... [Though central to Billy's history]

- Unaware of the specifics of the Fritz life insurance policy case, and how it entangled legally McSween and Tunstall

- Unaware of McSween's protector: Deputy Sheriff Adolph Barrier

- Error-filled specifics of Tunstall murder ....
  [Examples: Unaware of why Tunstall was returning to
  Lincoln on his murder day; fabricates that Tunstall was in a
  wagon that day; and is unaware of Tunstall's murder along
  with his horse]

- Unaware of the original legal status of the Regulators as
  deputies or possemen to serve Tunstall's murder
  warrants
- Unaware of the proclamations of Governor Axtell
  outlawing the Regulators and removing Sheriff
  Copeland

- For the Morton-Baker capture, thinks the road back to
  Lincoln crossed the Capitan Mountains .... [The road
  skirted the mountains on flatlands; and Morton and Baker
  were killed there]

- Gets wrong specifics of the Regulators' Sheriff Brady
  ambush .... [All fabricated; wrong location, wrong gun
  taken from body, wrong motive, and wrong fellow-Regulator
  shot along with Billy. Unaware of concomitant Deputy
  Hindman killing]

- Unaware that Billy gave a deposition on the Tunstall
  murder to investigator, Frank Warner Angel

- Gets wrong all specifics of the Lincoln County War
  .... [Examples: Not knowing the cause, who constituted
  either side, which buildings were occupied, the geography of
  the town, and the specifics of the McSween house in which
  Billy and others were besieged; unaware that the military
  was not present until the last day and turned the tide;
  unaware that the military brought in a howitzer and Gatling
  gun, and that the commander coerced the Justice of the
  Peace into writing arrest warrants for McSweens, including
  Billy; unaware that black troops did not shoot; unaware that
  white soldiers fired a volley during the escape from the
  burning building; unknowing of the drama with the trapped

women and children in the burning McSween house]

- Unaware of Chapman murder specifics .... [Wrongly states Susan McSween was present]

- Unaware that Attorney Ira Leonard replaced Chapman

- Unaware of the specifics of Billy's Governor Wallace pardon promise deal .... [Example: Garbles the meeting place, and fabricates erroneously that he, as "Billy," was offered $1000 to give himself up to stand trial for the Brady murder]

- Unaware that Billy's 1879 arrest and imprisonment in the Patrón house were feigned

- Wrongly makes Billy's 1881 Mesilla trial lawyer - Albert Jennings Fountain - as Billy's attorney in 1879 .... [Then Billy had no attorney, and was just a witness testifying in the Grand Jury against Chapman's murderers in the Wallace pardon deal]

- Unaware of Billy's successful 1879 Grand Jury testimony

- Unaware of specifics of 1879 Court of Inquiry, including details of Billy's testimony, most importantly: unaware of firing white soldiers .... [Erroneously calls the proceeding a Court Martial]

- Fabricates an "escape" from that Patrón house imprisonment by "slipping out of handcuffs .... [Does not realize that no escape was needed. The arrest was feigned. Billy simply left.]

- Unaware of Attorney Ira Leonard in Billy's life

- Unaware of counterfeiter Dan Dedrick in Billy's life

- Unaware of the circumstances of Billy's 1880 self-defense killing of Joe Grant

- Unaware of the specifics of the 1880 ambushes on Billy and his companions by the White Oaks posse (thus, unaware of Coyote Spring and ignorant of the location of the Greathouse ranch)

- Unaware of the counterfeiting charge against Billy

- Unaware of Secret Service Agent, Azariah Wild

- Unaware of why Garrett was tracking down Billy (wrongly thinks it was the Carlyle murder)

- Unaware of the specifics of Garrett's Stinking Springs capture of Billy

- Unaware of details of Billy's Mesilla murder trial .... [Fabricates that witnesses lacked subpoenas]
- Unaware of the episodes or locations of Billy's long incarceration, including near tunneling out, and the hope of partisan rescues .... [Unaware that the Ring was awaiting railroad completion to prevent rescue during transport]

- Unaware of Billy's replevin case with Attorney Edgar Caypless for the posseman's theft of his bay mare .... [Or of the theft itself]

- Unaware of all details of Billy's great escape from the courthouse-jail on April 28, 1881

- Unaware of why Billy went to Fort Sumner after his escape

- Claimed love interest: Celsa Gutierrez, incorrectly called Saval Gutierrez's sister (was his wife) .... [Unaware of Billy's truelove, Paulita Maxwell]

- Unaware of Fort Sumner and Maxwell house lay-out .....

[Fabricates everything incorrectly]

- Says July 14, 1881 ambush was on a dark night ....
  [Actual full moon made it as bright as day]

- Said ambush's "innocent victim" was his friend, Billy
  Barlow .... [Fabrication]

- Gigantic cover-up conspiracy required for concealing the
  July 14, 1881 victim's identity, and involving: Garrett,
  Peter Maxwell, Deluvina, the six coroner's jurymen, the
  200 townspeople, and all legitimate historians

- Could not speak Spanish, in which Billy was
  accentlessly fluent.

- No photo-match with Billy's tintype

DEBUNKING

JOHN MILLER

JOHN MILLER'S SINGLE SHOT

HOAXBUST: The only "identity" between John Miller and Billy Bonney, was Miller's calling himself "Billy the Kid" to family and friends. And Miller threw in a bit of confabulated pseudo-history. His biographer, equally unenergetic, added wan hoaxing. Both omitted that Miller was born nine years too early, making him no "kid" in Billy's day. Though used by the Billy the Kid Case hoaxers for "survival suspicion," John Miller failed them, lacking their Garrett-friendship-playing-dead-on-bench death scene, thus, removing justification for his exhumation for DNA to match with their carpenter's workbench DNA of "playing-dead-Billy" (though they ignored that).

Pretender, John Miller, dead since 1937, with only one little book and no known living believers, was placed on history's stage by the Billy the Kid Case hoaxers, who, blocked in New Mexico courts from digging up Billy's and his mother's graves, needed bones and DNA to keep TV cameras rolling.

Buried in the Arizona Pioneers' Home Cemetery, in Prescott, Miller is still called "Johnny," presumably his nick-name when living in its attached nursing facility - until he died of a broken hip, and was buried in their cemetery.

"Johnny" Miller's biographer was Helen Airy. Her *Whatever Happened to Billy the Kid?* was published in 1993, when she was in her 80's. She is now deceased. Her book is a hoax by virtue of misinformation; but her frail effort is more a "hoaxlet." She relied on old-timer interviews; they remembered that John Miller had said he was Billy the Kid.

MAKING A CASE FOR MILLER

As with "Brushy Bill" Roberts, age was Miller's problem. He was born in December of 1850; nine years before real Billy. John Miller as Billy Bonney, would have been older than "his" boss John Tunstall, who himself died at almost 25. And Miller would have been the same age as Pat Garrett.

In addition, John Miller's birthplace was Fort Sill, Texas; which has no connection to real Billy's history. Helen Airy circumvented these problems by not mentioning them.

Beginning her book is a tiny sly death scene: "It was near midnight on July 14, 1881, when Sheriff Pat Garrett shot someone in Pete Maxwell's darkened bedroom in the old officers' quarters in Fort Sumner, where Maxwell lived."

Why that "someone" was not Billy is missing; though later, to John Miller, is attributed an accidental killing of an "Indian-dressed-similarly" death scene version.

Helen Airy adds that there was a cover-up of the victim's identity. What makes her think that occurred? She mentions an unreferenced, unknown document, and says: "When he was asked to sign an affidavit that it was the Kid he had shot, Garrett refused to sign."

She also malingers: "McKinney and Poe accused Garrett of shooting the wrong man;" adding McKinney to her own distortion of Poe's statement of initial identity concern.

Helen Airy concludes: "But all through the years since that night, there have been doubts that it really was Billy the Kid's body they buried the next day."

Why doubts? Airy says people "saw Billy" after the death date ("fuzzy factoid"); some Coroner's Jurymen signed with an X (so?); there was "irregularity" in filing the Coroner's Jury Report (untrue); and the corpse was seen by only a few people (untrue). For witnesses, she lists Garrett and his deputies, "immediate family members" (there were none), and snidely: "supposedly, members of the coroner's jury."

Omitting effort of formulating a full conspiracy theory, Helen Airy concludes, "Surely there was reason to wonder."

The rest of Helen Airy's 175 page book is about John Miller's irrelevant life after July 14, 1881; though little flashbacks of blighted Billy history are given - and prove nothing.

ROMANCE AND MURDER

In Helen Airy's telling, the "rescue character" is an Isadora (a "petite, dark-eyed Mexican girl," and John Miller's real wife).

Airy writes: "Isadora later told friends and neighbors that some days before the shoot-out at Pete Maxwell's house the Kid had been wounded and she had taken him to her house in Fort Sumner."

Stop. That means Miller-Billy was shot *some days prior* to the Garrett killing. There goes his candidacy for the Billy the Kid Case carpenter's bench scenario - though it did not stop the hoaxers from digging him up.

Isadora is called the widow of Charlie Bowdre; though that widow's name was Manuela; and that Manuela had left Fort Sumner after her husband's murder by Garrett in 1880.

But why should we think John Miller was Billy?

Helen Airy says there were similarities: light eyes, a bad temper, and a tendency to point his rifle at people!

Another "proof" would have been offensive to real Billy. Miller's last shooting victim was his Mexican worker. Billy's bi-culturalism arguably brought Hispanic men to the McSween cause. One can recall the already cited quote of "Teddy Blue" Abbott, a cowboy contemporary of Billy's, who wrote *We Pointed Them North*. Abbott stated: "The Lincoln County troubles was still going on, and you had to be either for Billy the Kid or against him. It wasn't my fight ... it was the Mexicans that made a hero of him."

Helen Airy also touts "remarkable" resemblance of Miller to Billy. As evidence, she says Miller wore the same hat! That peculiar, high crowned, short brimmed one, worn by real Billy in his tintype, was probably the photographer's prop - since real Billy wore a sombrero - but Miller had his own tintype-style hat for posturing.

Of course, Miller had crooked front teeth. Also he did a rope trick for "handcuff" slipping. Wisely unmentioned is his long scrawny neck, since Billy had a short thick one. Miller's dark brows are compared favorably to those in the fake Catherine Antrim photo; though Airy also contradicts that match by saying that Miller had a Cherokee mother - a possible truth.

Photos of wax busts made by a sympathetic artist, prove that, by tweaking real Billy and John Miller, a resemblance for photographs can be achieved; though Billy suffers most.

OLD-TIMERS HAVE THEIR SAY

After page 33 of *Whatever Happened to Billy the Kid?*, Airy's only "proof" is old-timer recollections. Most merely say he *told them* he was Billy - and his wife, Isadora, vouched for it.

The oddest old-timer is a Herman Tecklenburg, who claims *he* knew John Miller in Fort Sumner as Billy the Kid; and was later his "most trusted friend." Tecklenburg seems to have had a follie a deux with Miller; meaning *both* were delusional.

John Miller himself, apparently, barely elaborated Billy history. But he would strip to show twelve bullet scars on his chest; though real Billy - other than a leg wound courtesy of Deputy Jacob Basil Matthews at the Sheriff Brady shooting - acquired his single chest one on July 14, 1881!

A rare elaboration does come from a Frank Burrard Creasy, prefaced with: "The following is an actual account of Billy the Kid as I know it" - and is pure fabrication. He states: "The first time anyone really heard the name of Billy the Kid was in 1871, when he was twelve years old. A deputy sheriff apparently insulted Billy's mother for which Billy promptly shot him and fled to the hills."

Creasy also provides a Miller-made death scene:

Pat Garrett, who was the marshal of Lincoln at the time, and a well known bounty hunter, heard that Billy was in town and along with two of his deputies laid in waiting near the side of beef. When the Indian boy stepped up onto the veranda of the house, he was shot down by Pat Garrett, who had apparently mistaken him for Billy. Billy [Miller] told me once that he and the Indian were dressed alike to confuse people. Pat Garrett was afraid of the reaction of townspeople and immediately buried the body.

Absolutely nothing in the rendition is true.

But Frank Burrard Creasy inspired Helen Airy to a vehement crescendo. She wrote:

To date, American historians maintain Sheriff Pat Garrett killed Billy the Kid in Lincoln County, New Mexico. But according to Creasy's account Garrett killed the wrong man, concealed the error and collected the reward ... For reasons unknown, historians in the United States failed to follow up on the leads Frank Creasy furnished about John Miller's claim that he was Billy the Kid.

Helen Airy's ignorance shows. She thinks the Billy shooting was in *Lincoln County*, not San Miguel County; where Fort Sumner was - over 150 miles away.

Frank Creasy even ends Airy's book with a photo of his cherished "gun of Billy the Kid": a single action Colt .45, which John Miller gave him.

Whatever Happened to Billy the Kid? has a small Appendix of misinformation containing tabloid-like *El Paso Times* articles from the 1920's to 1960's.

For example, the Billy the Kid grave is said to have been "marked by a rude cross, that was to prove to Billy's sister that he was still alive." Billy had no sister. And he was dead!

But by 2005, the clock was ticking on how much longer John Miller would repose in the sacrosanct peace of his own grave. The modern Billy the Kid Case hoaxers needed his DNA.

JOHN MILLER'S BONES

After John Miller's burial in 1937, he would have disappeared into deserved oblivion - Helen Airy's *Whatever Happened to Billy the Kid?* notwithstanding - had it not been for the Billy the Kid Case hoaxers.

By the 2003 start of their gambit, they had John Miller half-heartedly in their sights, as was seen above in their already cited "Seventy-Seven Days of Doubt" initial draft of a Probable Cause Statement for their Lincoln County Sheriff's Department Case No. 2003-274. There, Miller's brief and anemic presence was merely for "survival suspicion," and as a foil for "Brushy Bill" Roberts.

By 2005, "Johnny" Miller looked much better to the Billy the Kid Case hoaxers.

With legal blockade to the gravesites of Billy and his mother, they needed to exhume anyone else to continue their media circus. And they had achieved step one of the hoax despite no access to remains: getting DNA. They alleged that Dr. Henry Lee had provided them with DNA of Billy the Kid scraped from an old carpenter's bench on which they claimed shot Billy had been laid out (while playing dead).

It should be noted again that Dr. Lee, under my 2006 investigation by the American Academy of Forensic Sciences Ethics Committee for his work in the Billy the Kid Case, denied making any of the statements attributed to him! (There went that "bench-DNA of Billy the Kid!")

Using fake Billy DNA did not faze the hoaxers; neither did the fact that Miller had never claimed, in his Billy death scene version, to have been in an escape plot with Garrett, or to have been shot and laid out while playing dead. The hoaxers needed any exhumation. The same production company which had made their 2004 hoax-promoting film for the History Channel, "Investigating History: Billy the Kid," was ready to shoot some digging. And the Director of Orchid Cellmark Lab, which had extracted DNA from Lee's carpenter's bench handiwork, was ready to collect bones for DNA comparison (and to get on TV).

More importantly, Governor Bill Richardson, head hoaxer, was pals with Arizona's then governor, Janet Napolitano. And Miller's resting place - the Prescott, Arizona Pioneers' Home Cemetery - was state run, and under her auspices.

So the hoaxers, not even bothering to call him John Miller - using "Billy the Kid" instead - avoided court and Medical Examiner scrutiny or permission, and went straight to the backhoe. They claimed legality by misstating an Arizona law allowing cemetery exhumations to establish identity of remains. That law was to confirm gravesite markers. It was not to check the lifetime delusions of corpses, who thought they were Napoleon or Billy the Kid. Nevertheless, skeletal John got dug up on May 19, 2005 under a "Lincoln County Sheriff's Department Supplemental Report for Case No. 2003-274."

Since John Miller's cemetery area lacked any markers, the hoaxers simply guessed where to excavate. They found one body. Then, for good measure, they went after another. That bonus body was a William Hudspeth.

So hapless Hudspeth entered Billy the Kid pretender history. According to *Tucson Weekly* reporter, Leo Banks, in his April 13, 2007 article, "The New Billy the Kid," Orchid Cellmark Lab could not extract DNA from John Miller's bones; but succeeded with William Hudspeth.

So the Billy the Kid Case hoaxers matched random man William Hudspeth, with Dr. Henry Lee's fake Billy bench DNA. They even claimed a match of "80%" to Governor Janet Napolitano's office! (Though 80% meant *no identity match!*)

Things got worse for the hoaxers when an Arizona citizen filed criminal charges against them for disturbing remains and grave robbing. It apparently took Governor Bill Richardson's and Governor Janet Napolitano's political arm-twisting with the prosecutor to thwart that potential legal and political debacle.

Later, as covered in my book *MegaHoax*, the whole fiasco of preposterous pretender John Miller, outrageously exhumed William Hudspeth, and the hoaxer's brush with an Arizona slammer were allowed to sink below public memory.

The hoaxers had lost interest in "Johnny" Miller anyway. By 2007, they were after "Brushy Bill" himself.

What's It All About, "Johnny?"

One can say that John Miller ranks as the unluckiest of the dozens of Billy the Kid pretenders; if imposters expect to lie in peace in their graves.

And, despite the obvious absurdity of Miller's claims, comedian George Carlin's warning must be heeded: "Just because you got the monkey off your back, doesn't mean the circus has left town."

So, "Johnny" Miller may again rise from the dead, if needed again for another media circus. After all, the Billy the Kid Case hoaxers still have their production company's exhumation film waiting in the can.

Nevertheless, John Miller's" total failure in impostorship is summarized below.

JOHNNY" JUMBLES BILLY

SUMMARIZED DEBUNKING OF JOHN MILLER

- Birth Date: December (unknown day), 1850 ....
  [Billy's Birthdate: November 23, 1859]

- Birthplace: Fort Sill, Texas .... [Billy's Birthplace: New York City, New York]

- Named John Miller; used "Billy the Kid" .... [Billy's names: William Henry McCarty, Henry Antrim, William Henry "Billy" Bonney, nickname "Kid." Never used "Billy the Kid"]

- Cherokee mother .... [Billy had an Irish mother]

- Had only a sister .... [Billy had no sister. He had a brother]

- Unaware of Billy's childhood and Silver City history

- Stated when Billy was 12 he shot a deputy sheriff .... [Fabrication]

- Apparently near illiterate .... [Billy was highly literate]

- Racist (murdered his Mexican worker) .... [Billy was pro-Hispanic]

- Called self an "outlaw" .... [Billy considered himself a soldier, deputy constable, and posseman]

- Claimed 12 bullet wounds .... [Billy had a leg wound and a death wound!]

- Unaware of all Lincoln County War history

- Unaware of Dudley Court of Inquiry

- Unaware of Secret Service Agent, Azariah Wild

- Unaware of specifics of Garrett's capture of Billy

- Unaware of Billy's Mesilla trial

- Unaware of all details of Billy's great escape of April 28, 1881

- Love interest: Isabella (his actual wife) .... [Unaware of Billy's truelove, Paulita Maxwell]

- Claims being shot by an unknown attacker days before July 14, 1881; and his "Indian friend" was the "innocent victim"

- Claims Garrett killed his "Indian friend" near the side of beef, mistaking him for "Billy" .... [Fabrication]

- Claims the "innocent victim's" body was buried immediately without witnesses .... [Fabrication]

- Gigantic cover-up conspiracy required for concealing the July 14, 1881 victim's identity, and involving: Garrett, Peter Maxwell, Deluvina, the six coroner's jurymen, the 200 townspeople, and all legitimate historians

- Could not speak Spanish, in which Billy was accentlessly fluent.

- No photo match to Billy's tintype

DRAWING
CONCLUSIONS

IFS, WHYS, AND CLOWNS

HOAXBUST: Oliver "Brushy Bill" Roberts and John Miller presented no accurate biographical, physical, or historical evidence supporting their impostorships. And the Billy the Kid Case hoaxers backed them just to keep their media circus on the road. However, had the Billy the Kid Case hoaxers' scam not been blocked, by now "Brushy" might have been dubbed "Billy the Kid." And the temptation of John Miller as Billy appeared, at times, to beckon to those modern hoaxers also.

With "Brushy Bill" Roberts and John Miller, it is easy to conclude that they were not Billy the Kid.

If they were Billy, they would have been born in different decades; would not have made preposterous mistakes in telling his history; would have looked identical to him, would have reflected his articulate intelligence, instead of their own semi-literate coarseness; and would have expressed his revolutionary zeal and multi-cultural world view.

Why they could not "become Billy" had to do with bad timing: they lived almost 50 years too early, and missed all the historical research which could have fancied-up their impostorships.

Why they wanted to be Billy the Kid, however, is the most fascinating part, because, packaged with their confabulatory derangement, came their hoaxing authors and their fervent, conspiracy theorist believers. Motivating the pretenders and their authors were Billy's reflected acclaim, and the possibility of monetary profit. And for their true believers, there was an opportunity to crystallize an anti-authority world view into an anti-history story. But that made mind-changing impossible - no matter what damning contradictory truths exist.

Why becomes more cynical when it comes to the Billy the Kid Case hoaxers - other than Governor Bill Richardson's Texan political backer, Attorney Bill Robins III, as a possible "Brushy Bill" true-believer. They appear to have been merely opportunists. Bill Richardson was after political fodder; the rest were gobbling profits in cash or kind; or playing protectively along out of fear and favor engendered by New Mexico's modern incarnation of the Santa Fe Ring.

And despite all efforts at debunking, "Brushy Bill" Roberts, "Johnny" Miller, and the Billy the Kid Case hoaxers have probably embedded themselves in national TV consciousness as life's little nuisances - like mold and bellybutton lint and hard to open jars.

So join in with Stephen Sondheim:

> But where are the clowns?
> Quick send in the clowns.
> Don't bother, they're here.

APPENDIX

ANNOTATED PRIMARY DOCUMENTS

APPENDIX: 1: Lincoln County Sheriff's Department Probable Cause Statement For Case No. 2003-274. Signed December 31, 2003 by Sheriff Tom Sullivan and Deputy Steve Sederwall

LINCOLN COUNTY SHERIFF'S DEPARTMENT
CASE # 2003-274
Probable Cause Statement

In the struggle dubbed the "Lincoln County War" investigators

[AUTHOR'S COMMENT: Taken to mean the law enforcement document signers: Lincoln County Sheriff Tom Sullivan and Lincoln County Deputy Steve Sederwall.]

soon learned that nothing was as seemed.

[AUTHOR'S COMMENT: This is "alien invasion illogic suspicion."]

As they poured through the volumes of information, documents, paperwork, reports, county records, books and examined newly discovered evidence, it became apparent no clear lines could be drawn as to who was working with or for whom. What first appeared to be clear quickly became clouded as new information was uncovered,

[AUTHOR'S COMMENT: More "alien invasion illogic" with unsubstantiated and irrelevant "suspicion." And the "newly discovered evidence" is never presented.]

it's difficult to judge who the "good guys" and the "bad guys" were. One would think that the Lincoln County Sheriff's Department would be on the side of the law. However, it was a duly sworn posse of Lincoln County Deputies that shot and killed John Tunstall, in what investigators in clean conscience can only cauterize [sic] as an unprovoked murder.

> [AUTHOR'S COMMENT: Tunstall's murder is irrelevant. It occurred when William Brady was Sheriff of Lincoln County; and was 3 ½ years before Garrett killed the Kid.]

> [AUTHOR'S COMMENT: This guise of "research" is added to "alien invasion illogic suspicion." But Brady's being a dishonest sheriff remains irrelevant to Garrett.]

Evidence shows that posse-men, Hill and Morton

> [AUTHOR'S COMMENT: Error: Tom Hill was not Brady's official posseman; he was in Jessie Evans's criminal gang. Sheriff Brady, by a written declaration, stated that he used no known outlaws on that posse.]

committed murder when *"Hill called to him* (Tunstall) *to come up and that he would not be hurt; at the same time both Hill and Morton threw up their guns, resting their stocks on their knees; that after Tunstall came nearer, Morton fired and shot Tunstall through the breast, and then Hill fired and shot Tunstall through the head ..."* [1]([1]Deposition of Albert Howe, Angel Report) Although these deputies were acting under the color off the law they were not acting within the law. This behavior permeates the Lincoln County War and investigators will not make judgments on that behavior but rather uncover the facts and present the facts without varnish.

> [AUTHOR'S COMMENT: Repeating that lawman are not always honest, is irrelevant to a Garrett murder contention.]

No one from the Governor to the District Attorney to the Sheriff of Lincoln County is beyond suspicion of deception and covering up the true facts in this case.

[AUTHOR'S COMMENT: Again, "alien invasion illogic suspiciousness" is irrelevant to a Garrett murder.]

This can be seen in a number of examples. In a letter to Riley and Dolan of the Murphy-Dolan faction from District Attorney W. L. Rynerson of the 3rd Judicial District, the attorney clearly demonstrates he himself plays a part in the hostile actions when he writes, "*Shake that McSween outfit up until it shells out and squares up and then shake it out of Lincoln. I will aid to punish the scoundrels all I can.*"[2] ([2]Rynerson letter to Riley and Dolan, Feb. 7, 1878, University of Arizona Special Collection)

[AUTHOR'S COMMENT: Error: The letter is dated February 14, 1878. It is irrelevant to alleging a Garrett murder in 1881.]

When investigators began to look at the murder of Deputy Sheriff J.W. Bell and Deputy Robert Olinger on April 28, 1881, it was found that much of the information we now know as "history" came from Pat F. Garrett's book, "The Authentic Life of Billy the Kid" published in 1882.

[AUTHOR'S COMMENT: Error: Information about the Bell/Olinger murders did not rely on Garrett, who was away at White Oaks. It came from eyewitness accounts of townsman, Gottfried Gauss, the building's caretaker, and the jail's Tularosa Ditch War prisoners.]

Investigators learned that much of this history is flawed for the reason historian Robert Utley writes: "*Although not many copies of the Authentic Life were sold, it nevertheless had a decisive impact on the Kid's image. More than any other single influence, the Garrett-Upson book fed the legend of Billy the Kid. As the legend blossomed, writers turned to the Authentic Life for details. Ash Upson's fictions became implanted in hundreds of " histories" that followed. For more than a century, only a few students thought to question the wild fantasies that flowed from Ash's imagination. In the evolution of the Kid's image, the Authentic Life is a book of enormous consequence."[3]* ([3]Robert M. Utley. Billy the Kid a short and violent life. University of Nebraska Press, 1989.)

> [AUTHOR'S COMMENT: Utley is merely describing development of the Billy the Kid legend. And Garrett's ghostwritten book, though in dime novel style, of course, gives his shooting of Billy. True historical research was done by Robert Mullin, Walter Noble Burns, and Maurice Garland Fulton in the 1920's, and later by Frederick Nolan, Leon Metz, and Robert Utley himself. They all confirm that Garrett fatally shot Billy the Kid.]

On March 23, 1879, Governor Lew Wallace met with William Bonney (Kid) in Lincoln.

> [AUTHOR'S COMMENT: Error: Meeting occurred on March 17, 1879]

In this meeting it is demonstrated that Wallace convinced the Kid that it would be to his advantage to work for the government.

> [AUTHOR'S COMMENT: False. Billy proposed to Wallace, by a letter of about March 13, 1879, to give court testimony against murderers of Huston Chapman in exchange for Wallace's annulling his Lincoln County War indictments. The hoaxers, however, are setting up their straw man argument below.]

The Kid becomes, what would be referred to in today's terminology as a "Confidential Informant." In Governor Wallace's hand we read "Statements made by Kid, Made Sunday night March 23, 1879."[4] ([4]Statements by Kid, Lew Wallace Collection, Indiana Historical Society Library) It was through this meeting Wallace devised a plan and attempted to deceive when he and the Kid entered into an agreement where by the Kid would appear to have been arrested.

[AUTHOR'S COMMENT: Saying there was an attempt "to deceive" is a misleading switcheroo. The hoaxers have admitted to Billy's confidential informant status. The arrest plan was devised by both Wallace and Billy to prevent Billy's being killed before giving testimony against Chapman's murderers: James Dolan and Billy Campbell. The hoaxers, however, are still pumping the irrelevant claim that everyone was deceptive. Of course, that is irrelevant to a Garrett murder contention.]

The Kid later talks of this and says he was allowed to wear his guns and he left when he wanted to leave.

David S. Turk, Historian for the United States Marshals Service has discovered other such deceptions in his study of official records.

[AUTHOR'S COMMENT: This reference to "other such deceptions" is another hoaxer technique: Falsehoods are presented, and later used as a "proven facts" to build additional falsehoods. David Turk's "other deceptions" are never presented.]

[AUTHOR'S COMMENT: David Turk's hoax participation is discussed in *MegaHoax*.]

It is commonly believed

[AUTHOR'S COMMENT: Misstatement: It is a known historic fact, confirmed by Garrett's possemen and the Maxwell family.]

that Lincoln County Sheriff Pat F. Garrett arrested the Kid in December of 1880 in Stinking Springs near Fort Sumner. But the records show that Garrett was elected in November of 1880 and

did not take office until January of 1881.[5] ([5]Lincoln County Commissioners Records, November 8, 1880).

[AUTHOR'S COMMENT: So what?]

218

He went to Fort Sumner as a Deputy United States Marshall, but even that Commission and authority are now questioned.

> [AUTHOR'S COMMENT: By whom? Garrett was made a U.S. Deputy Marshall in November or December of 1880 by Secret Service Operative Azariah Wild, sent to New Mexico Territory as a counterfeiting investigator for the U.S. Treasury Department. Wild appointed Garrett because of his urgent need to capture Billy and his alleged counterfeiter gang. Wild believed that the Lincoln County Sheriff, George Kimbrell, was partisan to Billy; and, with Garrett just elected as Sheriff on November 2, 1880, he would not have assumed duties until January 1, 1881. Also, Wild's appointment of Garrett - fully accepted in his day, and reported to Secret Service Chief James Brooks, - gave Garrett Territory-wide jurisdiction to arrest Billy Bonney when and where he did.]

> [AUTHOR'S COMMENT: Also, this misinformation and sly innuendo is irrelevant to whether Garrett was a murderer. If anything, it proves that Wild believed Garrett's fitness for the marshal's title.]

Secret Service Special Operative Azariah F. Wild of New Orleans writes in his daily logs *"I this day went to Lincoln to meet Capt. Lea & Garrett who are to organize the Posse Comatatus (sic) to make a raid on Fort Sumner to arrest counterfeiters."*[6] ([6]Report of Azariah F. Wild, November 11, 1880, Record Group 87, National Archives) Garrett shot and killed Charles Bowdre and Tom O'Folliard during the chase and arrested the Kid. Later, Secret Service Special Operative Azariah F. Wild writes to his superior and admits he was deceptive in his commission of Garrett. *"I will respectfully state that I applied to Marshall Sherman to appoint P.F. Garrett as a Deputy Marshall to which he paid no attention. I was in great need of Mr. Garrett*

> [AUTHOR'S COMMENT: Error: Actual quote reads "Mr. Garrett's aid."]

at that time and took one of the Commissions Sherman sent to John Hurley (he having sent two) and substituted P.F. Garrett the very man who has rendered the Government such a valuable service in killing and arresting these men who I was in pursuit."[7] ([7]Report of Azariah F. Wild, January 4, 1881, Record Group 87, National Archives)

> [AUTHOR'S COMMENT: Error: Report is dated January 3, 1881.]
>
> [AUTHOR'S COMMENT: Though this paragraph is irrelevant to whether Garrett was a murderer, it implies, falsely, that Wild was deceptive. In fact, there was no deception. Wild was following proper procedure. One of only 40 Special Operatives in the country, he was answerable only to the Secret Service Chief, James Brooks. The Secret Service powers were flexible, and extended beyond counterfeiting. In Billy's case, Wild's pursuit of him included alleged large-scale rustling. For that - as Wild reported to his Chief - he needed Garrett's services. Note also the mention of Charles Bowdre, killed by Garrett on December 22, 1880. Billy's gravesite is contiguous with his. This was later an issue in the hoaxers' exhumation attempts.]

No one in 122 years has been able to speak with clear certainty where the gun came from that William Bonney used to kill Deputy J.W. Bell.

> [AUTHOR'S COMMENT: Hold your hat for this whip-lash subject change. It begins the accusation of Garrett as deputy murder accomplice.]

With the information investigators have seen they question Garrett's involvement in the Kid obtaining a weapon.

> [AUTHOR'S COMMENT: Why? You will not find out later, though such "information" is the crux accusing Garrett of "involvement" in providing Billy's "weapon" for the jail break. Instead, what follows is "alien invasion illogic" to fake Garrett's murder motive.]

220

It would go to reason that if the body in Fort Sumner is anyone other than William Bonney then Garrett no doubt had a hand in allowing the Kid to escape on July 14, 1881.

> [AUTHOR'S COMMENT: Catch your breath on this near-genius switcheroo. No legitimate historian says the body in Billy's grave is "anyone other than William Bonney." But the hoaxers need that for their murder claim; so they slip it in here – by "alien invasion illogic": "*If* the body in Fort Sumner is not Billy's, Garrett *might* have given it to the Kid for an escape."]

If the body at Fort Sumner is anyone other than William Bonney, then Garrett, whether by accident or design, is responsible for homicide of the person resting in that grave.

> [AUTHOR'S COMMENT: Another leap of "ifs." But no credible source says the body is not Bonney's; and the hoaxers' double-talk provides nothing contrary.]

If it is not Bonney in the grave at Fort Sumner it would also go to reason that Garrett would be looked at as a suspect in furthering the escape of the Kid on April 28, 1881 when the two Lincoln County Sheriffs were murdered.

> [AUTHOR'S COMMENT: Another world-class switcheroo. Now the fake "if" is used as fact: "if it is not Bonney" - merely building a house of cards.]
> [AUTHOR'S COMMENT: There you have it: the hoaxers' best shot at "probable cause for Garrett as a murderer": only "alien invasion illogic ifs" to fake a friendship motive: *If* Garrett gave Billy the escape gun, he was a friend. *If* he was a friend, he would later murder someone else to protect Billy again. But the giving of the gun and the friendship are just fabrications. No evidence been given – and none exists. And Pat and Billy were not friends.]
> [AUTHOR'S COMMENT: What follows is built on the hoaxers' false claims that (1) they established Garrett's murder motive, and that (2) they established need to check Billy's grave for Garrett's unidentified victim.]

Although the investigation will deal with what happened in the Lincoln County court house on April 28, 1881, this writing will deal with the alleged shooting of William Bonney at Fort Sumner on the night of July 14, 1881.

[AUTHOR'S COMMENT: Do not let that fast-one slip by. The "sub-investigation" of the deputy murders consisted merely of (1) firing a gun inside to test if it could be heard across the street, and (2) bringing in a forensic consultant who, is claimed, without basis, to have found "blood" in floorboards in an upstairs hallway. The hoaxers further claimed, without basis, that the "blood" was Bell's. Also left out is that this "investigation" has nothing to do with the gun used to shoot Bell. And, even if it did, that would have nothing to do with whether Garrett gave it to Billy, or whether Garrett shot an innocent victim 2½ months later, making him a murderer. Later in the hoax, this "deputy murder investigation" was recycled by claiming it *was the entire Billy the Kid case*. The truth is that there is was no gun ever found, and no way to prove its source; and the hoaxers have offered nothing contrary in the years the case has progressed. What is known is that Garrett was not present at the murder of Deputies Bell and Olinger. He left Lincoln to collect taxes in White Oaks on April 27, 1881. Billy's escape, after murdering the deputies, occurred the next day, the 28th. Garrett did not return to Lincoln until April 30th.]

[AUTHOR'S COMMENT: At this point, the hoaxers abandon the deputy murder issue and Garrett murder motive, though pretending the his friendship, his escape weapon providing, and his innocent victim.]

This writing will set forth probable cause as to why investigators question who is in the grave in Fort Sumner and seek DNA from Catherine Antrim.

[AUTHOR'S COMMENT: Probable cause pertains to the murder, and has not been established. But this double exhumation is a hoped-for publicity coup.]

[AUTHOR'S COMMENT: What follows is the hoaxers' attempt to fake that someone other than William Bonney was shot by Garrett. It is back to the following "alien invasion illogic": *If* there was any inconsistency in reporting of events around the murder, something is "suspicious;" ergo, Garrett killed someone else. But inconsistencies can be merely reporting errors. Also, the hoaxers never establish a single inconsistency, presenting only their fabricated ones!]

The detractors of this investigation hold up the statements of Lincoln County Sheriff Pat F. Garrett, Deputy Sheriff John W. Poe, and the Coroner's Jury report as proof it is William H. Bonney that Sheriff Garrett shot and killed on July 14, 1881 and that the Kid is buried in Ft. Sumner.

[AUTHOR'S COMMENT: Using their straw man-style arguing, the hoaxers give this threadbare list, cagily omitting witnesses and historical information proving that Garrett shot Billy. Later, in this document, in slip-ups, some of that proof is accidentally presented!]

Historian Philip J. Rash [sic - Rasch] tells the story history puts forth about the shooting of the Kid in the following manner:

Garrett led them to the mouth of Taiban Arroyo, arriving after dark on 13 July. When Brazil failed to appear, Poe, who was unknown in the area, agreed to ride into fort Sumner the next morning to see what he could learn. Finding the inhabitants suspicious and uncommunicative, he proceeded to Sunnyside, about seven miles north, to visit Milnor Rudolph, the postmaster and an old friend of Garrett's. Rudolph was nervous and evasive. He denied all knowledge of the Kid's whereabouts, but Poe was sure he was concealing something.[8] ([8] Poe, John W. *The Death of Billy the Kid*. New York: Houghton Mifflin Company, 1933) *There is a curious story that while the officer was on the way to Sunnyside, John Collins (Abraham Gordon Graham), a former member of Billy's gang, headed to Lobato's camp to warn the outlaw that officers were in the vicinity. On the way he met the Kid, bound for Fort Sumner.*

"Billy," he warned, *"don't go down there. I just saw Poe,*

[AUTHOR'S COMMENT: Recall that Poe was unknown to the locals, so this irrelevant "fuzzy factoid" story further lacks credibility.]

and no doubt Pat Garrett and a posse are around town looking for you."

The Kid merely laughed and answered, "Oh, that's O.K. I'll be alright," and rode on, leaving Collins badly puzzled."[9] ([9]Ben Kemp. *Dead Men, Who Rode Across the Border.* Unpublished. No date.)

That night Poe rendezvoused with Garrett and McKinney at La Punta de la Glorietta [sic], four miles north of Fort Sumner. Poe's report of both his failure to learn anything definite and his suspicions that there was so much smoke there must be some fire only increased the sheriff's skepticism. After some discussion he commented that the Kid was a frequent visitor to the house of Celsa Gutierrez (sister of Pat's wife Polineria [sic] Gutierrez) and suggested that they watch her home. Their vigil proved fruitless. As midnight approached Garrett and Poe decided that there was only one other possible source of information - Peter Maxwell, the town's most prominent citizen.

The officers arrived at his home about 12:30 AM on Friday, the 15th [sic]. Pat instructed Poe and McKinney to wait outside while he went in to talk to Maxwell. Sitting down on the edge of the bed, he asked in a low voice whether the Kid was on the premises. Maxwell became very agitated, but answered that he was not. At that point a bare headed, bare footed man in his shirt sleeves, carrying a butcher's knife in his left hand and a revolver in his right sprang through the door and asked Maxwell who the two men outside were.

Maxwell whispered, "That's him."

[AUTHOR'S COMMENT: Note the hoaxer slip-ups in presenting this source: (1) Their Garrett cannot recognize Billy, though they claimed he and Billy are such good friends that Garrett killed for him; and (2) Peter Maxwell identifies the victim as Billy!]

224

Sensing a third person in the room, the intruder backed toward the door, at the same time demanding, "Quien es? Quien es?"

Pat jerked his gun and fired twice.[10][11] *([10]Las Vegas Daily Optic, July 18, 1881. [11]Santa Fe Daily New Mexican, July 21, 1881) As the man fell Maxwell plunged over the foot of the bed and out the door, closely followed by the sheriff. Maxwell would surely have been shot by Poe if Garrett had not struck the latter's gun down saying, "Don't shoot Maxwell." He added, "That was the Kid that came in there onto me, and I think I have got him."*

[AUTHOR'S COMMENT: This is Maxwell's second Billy identification; and not contradicting Garrett's.]

Poe was not so sanguine. "Pat," he answered, "the Kid would not come to this place, you shot the wrong man." All was quiet inside. After some persuasion Maxwell brought a tallow candle and placed it on the outside of the window sill. By its light the body of a man could be seen. Deluvina Maxwell, a Navajo servant, entered the room, examined the body, and found that it was indeed the Kid's.

[AUTHOR'S COMMENT: Another inadvertent hoaxer error is here: their third identification of the victim as Billy! And Billy was well known to Deluvina, a fact the hoaxers will later confirm themselves. And the Poe quote, from his wife's posthumous biography of him, merely gives the truth: he could not identify Billy. But his simple disbelief is misused by the hoaxers to fake their claim of a non-Billy victim.]

Garrett's first shot had struck him in the left breast just above the heart; the second had gone wild. Later it was learned that Billy had been staying at the house of Juan Chavez.

[AUTHOR'S COMMENT: A fourth Billy identification!]

Becoming hungry, he had gone to Maxwell's to slice a steak from a yearling Pete had killed that morning.

The corpse was taken to a carpenter's shop and laid on the work bench.

[AUTHOR'S COMMENT: This workbench will later become the hoax's key ingredient.]

Fearing an assault from Billy's friends, the officers remained awake and on guard the rest of the night. However, it passed without incident.

[AUTHOR'S COMMENT: Note the hoaxer slip-up. The quote demonstrates that the body was viewed by townspeople, already identified as "Billy's friends." There were potentially 200 of them. Note also that Garrett makes no attempt to conceal the body of the supposed innocent victim of his heinous crime.]

When morning came, Justice of the Peace Alejandro Segura convened a jury, with Rudolph as president.

[AUTHOR'S COMMENT: Note that the Justice of the Peace convenes the Coroners Jury. Later the hoaxers will do a switcheroo with this fact.]

They rendered a verdict that William Bonney, Alias "Kid," had been killed by Garrett and were "unanimous in the opinion that the gratitude of the whole community is due the said Garrett for his act and that he deserves to be rewarded".

[AUTHOR'S COMMENT: Note that the obligation of a Coroners' Jury was to identify the body. And they did. Billy was known to them. The hoaxers already quoted Rasch saying Rudolph was nervous when interviewed by Poe, indicating he knew Billy, and knew he was in the area. Crucial also is the fact that the Coroner's Jury declared the killing justifiable homicide. That closed the case legally. Re-opening it would be double jeopardy: precisely what the hoaxers are doing.]

That afternoon Jesus Silva and Vincente Otero dug a grave for the outlaw in the old military cemetery.[12] (*[12]Philip Rasch. Trailing Billy the Kid* by Philip J. [sic] Outlaw-lawman research series Volume 1, University of Wyoming, Laramie, Wyoming, 1993.)

226

On face value this looks to be the truth. However, if you study the statements of the eye witness [sic] and the documents they do not match up and both can not be true.

> [AUTHOR'S COMMENT: This unsubstantiated claim is followed by faked "inconsistencies." But it will be used by the hoaxers in their conclusion, as if proved.]

Deputy John Poe says the following:

It was understood when I left my companions in the morning that in case of my being unable to learn any definite information in Fort Sumner, I was to go to the ranch of Mr. Rudolph (an acquaintance and supposed friend of Garrett's) whose ranch was located some seven miles north of Fort Sumner at a place called "Sunnyside," with the purpose of securing from him, if possible, some information as to the whereabouts of the man we were after. Accordingly I started from Fort Sumner about the middle of the afternoon for Rudolph's ranch,

> [AUTHOR'S COMMENT: Remember this "in the middle of the afternoon," because it will later become a switcheroo, with Poe leaving for Rudolph's at night.]

arriving there sometime before night. I found Mr. Rudolph at home, presented the letter of Introduction which Garrett had given me, and told him that I wished to stop overnight with him.[13] ([13]Poe, John W. Billy the Kid. Privately published by E.A. Brininstool. Los Angeles, CA.)

> [AUTHOR'S COMMENT: With this unpublished, Brininstool source - and probable assumption of its unavailability to everyone - the hoaxers are about to construct another straw man.]

In this part of Deputy Poe's statement he tells us he was sent to Rudolph's ranch by Garrett because Rudolph was *"an acquaintance and supposed friend of Garrett's,"* that the ranch was located seven miles north of Ft. Sumner, at Sunnyside. Poe also tells Rudolph he is going to spend the night at the ranch.

[AUTHOR'S COMMENT: The fakery here is omission of part of the historical quote. The Brininstool information is as follows: There was <u>no</u> "Brininstool book." Poe wrote his account - which included the Rudolph episode - for Charles Goodnight in 1917. In 1919, an Edward Seymour in New York contacted Goodnight for a reliable source of information on the Kid. Goodnight referred him to Poe. Poe sent a copy of his account of Billy's death to Seymour, who in turn sent it to Brininstool, who secured its publication in *Wild World Magazine*, a British publication, in December of 1919, and later disseminated it as a brochure. The identical version was used in in Poe's book, *The Death of Billy the Kid*, which the hoaxers cited earlier, so it too was available to them. In it, Poe states he <u>declined</u> the invitation to spend the night. That Poe quote is on page 22. The hoaxers omitted pages 25-26. Poe states: "Darkness was now approaching, and I said to Mr. Rudolph that inasmuch as myself and my horse were by this time pretty well rested, having had a good meal, I had changed my mind, and instead of stopping with him, would saddle up and ride during the cool of the evening to meet my companions. This I accordingly did, much, I thought, to the relief of Rudolph."]

In Sheriff Garrett's statement he gives about the same facts of where he was headed and how far it was from Ft. Sumner. Garrett differs with Poe in one area when he says he "arranged with Poe to meet us that night at moonrise" rather then spend the night with Rudolph, as can be seen below:

[AUTHOR'S COMMENT: This is to fake Garrett contradictions. But Poe *did not* spend the night. The hoaxers merely omitted Poe's quote saying that.]

I advised him (Poe) *also, to go to Sunnyside, seven miles above Sumner, and interview M. Rudolph Esq. In whose judgment and discretion I had great confidence. I arranged with Poe to meet us that night at moonrise, at La Puenta de la Glorietta, four miles north of Fort Sumner.*[14] ([14]Garrett, Pat F. The Authentic Life of Billy the Kid. University of Oklahoma Press, Norman. Oklahoma. 2000)

228

[AUTHOR'S COMMENT: That was it: the hoaxers' supposed inconsistency: whether Poe did or did not spend the night at Rudolph's. But both Poe and Garrett agree that he did not. There is no inconsistency. Nevertheless, the hoaxers' same double-talk is later repeated on the same subject.]

Deputy Poe then gives his account of when he says he first saw the Kid when he writes:

I observed that he was only partly dressed, and was both bare-headed and bare-footed - or rather, had only socks on his feet, and it seemed to me that he was fastening his trousers as he came toward me art a very brisk walk.

As Maxwell's was the one place in Fort Sumner that I considered above suspicion of harboring "The Kid," I was entirely off my guard, that thought coming into my mind that the man approaching was either Maxwell

[AUTHOR'S COMMENT: This quote dovetails with Poe's question about the right man, since he was unable to identify Billy. Note his lack of alarm, since it will be misstated by the hoaxers.]

or some guest of his who might have been staying there. He came on until he was almost within arm's length of where I sat before he saw me, as I was partly concealed from his view by the post of the gate. Upon his seeing me he covered me with his six-shooter as quick as lightening, sprang onto the porch, calling out in Spanish, "Quien es?" (Who is it?), at the same time backing away from me toward the door through which Garrett only a few seconds before had passed, repeating his query, "Quien es?" in Spanish several times. At this I stood up and advanced toward him, telling him not to be alarmed: that he should not be hurt, and still without the least suspicion that this was the very man we were looking for.

This statement raises many questions with investigators. Poe says he sees a man "*partially dressed, and was bare-headed and bare-footed - or rather, had only socks on his feet, and it seemed to me that he was fastening his trousers as he came toward me art a very brisk walk.*" Then the man covers him with his six shooter. Where did the man put the "*six-shooter*" when he was "*fastening his trousers*"?

> [AUTHOR'S COMMENT: This is an inadvertently hilarious hoaxer contrivance of the impossibility of doing two things at once! Actually, it is easy to hold a Colt .44 - or Colt .41 Thunderer - and button your pants. In addition, Billy was both a skilled gunman and ambidextrous, so even more able to multi-task!]

He did not stop and lay it down because Poe says he "*he came toward me art a very brisk walk.*"

> [AUTHOR'S COMMENT: Triple tasking!]

Another question that investigators struggle with is would it not go without saying Poe would have had a description of the Kid as he ventured into Ft. Sumner to scout around and gather information. It is beyond reason that he would go searching for a man without at least having a description of the man for whom he was searching?

> [AUTHOR'S COMMENT: It is not beyond reason. Garrett was not an experienced lawman. More to the point, Poe's task was not to search for Billy, but to gather information from locals about Billy's whereabouts.]

In a town of about 200 people, many of which were Hispanic would Poe be unable to recognize the Kid from this description as he claims?

> [AUTHOR'S COMMENT: What description? It seems Poe had none. Also, is unconscious racism creeping in? Many of Hispanic background are Spanish, and could be as fair as Billy was.]

Deputy Poe continues his statement with these words:

As I moved toward him trying to reassure him, he backed up into the doorway of Maxwell's room, where he halted for a moment, his body concealed by the thick adobe wall at the side of the doorway, from whence he put his head out and asking in Spanish for the fourth or fifth time who I was. I was within a few feet of him when he disappeared into the room.

When the Kid asks Poe who he is in Spanish and has his pistol pointed at the deputy, what is Deputy McKinney doing at this time? Why is he not shouldering his rifle, and at least deploying to the side to cover his partner Deputy Poe from this very real threat? Today the shooting policy for police officers is tight and narrow: in 1881 a shooting policy was non-existent. Investigators believe the deputies had to have a description for whom they were searching. With a threat such as Poe describes, a man with a gun, added to the description of the most wanted man in New Mexico, there would have been cause for both deputies to have fired on the suspect.

[AUTHOR'S COMMENT: Here comes a straw man. Who says Poe had the description, or thought the gun was a threat? Back then, most men were armed. Poe even shows lack of alarm by reassuring the stranger. And it seems that McKinney, for whatever reason, was unavailable for the hoaxers' fantasized shoot-out!]

Even if the deputies chose not to fire, would they have allowed the man who was threatening their lives with a gun

[AUTHOR'S COMMENT: Note this switcheroo from faked alarm of "threatening their lives," to it as a fact.]

to walk in on the unaware Sheriff in the dark? If they chose to allow the man with a gun to walk in on the Sheriff would these seasoned lawmen

[AUTHOR'S COMMENT: Kinney was just a hog farmer friend of Garrett's.]

not at least have warned the Sheriff of the danger?

[AUTHOR'S COMMENT: No danger is established.]

In Garrett's statement he relates the following:

From his step I could perceive he was either barefooted or in his stocking feet and held a revolver in his right hand and butcher knife in his left.

He came directly towards me. Before he reached the bed, I whispered, "Who is it Pete?"

> [AUTHOR'S COMMENT: This again eliminates the best buddies, murder plot, if Garrett is unsure of Billy. Note also that Peter Maxwell identifies Billy. Again the hoaxers accidentally undo their own arguments.]

But I received no response for a moment. It struck me that it might be Pete's brother-in-law. Manuel Abrea [sic], who had seen Poe and McKinney and wanted to know their business. The intruder came close to me, leaned both hands on the bed, his right and almost touching my knee, and asked in a low tone: "Who are they, Pete?" At the same moment Maxwell whispered to me, "That's him!" Simultaneously the Kid must have seen, or felt, the presence of a third person at the head of the bed. He raised quickly his pistol, a self cocker, within a foot of my breast. Retreating rapidly across the room he cried: "Quien es? Quien es? (Who's that? Who's that?) All this occurred in a moment. Quickly as possible I drew my revolver and fired, threw my body aside, and fired again. The second shot was useless: The Kid fell dead ..."

Investigators find it hard to believe that Garrett could see a 6 inch knife in the Kid's hand.

> [AUTHOR'S COMMENT: That night had an unusual full moon that stayed close to the horizon. It would have been almost as light as day. When Billy opened the door, he and a held weapon would have been visible. Also July is hot in Fort Sumner. It is unlikely that draperies would have been fully closed. Garrett's real problem was staying unseen himself.]

Yet the Kid could not see a six foot, five inch man.

[AUTHOR'S COMMENT: Sheriff Pat Garrett was 6'4".
This confirms only that the big man was hiding.]

[AUTHOR'S COMMENT: Note that as yet nothing
indicates that the victim was not Billy.]

Deputy Poe talks about what happened after the shooting of the
Kid. He writes:

[AUTHOR'S COMMENT: Quote has no footnote]

*Within a very short time after the shooting, quite a number of
the native people had gathered around, some of them bewailing the
death of their friend,*

[AUTHOR'S COMMENT: This is another hoaxer slip-
up. These people, who can recognize Billy, will later
be given his body to lay out.]

*while several women pleaded for permission to take charge of the
body, which we allowed them to do. They carried it to the yard to a
carpenter's shop, where it was laid on a workbench, the women
placing candles lightened around it, according to their ideas of
properly conducting a "wake" for the dead.*

[AUTHOR'S COMMENT: By this point, there are
profuse eye-witness identifications of Billy!]

Investigators keep Deputy Poe's statement in mind as they
studied the Coroner's Jury Report:

Greetings
:

*On this 15th day of July, A.D. 1881, I, the undersigned, Justice
of the Peace of the adobe named precinct, received information
that a murder had taken place in Fort Sumner, in said precinct,
and immediately upon receiving said information I proceeded to
the said place and named Milnor Rudolph, Jose Silva, Antonio
Sevedra, Pedro Antonio Lucero, Lorenzo Jaramillo and Sabal
Gutierres a jury to investigate the case and the above jury*

convened in the home of Luz B. Maxwell and proceeded to a room in the said house where they found the body of William Bonney alias "Kid" with a shot in the left breast and having examined the body they examined the evidence of Pedro Maxwell, which evidence is as follows: "I being in my bed in my room, at about midnight on the 14th day of July, Pat F. Garrett came into my room and sat down. William Bonney came in and got close to my bed with a gun in his hand and asked me "who is it" and then Pat F. Garrett fired two shots at the said William Bonney and the said William Bonney fell near my fire place and I went out of the room and when I came in again about three or four minutes after the shots the said William Bonney was dead."

[AUTHOR'S COMMENT: Note the definitive Jury plus Peter Maxwell identifications of the victim as William Bonney.]

The jury has found the following verdict: We the jury unanimously find that William Bonney

[AUTHOR'S COMMENT: The jurymen's identification]

has been killed by a shot on the left breast near the region of the heart, the same having been fired with a gun in the hand of pat F. Garrett and our verdict is that the deed of said Garrett was justifiable homicide and we are unanimous in the opinion that the gratitude of all the community is due to the said Garrett for his deed and is worthy of being rewarded.

M. Rudolph, President   *Anto, Sevedra(signature)*
Pedro Anto. m. Lucero (signature)
Jose Silba (x)   *Sabal Gutierrez (x)*
Lorenzo Jaramillo (x)

All said information I place to your knowledge.

Alejandro Segura Justice of the Peace (signature)

234

[AUTHOR'S COMMENT: This is a legally binding document. To reopen the case is double jeopardy. Further confirmation of jurymen's certainty, is that no indictment was subsequently made with the District Attorney against Garrett for a murder.]

Investigators remembered Deputy Poe's statement and Sheriff Garrett's statement as to where Poe had been that night.

[AUTHOR'S COMMENT: The hoaxers are hoping the reader believed their fake contention that Poe spent the night at Rudolph's. What follows is more fakery in attempt to manufacture "inconsistencies."]

Earlier that evening

[AUTHOR'S COMMENT: The time was afternoon, as quoted by the hoaxers earlier, and tagged by me in preparation for this switcheroo which they require to make their fake argument work.]

Garrett had dispatched Deputy Poe to interview M. Rudolph in Sunnyside, seven miles north of Fort Sumner. Poe says he left Rudolph and rode to meet Garrett and McKinney. All records show that the shooting took place about midnight and Historian Philip I. Rash [sic] sets the time at 12:30 AM on July 15th. If this were true then the time does not allow for the statement of Poe and the coroner's jury report to both be true.

[AUTHOR'S COMMENT: Their time switcheroo is being done to discredit the Coroner's Jury Report, their bugbear. But, even if granted them, it does not work. It would have been about an hour and a half ride for Poe to cover the seven miles to Sunnyside. Puenta de la Glorietta was four miles north of Fort Sumner on the way to Sunnyside. So Poe's return journey to meet his companions was only three miles, or about forty five minutes. He had plenty of time to meet them by evening, a fact he and Garrett confirmed.]

If, after the shooting, Garrett had to get some order to the scene, locate a rider to ride to Sunnyside to get Rudolph,

[AUTHOR'S COMMENT: The above Coroner's Jury Report clearly states that the appointment, and probable contact, of Rudolph was a legal duty performed by the appropriate official: Justice of the Peace, Alejandro Segura, certainly not Garrett, at that point the murder suspect being evaluated.]

and the rider then had to get his horses [sic] caught, saddled and ready to go all of which would take the better part of an hour,

[AUTHOR'S COMMENT: This is fabricated time. Maxwell had a stable - not just a corral - and workers. A horse could be readied quickly.]

the time would be 1:30 am.

[AUTHOR'S COMMENT: The hoaxers are creating another straw man argument about "inconsistency" by time fakery. Yet they know that the Coroner's Jury met sometime during daytime of the 15th. There was no need for middle-of-the night urgency; and no evidence that it occurred.]

It would take a rider who was in shape, on a good horse, and riding fast, an hour and a half to cover the seven miles to Rudolph's ranch, putting the time at 2:30 am. Adding an hour for the rider to wake Rudolph up and for Rudolph to catch his horse and saddle the horse the time would be 3:30 am. If Rudolph was in good shape, on a good horse it would be another hour and a half on the return trip to Fort Sumner putting the time at 4:30 am. Add another hour to put together a jury, and the time is now 5:30 am. This is if everyone worked smoothly.

In the jury's report we find the words:

... a jury to investigate the case and the above jury convened in the home of Luz B. Maxwell and proceeded to a room in the said in said house where they found the body of William Bonney alias "Kid"...

Either the jury found the Kid in the Maxwell's home, or he was not given to the women to put on the carpenters workbench as Poe says, or the jury report is deceptive.

[AUTHOR'S COMMENT: Obviously the hoaxers hope they convinced readers of that conclusion. But, in fact, there was easily enough time to carry the corpse from the Maxwell house, across about 300 yards of parade ground, to the carpenter's shop. In the morning, it could be returned to the Maxwell's house for the jurymen.]

Deputy Poe also says:

The next morning we sent for the justice of the peace,

[AUTHOR'S COMMENT: Oddly, the hoaxers undo their own elaborate scenario of middle of the night riding by giving this quote about the next morning.]

who held an inquest over the body, the verdict of the jury being such as to justify the killing, and later, on the same day, the body was buried in the old military burying ground at Fort Sumner.

If the Kid's body was taken to the carpenter shop then the jury did not find the body at Maxwell's house as stated and makes investigators wonder why they would lie in the report.

[AUTHOR'S COMMENT: This fabrication leads to a "lie" accusation. But nothing indicates that the body was not brought to the house from the carpenter's shop. But the hoaxers are still struggling to discredit the Coroner's Jury Report by "contradictions," though, of course, that is irrelevant to establishing the victim's identity.]

Deputy Poe says something else that raised investigators suspicions when he writes about the shooting itself:

[AUTHOR'S COMMENT: This quick switcheroo acts as a distraction from the sly misstatements just slipped past. In addition, though the hoaxers never say what is "suspicious" in the Poe quote - which merely repeats Garrett's description - they are setting the stage for their fake "investigation" to be described next.]

An instant later a shot was fired in the room, followed immediately by what everyone within hearing distance thought was two shots fired, the third report, as we learned afterward, being caused by the rebound of the second bullet which had struck the adobe wall and rebounded against the headboard of the wooden bedstead.

[AUTHOR'S COMMENT: It is important to take stock at this point. Nothing so far has indicated that the shooting victim was anyone other than profusely identified William Bonney. In addition, the hoaxers have provided no contradictions to that, as promised. It should also be noted that subsequently, as their case foundered, they recklessly did a switcheroo, contradicting this entire document: they stated that William Bonney *was* shot, but just played dead!]

[AUTHOR'S COMMENT: Note that the second bullet site is in the bed's headboard. The hoaxers will soon do fake forensics on a wash stand instead!]

[AUTHOR'S COMMENT: Next follows faked CSI-style investigation.]

On August 29, 2003, Deputy Sederwall of the Lincoln County Sheriff''s Department

[AUTHOR'S COMMENT: Note Sederwall doing the investigation in official capacity. That will later be denied by the hoaxers.]

located the carpenter bench where the Kid's body was placed on July 14, 1881.

[AUTHOR'S COMMENT: Error: the earliest morning hours of July 15th]

[AUTHOR'S COMMENT: Since the bench will later become the center of the hoax's next phase, it should be noted that the one in possession of Maxwell family descendents, was first identified in the late 1920's by Robert Mullin and photographed by Maurice Garland Fulton. There is no proof that it is really the one on which Billy was laid out. In addition, one should not miss that the hoaxers are here switching from Garrett's "innocent victim," who should be the one on the bench, to real Billy on the bench - thereby undoing their own murder contention.]

On September 13, 2003, investigators located all the furniture that was in Pete Maxwell's bedroom the night of the shooting, July 1881.

[AUTHOR'S COMMENT: Though this information is irrelevant to the claim of whether Billy was Garrett's victim, this Maxwell furniture - including the carpenter's bench - became pivotal to the survival of the hoax. But the furniture's certain provenance for Billy the Kid's carpenter shop vigil is unprovable.

Maxwell Fort Sumner holdings were sold at public auction on January 15, 1884, and bought by Lonny Horn, Sam Doss, Daniel Taylor and John Lord in partnership with the New England Cattle Company which transferred its operations there. The Maxwell house (with the fateful bedroom) was torn down about 1887, and some of the timber was used to build the Pigpen Ranch south of Melrose, New Mexico.

Pete Maxwell died in 1898. A brother-in-law, Manuel Abreu, lived in the area, and *may* have taken some furniture. In the 1920's, after the writings of historian, Robert Mullin, the family claimed to have the bedroom furniture and carpenter's bench in storage in a shed - and they were pictured in a 1930 article.

But this was the period in which Billy's fame was in recrudescence, and unsubstantiated claims were being made about many alleged Billy artifacts. All one can say is that about 50 years after the killing, Maxwells alleged possession of Billy the Kid-related objects.]

Among these items is the headboard of the bed that was in Maxwell's room that night. There is no bullet hole in the headboard.

[AUTHOR'S COMMENT: That finding, though irrelevant to the murder victim, contradicts Poe's statement that the headboard was hit; thus, invalidating the furniture's authenticity!]

In a statement made by Deluvina Maxwell she says the following:

… There was a washstand with a marble top in Pete Maxwell's bedroom, which Garrett had seen in the moonlight

[AUTHOR'S COMMENT: A hoaxer slip. Earlier, they denied that Garrett could have clearly seen Billy, yet here they confirm moonlit visibility. Note that they are trying to validate the washstand. It will be used for a fake investigation, though the headboard was shot.]

and shot at, thinking it was Bonney trying to get up. It was an old Spanish custom that the night before the burial of a person, people would take turns staying with the body and reciting prayers. William Bonney had a proper funeral. The people took turns and stayed through the night.

[AUTHOR'S COMMENT: Note the hoaxer slip. Again the hoaxers confirm identity by eyewitnesses.]

He was buried in the old government cemetery in Fort Sumner. For many years Deluvina left flowers on his grave in the summer time. [15]

240

[AUTHOR'S COMMENT: The last sentence is not Deluvina's quote.]

(^{15}Deluvina Maxwell's story as related to Lucien B. Maxwell grandchildren, unpublished.)

[AUTHOR'S COMMENT: Note that unreliable reporting by grandchildren is used as the only "proof" of wash stand validity. Also, the entire story is irrelevant to victim identity, though it repeats, to hoaxer detriment, the vigil and corpse witnessing scenario.]

Deluvina lends credibility to the story of the Kid's body being laid on the carpenter bench.

[AUTHOR'S COMMENT: Note the hoaxer slip. That information ends their case: Billy's corpse on bench!]

She also mentions, *"There was a washstand with a marble top in Pete Maxwell's bedroom, which Garrett had seen in the moonlight and shot at, thinking it was Bonney trying to get up."* In the items investigators located on September 13, 2003 was that wash stand.

[AUTHOR'S COMMENT: The wash stand is unsubstantiated as coming from Pete Maxwell's room - as is the rest of the furniture. And Deluvina apparently only said the wash stand was "shot at," not shot. And Poe claimed the bed's headboard as hit. But what follows is a fake mimicking of crime scene investigation based on "certainty" of the wash stand.]

The was stand was dark in color and 291/2 inches wide, with a splash board on the back that measured 5 inch at the middle and tapered down to the ends in a decorative curve. From front to back the wash stand measured 16 inches. It stood 29 inches with three drawers with rusted locks on each drawer. There was what appeared to be a bullet hole through the stand.

Deputy Sederwall removed a .45 caliber pistol round from his deputy weapon and noticed the round was just a little bit bigger than the hole. The night of the shooting Sheriff Garrett was shooting a Colt Single Action Army Revolver, Serial Number 55093, caliber .44/40.[16] ([16]Typed letter from P.F. Garrett dated April 16, 1906. James H. Earl [sic - Earle] Collection, from County Clerk's office, El Paso, Texas.)

> [AUTHOR'S COMMENT: Note that there is no bullet, just a hole. That cannot establish precise caliber size. The claim of .44/40 ammunition is a faking of a match to the caliber in Garrett's known weapon. Here, it is as absurd to link the shot to Garrett, as to link the washstand to Peter Maxwell. It is even more absurd to link it to the shooting of anyone, since accidental discharges occurred in New Mexico where most had guns from the 19th century to the present – the same time frame during which the stand could have been shot! And the washstand is tiny – like a child's!]

The bullet pierced the left side of the washstand, both sides of the drawer and exited out the right side of the stand.

The bullet struck the left side of the stand 22 1/4 inches on the center up from the bottom and 6 1/2 inches on the center of the back of the stand. The bullet exited to the right side 20 1/2 inches on the center up from the bottom and 6 1/2 inches on center from the back of the washstand. On the inside of the left side panel the wood was somewhat splintered indicating that was where the bullet entered the stand. On the right side panel the outside of the panel was splintered indicating the exit of the bullet.

The owner of the washstand, whose name investigators do not wish to release at this time

> [AUTHOR'S COMMENT: Periodically the hoaxers nervously claimed secrecy, then forgot, and gave the information; in this case the Maxwell family.]

says it was inherited along with the bed from Maxwell's bedroom. The discovery of this evidence makes Deluvina's statement believable.

> [AUTHOR'S COMMENT: Historically real or not, the furniture examination is irrelevant to Garrett's victim.]

Many questions remain. Why would the coroner's jury report and the eye witness reports be so at odds?

> [AUTHOR'S COMMENT: They are not at odds. And the hoaxers have not demonstrated otherwise. But the hoaxers are heading again into a straw man argument.]

A hint can be found in a document discovered in July of 1989 by Joe O. Bowlin.

> [AUTHOR'S COMMENT: This is a low blow to a dead man. Joe Bowlin, with his wife Marlyn, founded the Billy the Kid Outlaw Gang, dedicated to the preservation, protection, and promotion of the true history of Billy Bonney and Pat Garrett. This hoax represents everything Bowlin opposed. What follows is a misrepresentation of the book which Bolin published for its author, Paco Anaya.]

The document is a story, according to Louis Anaya of Clovis, New Mexico as told to his father, Paco Anaya, a friend of Billy the Kid.

> [AUTHOR'S COMMENT: Note the admitted friendship of Anaya and Billy. It will cause another hoaxer slip-up.]

This story was translated from Spanish and then printed in book form. In this transcript you will find the following:

Also, I will have to tell you a lot in reference to the reports that Pat Garrett made about the sworn declaration that appears in the records of the Secretary of State and more, concerning what he said about the Coroners Jury that investigated the death of Billy the Kid when Pat killed Billy.

In this report, I find that the Coroners Jury that investigated the death of Billy the Kid when he was dead is not part of the same report that acted as a Coroners Jury, neither the form or the

verdict of the Coroners Jury. The verdict is recorded in the office of the Secretary of State in Spanish, and they (the jury) are not the same men. There are two that did not even live in Fort Sumner.[17]
([17]Anaya, A. P. *I Buried Billy.* Creative Publishing Company. 1991.)

Paco Anaya goes on to list the members of the Jury that he remembered holding the inquest over the body. They are not the same as the jury report as is held up as proof that Garrett killed the Kid.

> [AUTHOR'S COMMENT: Note this fast one done to create another straw man. There are many other corpse identifications for Billy. In fact, most have already been accidentally quoted in this document by the hoaxers!]

One of the differences is Illeginio Garcia [sic - poor legibility - unclear spelling] as the Jury President and not M. Rudolph.

Paco Anaya says that Garrett wrote the first version in English himself. Anaya says that Garrett later came back and wrote another report in Spanish with the help of "Don Pedro Maxwell and Don Manuel Abrea [sic]," Maxwell's brother-in-law.

This makes the investigators ask, if Garrett wrote the verdict is that why the words are found, *"…we are unanimous in the opinion that the gratitude of all the community is due to the said Garrett for his deed and is worthy of being rewarded"?*

It should be noted that in the Coroners Jury Report that Garrett puts forth

> [AUTHOR'S COMMENT: Note the switcheroo. Garrett did not put it forth. It was a legal document done under Justice of the Peace, Alejandro Segura. Garrett was the *subject* of their investigation. The document might have been available to him after the inquest. It surely would not have been available to humble citizen Anaya.]

244

it is interesting to note that two of those listed were in Garrett's wedding, Sabal Gutierrez is his brother-in-law, and Garrett admits in his statement that Rudolph is a close friend.

[AUTHOR'S COMMENT: Note the falsehood. Garrett did not pick the jurymen; the Justice of the Peace did.]

[AUTHOR'S COMMENT: With continuing sly innuendo, the hoaxers end their discussion of the Coroner's Jury Report here. Nothing has indicated that Garrett murdered anyone other than Billy. A hoaxer hope is that the reader will fill in their blanks, and conclude the report is fishy; though, even that, is irrelevant to victim identity. But their ploy is even more flawed. The reader would then have to postulate a preposterous conspiracy including Justice of the Peace Segura; Milnor Rudolph; the other jurymen; Peter Maxwell; and his brother-in-law, Manuel Abreu; and Deluvina, all in the service of helping Garrett get away with the murder of the unknown victim (whose corpse had been seen by possibly 200 townspeople, so they would all need to be in on the conspiracy too)!]

[AUTHOR'S COMMENT: More to the point, is the hoaxers' use of Paco Anaya. Like many old-timer accounts, his was written long after the events; in this case, in 1930, forty-nine years later. Since he would not have been privy to the legal details of the Coroner's Jury, and since his memory may have failed him, his inaccuracies are explainable. In fact, his entire memoir is an inaccurate rendition of the history of the Lincoln War. What is undeniable is that he knew Billy well, saw his body, and named his book *I Buried Billy*! Once again the hoaxers accidentally contradict their contention.]

[AUTHOR'S COMMENT: What follows is the hoaxer' last effort. And, to this point, nothing at all has indicated that the victim was other than Billy. David Turk, historian for the U.S. Marshals Service, was a hoax participant.]

David Turk, Historian for the United States Marshal's Service has pointed out other documents

> [AUTHOR'S COMMENT: Note that only one will be presented, though this hints at David Turk's role in the hoax as writer, participant, and voucher in the press.]

bringing into question Garrett's involvement in the Kid's escape.

> [AUTHOR'S COMMENT: Note the switcheroo. Who said Billy escaped? Up to now he has been a corpse.]

Mr. Turk has produced a Works Progress Administration, Federal Writer's Project interview where the following statement was taken:

> *The people around Lincoln*

> [AUTHOR'S COMMENT: The murder was 150 miles from Lincoln; and Turk's old-timer claims no first-hand knowledge, giving "fuzzy factoid" only.]

say Garrett didn't kill Billie (sic) the Kid. John Poe was with Garrett the night he was supposed to ... said that he didn't see the man that Garrett killed.

> [AUTHOR'S COMMENT: Besides the fact that Poe's statements all refer to seeing the victim, it should be remembered that Poe did not know Billy.]

I can take you to the grave in Hell's High Acre, an old government cemetery, where Billie (sic) was supposed to be buried and show you the grave.
The cook at Pete Maxwell's was always putting flowers on the grave and praying at it. This woman thought a lot of Billie (sic), but after Garrett killed the man at Maxwell's home her grandson was never seen again

> [AUTHOR'S COMMENT: Whose grandson?]

and Billie (sic) was seen by Bill Nicholi an Indian scout. Bill saw him in Mexico.[18] ([18]Frances E. Tolly, comp. "Early Days in Lincoln County," Charles Remark Interview. February 14, 1938, Works Progress Administration, Federal Writer's Project, Folklore-Life Histories, Manuscript Division. Library of Congress.)

> [AUTHOR'S COMMENT: There you have it: the only document the hoaxers provide, so far, which says Garrett did not kill Billy. But it is merely an old-timer recollection, 57 years later, by someone with no historical connection to the event, aptly titled in its archive as "folklore." This old-timer merely "thinks" someone saw Billy in Mexico. It should be noted that, by 1938, Billy the Kid was famous, and slews of old-timers were fabricating connections to him, or claiming to be him. In fact, old-timer unreliability is illustrated in the Overton affidavit attached to this Probable Cause Statement.]

> [AUTHOR'S COMMENT: Next comes the conclusion. Note hoaxer feigning that their contentions had been proved - when not a single one was.]

Discovering the headboard of Maxwell's bed that does not have a bullet hole in it, as Deputy Poe says it did, leads investigators to question if Poe was in fact in the room after the shooting of William Bonney as he said.

> [AUTHOR'S COMMENT: More obvious is that this headboard is probably not from the Maxwell bedroom murder scene. And "if the headboard was not shot, Poe was not in the room" is only "alien invasion illogic," and is irrelevant to the hoaxers' murder claim.]

However, the discovery of the Maxwell wash stand with the bullet hole through it indicates someone was shot in Maxwell's room on the night of July 14, 18821.

[AUTHOR'S COMMENT: Why? Even if it was from the bedroom, a bullet hole in a wash stand does not indicate that a person was shot. Of course, this is irrelevant to whether Garrett shot Billy.]

The question remains as to who is in William H. Bonney's grave at Fort Sumner.

[AUTHOR'S COMMENT: No question remains. The hoaxers have simply made it up - unsubstantiated. The purpose of this probable cause statement for murder was to justify Garrett as a suspect, and that the victim was other than Billy. They have failed both: the first by motive or evidence, the second by reasonable doubt of victim identity.]

Investigators believe with the conflicts of Sheriff Pat F. Garrett and Deputy John Poe and the fact that these statements are at odds with the Jury Report as shown above,

[AUTHOR'S COMMENT: This is fakery. The "conflicts" do not exist. More to the point, the hoaxers never even explained how "conflicts" in reporting would indicate that Garrett shot anyone other than Billy.]

coupled with the evidence discovered by deputies,

[AUTHOR'S COMMENT: What evidence? The hoaxers have some unsubstantiatable antique furniture; and it is irrelevant, even if real, as to a murder victim. And their period quotes are either irrelevant or misrepresented.]

probable cause exist [sic] to warrant the court to grant investigators the right to search for the truth in criminal investigation 2003-274 through DNA samples obtained from Catherine Antrim.

[AUTHOR'S COMMENT: Without any probable cause of a murder, the hoaxers have headed to their objective: exhumation of Billy and his mother.]

248

[AUTHOR'S COMMENT: Two signatures follow; each typed and written.]

Steven M. Sederwall: Deputy Sheriff, Lincoln County (12/31/03)

Tom Sullivan: Sheriff Lincoln County (12/31/03)

[AUTHOR'S COMMENT: The signature date is noteworthy, being three months after their exhumation case began. It appears possible that hoax participant, U.S. Marshals Service Historian David Turk, came to Lincoln County to help finish the document.]

* * * * * * *

OVERTON AFFIDAVIT

Completing the Probable Cause Statement is a two page, typed, old-timer affidavit by a Homer Overton. Note that the widow of Pat Garrett, Apolinaria Gutierrez Garrett, died in 1936, four years *before* Overton's alleged conversation with her in 1940 (b.1861 - d.1936)! She is buried in the Masonic Cemetery in Las Cruces, New Mexico, where Garrett is also buried.

Overton's florid elaborations, implying confabulation, include details like a Garrett report to Texas Rangers, the corpse with blasted face, and, of course, his murder of someone other than Billy. Overton's claims have more subtle absurdity. Garrett's wife protected his earned fame. After his death in 1908, she even legally reclaimed his 7 ½ inch barrel, Colt .44, single action revolver, serial number 55093, from a saloonkeeper to whom he had lent it. She would not have undermined Garrett's glory.

Later, this "murder scene" description would contradict the Billy the Kid Case hoax's new, and completely different, "murder scene."

* * * * * * *

December 22, 2003

Tom Sullivan
Lincoln County Sheriff
P.O. Box 278
Carrizozo, NM 88301

Tom,

It was good talking to you on the phone and, as promised, I am sending this letter as promised to present this Statement of Facts.

Fact: I was born in Pecos, Texas in the year 1931 and lived there until the later [sic] part of 1941. In the summer of 1940, I was invited to spend the summer with Bobby Talbert and his mother, who had moved from Pecos to Las Cruces, New Mexico earlier that year.

> [AUTHOR'S COMMENT: Note time specificity. Overton was not in Las Cruces earlier than 1940.]

The time I spent there was wonderful, but one thing happened that summer that made the summer unforgettable.

Bobby's next door neighbor was a lady who introduced herself as Mrs. Garrett, the widow of Pat Garrett. Mrs. Garrett would invite us over to have iced tea with mint leaves in it, and told us stories about her life with Pat. I recall her having a parrot that had belonged to Pat which she said was very old. She told us some parrots live to be over 100 years.

That afternoon, she brought out a gun to show us and said it had belonged to Pat. As I recall, the gun appeared to be a Colt single action revolver. At that point I asked her if that was the gun used to kill Billy the Kid. At this point she got an unusual look on her face and stated that she was going to tell us something we would have to promise to keep a secret, and never to tell anyone. We both promised, and until this day I have never told anyone but my immediate family.

Mrs. Garrett proceeded to tell us the following facts concerning her husband and Billy:

Mrs. Garrett said, "Pat did not shoot Billy". She said there was a very close relationship between Pat and Billy, almost like a father and son relationship. She further stated that the night Pat was supposed to kill Billy, that they were in Ft. Sumner and had made a plan to make it look like Pat killed Billy so Billy could go to Mexico and live with no one looking for him any more. She said that Pat had seen a drunk Mexican lying in the street on his way to talk to Billy. So they planned to use the Mexican and claim that he was in fact Billy the Kid. She didn't state if the Mexican was dead or not, but said that they shot him in the face so he couldn't be recognized. They dressed him in Billy's clothes and Pat signed a paper for the Texas Rangers stating that he had killed Billy the Kid and that this was his body. The Mexican was then buried in Fort Sumner and identified as Billy.

Mrs. Garrett struck me as being very sincere when she told us this and she stated that she had never told anyone before. I have kept this secret for sixty-three years and feel it is time to disclose this story. I hope it will be helpful to you in your quest to find the truth about Billy, as I believe what Mrs. Garrett told us that day was the absolute truth.

All that I have told you is as I recall it related to me sixty-three years ago when I was nine years old. It made such an impression on me that I have remembered it in detail these sixty-three years.

Sincerely,
Homer D. Overton
AKA: Homer D. Kinsworthy
CONTACT INFORMATION

Witnessed by: Jerry Raffee, NOTARY
on December 27th 2003

SEAL AFFIXED

APPENDIX: 2. "Billy the Kid's Pre-Hearing Brief." Filed January 5, 2004. Attorney Bill Robins III and Attorney David Sandoval.

SIXTH JUDICIAL DISTRICT COURT
STATE OF NEW MEXICO
COUNTY OF GRANT

NO. MS 2003-11
IN THE MATTER OF CATHERINE ANTRIM

BILLY THE KID'S PRE-HEARING BRIEF

COME NOW, Bill Robins, III and David Sandoval, of the law firm of Heard, Robins, Cloud, Lubel & Greenwood, LLC, and on the behalf of the estate of William H. Bonney, aka "Billy the Kid",

[AUTHOR'S COMMENT: Billy the Kid had no estate. That means posthumous property to be dealt with in a probate court. This fakery was the lead-up to Robins's segue into dead Billy himself as his client.]

file this Pre-Hearing Brief and state as follows:

I. INTRODUCTION

The Court asks the undersigned counsel to brief several questions as follows:

1. The Governor's right to assign an Attorney to Represent the Interests of Billy the Kid and the Associated Zone of Public Interest;

2. Who is the Real Party in Interest Represented by Counsel;

3. What Stake Does that Party Have in Intervening in This Cause;

4. Billy the Kid's Interest as Defined in the Law Relating to Standing; and

5. The Effect of *In Re: Application of Lois Telfer, for the Removal of the Body of William H. Bonney*

[AUTHOR'S COMMENT: These questions by the judge are an hilarious parody of judicial gravitas. Judge Quintero well knows that Governor Richardson had no right to appoint an attorney to his court, knows that Robins has no "real party" as a client, only a ghost; knows that the dead do not appear in court and have no standing; and knows that the Telfer exhumation case in Fort Sumner blocked all future exhumation attempts there by stating that the grave location was uncertain and contiguous remains would be disturbed.]

The Points and Authorities section below does so as follows: **Point One** provides introductory legal analysis, **Point Two** addresses Question 1, **Point Three** addresses Questions 2, 3, and 4, and **Point Four** addresses Question 5. **Point 5** supports the merits of the Petition for Exhumation.

II. POINTS AND AUTHORITIES

Point One
Initial Discussion as to the Nature of This Proceeding

This is an interesting proceeding in that the relief sought here is not exclusively judicial.

[AUTHOR'S COMMENT: That is understatement! What will follow has nothing to do with a court of law, and is double talked fakery. But New Mexico taxpayers would be footing its bills for almost a decade.]

New Mexico allows the state registrar or state medical examiner to issue permits for disinterment. 1978 NMSA §24-14-23D. The statute does not identify who may make such a request nor specify the showing that needs to be made in order to obtain the permit. Rather than proceeding with this simple and non-adversarial process, Petitioners here have invoked this Court's equity jurisdiction for an order allowing the exhumation of Billy the Kid's mother, Catherine Antrim. See, *Hood v. Spratt,* 357 So.2d 135 (Miss. 1978) (request for disinterment "is particularly one for a court of equity") citing *Theodore v. Theodore,* 57 N.M. 434, 259 P.2d 795 (1953).

"[N]ormally a district court would not become involved in such matters unless a protesting relative or interested party files an injunction or takes some other legal action to halt the autopsy or disinterment," *In Re Johnson,* 94 N.M. 491, 494, 612 P.2d 1302 (1980). Petitioners should thus be commended for bringing this Court into the picture and in doing so, offering the town of Silver City, a relative of another descendent buried in the cemetery, and the legal interests of Billy the Kid, an opportunity to participate in the process.

[AUTHOR'S COMMENT: This sanctimonious fakery implies that the hoax is doing a favor for Silver City - in court to oppose exhumation - and even a favor to dead Catherine Antrim. And dead Billy has no "legal interests," being dead!]

The questions the Court asked briefed, however, suggest the possibility that the court may not allow Billy the Kid to be heard.

[AUTHOR'S COMMENT: At this point, the hoaxers were going through the motions. They had every reason to believe that Judge Quintero was in their pocket.]

As will be shown clearly, Billy the Kid's interests are real, legitimate, proper for consideration, and we respectfully ask the Court to recognize them as such.

[AUTHOR'S COMMENT: And if you believe a dead man has real interests on earth, Robins and his compatriots probably have a bridge to sell you in New York.]

A challenge to a governor's appointment power is made in a *quo warranto* proceeding.

> [AUTHOR'S COMMENT: Robins is here faking legitimacy of appointment as dead Billy's attorney. In fact, only the judge can appoint an attorney for a court client - if the client is indigent. Governor Richardson, by appointing Robins here, used *ultra vires,* overstepping his executive power for judicial intervention.]

New Mexico Judicial Standards Commission v. Governor Bill Richardson and Espinoza, 134 N.M. 59, 73 P.2d 197 (2003); see also, 1978 NMSA. §§44-3-1 *et. seq. (quo warranto* action proper when "any person shall usurp, intrude into or unlawfully holds or exercise any public office, civil or military, or any franchise within this state.")

The *quo warranto* statute contains specific procedures that the Town has not properly followed, nor could follow because the Town is not a "private person."

> [AUTHOR'S COMMENT: This fact demonstrates that Robins is misapplying the law to the town with his false argument.]

Standing to bring such a proceeding lies first with the attorney general or district attorney. 1978 NMSA, §44-3-4; *Beese v. District Court,* 31 N.M. 82, 239 P. 452 (1925). Those public officials do not present any challenge here.

A private person can bring a *quo warranto* action only when he has requested the aforementioned public officials to bring action and they have refused. 1978 NMSA, §44-3-4. The only private person in this matter is Ms. Amos-Staadt and she has not challenged the Governor's appointment, much less shown compliance with the procedural requisites of the *quo warranto* statute.

As noted, the challenge to the Governor comes from the Town of Silver City. It simply has no standing to bring a *quo warranto* proceeding. 1978 NMSA, §44-3-4. The validity of

Governor Richardson's appointment of the undersigned counsel is thus not before this Court.

> [AUTHOR'S COMMENT: An inappropriately appointed lawyer representing a corpse as client should indeed have been taken up by the Court - and Robins should have been kicked out on his petard.]

To the extent that the Court remains concerned with the presence of Billy the Kid in this litigation,

> [AUTHOR'S COMMENT: Robins here switches from the "estate" of Billy the Kid to the dead Kid as client.]

it is a matter that can be more properly addressed pursuant to legal requirements of standing and intervention, which the discussion below shows the Kid satisfies.

> [AUTHOR'S COMMENT: Robins advances his client, dead Billy, who now, he claims, is able to have court standing and perform intervention.]

(Given the express direction to brief the question, however, the discussion below sets forth the proper gubernatorial powers at play here.)

C. *The Governor's Powers*

As noted above, the governor is the supreme executive officer of the state. There can be no question that in that capacity Governor Richardson has authority to engage the services of professionals to assist him in accomplishment of those duties. Lawyers are certainly within that group, as is witnessed by Geno Zamora, the Governor's chief legal counsel.

> [AUTHOR'S COMMENT: Robins is here making a false argument based on omission. The governor can engage an attorneys services. But the matter here is not services, but violating the division of executive and judicial powers. The omission is the illegal nature of Robins's appointment.]

256

The source of power behind such appointments is likely found in the "inherent general power of appointment in the executive." *Matheson v. Ferry*, 641 P.2d 674, 682 (Ut 1982); *Hadley v. Washburn*, 67 S.W. 592 (Mo. 1902) (appointment of election commissioners is an inherent executive power); *Application of O'Sullivan*, 158 P.2d 306, 309 (Mont. 1945) ("the power of appointment is an executive function which cannot be delegated to the judiciary); *State v. Brill*, 111 N.W. 294, (1907) (legislature prohibited from requiring judges at appoint members to a board of control unrelated to the judiciary on a separation of powers theory grounded in the presumption that the power of appointment is inherently executive).

> [AUTHOR'S COMMENT: Robins, wildly spewing irrelevant legal cases, is omitting something else in his argument here: the U.S. Constitution which guarantees separation of powers!]

This inherent power must also allow the Governor to appoint attorneys to address his concerns and/or further his interests outside his immediate circle.

> [AUTHOR'S COMMENT: Robins gives dramatic proof that this Billy the Kid Case was Richardson's baby. Then he jumps with a legal *non sequitor*, but to the ulterior motive of the whole publicity-seeking hoax: the Billy the Kid pardon.]

The governor has the "power to grant reprieves and pardons." N.M. Const. Art. V Sec. 6. Undersigned counsel intends on seeking a pardon for Billy the Kid. Certainly Governor Richardson is within his inherent appointment power to hire counsel to advise him on the merits of such a pardon.

> [AUTHOR'S COMMENT: Tricky Robins omits that pardon advising gives no legal justification to be appointed to this court seeking the exhumation of Catherine Antrim. He is just functioning as an amateur historian.]

That the power extends to pardons of long-dead individuals is clear because our Constitution extends that power to pardon offences under the Territorial Laws of New Mexico. N.M. Const. Art. XXII Sec 5. (Footnote: Posthumous pardons are not unusual. In fact, Lenny Bruce was pardoned by Governor Patake in New York just last month.)

> [AUTHOR'S COMMENT: Robins is omitting that Territorial law left pardon to the discretion of the Governor. All Richardson had to do was to pardon Billy if he wanted to. The rest of the hoaxers' exhumation gambit was just a dog and pony show for publicity.]

That the appointment is consistent with the statutorily granted powers is shown by consideration of two different status. Counsel's appointment here is in the nature of an appointment as a public defender; a portion of their work effort will go towards exposing the merits of a pardon. 1978 NMSA §§31-15-1, et. seq. The public defender department is within the executive branch and is headed [sic-by] an appointee of the governor. 1978 NMSA §§31-15-4A. The duty and function of the department is to have attorneys serve as defense counsel "as necessary and appropriate." 1978 NMSA §§31-15-7B(10).

> [AUTHOR'S COMMENT: Robins transcends to the absurd: saying he is in an exhumation court to decide on a pardon; saying he is a public defender of a corpse; saying that all that makes his non-constitutional appointment justified.]

The Governor has apparently deemed it necessary and appropriate to seek guidance from undersigned counsel on matters related to the Kid and potential pardon.

Similarly, the Governor has authority to request the appointment of prosecutorial attorneys. 1978 NMSA, Section 8-5-2B provides that a governor may request the attorney general to appoint counsel in "all actions civil or criminal" in which the governor believes the state is "interested." The governor's pardon power gives the state an interest [sic- in] legal matters involving a potential candidate for pardon and Governor Richardson could rely on Section 8-5-2B's power at the appropriate time. This should not be read to mean that Governor Richardson is assuming power to appoint attorneys to act on behalf of the State, a power that lies exclusively with the Attorney General. It is referenced here as another example of how the governor is authorized in several instances to procure the assistance of attorneys.

> [AUTHOR'S COMMENT: Though he managed to slip in the raison d'être for the Billy the Kid Case - pardon (plus publicity) - Robins has not justified his appointment for this exhumation court.]

Point Three
What Interests Are of Importance Here

A. *The Law of Standing*

As has been established, this is an action in equity. New Mexico's Supreme Court wrote: "The equity right of intervention in proper cases has always been recognized. The equitable test is, 'Does the intervener stand to gain or lose by the judgment.' " *Stovall v. Vesely*, 38 N.M. 415, 34 P.2d 862, 864 (1934)

> [AUTHOR'S COMMENT: The actual test here is that Robins has no client to have an interest.]

Billy the Kid's interest here is his legacy.

> [AUTHOR'S COMMENT: The actual test here is also for the level of Judge Quintero's morals. That single sentence says it all: the use of Quintero's court for an illegally appointed attorney, speaking for a dead man, whose "interest" is not a legal one, but a sentimental "legacy" - whatever that means. And Robins and Quintero both failed their credibility tests.]

As noted in previous briefing the very question of his life and death will be impacted by the results of the Petitioners' investigation.

[AUTHOR'S COMMENT: Robins's argument is irrelevant but revealing of hoax motive: the thrust always seemed to establish long-discredited pretender, "Brushy Bill" Roberts as Billy the Kid - and give him the pardon. Robins, throughout the Billy the Kid Case, gave hints of being a "Brushy" believer.]

B. *The Planned Request For Pardon Confers Standing Here*

Undersigned counsel intends to ask Governor Richardson that he pardon Billy the Kid for the murder conviction of Sheriff Brady on several known bases including the fact that then Territorial Governor Lew Wallace reneged on his promise to pardon the Kid.

[AUTHOR'S COMMENT: Here it comes, folks. This is the leap that finally cracked the hoax for me. See that Robins seemed to be talking about the pardon for Billy Bonney. He will immediately segue into the pretenders - as if one is really Billy. So the pardon he is discussing is not for the real Billy at all! That switcheroo is followed by his irrelevant and meaningless legal blather.]

There were at least two individuals that laid claim to Billy the Kid's identity years after his alleged shooting by Garrett. **Both of them apparently led long and peaceful and crime-free lives.** [author's boldface]

As was recently recognized by the court in *Mestiza v. DeLeon*, 8 S.W. 3d 770 (Tx. Ct. App. - Corpus Christi - (1999) this interest is sufficient to properly confer standing. There an inmate imprisoned on murder conviction sought the exhumation of the victim's body on the basis that the exhumation could lead to new evidence to support a habeas corpus claim. While not deciding the merits, the Texas court determined that the inmate's interest in showing the improper conviction was sufficient to confer standing. That certainty is an analogous situation here.

The reasons that the exhumation is sought is to disinter the remains of Billy the Kid's mother for the extraction of Mitochondrial DNA.

As such, Ms. Antrim presents the only source of such DNA. Should the exhumation be denied, Billy the Kid will be forever denied the opportunity to make use of modern technology to shed light on his life and death.

> [AUTHOR'S COMMENT: Do not miss that the issue here is merely an argument for a Billy the Kid pretender: namely that Billy's death is in question. Omitted is that there exists no historical reason for doubt Billy's killing by Pat Garrett.]

Should the DNA extracted from Ms. Antrim confirm that one of the potential Kids was in fact Billy the Kid, undersigned counsel will be able to make an even stronger argument for pardon by citing to the long years of law abiding life. [author's boldface]

> [AUTHOR'S COMMENT: **HERE IS THE SENTENCE THAT CRACKED THE BILLY THE KID CASE HOAX.** And here is the almost full-blown hoax plot: prove a pretender by faking DNA, then pardon him: "Oliver "Brushy Bill" Roberts - as THE Billy the Kid.]

C. A Comparison of Interests

This Court has allowed the intervention of the Town of Silver City in this matter. The municipal politicians there have apparently authorized the Town's Mayor to oppose the exhumation. Billy the Kid acknowledges the existence of case law that accords standing to the owners of the cemetery concerned in such proceedings.

> [AUTHOR'S COMMENT: Do not miss Robins's sly and crazy switch from "Billy the Kid's estate" to channeling dead Billy, who is now speaking along with him - in apparent legal agreement!]

What is of interest here, is that such standing is often given to the cemetery owner because it may be the only entity that can represent the wishes of the deceased, an element typically considered in whether to order an exhumation. *Theodore*, 57 N.M. at 438, *Estate of Conroy*, 530 A2d 212, 530 N.Y. S.2d 668 (N.Y.Super. 1988)

As expected, the Mayor here opposes the exhumation and is positioned to present evidence in support of its objection. Whether or not that truly represents the interests of Ms. Antrim can never be known. Given the identity of the decedent and the time that has passes since her death, the Mayor cannot possibly have any direct evidence of Ms. Antrim's wishes. As such, the evidence that is presented by the Mayor can be viewed as best, supposition, or at worst, utterly unreliable.

> [AUTHOR'S COMMENT: Do not miss the bizarreness of this argument. In the real world, the Mayor is obligated to protect the remains in the cemetery under his authority. However, according to Robins, the Mayor actually needs to mind-read corpse Catherine to find out if she really really wants to be dug up. Or better, Robins implies, the Mayor should channel her, like Robins does Billy, so she could speak her mind right in Court!]

One is left to question why such a party with such a remote interest and lack of express knowledge about the decedent's wishes is conferred standing while the interests of Billy the Kid go unheard if this Court denier him standing. Allowing such a party to appear and present evidence while denying the same opportunity to a party that has been appointed to represent the interests of the decedent's son does not seem prudent nor fair.

> [AUTHOR'S COMMENT: This argument is so crazy that a reader might be tempted to rationalize that it cannot be as crazy as it sounds.
> Robins is saying that dead Billy has more credibility to let his wishes be known, than the live Mayor whose obligation it is to protect the cemetery.
> And by the way, Robins himself can tell the exact wishes of the dead, unlike the more limited Mayor.
> And also, by the way, this adds up to corpse Billy the Kid having standing - better justification to speak in Court than the Silver City Mayor!]

Point Four
The *Telfer* Case and Impact on This Case

The *Telfer* case is of no major consequence here.

[AUTHOR'S COMMENT: This statement is evidence that Robins has nerve as well as nuttiness. The *Telfer* case was fatal to the Catherine Antrim exhumation for two reasons. First, the blocked exhumation attempt on the Billy the kid grave of Lois Telfer from 1961 to 1962, established precedent for that grave being permanently blocked because of uncertain location and risk of disturbing remains. Second, the Catherine Antrim exhumation intended to match remains to that grave. Being blocked, it removed the need to exhume her. And the pretenders did not need to be exhumed to prove that they were not Billy - their non-matching histories and preposterous tales alone undid them. And, in what follows, Robins conceals all that.]

First, since neither of the parties here were parties there, the doctrines of res judica and collateral estoppel cannot possibly apply against the current litigants. *Brantley Farms v. Carlsbad Irrigation District*, 124 N.M. 698, 702, 954 p.2d 763 (1998).

Second, the body sought to be exhumed there was the purported body of Billy the Kid and not the subject of this request, his mother. Third, the basis for the request was that the Ft. Sumner burial site had been abandoned and not maintained for years. The petitioner's desire was to re-inter the body in a "decent and respectable burial place" in Lincoln, New Mexico. The factual and legal matters there are thus distinct to those here. That one was denied cannot serve to prohibit the exhumation of the other.

The opponents of exhumation may rely on the *Telfer* court's finding that "it is no longer possible to locate the site of the grave of the said William H. Bonney" as a means to argue that the exhumation of Ms. Antrim for DNA would be futile. Even if such a factual finding was true and correct the technology available now as opposed to 1962 is such that a new factual inquiry would be likely to yield different results.

263

[AUTHOR'S COMMENT: This argument about "new technology" is misstatement. Technology cannot show where Billy Bonney himself rests in the Fort Sumner cemetery. Technology cannot prevent disturbing overlapping remains of Charles Bowdre or other unknown remains. But more to the point, there is no need for exhumation, since the premise that Billy was not killed by Pat Garrett is false.]

Even if the body buried in Ft., Sumner cannot possibly be exhumed for comparable DNA, a denial here is not called for. As has been mentioned there are at least two other individuals who claim to have been the Kid. Surely *Telfer* would not be a binding precedent to deny exhumations of grave sites in Texas or Arizona.

[AUTHOR'S COMMENT: Robins is back on track to his real goal: getting to the pretender graves. But his argument makes no sense. Why should Catherine Antrim be dug up to compare withy crazy old coots who can easily be debunked historically?]

Point Five
Exhumation is Proper

The Sheriffs invoke the jurisdiction of this Court in an attempt to exhume the remains of Catherine Antrim. The Court has express statutory authority to so order. It is a crime in New Mexico to knowingly and willfully disturb or remove remains of any person interred in a cemetery. 1978 NMSA, § 30-12-12. The criminal statute, however, recognizes three exceptions. Disinterment is allowed "pursuant to an order of the district court, the provisions of Section 24-14-23 NMSA 1978 or as otherwise permitted by law." This request falls into the first and last exceptions.

[AUTHOR'S COMMENT: By the time of this Brief, Robins must be aware that the exhumation is being blocked by the Office of the Medical Investigator, and that Attorney Sherry Tippett had lied about getting its permission. He is, thus. attempting to get the court to act independently of the OMI.]

264

The leading exhumation case in New Mexico is *Theodore*, 57, N.M. 434 and sets forth as follows:

[AUTHOR'S COMMENT: The *Theodore* case, whose description follows, has to do with <u>digging up and relocating</u> a body - absolutely noting to do with the Antrim exhumation at hand.].

> In determining whether authority to disinter a body **and bury it elsewhere** should be granted, controlling consideration seems generally to be given by the courts to the following factors, (1) the interest of the public; (2) wishes of the decedent; (3) rights and feelings of those entitled to be heard by reason of relationship; (4) the rights and principles of religious bodies or other organizations which granted the right to inter the body in the first place of burial, and (5) the question of whether or not consent was given to the burial in the first place of interment by the one claiming the right of removal.

(emphasis added).

The bolded language is important because it shows that *Theodore* is not directly on point.

[AUTHOR'S COMMENT: More than "not on point," it is totally irrelevant - which Robins next blithely admits himself. Apparently, however, he needed filler, since he lacks arguments or precedents for representing a corpse as his sole client, digging up someone else for no reason, and having no standing to even be in court for himself or dead Billy.].

The exhumation there was for the purpose of moving remains from one grave site (preferred by the decedent's brother) to another site (preferred by the plaintiff's widow). That is not the case here. Petitioners asking for an exhumation that is of importance in their investigation surrounding the Lincoln County Wars [sic] and the shooting of Billy the Kid.

The distinction renders some of the *Theodore* factors of no consequence and the others of limited precedential value. Since the Ms. Antrim remains will be replaced in the same burial site, the 4th and 5th factor, which involves the decedent's ties to the "first place of burial" sought to be abandoned are of no consequence here. The first three factors remain.

1st Factor Public Interest, Billy the Kid's name is forever tied to New Mexico and to that of another legendary figure of the Old West, Sheriff Pat Garrett. A commonly held version of history paints a picture of an ambush in which Garrett killed the Kid in Ft. Sumner where most believe the Kid still lies at rest. This version has been questioned. It is the investigation into whether Garrett killed the Kid that has prompted these investigators to seek exhumation.

> [AUTHOR'S COMMENT: This is pure hoaxer illogic. The only ones to "question" history are the hoaxers themselves for their stunt. There is no "public interest" - meaning value - there is only the self-serving motives of the hoaxers.]

2nd Factor, the Decedents wishes. In spite of Silver City's position to the contrary, we simply do not know what the decedent's wishes would be. Given the present circumstances, however, where her remains could possibly provide critical evidence to be used by modern day advocates to clear her son's name, one might easily surmise that Silver City's dogged attempt to resist exhumation would not be appreciated by Ms. Antrim.

> [AUTHOR'S COMMENT: This is Robins at his most slippery. First of all, he is now near-channeling Catherine Antrim to express "her wishes." Secondly he is misstating Silver City's position. The Mayor has standing not to guess "wishes," but to protect the sanctity of her grave from exactly the groundless

publicity stunt that the hoax represents. Thirdly, Robins is floating pure hoaxer illogic. The only ones "questioning" history are the hoaxers themselves for their stunt. There is no "public interest" - meaning value - there is only the self-serving motives of the hoaxers. Fourthly, is the most outrageous thrust: that Catherine Antrim would want to be dug up to "prove" that he son was the old and crazy faker "Brushy Bill."]

3rd Factor, Surviving Relatives Wishes. There are no relatives of Ms. Antrim currently before the Court. This Court can take judicial notice from the *Telfer* case, that at least one of her claimed relatives was not adverse to the concept of exhumation since the disinterment of Billy the Kid was sought in 1962 [sic - 1961, denied in 1962]

[AUTHOR'S COMMENT: Robins is omitting that Lois Telfer was never established as kin to Billy the Kid. And no opinion was expressed by her as the exhuming Catherine Antrim anyway - faked kinship notwithstanding.]

The closest party currently before the Court is in fact Billy the Kid as represented by the undersigned counsel. As is apparent from the arguments set forth in this brief, the kid's [sic] interests would be furthered by the exhumation.

[AUTHOR'S COMMENT: Here it is again folks. Robins is channeling - without shame - dead Billy to say that HE wants his mom dug up!]

The "limitation of "currently before the Court" was used above because of undersigned counsel is aware of certain individuals who claim to be related to Ms. Antrim who at worst will likely testify in support of exhumation and may even attempt to intervene in this matter.

[AUTHOR'S COMMENT: Robins is apparently referring to Elbert Garcia (who was included in the list of those receiving a copy of this brief, but was called "Albert), a Santa Rosa, New Mexico, resident who wrote an incoherent book claiming that his grandmother, Abrana Garcia, had an illegitimate child fathered by Billy. And he believes he is the descendant of that man. But Bert Garcia has never done the more obvious exhumation to explore his hopes for a more exciting family tree: exhuming Abrana's husband, his putative grandfather. Bert Garcia adds to his silliness, by having photos in his book of things left to the family by Billy. Among them is a bolo tie; the bolo being invented in 1940!]

Billy the Kid believes that the evidence adduced at the exhumation hearing will certainly support an order of exhumation here.

[AUTHOR'S COMMENT: Oops, Robins has crossed into the "Exorcist" movie's territory. He has "disappeared" as an entity; only dead Billy is talking now. The creepy thought is that Robins not be faking. He may really think he IS "Brushy Bill" incarnate.]

As such, Billy the Kid's mother's name, will forever be tied with other famous names and legendary figures: Czar Nicholas II of Russia and his family, John Paul Jones, President Zachary Taylor, Jesse James, Butch Cassidy and the Sundance Kid. All these individuals were themselves exhumed for various reasons. Other lesser known, or perhaps less colorful figures, have also been exhumed. They include Samuel Mudd (conspirator in the assassination of Abraham Lincoln), Haile Selassie (former emperor of Ethiopia), Czar Lazar (14th century Serbian monarch), Medgar Evers (civil rights leader), Carl A. Weiss (alleged assassin of Huey Long). Those whose exhumation has been proposed at various times in the past include, Meriwether Lewis. John Wilkes Booth, John F. Kennedy, Lee Harvey Oswald and J. Edgar Hoover.

[AUTHOR'S COMMENT: Just because other name-recognition people have been exhumed (some for the same type of frivolous publicity stunt being tried here), is irrelevant to exhuming Catherine Antrim for no reason. In fact, one is left with a suspicion that other corpses, here listed, fell victim to the same senseless desecration and selfish profit being attempted by Robins and the other hoaxers. One can also

268

contemplate that for some of the poor bunch of bodies above, no one cared enough about their dignity to protect them from their own attacks of shovels.]

Clearly, exhumation as a truth seeking device has been used throughout history. Exhumation has also been the subject of case law and legal discourse. See, 61 U. Colo.L.Rev. 567, Evidentiary Autopsies, 1990; 21 A.L.R.2d. 538, *Annotation*, Power of a Court to Order Disinterment and Autopsy or Exhumation for Evidential Purpose in a Civil Case."

> [AUTHOR'S COMMENT: Again Robins is using irrelevant legal precedent. First of all, this is allegedly a criminal murder case, not a civil one. More important, the murder case is a groundless hoax: there is no matter to solve. Billy was killed, not an innocent victim to allow Robin's fantasized "Brushy" to live on.]

The current state of knowledge and technology, and its expected refinement and expansion, will likely make it even more of a common occurrence in the future. It is proper to allow such an inquiry here.

III. CONCLUSION

The foregoing has established that the undersigned counsel may legally and properly appear in these proceedings on behalf of, and to represent the interests of Billy the Kid. They are ready to present testimony and evidence to further support their interests that the exhumation of the Kid's mother, Ms. Catherine Antrim be allowed to proceed.

> [AUTHOR'S COMMENT: Only in his fevered and delusional "Brushy Bill" dreams, has Robins established anything at all "legal" to justify being in Court and channeling dead Billy. One is left with the eerily echoing "They are ready ..." Are "they" Robins and his dead buddy Ollie Roberts (creepily as Billy), or just Robins and his co-counsel, David Sandoval - present with his New Mexico law license and signature because Robins had just a Texas one?]

Respectfully submitted this _5th_ day of January, 2004.

Heard, Robins, Cloud, Lubel & Greenwood, L.L.P.

By: _David Sandoval_

Bill Robins III

David Sandoval

Address and Telephone Numbers

ATTORNEYS FOR BILLY THE KID

[AUTHOR'S COMMENT: Really - in boldface, Robins and Sandoval are listed as Billy's lawyers! And New Mexico taxpayers footed the district court bill for these hoaxing antics.]

SOURCES

ANNOTATED BIBLIOGRAPHY

FOR HISTORY OF BILLY THE KID AND THE LINCOLN COUNTY WAR

GLOBAL HISTORICAL REFERENCES FOR BILLY THE KID AND THE LINCOLN COUNTY WAR

Nolan, Frederick. *The Lincoln County War: A Documentary History.* Norman: University of Oklahoma Press. 1992.
_____. *The West of Billy the Kid.* Norman: University of Oklahoma Press. 1998.

GLOBAL HISTORICAL REFERENCES FOR WILLIAM HENRY BONNEY ("BILLY THE KID")

AUTHORSHIP / TESTIMONY / INTERVIEWS

HOYT BILL OF SALE

Bonney, W H. "Know all persons by these presents ..." (for Henry Hoyt). Thursday, October 24, 1878. Collection of Panhandle-Plains Historical Museum, Canyon, Texas. (Item No. X1974-98/1)

LETTERS TO LEW WALLACE

Bonney, W H. "I have heard you will give one thousand $ dollars for my body which as I see it means alive ..." March 13 (?), 1879. Fray Angélico Chávez Historical Library, Santa Fe, New Mexico. Lincoln County Heritage Trust Collection. (AC481).
_____. "I will keep the keep the appointment ..." March 20, 1879. Indiana Historical Society. Lew Wallace Collection. M0292.
_____. "... on the Pecos." ("Billie" letter fragment). March 24 (?), 1879. Indiana Historical Society. M0292.
_____. "I noticed in the Las Vegas Gazette a piece which stated that 'Billy the Kid' ..." December 12, 1880. Indiana Historical Society. Lew Wallace Collection. M0292.
_____. "I would like to see you ..." January 1, 1881. Indiana Historical Society. Lew Wallace Collection. M0292.
_____. "I wish you would come down to the jail and see me ..." March 2, 1881. Fray Angélico Chávez Historical Library, Santa Fe, New Mexico. Lincoln County Heritage Trust Collection. (AC481).

_____. "I wrote you a little note day before yesterday ..." March 4, 1881. Indiana Historical Society. Lew Wallace Collection. M0292.
_____. "For the last time I ask ..." March 27, 1881. Indiana Historical Society. Lew Wallace Collection. M0292.

LETTER TO JOHN "SQUIRE" WILSON

Bonney, W H. "Friend Wilson ..." March 20, 1879. Indiana Historical Society. Lew Wallace Collection. M0292.

LETTER TO EDGAR CAYPLESS

Bonney, W. H. "I would have written before ..." April 15, 1881. Copy in William Kelleher's *Violence in Lincoln County;* originally reproduced in Griggs *History of the Mesilla Valley.* **(Original is lost)**

LETTER (POSSIBLY DICTATED) FOR EDGAR WALZ

Regulator. "Mr. Walz. Sir ..." Letter to Edgar Walz. July 13, 1878. Adjutant General's Office. File 1405 AGO 1878. (Quoted in Maurice Garland Fulton, *History of the Lincoln County War.* Tucson: University of Arizona Press. 1975. pages 246-247, and Frederick Nolan, *The Lincoln County War: A Documentary History*, page 310.)

NEWSPAPER INTERVIEWS (CHRONOLOGICAL)

Wilcox, Lucius "Lute" M. (city editor, owner, J.H. Koogler). "The Kid. Interview with Billy Bonney The Best Known Man in New Mexico." Las Vegas *Gazette.* December 28, 1880. **(Has quote about "the laugh's on me this time")**
_____. Interview, at train depot. Las Vegas *Gazette.* December 28, 1880. **(Has "adios" quote)**
No Author. "At least two hundred men have been killed in Lincoln County during the past three years ..." Santa Fe *Daily New Mexican.* March 28, 1881.
No Author. "Something About the Kid." Santa Fe *Daily New Mexican.* April 3, 1881. **(With quotes "this is the man" and "two hundred men have been killed ... he did not kill all of them")**
No Author. "I got a rough deal ..." *Mesilla News.* April 15, 1881.
Newman, Simon N. Ed. Interview with "The Kid." *Newman's Semi-Weekly.* April 15, 1881.
_____ . Departure from Mesilla. *Newman's Semi-Weekly.* April 15, 1881.
No Author. "Advise persons never to engage in killing." *Mesilla News.* April 16, 1881.

TESTIMONY

Angel, Frank Warner. *In the Matter of the Examination of the Causes and Circumstances of the Death of John H. Tunstall a British Subject.* Report filed October 4, 1878. Angel Report. Microfilm File Case Number 44-4-8-3. Record Group 060. Microfilm No. M750. Roll 1. National Archives and Records Administration. U. S. Department of Justice. Washington, D.C. **(Deposition of William H. Bonney. June 8, 1878. Pages 314-319)**
No Author. *Dudley Court of Inquiry. (May 2, 1879 - July 5, 1879).* 16W3/16/28/6. Boxes 1923-1923A. File Number QQ1284. National Archives and Records Administration. Old Military and Civil Branch. Records of the Office of the Judge Advocate General. Washington, D.C. **(Testimony of William H. Bonney. May 28 and 29, 1879)**

WILLIAM BONNEY BIOGRAPHICAL BOOKS

Abbott, E.C. ("Teddy Blue") and Helena Huntington Smith. *We Pointed Them North: Recollections of a Cowpuncher.* Norman, Oklahoma: University of Oklahoma Press. 1955. (**Billy the Kid's multiculturalism, Page 47**)

Anaya, Paco. *I Buried Billy.* College Station, Texas: Creative Publishing Company. 1991.

Ball, Eve. *Ma'am Jones of the Pecos.* Tucson: University of Arizona Press. 1969.

Bell, Bob Boze. *The Illustrated Life and Times of Billy the Kid.* Cave Creek, Arizona: Boze Books. 1992. (Frank Coe quote about the Kid's cartridge use, page 45.)

Bell, Bob Boze. *The Illustrated Life and Times of Billy the Kid.* Second Edition. Phoenix, Arizona: Tri Star-Boze Publications, Inc. 1996.

Burns, Walter Noble. *The Saga of Billy the Kid.* Stamford, Connecticut: Longmeadow Press. 1992. (Original printing: 1926, Doubleday)

_____. "*I also know that the Kid and Paulita were sweethearts.*" Unpublished letter to Jim East. June 3, 1926. Robert N. Mullin Collection. File RNM, IV, NM, 116-117. Nita Stewart Haley Memorial Museum, Haley Library. Midland, Texas.

Coroner's Jury Report for William Bonney. July 15, 1881. (Copy) Herman Weisner Collection. Lincoln County Papers. New Mexico State University Library at Las Cruces. Rio Grande Historical Society Collection. Box No. 1. Folder Name: Billy the Kid Legal Documents. Folder No. 14C. 26.

Garrett, Pat F. *The Authentic Life of Billy the Kid The Noted Desperado of the Southwest, Whose Deeds of Daring and Blood Made His Name a Terror in New Mexico, Arizona, and Northern Mexico.* Santa Fe, New Mexico: New Mexico Printing and Publishing Co. 1882. (Reprint used: New York: Indian Head Books. 1994.)

Hendron, J. W. *The Story of Billy the Kid. New Mexico's Number One Desperado.* New York: Indian Head Books. 1994.

Jacobsen, Joel. *Such Men as Billy the Kid. The Lincoln County War Reconsidered.* Lincoln and London: University of Nebraska Press. 1994.

Kadlec, Robert F. *They "Knew" Billy the Kid. Interviews with Old-Time New Mexicans.* Santa Fe, New Mexico: Ancient City Press. 1987.

Keleher, William A. *Violence in Lincoln County 1869-1881.* Albuquerque, New Mexico: University of New Mexico Press. 1957. (**Pardon agreement: Pages 212, 216, 335; comparison with Wallace: Page 221; Court of Inquiry testimony: Page 233; Las Vegas *Gazette* article of December 28, 1880, "The Kid. Interview with Billy Bonney The Best Known Man in New Mexico": Pages 293-295; Las Vegas *Gazette* article of December 28, 1880. Untitled - at train station. Pages 296-297; great escape: Page 333**)

McFarland, David F. Reverend. *Ledger: Session Records 1867-1874. Marriages in Santa Fe New Mexico. "Mr. William H. Antrim and Mrs. Catherine McCarty." March 1, 1873.* (Unpublished). Santa Fe, New Mexico: First Presbyterian Church of Santa Fe.

Meadows, John P., Ed. John P. Wilson. *Pat Garrett and Billy the Kid as I Knew Them: Reminiscences of John P. Meadows.* Albuquerque: University of New Mexico Press. 2004.

Mullin, Robert N. *The Boyhood of Billy the Kid.* Monograph 17, Southwestern Studies 5(1). El Paso, Texas: Texas Western Press. University of Texas at El Paso. 1967.

Poe, John W. *The Death of Billy the Kid.* (Introduction by Maurice Garland Fulton). Boston and New York: Houghton Mifflin Company. 1933.

_____. "The Killing of Billy the Kid." (a personal letter written at Roswell, New Mexico to Mr. Charles Goodnight, Goodnight P.C., Texas) July 10, 1917. Earle Vandale Collection. 1813-946. No. 2H475. Center for American History. University of Texas at Austin.

Rakocy, Bill. *Billy the Kid.* El Paso, Texas: Bravo Press. 1985.

Rasch, Phillip J. *Trailing Billy the Kid.* Laramie, Wyoming: National Association for
Outlaw and Lawman History, Inc. with University of Wyoming. 1995.
Russell, Randy. *Billy the Kid. The Story - The Trial.* Lincoln, New Mexico:
The Crystal Press. 1994.
Siringo, Charles A. *The History of Billy the Kid.* Santa Fe: New Mexico. (Privately
Printed) 1920.
Tuska, Jon. *Billy the Kid. His Life and Legend.* Westport, Connecticut: Greenwood
Press. 1983.
Utley, Robert M. *Billy the Kid. A Short and Violent Life.* Lincoln and London:
University of Nebraska Press. 1989.
Weddle, Jerry. *Antrim is My Stepfather's Name. The Boyhood of Billy the Kid.*
Monograph 9, Globe, Arizona: Arizona Historical Society. 1993. (**Quotes from
Mary Richards about Billy on Pages 19-20**)
Wild, Azariah F. "Daily Reports of U. S. Secret Service Agents, Azariah F. Wild."
Microfilm T-915. Record Group 87. Rolls 306 (June 15, 1877 - December 31, 1877),
307 (January 1,1878 - June 30, 1879), 308 (July 1, 1879 - June 30, 1881), 309
(July 1, 1881 - September 30, 1883), 310 (October 1, 1883 - July 31, 1886).
National Archives and Records Department. Department of the Treasury. United
States Secret Service. Washington, D. C.
No Author. "The Prisoners Who Saw the Kid Kill Olinger." Herman Weisner Collection.
Accession No. MS249. Lincoln County Papers. New Mexico State University
Library at Las Cruces. Rio Grande Historical Collections. Box No. 30. Folder
Name: The Prisoners who saw the Kid Kill Olinger. Box No. T-8.

WILLIAM BONNEY BIOGRAPHICAL
NEWSPAPER ARTICLES (CHRONOLOGICAL)

No Author. Grant County *Herald.* May 10, 1879. Results of the Lincoln County Grand
Jury. (**Also published in the Mesilla** *Thirty Four.* **Confirmation of the
William Bonney testimony and James Dolan and Billy Campbell murder
indictments, from page 224 of William Keleher,** *Violence in Lincoln
County.*)
No Author. Editorial. "Powerful Gang of Outlaws Harassing the Stockman." Las Vegas
Gazette. December 3, 1880. (**Condemnation of William Bonney as an outlaw
leader; and resulting, according to William Keleher, who quotes it in his**
Violence in Lincoln County, **on Pages 286-288, as motivating Bonney's
response letter of December 12, 1880 to Governor Lew Wallace**)
Wallace, Lew. "Billy the Kid: $500 Reward." December 22, 1880. Las Vegas *Gazette.*
No Author. "A Big Haul! Billy Kid, Dave Rudabaugh, Billy Wilson and Tom Pickett in
the Clutches of the Law." *The Las Vegas Daily Optic.* Monday, December 27, 1880.
Vol. 2, No. 45. Page 4, Column 2.
No Author. "Outlaws of New Mexico. The Exploits of a Band Headed by a New York
Youth. The Mountain Fastness of the Kid and His Followers - War Against a Gang
of Cattle Thieves and Murderers - The Frontier Confederates of Brockway, the
Counterfeiter." *The Sun.* New York. December 22, 1880. Vol. XLVIII, No. 118,
Page 3, Columns 1-2.
No Author. " 'The Kid.' The greatest excitement prevailed yesterday when the news
was abroad that Pat Garrett and Frank Stewart had arrived in town bringing
with them Billy 'the Kid.' " Las Vegas *Gazette.* December 27, 1880.
Wilcox, Lucius "Lute" M. "Interview With The Kid." *Las Vegas Gazette.* December 28,
1880.(From "Billy the Kid: Las Vegas Newspaper Accounts of His Career, 1880-
1881." W.M. Morrison – Books, Waco, Texas. 1958.) (**With "laugh's on me"
quote, and mention of the dead horse blocking escape at Stinking
Springs**)

No Author. "A Bay-Mare. Everyone who has heard of Billy 'the kid' has heard of his beautiful bay mare." *Las Vegas Morning Gazette.* Tuesday, January 4, 1881.

No Author. "The Kid. Billy 'the Kid' and Billy Wilson were on Monday taken to Mesilla for Trial." *Las Vegas Morning Gazette.* Tuesday, March 15, 1881.

Newman, Simon. "In the Name of Justice! In the Case of Billy Kid." *Newman's Semi-Weekly.* Saturday, April 2, 1881.

No Author. "Billy the Kid. Seems to be having a stormy journey on his trip Southward." *Las Vegas Morning Gazette.* Tuesday, April 5, 1881.

Koogler, J. H. "Interview with Governor Lew Wallace on 'The Kid.'" *Las Vegas Gazette.* April 28, 1881.

No Author. "The Kid." *Santa Fe Daily New Mexican.* May 1, 1881. Vol. X, No. 32, Page 1, Column 2.

No Author. "Billy Bonney. Advices from Lincoln bring the intelligence of the escape of 'Billy the Kid.'" *Las Vegas Daily Optic.* Monday, May 2, 1881.

No Author. "The Kid's Escape." *Santa Fe Daily New Mexican.* Tuesday Morning, May 3, 1881. Vol. X, No. 33, Page 1, Column 2.

Wallace, Lew. "Billy the Kid. $500 Reward." *Daily New Mexican.* May 3, 1881. Vol. X, No. 33, Page 1, Column 3.

No Author. "Dare Devil Desperado. Pursuit of 'Billy the Kid' has been abandoned." *Las Vegas Daily Optic.* May 4, 1881.

No Author. "More Killing by Kid." Editorial. *Santa Fe Daily New Mexican.* Wednesday Morning, May 4, 1881. Vol. X, No. 34, Page 1, Column 2.

No Author. "Kid was then in Albuquerque ..." *Santa Fe Daily New Mexican.* May 5, 1881. Page 4, Column 1.

No Author. "The question if how to deal with desperados who commit murder has but one solution - kill them." *Las Vegas Daily Optic.* Tuesday, May 10, 1881.

No Author. "Billy 'the Kid.'" Las Vegas *Gazette.* Thursday, May 12, 1881.

No Author. "The Kid was in Chloride City ..." *Santa Fe Daily New Mexican.* May 13, 1881. Page 4, Column 3.

No Author. "Billy 'the Kid' is in the vicinity of Sumner." Las Vegas *Gazette.* Sunday, May 15, 1881.

No Author. "The Kid is believed to be in the Black Range ..." *Santa Fe Daily New Mexican.* May 19, 1881. Page 4, Column 1.

No Author. "Billy the Kid was last seen in Lincoln County ..." *Santa Fe Daily New Mexican.* May 19, 1881. Page 4, Column 1.

No Author. " 'Billy the Kid' has been heard from again." *Las Vegas Daily Optic.* Friday, June 10, 1881.

No Author. " 'Billy the Kid.' He is Reported to Have Been Seen on Our Streets Saturday Night." *Las Vegas Daily Optic.* Monday Evening, June 13, 1881. Vol. 2, No. 188, Page 4, Column 2.

Wilcox, Lute, Ed. "Billy the Kid would make an ideal newspaper-man in that he always endeavors to 'get even' with his enemies." *Las Vegas Daily Optic.* Monday Evening, June 13, 1881. Vol. 2, No. 188, Page 4, Column 1.

No Author. "Land of the Petulant Pistol. 'Billy the Kid' as a Killer." *Las Vegas Daily Optic.* Wednesday Evening, June 15, 1881. Vol. 2, No. 190.

No Author. "Barney Mason at Fort Sumner states the 'Kid' is in Local Sheep Camps." *Las Vegas Morning Gazette.* June 16, 1881.

No Author. "The Kid." *Santa Fe Daily New Mexican.* June 16, 1881. Vol. X, No. 90, Page 4, Column 2.

No Author. "Billy the Kid." *Las Vegas Daily Optic.* Thursday, June 28, 1881.

No Author. " 'The Kid' Killed." *Las Vegas Daily Optic.* July 18. 1881.

Wallace, Lew. "Old Incident Recalled," *The* (Crawfordsville) *Weekly News-Review,* December 20, 1901. Lew Wallace Collection. Indiana Historical Society. MO292.

_____. "General Lew Wallace Writes a Romance of 'Billy the Kid' Most Famous Bandit of the Plains: Thrilling Story of the Midnight Meeting Between Gen Wallace, Then Governor of New Mexico, and the Notorious Outlaw, in a

Lonesome Hut in Santa Fe." *New York World Magazine.* Sunday, June 8, 1902. Indiana Historical Society. Lew Wallace Collection. MO292.

LEW WALLACE WRITINGS ABOUT/TO WILLIAM BONNEY

LETTERS (CHRONOLOGICAL)

Wallace, Lew. Letter to W H. Bonney. "Come to the house of Squire Wilson ..." March 15, 1879. Indiana Historical Society. Lew Wallace Collection. MO292. Box 4. Folder 6.

_____. Letter to W. H. Bonney. "The escape makes no difference in arrangements ..." March 20, 1879. Indiana Historical Society. Lew Wallace Collection. MO292. Box 4. Folder 6.

_____. Letter to Carl Schurz. "A precious specimen named 'The Kid,' whom the sheriff is holding ..." March 28, 1879. Letters to Carl Schurz. Herman Weisner Collection. Lincoln County Papers. New Mexico State University Library at Las Cruces. Rio Grande Historical Collections. Box No. 7. Folder Name: Interior Dept. 1851 1914. Folder No. L2. From Department of the Interior, Washington, D. C. Territorial Papers, M-364. Group 48. Roll 8.

_____. Letter to Carl Schurz. "A precious specimen nick-named 'The Kid'." March 31, 1879. Indiana Historical Society. Lew Wallace Collection. MO292. Box 4. Folder 1.

_____. Request for draft of "Billy the Kid" $500 Reward Proclamation. December 13, 1880. Herman Weisner Collection. Lincoln County Papers. New Mexico State University Library at Las Cruces. Rio Grande Historical Collections. Box No. 13. Folder Name: Wallace, Gov. N. M. Box No. W3. From Lew Wallace Papers. New Mexico State Records Center. Santa Fe, New Mexico.

INTERVIEW NOTES

Wallace, Lew. "Statements by Kid, made Sunday night March 23, 1879." March 23, 1879. Indiana Historical Society. Lew Wallace Collection. M0922. Box 4. Folder 7.

DEATH WARRANT FOR WILLIAM BONNEY

Wallace, Lew. "To the Sheriff of Lincoln County, Greeting ..." April 30, 1881. Indiana Historical Society. Lew Wallace Collection. M0292. Box 9, Folder 11.

REWARD NOTICES

Wallace, Lew. "Billy the Kid: $500 Reward." Las Vegas *Gazette.* December 22, 1880.

_____. "Billy the Kid. $500 Reward." May 3, 1881. *Daily New Mexican.* Vol. X, No. 33. Page 1, Column 3.

REWARD POSTERS

Greene, Chas. W. "To the New Mexican Printing and Publishing Company." May 20, 1881. (Bill sent to Lew Wallace for printing reward posters for "Kid"). Indiana Historical Society. Lew Wallace Collection. M0292. Box 4, Folder 18.

_____. "I enclose a bill ..." Letter to Lew Wallace for "Kid" wanted posters. June 2, 1881. Indiana Historical Society. Lew Wallace Collection. M0292. Box 4, Folder 18.

ARTICLES (CHRONOLOGICAL)

"Wallace's Words ..." (interview with Lew Wallace in Washington, D.C. on January 3, 1881), Chicago *The Daily Inter Ocean*, January 4, 1881, Page 2, Column 4.

(Richard Dunham's May 2, 1881 encounter with Billy the Kid), *Santa Fe Daily New Mexican*, May 5, 1881, Page 4, Column 3.

(O.L. Houghton's Conversation with Lew Wallace, before May 26, 1881), *The Las Vegas Daily Optic*, May 26, 1881, Page 4, Column 4.

"Billy the Kid ..." (Lew Wallace interviewed on June 13, 1881), Crawfordsville (Indiana) *Saturday Evening Journal*, June 18, 1881. Indiana Historical Society. Lew Wallace Collection. MO292.

"Street Pickings," *Crawfordsville* (Weekly) *Review - Saturday Edition*, January 6, 1894. Lew Wallace Collection. Indiana Historical Society.

Wallace, Lew. "Old Incident Recalled," *The* (Crawfordsville) *Weekly News-Review*, December 20, 1901. Indiana Historical Society. Lew Wallace Collection. MO292.

_____. "General Lew Wallace Writes a Romance of 'Billy the Kid' Most Famous Bandit of the Plains: Thrilling Story of the Midnight Meeting Between Gen Wallace, Then Governor of New Mexico, and the Notorious Outlaw, in a Lonesome Hut in Santa Fe." *New York World Magazine*. Sunday, June 8, 1902. Page 4. Indiana Historical Society. Lew Wallace Collection. MO292.

OTHER HISTORICAL FIGURES (PERIOD)

ANGEL, FRANK WARNER

PRESIDENT HAYES MEETING

Mullin, Robert N. Re: Frank Warner Angel Meeting With President Hayes August, 1878. Binder RNM, VI, M. (Unpublished). Midland, Texas: Nita Stewart Haley Memorial Library and J. Everts Haley History Center. (Undated).

LETTER

Angel, Frank Warner. "I am in receipt of a copy of a letter sent you by one Wm McMullen ..." Letter to Carl Schurz. September 9, 1878. The Papers of Carl Schurz 1842 - 1906 in 165 Volumes. Library of Congress 1935. General Correspondence July 26, 1878 - October 7, 1878. Shelf Accession No. 14,803. Container 45.

PAPERS

McMullen, William. "In view of the existing troubles in our territory I appeal ..." Letter to Carl Schurz. August 24, 1878. The Papers of Carl Schurz 1842 - 1906 in 165 Volumes. Library of Congress 1935. General Correspondence. July 26, 1878 - October 7, 1878. Shelf Accession No. 14,803. Container 45.

McPherson, Mary E. Letters and Petitions to President Rutherford B. Hayes re: Removal Governor Axtell and the Santa Fe Ring. Frank Warner Angel File. Microfilm File Case Number 44-4-8-3. Record Group 060. Microfilm Roll M750. National Archives and Records Administration. U.S. Department of Justice. Washington, D. C.

REPORTS

Angel, Frank Warner. Examination of charges against F. C. Godfroy, Indian Agent, Mescalero, N. M. October 2, 1878. (Report 1981, Inspector E. C. Watkins; Cited as Watkins Report). M 319-20 and L147, 44-4-8. Record Group 075. National Archives and Records Administration. U. S. Department of Justice. Washington, D. C.

_____. In the Matter of the Examination of the Causes and Circumstances of the Death of John H. Tunstall a British Subject. Report filed October 4, 1878. Angel Report. Microfilm File Case Number 44-4-8-3. Record Group 060. Microfilm No. M750. Roll 1. National Archives and Records Administration. U.S. Department of Justice. Washington, D.C.

_____. In the Matter of the Investigation of the Charges Against S. B. Axtell Governor of New Mexico. Report and Testimony. October 3, 1878. Angel Report. Microfilm Case File No. 44-4-8-3. Record Group 060. Microfilm Roll M750. National Archives and Records Administration. U. S. Department of Interior. Washington, D.C.

_____. In the Matter of the Lincoln County Troubles. To the Honorable Charles Devens, Attorney General. October 4, 1878. Angel Report. Microfilm Case File No. 44-4-8-3. Record Group 060. Microfilm Roll M750. National Archives and Records Administration. U. S. Department of Justice. Washington, D. C.

NOTEBOOK

Theisen, Lee Scott. "Frank Warner Angel's Notes on New Mexico Territory, 1878." *Arizona and the West*, 18 (4) (Winter 1976) 333-370.

AXTELL, SAMUEL BEACH

Angel, Frank Warner. *In the Matter of the Investigation of the Charges Against S. B. Axtell Governor of New Mexico*. Report and Testimony. October 3, 1878. Angel Report. Microfilm Case File No. 44-4-8-3. Record Group 060. Microfilm Roll M750. National Archives and Records Administration. U.S. Department of Interior. Washington, D.C.

_____. "The Honorable C. Schurz ... I enclose copies of letter received by me from Gov. Axtell (marked A) and my reply there to (marked B)." August 24, 1878. Microfilm Roll M750. National Archives and Records Administration Record Group 060. Microfilm Case Number 44-4-8-3. U. S. Department of Interior. Washington D. C.

_____. "The Hon. C. Schurz, Secretary of the Interior, Sir: I have just been favored by a call from W. L. Rynerson Territorial Dist. Attorney 3rd District New Mexico - in the interest of Gov. Axtell." (Letter) September 6, 1878. Microfilm M750. National Archives and Records Administration Record Group 060. Microfilm Case Number 44-4-8-3. U. S. Department of Interior. Washington D. C.

Axtell, Samuel B. "Hon. Carl Schurz. Sir: I have today mailed to you a reply to the charges on file in your Dept against me." (Letter regarding charges in Colfax County). Microfilm Roll M750. National Archives and Records Administration Record Group 060. Microfilm Case Number 44-4-8-3. U.S. Department of Interior. Washington D. C.

_____. "To the President. I am unable to enforce the law ..." (Telegram). March 3, 1878. Microfilm Roll M750. National Archives and Records Administration Record Group 060. Microfilm Case File Number 44-4-8-3. U.S. Department of Interior. Washington D. C.

Bradstreet, George P. "Referring to the nomination of Sam'l B. Axtell of Ohio to be Chief Justice of the Supreme Court of New Mexico ... he is alleged to have been removed by President Hayes ..." (Presentation to the U.S. Senate Chamber). Microfilm Roll M750. National Archives and Records Administration Record Group 060. Microfilm Case Number 44-4-8-3. U.S. Department of Interior. Washington D. C.

Elkins, Stephen B. "To the President. Referring to a conversation had with you last week ... Hon S. Elkins favors appointment Axtell, Ex Gov. as Gov'r of New Mexico". (Letter) March 23, 1881. (Received Executive Mansion April 6, 1881). Microfilm Roll M750. National Archives and Records Administration Record Group 060. Microfilm Case Number 44-4-8-3. U. S. Department of Interior. Washington D. C.

Springer, Frank. "Hon Carl Schurz, Secretary of the Interior. Sir: I endorse herewith, directed to the President charges against S. B. Axtell Governor of New Mexico ..." (Letter) June 10, 1878. Frank Warner Angel File. Microfilm Roll M750. National Archives and Records Administration Record Group 060. Microfilm Case Number 44-4-8-3. U. S. Department of Interior. Washington D. C.

BRADY, WILLIAM

Brady, William. Affidavit of July 2, 1876 concerning appointment as Administrator for the Emil Fritz Estate. Copied from the original District Court Record. (Private collection)
_____. Affidavit of August 22, 1876 documenting business debts to L.G. Murphy and Co. pertaining to the Emil Fritz Estate. Copied from the original District Court Record. (Private collection)
_____. Affidavit of July__, 1876 of Resignation as Emil Fritz Estate Administrator. Copied from the original District Court Record. (Private collection)
_____. Affidavit of August 22, 1876 confirming giving Alexander McSween the books of the L.G. Murphy Company for the purpose of making business debt collections. Copied from the original District Court Record. (Private collection)
_____. "List of Articles Inventoried by Wm Brady sheriff in the suit of Charles Fritz & Emilie Scholand vs A.A. McSween now in the dwelling house belonging to A.A. McSween." (undated) (Private Collection)
Bristol, Warren. "Action of Assumpsit to command Sheriff Brady of Lincoln County to attach goods of Alexander A. McSween." February 7, 1878. District Court Record. (Private Collection)
_____. Preprinted form for "Writ of Attachment" (Printed and sold at the office of the Mesilla News) filled out to command the Sheriff of Lincoln County to attach goods of Alexander McSween for a suit of damages for ten thousand dollars. February 7, 1878. District Court Record. (Private Collection)
Lavash, Donald R. *Sheriff William Brady. Tragic Hero of the Lincoln County War.* Santa Fe, New Mexico: Sunstone Press. 1986.

CASEY FAMILY

Klasner, Lilly. Eve Ball. Ed. *My Girlhood Among Outlaws.* Tucson, Arizona: University of Arizona Press. 1988.

CATRON, THOMAS BENTON

Cleaveland, Norman, *A Synopsis of the Great New Mexico Cover-up.* Self-printed. 1989.
_____ . *The Great Santa Fe Cover-up. Based on a Talk given Before the Santa Fe Historical Society on November 1, 1978.* Self-printed. 1982.

_____. *The Morleys - Young Upstarts on the Southwest Frontier.* Albuquerque, New Mexico: Calvin Horn Publisher, Inc. 1971.

Dunham, Harold H. "New Mexican Land Grants with Special Reference to the Title Papers of the Maxwell Grant." *New Mexico Historical Review.* (January, 1955) Vol. 70. No. 1. pp. 1 - 23.

Hefferan, Vioalle Clark. *Thomas Benton Catron.* Albuquerque, New Mexico: University of New Mexico. Zimmerman Library. Unpublished Thesis for the Degree of Master of Arts. 1940.

Keleher, William A. *The Maxwell Land Grant. A New Mexico Item.* Albuquerque, New Mexico: University of New Mexico Press. 1964.

Lamar, Howard Robert N. *The Far Southwest 1846 - 1912. A Territorial History.* New Haven and London: Yale University Press. 1966.

Montoya, María E. *Translating Property. The Maxwell Land Grant and the Conflict Over Land in the American West, 1840-1900.* Berkeley and Los Angeles: University of California Press. 2002.

Mullin, Robert N. "A Specimen of Catron's Dirty Work. Sworn Affidavit of Samuel Davis." October 1, 1878. Binder RNM IV, EE. (Unpublished). Midland, Texas: Nita Stewart Haley Memorial Library and J. Everts Haley Historical Center.

_____. "Catron Embarrassed Throughout His Life by an Affliction." (Date Unknown). Binder RNM, IV, M. (Unpublished). Midland, Texas: Nita Stewart Haley Memorial Library and J. Everts Haley Historical Center.

_____. Catron letter to Governor S. B. Axtell to intervene in Lincoln County. May 30, 1878. Binder RNM IV, EE (Unpublished). Midland, Texas: Nita Stewart Haley Memorial Library and J. Everts Haley Historical Center.

_____. "Prior to Lincoln County War Catron Had Defended Colonel Dudley." (No Date). Notes from "Lincoln County War Cast of Characters." Midland, Texas: Nita Stewart Haley Memorial Library and J. Everts Haley Historical Center.

Murphy, Lawrence R. *Lucien Bonaparte Maxwell. Napoleon of the Southwest.* Norman: University of Oklahoma Press. 1983.

Pearson, Jim Berry. *The Maxwell Land Grant.* Norman: University of Oklahoma Press. 1961.

Sluga, Mary Elizabeth. *Political Life of Thomas Benton Catron 1896-1912.* Albuquerque, New Mexico: University of New Mexico. Zimmerman Library. Unpublished Thesis for the Degree of Master of Arts. 1941.

Westphall, Victor. "Fraud and Implications of Fraud in the Land Grants of New Mexico." *New Mexico Historical Review.* 1974. Vol. XLIX, No. 3. 189 - 218.

_____. *Thomas Benton Catron and His Era.* Tucson, Arizona: University of Arizona Press. 1973.

Wooden, John Paul. *Thomas Benton Catron and New Mexico Politics 1866-1921.* Albuquerque, New Mexico: University of New Mexico. Zimmerman Library. Unpublished Thesis for the Degree of Master of Arts. 1959.

No Author. Catron Files Statement of Sole ownership of Carrizozo Ranch in Tax Dispute Case. Herman Weisner Collection. Lincoln County Papers: New Mexico State University Library at Las Cruces. Rio Grande Historical Collections. Box No. 2. Folder Name "T. B. Catron Tax Troubles." Folder No. C-8.

CHAPMAN, HUSTON

Chapman, Huston. Letter to Governor Lew. Wallace. November 29, 1878. Herman Weisner Collection. Lincoln County Papers: New Mexico State University Library at Las Cruces. Rio Grande Historical Collections. Box No. 2. Folder Name H. J. Chapman. Box No. C-9.

CHISUM, JOHN SIMPSON

Hinton, Harwood P., Jr. "John Simpson Chisum, 1877-84." *New Mexico Historical Review* 31(3) (July 1956): 177 - 205; 31(4) (October 1956): 310 - 337; 32(1) (January 1957): 53 - 65.
Klasner, Lilly. Eve Ball. Ed. *My Girlhood Among Outlaws.* Tucson, Arizona: The University of Arizona Press. 1988.

COE FAMILY

Coe, George. Doyce B. Nunis, Jr. Ed. *Frontier Fighter. The Autobiography of George Coe Who Fought and Rode With Billy the Kid.* Chicago: R. R. Donnelley and Sons Company. 1984. (**Original copyright, 1934.**) (**Quote about Billy's seeming "college-bred," singing and dancing. Pages 49-50**)
Coe, Frank. "He was a wonder ..." Letter to William Steele Dean. August 3, 1926. Museum of New Mexico History Library. Santa Fe. Unpublished. (Excerpt in Frederick Nolan's *The West of Billy the Kid.* Page 135)
Coe, Wilbur. *Ranch on the Ruidoso. The Story of a Pioneer Family in New Mexico, 1871 - 1968.* New York: Alfred A. Knopf. 1968.

DEDRICK BROTHERS

No Author. "Arrests of Dedricks. Legal Documents." Herman Weisner Collection. Lincoln County Papers. New Mexico State University Library at Las Cruces. Rio Grande Historical Collections. Box 1. Folder Name Lincoln County Bonds. Folder No. B-8.
Upham, Elizabeth. (Related by marriage to Daniel Dedrick). Personal interviews. 1998.
Upham, Marquita. (Relative by marriage to Daniel Dedrick). Personal interview. 1998.

DOLAN, JAMES J.

Angel, Frank Warner. *In the Matter of the Examination of the Causes and Circumstances of the Death of John H. Tunstall a British Subject.* Report filed October 4, 1878. Angel Report. Microfilm File Case Number 44-4-8-3. Record Group 060. Microfilm No. M750. Roll 1. National Archives and Records Administration. U. S. Department of Justice. Washington, D.C. (James J. Dolan Deposition. June 20, 1878. pp. 235-247.)
Dolan, James. "Confidential Letter to Lew Wallace." December 31, 1878. Herman Weisner Collection. Lincoln County Papers: New Mexico State University Library at Las Cruces. Rio Grande Historical Collections. Box No. 4. Folder Name. Fulton's File. Folder No. F3.
Murphy, Lawrence G. "Will of Lawrence G. Murphy." Herman Weisner Collection. Lincoln County Papers. Accession No. MS 249. New Mexico State University Library at Las Cruces. Rio Grande Historical Collections. Box No. 11. Folder Name: Murphy, Lawrence G. No. P15.
Nolan, Frederick. Biographical information on James Dolan. Unpublished. Personal communication 2005.
No Author. *Proceedings of a Court of Inquiry in the Case of Col. N.A.M. Dudley (May 2, 1879-July 5, 1879).* File Number QQ1284. (Boxes 3304, 3305, 3305A). Court Martial Case Files 1809-1894. Records of the Office of the Judge Advocate General - Army. Record Group 153. National Archives and Records Administration. Old Military and Civil Branch. Washington, D.C. (James J. Dolan Testimony. June 5, 1879.)

Wild, Azariah F. "Daily Reports of U. S. Secret Service Agents, Azariah F. Wild."
Microfilm T-915. Record Group 87. Rolls 307 (January 1,1878 - June 30, 1879)
and 308 (July 1, 1879 - June 30, 1881). National Archives and Records
Department. Department of the Treasury. United States Secret Service.
Washington, D. C.

DUDLEY, NATHAN AUGUSTUS MONROE

Kaye, E. Donald. *Nathan Augustus Monroe Dudley: Rogue, Hero, or Both?* Parker,
Colorado: Outskirts Press, Inc. 2007.
No Author. *Dudley Court of Inquiry. (May 2, 1879 - July 5, 1879).* Record No.
16W3/16/28/6. Boxes 1923 - 1923A. File No. QQ1284. National Archives and
Records Administration. Old Military and Civil Branch. Records of the Office of
the Judge Advocate General. Washington, D. C.

ELKINS, STEPHEN BENTON

BIOGRAPHY

Cleaveland, Norman, *A Synopsis of the Great New Mexico Cover-up.* Self-printed. 1989.
_____ . *The Great Santa Fe Cover-up. Based on a Talk given Before the*
Santa Fe Historical Society on November 1, 1978. Self-printed. 1982.
_____. *The Morleys - Young Upstarts on the Southwest Frontier.*
Albuquerque, New Mexico: Calvin Horn Publisher, Inc. 1971.
Lambert, Oscar Doane. *Stephen Benton Elkins. American Foursquare.* Pittsburgh,
Pennsylvania: University of Pittsburg Press. 1955.
Montoya, María E. *Translating Property. The Maxwell Land Grant and the Conflict*
Over Land in the American West, 1840-1900. Berkeley and Los Angeles:
University of California Press. 2002.
Westphall, Victor. *Thomas Benton Catron and His Era.* Tucson, Arizona: University of
Arizona Press. 1973.

LETTERS

Devens, Charles. "To honorable S. B. Elkins re. T. B. Catron continuing to act as U. S.
Attorney." November 12, 1878. Angel Report. Microfilm File Case No. 44-4-8-3.
Record Group 060. National Records and Archives Administration. Microfilm No.
M750. Roll 1. U. S. Department of Justice. Washington, D. C.
Elkins, Stephen B. "Asking delay of action upon charges against U. S. Atty. Catron
..." September 24, 1878. Angel Report. Microfilm File Case No. 44-4-8-3. Record
Group 060. National Records and Archives Administration. Microfilm No. M750.
Roll 1. U. S. Department of Justice. Washington, D. C.
_____. "Regarding Attorney General's decision on T. B. Catron." Letter.
September___, 1878. Angel Report. Microfilm File Case No. 44-4-8-3. Record
Group 060. National Records and Archives Administration. Microfilm No. M750.
Roll 1. U. S. Department of Justice. Washington, D. C.
_____. "Relative to resignation of T. B. Catron U. S. Attorney." Letter.
November 10, 1878. Angel Report. Microfilm File Case No. 44-4-8-3. Record
Group 060. National Records and Archives Administration. Microfilm No. M750.
Roll 1. U. S. Department of Justice. Washington, D. C.
_____. "To the President. Referring to a conversation had with you last
week ... Hon. S. B. Elkins favors appointment Axtell, ExGov. as Gov'r of New
Mexico." (Letter) March 23, 1881. (Received Executive Mansion April 6, 1881).
Microfilm Roll M750. National Archives and Records Administration. Record
Group 060. Microfilm Case File Number 44-4-8-3. U. S. Department of Interior.
Washington, D. C.

EVANS, JESSIE

McCright, Grady E. and James H. Powell. *Jessie Evans: Lincoln County Badman.* College Station, Texas: Creative Publishing Company. 1983.
No Author. "Charges against Jessie Evans and John Kinney." Doña Ana County Criminal Docket Book. August 18, 1875 to November 7, 1878. Herman Weisner Collection. Accession No. MS249. Lincoln County Papers: New Mexico State University Library at Las Cruces. Rio Grande Historical Collections. Box No. 13. Folder Name: Venue, Change of. Folder No. V3.

FOUNTAIN, ALBERT JENNINGS

Gibson, A. M. *The Life and Death of Colonel Albert Jennings Fountain.* Norman: University of Oklahoma Press. 1965.

FRITZ FAMILY (CHARLES FRITZ AND EMILIE SCHOLAND)

Fritz, Charles. Affidavit of September 18, 1876 claiming that Emil Fritz had a will. Probate Court Record. (Private Collection)
_____. Affidavit of September 26, 1876 Authorizing Alexander McSween to Receive Payments for the Emil Fritz Estate. Probate Court Record. (Private Collection)
_____. Affidavit of December 7, 1877 to order Alexander McSween to pay the Emil Fritz insurance policy money. Probate Court Record. (Private Collection)
_____. Affidavit sworn before John Crouch, Clerk of Doña Ana District Court, for Writ of Attachment issued against property of Alexander A. McSween. Probate Court Record. February 6, 1878. (Private Collection)
_____ and Emilie Scholand. Attachment Bond sworn before John Crouch, Clerk of Doña Ana District Court, against Alexander A. McSween for indebtedness to them. February 6, 1878. (Private Collection)
Scholand, Emilie and Charles Fritz. Affidavit of September 26, 1876 appointing McSween to collect debts for the Emil Fritz Estate. Copied from the original District Court Record. (Private Collection)
Scholand, Emilie. Affidavit of December 21, 1877 Accusing Alexander McSween of Embezzlement. Copied from the original District Court Record. (Private Collection)
No Author. Diagram showing parcels of land to each of the heirs of Emil Fritz. Herman Weisner Collection. Accession No. MS249. Lincoln County Papers: New Mexico State University Library at Las Cruces. Rio Grande Historical Collections. Box No. 11. Folder Name. Charles Fritz Estate. Box No. P1.

GARRETT, PATRICK FLOYD

Garrett, Pat F. *The Authentic Life of Billy the Kid The Noted Desperado of the Southwest, Whose Deeds of Daring and Blood Made His Name a Terror in New Mexico, Arizona, and Northern Mexico.* Santa Fe, New Mexico: New Mexico Printing and Publishing Co. 1882.
Metz, Leon C. *Pat Garrett. The Story of a Western Lawman.* Norman: University of Oklahoma Press. 1974.
Mullin, Robert N. "Killing of Joe Briscoe." Letter to Eve Ball. January 31, 1964. (Unpublished). Binder RNM, VI, H. Midland, Texas: Nita Stewart Haley Memorial Library and J. Everts Haley Historical Center.
_____. "Pat Garrett. Two Forgotten Killings." *Password.* X(2) (Summer, 1965). Pages 7 - 65.

_____. "Skelton Glen's Manuscript Entitled 'Pat Garrett As I Knew Him on the Buffalo Ranges.'" (Unpublished). Binder RNM, III B, 20. Midland, Texas: Nita Stewart Haley Memorial Library and J. Everts Haley Historical Center.

Upson, Ash. Letter from Garrett's Ranch to Upson's Nephew, Frank S. Downs, Esq. re. "His Drawers and pigeon holes of his desk were full of letters, deeds, bills, notes, agreements, & C. I have burned bushels of them and am not through yet." October 20, 1888. (Unpublished). Binder RNM, V1-MM. Midland, Texas: Nita Stewart Haley Memorial Library and J. Everts Haley Historical Center.

Wild, Azariah F. "Daily Reports of U. S. Secret Service Agents, Azariah F. Wild." Microfilm T-915. Record Group 87. Rolls 306 (June 15, 1877 - December 31, 1877), 307 (January 1,1878 - June 30, 1879), 308 (July 1, 1879 - June 30, 1881), 309 (July 1, 1881 - September 30, 1883), 310 (October 1, 1883 - July 31, 1886). National Archives and Records Department. Department of the Treasury. United States Secret Service. Washington, D. C.

ARTICLE "[Pat F. Garrett] Recommended by Gen. Wallace," *The* (Crawfordsville) *Weekly News-Review*, December 20, 1901. Indiana Historical Society. Lew Wallace Collection. M0292.

HOYT, HENRY F.

Hoyt, Henry F. *A Frontier Doctor*. Boston and New York: Houghton Mifflin Company. 1929. **(Quote describing Billy's superior abilities, Pages 93-94)**

JONES, BARBARA ("MA'AM") AND FAMILY

Ball, Eve. *Ma'am Jones of the Pecos*. Tucson: University of Arizona Press. 1969.

KINNEY, JOHN

Mullin, Robert N. "Here Lies John Kinney." *Journal of Arizona History*. 14 (Autumn 1973). Pages 223 - 242.

No Author. "Charges against Jessie Evans and John Kinney." Doña Ana County Criminal Docket Book. August 18, 1875 to November 7, 1878. Herman Weisner Collection. Accession No. MS249. Lincoln County Papers: New Mexico State University Library at Las Cruces. Rio Grande Historical Collections. Box 13. Folder Name: File Name. Venue, Change of. Folder No. V-3.

No Author. "Obituary of John Kinney." *Prescott Courier*. August 30, 1919. Obituary Section.

No Author. Obituary. "Over the Range Goes Another Pioneer." *Journal Miner*. Tuesday Morning, August 26, 1919.

LEONARD, IRA

Nolan, Frederick. Biography and photograph of Ira Leonard. Unpublished. Personal communication 2005.

No Author. *Proceedings of a Court of Inquiry in the Case of Col. N.A.M. Dudley (May 2, 1879 - July 5, 1879)*. File Number QQ1284. (Boxes 3304, 3305, 3305A). Court Martial Case Files 1809-1894. Records of the Office of the Judge Advocate General - Army. Record Group 153. National Archives and Records Administration. Old Military and Civil Branch. Washington, D.C.

See also: WALLACE, LEW for letters

MATTHEWS, JACOB BASIL

Fleming, Elvis E. *J.B. Matthews. Biography of a Lincoln County Deputy*. Las Cruces, New Mexico: Yucca Tree Press. 1999.

MAXWELL FAMILY

Cleaveland, Norman. *The Morleys - Young Upstarts on the Southwest Frontier*. Albuquerque, New Mexico: Calvin Horn Publisher, Inc. 1971.

Dunham, Harold H. "New Mexican Land Grants with Special Reference to the Title Papers of the Maxwell Grant." *New Mexico Historical Review*. (January 1955) Vol. 30, No. 1. Pages 1 - 23.

Freiberger, Harriet, *Lucien Maxwell: Villain or Visionary*. Santa Fe: New Mexico. Sunstone Press. 1999.

Keleher, William A. *The Maxwell Land Grant. A New Mexico Item*. Albuquerque, New Mexico: University of New Mexico Press. 1964.

Lamar, Howard Roberts. *The Far Southwest 1846 - 1912. A Territorial History*. New Haven and London: Yale University Press. 1966.

Montoya, María E. *Translating Property. The Maxwell Land Grant and the Conflict Over Land in the American West, 1840-1900*. Berkeley and Los Angeles, California: University of California Press. 2002.

Murphy, Lawrence R. *Lucien Bonaparte Maxwell. Napoleon of the Southwest*. Norman: University of Oklahoma Press. 1983.

Pearson, Jim Berry. *The Maxwell Land Grant*. Norman: University of Oklahoma Press. 1961.

Poe, Sophie. *Buckboard Days*. Albuquerque, New Mexico: University of New Mexico Press. 1964.

Taylor, Morris F. *O. P. McMains and the Maxwell Land Grant Conflict*. Tucson, Arizona: The University of Arizona Press. 1979.

No Author. "Mrs. Paula M. Jaramillo, 65 Died Here Tuesday." *The Fort Sumner Leader*. Official Newspaper County of De Baca. December 20, 1929. No. 1158, Page 1, Column 1.

McSWEEN, ALEXANDER

Angel, Frank Warner. *In the Matter of the Examination of the Causes and Circumstances of the Death of John H. Tunstall a British Subject*. Report filed October 4, 1878. Angel Report. Microfilm File Case Number 44-4-8-3. Record Group 060. Microfilm No. M750. Roll 1. National Archives and Records Administration. U. S. Department of Justice. Washington, D.C. Deposition given June 6, 1878, pp. 5-183.

_____. *In the Matter of the Lincoln County Troubles. To the Honorable Charles Devens, Attorney General*. October 4, 1878. Angel Report. Microfilm File Case Number 44-4-8-3. Record Group 060. Microfilm No. M750. Roll 1. National Archives and Records Administration. U. S. Department of Justice. Washington, D. C.

Bristol, Warren. Action of Assumpsit to command Sheriff of Lincoln County to attach goods of Alexander A. McSween. February 7, 1878. District Court Record. (Private Collection)

_____. Preprinted form in his name for "Writ of Attachment" (Printed and sold at the office of the Mesilla News) filled out to command the Sheriff of Lincoln County to attach goods of Alexander McSween for a suit of damages for ten thousand dollars. February 7, 1878. (Private Collection)

Fritz, Charles. Affidavit sworn before John Crouch, Clerk of Doña Ana District Court, for Writ of Attachment issued against property of Alexander A. McSween. Probate Court Record. February 6, 1878. (Private Collection)
_____ and Emilie Scholand. Attachment Bond sworn before John Crouch, Clerk of Doña Ana District Court, against Alexander A. McSween for indebtedness to them. February 6, 1878. (Private Collection)
McSween, Alexander, *Will. February 25, 1878.* Herman Weisner Collection. Accession No. MS249. Lincoln County Papers. New Mexico State University Library at Las Cruces. Rio Grande Historical Collections. Box No. 10. Folder Name. Will and Testament A. McSween. Box No. M15.

POE, JOHN WILLIAM

Poe, John W. "The Killing of Billy the Kid." (a personal letter written at Roswell, New Mexico to Mr. Charles Goodnight, Goodnight P.C., Texas) July 10, 1917.
Poe, Sophie. *Buckboard Days.* Albuquerque, New Mexico: University of New Mexico Press. 1964.

TUNSTALL, JOHN HENRY

Angel, Frank Warner. *In the Matter of the Examination of the Causes and Circumstances of the Death of John H. Tunstall a British Subject.* Report filed October 4, 1878. Angel Report. Microfilm File Case Number 44-4-8-3. Record Group 060. Microfilm Roll No. M750. Roll 1. National Archives and Records Administration. U. S. Department of Justice. Washington, D.C.
_____. *In the Matter of the Lincoln County Troubles. To the. Honorable Charles Devens, Attorney General October 4, 1878.* Angel Report. Microfilm Case File No. 44-4-8-3. Record Group 060. Microfilm Roll No. M750. National Archives and Records Administration. U. S. Department of Justice. Washington, D. C.
Nolan, Frederick W. *The Life and Death of John Henry Tunstall.* Albuquerque, New Mexico: The University of New Mexico Press. 1965.

WALLACE, LEW

BOOKS - BIOGRAPHICAL

Jones, Oakah L. "Lew Wallace: Hoosier Governor of Territorial New Mexico. 1878-81." *New Mexico Historical Review. 59(1)* (January, 1984).
Morsberger, Robert E. and Katherine M. Morsberger. *Lew Wallace: Militant Romantic.* New York: McGraw - Hill Book Company. 1980.
Stephens, Gail. "Shadow of Shiloh: Major General Lew Wallace in the Civil War." Indianapolis: Indiana Historical Society Press. 2010.
Wallace, Lew. *An Autobiography. Vol. I.* New York and London: Harper and Brothers Publishers. 1997.
_____. *An Autobiography. Vol. II.* New York and London: Harper and Brothers Publishers. 1997.

PAPERS

Wallace, Lew. Collected Papers. Microfilm Project by the National Historical Publications Commission. Microfilm Roll No. 99. Santa Fe, New Mexico: New Mexico Records Center and Archives. 1974.
Wallace, Lew. Indiana Historical Society. Lew Wallace Collection. M0292.
Wallace, Lew. Lew Wallace Collection. Bloomington, Indiana, University of Indiana Lilly Library. Mss.

NOTES

Wallace, Lew. "Statements by Kid, made Sunday night March 23, 1879." March 23, 1879. Indiana Historical Society. Lew Wallace Collection. M0922. Box 4. Folder 7.

LETTERS (See Bonney, William for that correspondence)

TO JOHN "SQUIRE" WILSON

Wallace, Lew. "I enclose a note for Bonney." March 20, 1879. Indiana Historical Society. Lew Wallace Collection. M0922. Box 4. Folder 6.

TO CARL SCHURZ

Wallace, Lew. "As to the basis of the request which I have to prefer ..." October 5, 1878. Indiana Historical Society. Lew Wallace Collection. M0292. Box 3, Folder 15.
—————————. "I have the honor to report that affairs of the Territory are moving on quietly ..." December 21, 1878. Letter to Carl Schurz. The Papers of Carl Schurz 1842 - 1906 in 165 Volumes. Library of Congress 1935. General Correspondence November 30, 1878. Shelf No. 14,803. Container 47.
—————————. Letter to Carl Schurz. "A precious specimen nick-named 'The Kid'." March 31, 1879. Indiana Historical Society. Lew Wallace Collection. MO292. Box 4. Folder 1.

FROM AND TO EDWARD HATCH

Hatch, Edward. Letter to Lew Wallace. March 6, 1879. Indiana Historical Society. Lew Wallace Collection. M0292. Box 4, Folder 4.
Wallace, Lew. Letter to General Edward Hatch. March 6, 1879. Indiana Historical Society. Lew Wallace Collection. Box 9, Folder 10. (**Written on dead John Tunstall's letterhead stationery**)

TO AND FROM IRA LEONARD:

Leonard, Ira. "... the assassination of H.I. Chapman ..." February 24, 1879. Indiana Historical Society. Lew Wallace Collection. MO292.
Wallace, Lew. "It is important to take steps to protect the coming court." April 6, 1879. Indiana Historical Society. Lew Wallace Collection. MO292.
—————————. "To work trying to do a little good, but with the world against you, requires the will of a martyr. Indiana Historical Society. Lew Wallace Collection. MO292.
Leonard, Ira. "He is bent on going for the Kid ..." April 20, 1879. Indiana Historical Society. Lew Wallace Collection. MO292.
—————————. "... the Santa Fe Ring that has been so long an incubus on the government of this territory." May 20, 1879. Indiana Historical Society. Lew Wallace Collection. MO292.
—————————. "... we are pouring 'hot shot' into Dudley ..." May 23, 1879. Indiana Historical Society. Lew Wallace Collection. MO292.
—————————. "I am thoroughly and completely disgusted with their proceedings." June 6, 1879. Indiana Historical Society. Lew Wallace Collection. MO292.
—————————. "... they would not enter our objections ..." "... would not allow us to show the conspiracy formed with Dolan beforehand ..." "I tell you Governor as long as the present incumbent occupies the bench all that Grand Juries may do to bring to justice these men every effort will be thwarted by him and the sympathizers of that side." June 13, 1879. Indiana Historical Society. Lew Wallace Collection. MO292.

TESTIMONY

No Author. *Dudley Court of Inquiry.* *(May 2, 1879 - July 5, 1879).* Record No. 16W3/16/28/6. Boxes 1923-1923A. File Number QQ1284. National Archives and Records Administration. Old Military and Civil Branch. Records of the Office of the Judge Advocate General. Washington, D.C.

NOTEBOOK FOR WALLACE

Angel, Frank Warner. "To Gov. Lew Wallace, Santa Fe, N. M., 1878." (Cover of notebook written for Wallace reads "Gov. Lew Wallace, Santa Fe, N.M.") Microfilm No. F372. From a document now missing in original form from the Indiana Historical Society. Lew Wallace Collection. MO292.

Theisen, Lee Scott. "Frank Warner Angel's Notes on New Mexico Territory, 1878." *Arizona and the West,* 18 (4) (Winter 1976) 333-370.

ARTICLES (CHRONOLOGICAL)

Wallace, Lew. "General Lew Wallace Writes a Romance of 'Billy the Kid," Most Famous Bandit of the Plains." June 8, 1902. *New York Sunday World Magazine.* Page 4. Indiana Historical Society. Lew Wallace Collection. MO292.

"Wallace's Words ..." (interview with Lew Wallace conducted in Washington, D.C. on January 3, 1881), Chicago *The Daily Inter Ocean.* January 4, 1881. Page 2, Column 4. Indiana Historical Society. Lew Wallace Collection. MO292.

(Richard Dunham's May 2, 1881 encounter with Billy the Kid), Santa Fe Daily New Mexican, May 5, 1881, Page 4, Column 3. Indiana Historical Society. Lew Wallace Collection. MO292.

(O.L. Houghton's Conversation with Lew Wallace, before May 26, 1881), *The Las Vegas Daily Optic,* May 26, 1881, Page 4, Column 4. Indiana Historical Society. Lew Wallace Collection. MO292.

"Billy the Kid ..." (Lew Wallace interviewed on June 13, 1881), Crawfordsville (Indiana) *Saturday Evening Journal,* June 18, 1881. Indiana Historical Society. Lew Wallace Collection. MO292.

"Street Pickings," *Crawfordsville* (Weekly) *Review* – *Saturday Edition,* January 6, 1894. Indiana Historical Society. Lew Wallace Collection. MO292.

"An Old Incident Recalled," *The* (Crawfordsville) *Weekly News-Review,* December 20, 1901. Indiana Historical Society. Lew Wallace Collection. MO292.

DEATH WARRANT FOR WILLIAM BONNEY

Wallace, Lew. "To the Sheriff of Lincoln County, Greeting ..." April 30, 1881. Indiana Historical Society. Lew Wallace Collection. M0292. Box 9, Folder 11.

REWARD NOTICES FOR WILLIAM BONNEY

Wallace, Lew. "Billy the Kid: $500 Reward." Las Vegas *Gazette.* December 22, 1880.
_____. "Billy the Kid. $500 Reward." May 3, 1881. *Daily New Mexican.* Vol. X, No. 33. Page 1, Column 3.

REWARD POSTERS FOR WILLIAM BONNEY

Greene, Chas. W. "To the New Mexican Printing and Publishing Company." May 20, 1881. (Bill to Lew Wallace for Reward posters for "Kid"). Indiana Historical Society. Lew Wallace Collection. M0292. Box 4, Folder 18.

_____. "I enclose a bill ..." Letter to Lew Wallace for "Kid" wanted posters. June 2, 1881. Indiana Historical Society. Lew Wallace Collection. M0292. Box 4, Folder 18.

WILD, AZARIAH

Brooks, James J. *1877 Report on Secret Service Operatives.* (September 26, 1877). "On Azariah Wild." p.392. Department of the Treasury. United States Secret Service. Washington, D.C.

Wild, Azariah F. "Daily Reports of U. S. Secret Service Agents, Azariah F. Wild. Microfilm T-915. Record Group 87. Rolls 306 (June 15, 1877 - December 31, 1877), 307 (January 1, 1878 - June 30, 1879), 308 (July 1, 1879 - June 30, 1881), 309 (July 1, 1881 - September 30, 1883), and 310 (October 1, 1883 - July 31, 1886). National Archives and Records Department. Department of Treasury. United States Secret Service. Washington, D. C.

Wild, Azariah. Telegraph on counterfeit bills. January 4, 1881. Herman Weisner Collection. Lincoln County Papers. New Mexico State University Library at Las Cruces. Rio Grande Historical Collections. Box No. 11. Folder Name: Olinger, Robert and James W. Bell. Folder No. O-1.

HISTORICAL ORGANIZATIONS (PERIOD)

SANTA FE RING

Angel, Frank Warner. *Examination of Charges Against F. C. Godfroy, Indian Agent, Mescalero, N. M. October 2, 1878.* (Report 1981, Inspector E. C. Watkins; Cited as Watkins Report). M 319-20 and L147-44-4-8. Record Group 075. National Archives and Records Administration. U. S. Department of Justice. Washington, D. C.

_____. "To Gov. Lew Wallace, Santa Fe, N. M., 1878." (Cover of notebook written for Wallace reads "Gov. Lew Wallace, Santa Fe, N.M." Microfilm No. F372. From a document now missing from the Lew Wallace Collection (M0292), Indiana Historical Society.

_____. *In the Matter of the Examination of the Causes and Circumstances of the Death of John H. Tunstall a British Subject.* Report filed October 4, 1878. Angel Report. Microfilm File Case Number 44-4-8-3. Record Group 060. Microfilm No. M750. Roll 1. National Archives and Records Administration. U.S. Department of Justice. Washington, D.C.

_____. *In the Matter of the Investigation of the Charges Against S. B. Axtell Governor of New Mexico.* October 3, 1878. Angel Report. Microfilm File No. 44-4-8-3. Record Group 060. Roll M750. National Archives. U.S. Department of Interior. Washington, D.C.

_____. *In the Matter of the Lincoln County Troubles. To the Honorable Charles Devens, Attorney General. October 4, 1878.* Angel Report. Microfilm Case File No. 44-4-8-3. Record Group 060. Microfilm Roll M750. National Archives and Records Administration. U.S. Department of Justice. Washington, D. C.

Cleaveland, Norman, *Colfax County's Chronic Murder Mystery.* Santa Fe: New Mexico. The Rydel Press. 1977.

_____. *A Synopsis of the Great New Mexico Cover-up.* Self-printed. 1989.

_____. *Some Comments Norman Cleveland May Make to the Huntington Westerners on Sept. 19, 1987.* Unpublished.

_____. *Some Highlights of William R. Morley's Contribution to the Pioneer Development of the Southwest.* Self-printed. No Date.

_____. *The Great Santa Fe Cover-up.* Based on a Talk given Before the Santa Fe Historical Society on November 1, 1978. Self-printed. 1982.

Cleaveland, Norman and George Fitzpatrick. *The Morleys - Young Upstarts on the Southwest Frontier.* Albuquerque, New Mexico: Calvin Horn Publisher, Inc. 1971.

- Keleher, William A. *The Maxwell Land Grant. A New Mexico Item.* Albuquerque, New Mexico: University of New Mexico Press. 1964.

Lamar, Howard Robert N. *The Far Southwest 1846 - 1912. A Territorial History.* New Haven and London: Yale University Press. 1966.

Leonard, Ira. Letters to Governor Lew Wallace. "... the Santa Fe ring that has been so long an incubus on the government of this territory." May 20, 1879. Indiana Historical Society. Lew Wallace Collection. MO292.

_____. "... they would not enter our objections ..." "... would not allow us to show the conspiracy formed with Dolan beforehand ..." "I tell you Governor as long as the present incumbent occupies the bench all that Grand Juries may do to bring to justice these men every effort will be thwarted by him and the sympathizers of that side." June 13, 1879. Indiana Historical Society. Lew Wallace Collection. MO292.

Meinig, D. W. *The Shaping of America. A Geographical Perspective on 500 Years of History. Vol. 3. Transcontinental America 1850 - 1915.* New Haven and London: Yale University Press. 1998. **(Pages 127 and 132 are on the Santa Fe Ring)**

Milner, Clyde A. II, Carol A. O'Connor, Martha Sandweiss. Eds. *The Oxford History of the American West.* New York and Oxford: Oxford University Press. 1994.

Montoya, María E. *Translating Property. The Maxwell Land Grant and the Conflict Over Land in the American West, 1840-1900.* Berkeley and Los Angeles: University of California Press. 2002.

Naegle, Conrad Keeler. *The History of Silver City, New Mexico 1870-1886.* University of New Mexico Bachelor of Arts thesis. Pages 30-60. Unpublished. 1943. Collection of the Silver City Museum, Silver City, New Mexico.

Pearson, Jim Berry. *The Maxwell Land Grant.* Norman: University of Oklahoma Press. 1961.

Taylor, Morris F. *O. P. McMains and the Maxwell Land Grant Conflict.* Tucson, Arizona: The University of Arizona Press. 1979.

Theisen, Lee Scott. "Frank Warner Angel's Notes on New Mexico Territory, 1878." *Arizona and the West,* 18 (4) (Winter 1976) 333-370.

• Twitchell, Ralph Emerson. *The Leading Facts of New Mexico History.* Vol. I-II. Santa Fe: Sunstone Press. 2007. (Reprinted from 1912 edition) **(Reputed Ringman and its cover-up historian)**

Westphall, Victor. *Thomas Benton Catron and His Era.* Tucson, Arizona: University of Arizona Press. 1973.

See Also: THOMAS BENTON CATRON
See Also: STEPHEN BENTON ELKINS

SECRET SERVICE

Bowen, Walter S. and Harry Edward Neal. *The United States Secret Service.* Philadelphia and New York: Chilton Company Publishers. 1960.

Brooks, James J. *1877 Report on Secret Service Operatives.* (September 26, 1877). "On Azariah Wild." Page 392. Department of the Treasury. United States Secret Service. Washington, D.C.

Burnham, George P. *American Counterfeits. How Detected, And How Avoided. Comprising Sketches of Noted Counterfeiters, and Their Allies, Of Secret Agents, and Detectives; Authentic Accounts of the Capture of Forgers, Defaulters, and Swindlers; With Rules for Deciding Good and Counterfeit Notes, or United States Currency; A List of Terms and Phrases in Use Among This Fraternity of Offenders, &c., &c.* Springfield, Massachusetts: W. J. Holland. 1875.

_____. *Memoirs of the United States Secret Service With Accurate Portraits of Prominent Members of the Detective Force, Some of Their Most Notable Captures, and a Brie Account of the Life of Col. H. C. Whitley, Chief of the Division.* Boston: Lee, Shepard. 18??.

_____. *Three Years With Counterfeiters, Smugglers, and Boodle Carriers; With Accurate Portraits of the Prominent Members of the Detective Force in The Secret Service.* Boston: 560. John P. Dale & Co. 18??.

Johnson, David R. Illegal Tender. Counterfeiting and the Secret Service in Nineteenth Century America. Washington and London: Smithsonian Institution Press. 1995.

Wild, Azariah F. "Daily Reports of U. S. Secret Service Agents, Azariah F. Wild. Microfilm T-915. Record Group 87. Rolls 306 (June 15, 1877 - December 31, 1877), 307 (January 1, 1878 - June 30, 1879), 308 (July 1, 1879 - June 30, 1881), 309 (July 1, 1881 - September 30, 1883), and 310 (October 1, 1883 - July 31, 1886). National Archives and Records Department. Department of Treasury. United States Secret Service. Washington, D. C.

Wild, Azariah. Telegraph on counterfeit bills. January 4, 1881. Herman Weisner Collection. Lincoln County Papers. New Mexico State University Library at Las Cruces. Rio Grande Historical Collections. Box No. 11. Folder Name: Olinger, Robert and James W. Bell. Folder No. O-1.

NEW MEXICO TERRITORY REBELLIONS (PERIOD)

GRANT COUNTY REBELLION

Naegle, Conrad Keeler. *The History of Silver City, New Mexico 1870-1886.* University of New Mexico Bachelor of Arts thesis. Pages 30-60. Unpublished. 1943. Collection of the Silver City Museum, Silver City, New Mexico.

_____. "The Rebellion of Grant County, New Mexico in 1876." *Arizona and the West* (published by *Journal of the Southwest*). Autumn, 1968. Volume 10. Number 2. Pages 225-240.

Sullivan, A.P., "Diario del Consejo der Territorio de Neuvo Mejico, Session de 1871-1872. Santa Fe: *Santa Fe New Mexican.* January 8, 1872. Pages 144-154. (**A Ring expurgated document, with a copy found in 1942 by historian Conrad Naegle; confirms troops to "preserve peace"**)

Vincent, Wilson, Jr. *The Book of Great American Documents.* Brookville, Maryland: American History Research Associates. 1993.

No author. "Diario del Consejo der Territorio de Neuvo Mejico, Session de 1871-1872. Las Cruces: *Borderer.* January 24, 1872. Pages 110-113. (**Don Diego Archuleta, President of the Council, gives speech objecting to troops in legislature**)

_____. Grant County *Herald.* September 16, 1876. (**The intent to annex Grant County to Arizona was announced**)

_____. Grant County *Herald.* September 23, 1876. (**Need for school system stressed**)

_____. Grant County *Herald.* September 30, 1876. (**"Annexation Meeting" announced**)

_____. Grant County *Herald.* October 7, 1876. (**"Grant County Declaration of Independence" published**)

COLFAX COUNTY WAR

Caffey, David L. *Frank Springer and New Mexico: From the Colfax County War to the Emergence of Modern Santa Fe.* Texas A and M. University Press. 2007.

Cleaveland, Norman. *The Morleys - Young Upstarts on the Southwest Frontier.* Albuquerque, New Mexico: Calvin Horn Publisher, Inc. 1971.

294

Dunham, Harold H. "New Mexican Land Grants with Special Reference to the Title Papers of the Maxwell Grant." *New Mexico Historical Review.* (January 1955) Vol. 30, No. 1. Pages 1-23.

Keleher, William A. *The Maxwell Land Grant. A New Mexico Item.* Albuquerque, New Mexico: University of New Mexico Press. 1964.

Lamar, Howard Roberts. *The Far Southwest 1846 - 1912. A Territorial History.* New Haven and London: Yale University Press. 1966.

Montoya, María E. *Translating Property. The Maxwell Land Grant and the Conflict Over Land in the American West, 1840-1900.* Berkeley and Los Angeles, California: University of California Press. 2002.

Murphy, Lawrence R. *Lucien Bonaparte Maxwell. Napoleon of the Southwest.* Norman: University of Oklahoma Press. 1983.

Pearson, Jim Berry. *The Maxwell Land Grant.* Norman: University of Oklahoma Press. 1961.

Poe, Sophie. *Buckboard Days.* Albuquerque, New Mexico: University of New Mexico Press. 1964.

Taylor, Morris F. *O. P. McMains and the Maxwell Land Grant Conflict.* Tucson, Arizona: The University of Arizona Press. 1979.

No Author. "Mrs. Paula M. Jaramillo, 65 Died Here Tuesday." *The Fort Sumner Leader.* Official Newspaper County of De Baca. December 20, 1929. No. 1158, Page 1, Column 1.

LINCOLN COUNTY WAR

Angel, Frank Warner. *Examination of charges against F. C. Godfroy, Indian Agent, Mescalero, N. M. October 2, 1878.* (Report 1981, Inspector E. C. Watkins; Cited as Watkins Report). M 319-20 and L147, 44-4-8. Record Group 075. National Archives and Records Administration. U. S. Department of Justice. Washington, D. C.

_____. *In the Matter of the Examination of the Causes and Circumstances of the Death of John H. Tunstall a British Subject.* Report filed October 4, 1878. Angel Report. Microfilm File Case Number 44-4-8-3. Record Group 060. Microfilm No. M750. Roll 1. National Archives and Records Administration. U.S. Department of Justice. Washington, D.C.

_____. *In the Matter of the Investigation of the Charges Against S. B. Axtell Governor of New Mexico. October 3, 1878.* Angel Report. Microfilm No. 44-4-8-3. Record Group 060. Roll M750. National Archives. U. S. Department of Interior. Washington, D.C.

_____. *In the Matter of the Lincoln County Troubles. To the Honorable Charles Devens, Attorney General. October 4, 1878.* Angel Report. Microfilm Case File No. 44-4-8-3. Record Group 060. Microfilm Roll M750. National Archives and Records Administration. U. S. Department of Justice. Washington, D. C.

Cramer, T. Dudley. *The Pecos Ranchers in the Lincoln County War.* Orinda, California: Branding Iron Press. 1996.

Fulton, Maurice Garland. Robert N. Mullin. Ed. *History of the Lincoln County War.* Tucson, Arizona: The University of Arizona Press. 1997.

Jacobson, Joel. *Such Men as Billy the Kid. The Lincoln County War Reconsidered.* Lincoln and London: University of Nebraska Press. 1994.

Keleher, William A. *Violence in Lincoln County 1869-1881.* Albuquerque, New Mexico: University of New Mexico Press. 1957.

Mullin, Robert N. Re: Frank Warner Angel Meeting with President Hayes. August, 1878. Binder RNM, VI, M. (Unpublished). Nita Stewart Haley Memorial Museum. Haley Library. Midland, Texas.

Nolan, Frederick W. *The Life and Death of John Henry Tunstall.* Albuquerque, New Mexico: The University of New Mexico Press. 1965.

Rasch, Philip J. *Gunsmoke in Lincoln County.* Laramie, Wyoming: National Association for Outlaw and Lawmen History, Inc. with University of Wyoming. 1997.

_____. Robert K. DeArment. Ed. *Warriors of Lincoln County.* Laramie: National Association for Outlaw and Lawmen History, Inc. with University of Wyoming. 1998.

Utley, Robert M. *High Noon in Lincoln. Violence on the Western Frontier.* Albuquerque, New Mexico: University of New Mexico Press. 1987.

Wilson, John P. *Merchants, Guns, and Money: The Story of Lincoln County and Its Wars.* Santa Fe, New Mexico: Museum of New Mexico Press. 1987.

No Author. "Amnesty for Matthews and Long in the Third Judicial Court April Term 1879." Herman Weisner Collection. Lincoln County Papers. New Mexico State University at Las Cruces. Rio Grande Historical Collections. Box No. 1. Folder: Amnesty. Folder No. 4.

No Author. "Brady Inventory McSween Property." Herman Weisner Collection. Lincoln County Papers. New Mexico State University Library at Las Cruces. Rio Grande Historical Collections. Box No. 10. Folder Name: Will and Testament A. McSween. Folder No. M15.

No Author. "Charges against Jessie Evans and John Kinney." Doña Ana County Civil and Criminal Docket Book. August 18, 1875 to November 7, 1878. Herman Weisner Collection. Accession No. MS249. Lincoln County Papers. New Mexico State University Library at Las Cruces. Rio Grande Historical Collections. Box No. 13. Folder Name. Venue, Change Of. Folder No. V3.

No Author. "Dismissal of Cases Against Dolan, Matthews, Peppin, October 1879 District Court." Herman Weisner Collection. Lincoln County Papers. New Mexico State University Library at Las Cruces. Rio Grande Historical Collections. Box No. 13. Folder Name: Venue, Change Of. Folder No. V3.

"Disturbances in the Territories, 1878 - 1894. Lawlessness in New Mexico." Senate Documents. 67th Congress. 2nd Session. December 5, 1921 - September 22, 1922. pp. 176 - 187. Washington, D.C.: Government Printing Office. 1922.

No Author. *Dudley Court of Inquiry. (May 2, 1879 - July 5, 1879).* Record No. 16W3/16/28/6. Boxes 1923-1923A. File Number QQ1284. National Archives and Records Administration. Old Military and Civil Branch. Records of the Office of the Judge Advocate General. Washington, D.C.

No Author. "Killers of Tunstall. February 18, 1879." Herman Weisner Collection. Lincoln County Papers. New Mexico State University Library at Las Cruces. Rio Grande Historical Collections. Box No. 12. Folder Name: Tunstall, John H. Folder No. T1.

No Author. "Lincoln County Indictments July 1872 – 1881." Herman Weisner Collections. Lincoln County Papers. New Mexico State University Library at Las Cruces. Rio Grande Historical Collections. Box No. 8. Folder Name. Lincoln Co. Indictments. Folder No. L11.

WRITING, PAPER, AND IMPLEMENTS (PERIOD)

REFERENCE BOOKS

Thornton, Tamara Plakins. *Handwriting in America: A Cultural History.* New Haven and London: Yale University Press. 1996.

SPENCERIAN PENMANSHIP

Spencer, Platt Rogers. *Spencerian Penmanship.* New York: Ivison, Phinney, Blakemont Co. 1857.

_____. *Spencerian System of Practical Penmanship.* (New York: Ivison, Phinney, Blakemont Co. 1864). Reprinted by Milford, Michigan: Mott Media, Inc. 1985.

Spencer, H.C. (Prepared for the "Spencerian Authors) *Spencerian Key to Practical Penmanship*. New York: Ivison, Phinney, Blakemont, Taylor & Co. 1874.

_____. (Prepared for the "Spencerian Authors) *Theory of Spencerian Penmanship for Schools and Private Learners Developed by Questions and Answers with Practical Illustrations: Designed to Be Used by Pupils in Connection With the Use of Spencerian Copybooks*. New York: Ivison, Phinney, Blakemont, Taylor & Co. 1874.

Spencerian Authors. *Theory of Spencerian Penmanship for Schools and Private Learners Developed by Questions and Answers with Practical Illustrations: Designed to Be Used by Pupils in Connection With the Use of Spencerian Copybooks*. (New York: Ivison, Phinney, Blakemont, Taylor & Co. 1874.) Reprinted and modified by Milford, Michigan: Mott Media, Inc. 1985.

Sull, Michael, *Spencerian Script and Ornamental Penmanship*. Prairie Village: Kansas. (Unpublished, undated, modern manual).

FOR PRETENDERS' EXPOSÉ

Airy, Helen L. *Whatever Happened to Billy the Kid?* Santa Fe, New Mexico: Sunstone Press. 1993. (**John Miller as Billy the Kid**)

Garcia, Elbert A. *Billy the Kid's Kid. 1875-1964. The Hispanic Connection*. Santa Rosa, New Mexico: Los Products Press. 1999.

Jameson, W.C. and Frederic Bean. *The Return of the Outlaw Billy the Kid*. Plano, Texas: Republic of Texas Press. 1997. ("**Brushy Bill" Roberts as Billy the Kid**)

Kaplan, Harold I, M.D. and Benjamin J. Sadock, M.D. *Synopsis of Psychiatry*. Philadelphia: Lippincott Williams & Wilkins. 1994. (**Definition of "confabulation": Page 285**)

Sams, Dale. Arizona Pioneers' Home and Cemetery Administrator. Personal communication. January 12, 2010. (**Confirmed that records list John Miller's DOB as December – 1850; and birthplace as Fort Sill, Texas**)

Sonnichsen, C.L. and William V. Morrison. *Alias Billy the Kid*. Albuquerque, New Mexico: University of New Mexico Press. 1955. (**Oliver "Brushy Bill" Roberts as Billy the Kid**)

FOR BILLY THE KID CASE EXPOSÉ

(EXCERPTED FROM: *MegaHoax: The Strange Plot to Exhume Billy the Kid and Become President*)

BOOKS

Althouse, Bill. *Frozen Lightening: Bill Richardson's Strike on the Political Landscape of New Mexico*. Buckman, New Mexico: Thinking Out Loud Press. 2006.

Bugliosi, Vincent. *Outrage: The Five Reasons Why O.J. Simpson Got Away With Murder*. New York and London: W.W. Norton & Company. 1996. (**Exposé of Dr. Henry Lee pp. 47-49**)

Chamberlain, Kathleen, comp. *Billy the Kid and the Lincoln County War: A Bibliography*. Albuquerque, New Mexico: Center for the American West, University of New Mexico. 1997.

Cline, Donald. *Alias Billy the Kid: The Man Behind the Legend*. Santa Fe: New Mexico: Sunstone Press. 1986. (**Historian cited by the hoaxers as backing them**)

Garcia, Elbert A. *Billy the Kid's Kid 1875-1964, The Hispanic Connection*. Santa Rosa, New Mexico: Los Products Press. 1999. (**Participant in Billy the Kid Case as unsubstantiated kin of Billy the Kid**)

Miller, Jay. *Billy the Kid Rides Again: Digging for the Truth.* Santa Fe, New Mexico: Sunstone Press. 2005. (**Reprint of his syndicated articles from his column, "Inside the Capitol" - an exposé of the Billy the Kid Case hoax**)

Nolan, Frederick. *The West of Billy the Kid.* Norman: University of Oklahoma Press. 1998. (**See Page 7 for quote on the Eugene Cunningham hoaxed photo of Catherine Antrim**)

Palast, Greg. *The Best Democracy Money Can Buy.* New York: A Plume Book. 2004. (**Manny Aragon exposé is on page 214**)

_____. *Armed Madhouse.* New York: Penguin Group USA. 2007. (**Bill Richardson exposé**)

Poe, John W. *The Death of Billy the Kid.* (Introduction by Maurice Garland Fulton). Boston and New York: Houghton Mifflin Company. 1933. (**Pages 22 and 25-26 have Milnor Rudolph quote with the part omitted by hoaxers' from their Probable Cause Statement**)

Richardson, Bill, with Michael Ruby. *Between Worlds: The Making of an American Life.* New York: G.P. Putnam's Sons. 2005. ((**Bill Richardson "autobiography"**)

PAMPHLETS, ARTICLES (CHRONOLOGICAL ORDER)

Hutton, Paul Andrew. "Dreamscape Desperado." *New Mexico Magazine.* June, 1990. Volume 68. Number 6. pp. 44-58.

Turk, David S. Historian U.S. Marshals Service. "Research Report: The U.S. Marshals Service and Billy the Kid. To Be Added in its Present Entirety, with Exhibits, to Lincoln County, New Mexico Case # 2003-274." U.S. Marshals Service Executive Services Division. December, 2003.

Madrid, Patricia A. Attorney General. *Inspection of Public Records Act Compliance Guide. Fourth Edition. The "Inspection of Public Records Act" NMSA 1978, Chapter 14, Article 2: A Compliance Guide for New Mexico Public Officials and Citizens.* Santa Fe: Office of the Attorney General. January 2004.

No Author. "Preservation and Planning at Fort Stanton." Annual Report Historic Preservation Division: Preservation New Mexico. January, 2005. Volume 19. Number 6. Page 1.

Turk, David S. "Billy the Kid and the U.S. Marshals Service." *Wild West.* February 2007. Volume 19. Number 5. Pages 34 – 41. (**Link of U.S. Marshals Service Historian David Turk and Probable Cause Statement**)

Brenner, Charles H., Ph.D. "Forensic Mathematics of DNA Matching." May 4, 2009. http://dna-view.com/profile.htm.

PRESS RELEASE (GOVERNOR BILL RICHARDSON)

Richardson, Bill. "Governor Bill Richardson Announces State Support of Billy the Kid Investigation." June 10, 2003. (**Announcement at State Capitol of state backing of case # 2003-274 and listing of the participants: Tom Sullivan, Steve Sederwall, Gary Graves, Sherry Tippett, and Paul Hutton**)

LETTERS/FAXES: (CHRONOLOGICAL ORDER)

Pittmon, Geneva. December 16, 1987 letter to Joe Bowlin with hand copy of Roberts family Bible genealogy page. Private collection Frederick Nolan. (**Showing Oliver P. Roberts's date of birth and her statement that he was not Billy the Kid**).

Poe, John W. "The Killing of Billy the Kid." (a personal letter written at Roswell, New Mexico to Mr. Charles Goodnight, Goodnight P.C., Texas) July 10, 1917. Earle Vandale Collection. 1813-946. No. 2H475. Center for American History. University of Texas at Austin. (**Has Milnor Rudolph quote and the part misleadingly omitted from the Probable Cause Statement**)

De Baca County Commissioners. (Powhatan Carter III, Chairman; Joe Steele; Tommy Roybal; Nancy Sparks, County Clerk. To whom it may concern. "The De Baca County Commissioners are in full support of Village of Fort Sumner's stand against exhuming the body of Billy the Kid." September 25, 2003.

Kemper, Lisa. Kennedy Han, PC. Controller, (via fax). To Gale Cooper. "*In the Matter of Catherine Antrim,* 6th *Judicial Dist. Ct. Case No. MS 2003-001,* "This is to confirm our receipt of payment ..." Baker, Adam. Confirmation of payment of Attorney Sherry Tippett's Judge Henry Quintero sanction by Attorney Bill Robins III. September 1, 2004. (See "Order of Continuance. In the Matter of Catherine Antrim. Case No. MS 03-011.") Filed January 23, 2004. Sixth Judicial Court, County of Grant, State of New Mexico. Signed: H.R. Quintero, District Judge, Division 1." April 28, 2004, (**Here the Court sanctions Attorney Tippett, and Bill Robins III pays**)

Fortenberry, Terry D, Mayor; Thomas A. Nupp Councilor District 2; Steve May, Councilor District 4; Gary Clauss, Councilor District 3; Judy Ward, Councilor District 1; Alex Brown, Town Manager; Cissy McAndrew, Executive Director Chamber of Commerce; Frank Milan, Director Silver City Mainstreet Project; Susan Berry, Director Silver City Museum. "Open Letter to Governor Bill Richardson." June 21, 2004.

Sams, Dale. To George Thompson. "Subject: Disinterment." May 4, 2005. (**Confirms Sams has no idea where the Miller grave is located**)

Olson, Gary. Superintendent Arizona Pioneers' Home. To David Snell. "You recently asked the Arizona Pioneers' Home if a body in its cemetery had been exhumed ..." October 3, 2005. (**Confirms original cover-up of John Miller exhumation**)

Snell, David. To Shiela Polk. Yavapai County Attorney. "I feel it is my duty to report to you that graverobbers are plying their trade ..." March 11, 2006. (**Arizona citizen initiating criminal investigation of Miller/Hudspeth exhumations**)

Savona, Glenn A. Prescott City Prosecutor. To Shiela Sullivan Polk, Yavapai County Attorney. "Re: Police Department DR# 2006-12767 Arizona Pioneers' Home Cemetery." April 13, 2006. (**Calls exhumations potential felonies, and moves case up to County Attorney**)

Jacobson, Marcia. "To Anne Winter, Policy Advisor for Health, Office of the Governor, and Chief Randy Oaks, Prescott Police Department. Re: Disinterment of bodies at Arizona Pioneer's [sic] Home Cemetery." March 30, 2006. (**Attempted cover-up of John Miller and William Hudspeth exhumations**)

Cooper, Gale. To Detective Anna Cahall. Prescott Police Department. "Re: Exhumation of John Miller and adjacent grave for pursuing the New Mexico Billy the Kid Case." April 13, 2006.

_____. To Detective Anna Cahall. Prescott Police Department. "Re: Pertinent articles regarding exhumation of John Miller and remains from adjacent grave for alleged promulgation of the New Mexico Billy the Kid Case, a murder investigation." April 17, 2006.

_____. To Arizona Senate President Ken Bennett. (via fax). "RE: Billy the Kid Case Arizona Exhumations." April 20, 2006.

_____. To Carol Landis. (Office of the Yavapai County Prosecutor). "Re: Billy the Kid Case Arizona Exhumations." April 21, 2006.

_____. To Arizona Senate President Ken Bennett. (via fax). "RE: Billy the Kid Case Arizona Exhumations. As a Follow-up." April 25, 2006.

_____. To Deputy County Attorney Steve Jaynes and County Attorney Dennis McGrane. (via fax) "Re: Information on the New Mexico Billy the Kid Case pertinent to the Arizona John Miller exhumations." May 2, 2006.

_____. To Arizona Senate President Ken Bennett. (via fax). "Re: Follow-up on Prescott, Arizona John Miller exhumation." May 17, 2006.

299

_____. To Attorney Jonell Lucca (via fax). "Re: Case # CA20006020516. Follow-up to our telephone conversation of June 9, 2006, to address the issue of Permit for the exhumations of John Miller and the remains from an adjacent grave for promulgation of the New Mexico Billy the Kid Case, a murder investigation." June 12, 2006.

Hutton, Paul. To Jay Miller. "I was never the 'state historian' ..." June 20, 2006.

Miller, Jay. To Attorney Mark Acuña, Jaffe Law Firm. "Re: Follow-up on your legal participation in the New Mexico Billy the Kid Case ..." June 22, 2006. **(No response)**

"Jordan, Wilma" aka Gale Cooper. To David Turk, Historian U.S. Marshals Service. "Looking for the truth is good ..." June 15, 2006. **(Attempt to get the pamphlet.)**

Turk, David. Historian U.S. Marshals Service. To "Wilma Jordan." "Thank you for your thoughtful and thorough letter ..." July 3, 2006. **(Tracked "Wilma's" address; refuses to send his Billy the Kid pamphlet)**

Cooper, Gale. To Attorney Jonell Lucca (via fax). "Re: Case # CA20006020516. Follow-up to my fax of June 12, 2006, to address additional issues pertinent to the exhumations of John Miller and William Hudspeth, done for promulgation of the New Mexico Billy the Kid Case, an alleged murder investigation." July 11, 2006.

Miller, Jay. To Dr. Rick Staub, Director Orchid Cellmark Lab. "Re: The participation by you and Orchid Cellmark in the New Mexico Billy the Kid Case." August 8, 2006. **(No response)**

_____. To Attorney Mark Acuña, Jaffe Law Firm. "Re: Follow-up on my unanswered letter of June 22, 2006 with regard to your legal participation in the New Mexico Billy the Kid Case ..." August 8, 2006. **(No response)**

Cooper, Gale. To Attorney Jonell Lucca (via fax). "Re: Case # CA20006020516. Follow-up to my fax of July 11, 2006, to address issues pertinent to the promulgators of the New Mexico Billy the Kid Case (which resulted in the exhumations of John Miller and William Hudspeth); with added focus on its alleged forensic experts and co-participants." August 11, 2006.

_____. To New Mexico Congresswoman Heather Wilson and Campaign Manager Enrique Knell. "Re: Information relevant to campaign claims of Attorney General Patricia Madrid's corruption." September 11, 2006.

_____. To Attorney Jonell Lucca. "Re: Enclosed reference copy of Freedom of Information Act (FOIA) to Governor Janet Napolitano regarding her possible participation in the Prescott, Arizona exhumations of John Miller and William Hudspeth, and their legal issues related to Maricopa County Prosecutor's Office Case # CA20006020516." September 22, 2006.

_____. To New Mexico Congresswoman Heather Wilson and Campaign Manager Enrique Knell. "Re: Additional information relevant to the New Mexico Billy the Kid Case." September 22, 2006.

_____. To Kelly Ward, Campaign Manager for John Dendahl. "Re: For campaign perspective – Enclosed reference copy of Freedom of Information Act (FOIA)/New Mexico Inspection of Public Records Act (IPRA) request to Governor Bill Richardson." September 22, 2006.

_____. To Len Munsil, Arizona Republican candidate for governor. "Re: Enclosed reference copy of Freedom of Information Act (FOIA) request to Governor Janet Napolitano regarding her possible involvement in the Prescott, Arizona exhumations of John Miller and William Hudspeth, and their legal issues related to Maricopa County Prosecutor's Office Case # CA 2006020516." September 22, 2006. **(No response)**

Sullivan, Tom and Steve Sederwall. To Lincoln County Attorney Alan Morel. "The Dried Bean. 'You Believin' Us or Them Lyin' Whores.' " September 30, 2006. **(Exhibit 4 in IPRA response to me of October 11, 2006 from Sheriff Rick Virden through Lincoln County Attorney Alan Morel)**

300

Cooper, Gale. To Attorney Jonell Lucca. "Re: Information pertaining to Case # CA20006020516 (exhumations of John Miller and William Hudspeth) - American Academy of Forensic Science Ethics and Conduct Complaint against Dr. Henry Lee." October 2, 2006.

_____. To Senator John McCain. "New Mexico Billy the Kid Case and Governor Janet Napolitano." October 10, 2006.

_____. To Arizona Senate President Ken Bennett / Nick Simonetta. (via fax). "RE: Follow-up on Maricopa County Prosecutor's Office Case # CA 200602516 considering possible felony indictments ..." October 16, 2006.

Lucca, Jonell L. To Dr. Gale Cooper. "This letter is to inform you that the Maricopa County Attorney's Office has declined to file charges ..." . October 17, 2006. **(Switching of suspects to Jeanine Dike and Dale Tunnell)**

McCain, John. To Gale Cooper. "Your situation is under the jurisdiction of Governor Janet Napolitano ..." October 27, 2006.

Cooper, Gale. To Attorney Jonell Lucca. "Re: Maricopa County Case # CA20006020516." October 30, 2006. **(Confirmation of getting her case termination letter, and asking why she changed suspects. Never answered.)**

Iglesias, David C. U.S. Attorney and Mary L. Higgins, Assistant U.S. Attorney. To Gale Cooper, M.D. "Re: Copy of Documentation of RICO Complaint Concerning The 'Billy the Kid Case.' " November 16, 2006. **(Denial of my RICO complaint)**

Cooper, Gale. To John Dendahl. "RE: Documents Pertinent to Investigation of Billy the Kid Case Legal Improprieties." January 9, 2007.

_____. To Senator John McCain. "New Mexico Billy the Kid Case and possible involvement of Governor Janet Napolitano ..." January 9, 2007.

McCain, John. To Gale Cooper. "Members of Congress are precluded from inquiring into matters pending before the courts ..." January 25, 2007.

Cooper, Gale.. To Congressman Steve Pearce. "Bring to your attention an ongoing corruption case in Lincoln County ..." March 12, 2007.

_____. To New Mexico GOP Chairman Allen Weh. "RE: RICO Case." March 14, 2007.

_____. To Arizona Attorney General Terry Goddard. "Presentation of alleged prosecutorial improprieties relating to the exhumation of remains of John Miller and William Hudspeth at the Arizona Pioneers' Home Cemetery." March 21, 2007. **(No response.)**

_____. To Len Munsil, former Arizona Republican candidate for governor. "Re: Scandalous political cover-up by Governor Napolitano's Office and Maricopa County Prosecutor's Office ..." March 21, 2007. **(No response)**

_____. To State Senator Rod Adair. "Re: Overview of the Billy the Kid Case and its political scandal." April 3, 2007.

_____. To Hamilton, Texas, Mayor Roy Rumsey. (via fax). "Billy the Kid Case in a Nutshell." May 3, 2007. **(Background about current attempt to dig up "Brushy Bill")**

Virden, R.E. Lincoln County Sheriff. To Hamilton, Texas, Mayor Roy Ramsey [sic]. "This letter will inform you that Tom Sullivan and Steve Sederwall are both commissioned deputies ..." No date, but around May 2007. **(Confirms Virden's participation in the attempt to exhume "Brushy Bill" Roberts)**

Cooper, Gale. To Detective Anna Cahall. Prescott Police Department. "Re: Freedom of Information Act Request for Records of Prescott Police Department Case No. 06-12767. September 11, 2008.

_____. To Hamilton, Texas, Mayor Roy Rumsey. (via fax). "RE: Lincoln County Sheriff's Department's 2007 attempt to exhume Oliver "Brushy Bill" Roberts. September 11, 2008.

Rumsey, Roy. Hamilton Mayor. To Gale Cooper. (via fax). "RE: Lincoln County Sheriff's Department's 2007 attempt to exhume Oliver Roberts." September 12, 2008. **(Confirmation that the case is closed)**

E-MAILS (CHRONOLOGICAL ORDER)

Valdez, Jannay. "Re: Billy the Kid (Brushy Bill Roberts), To: Frederick Nolan "Author." September 12, 2004.

Utley, Robert M. "Billy Again." September 16, 2004. (**Sent to Jay Miller and forwarded to me regarding role of Paul Hutton in Billy the Kid Case**)

Tunnell, Dale. To Jeanine Dike. "Subject: RE: Disinterment of Wm Bonney." May 3, 2005.

Dike, Jeanine. To Dale Tunnell. "Subject: Disinterment of Wm Bonney." May 3, 2005.

_____. To Dale Sams. "Subject: FW: Disinterment Wm Bonney." May 3, 2005.

_____. To Dale Sams. "Subject: FW: Disinterment Wm Bonney." May 4, 2005.

Sederwall, Steven. To Misty Rodarte. "Subject: Billy the Kid." July 6, 2005.

Winter, Anne. "To: Tim Nelson; Alan Stephens. Subject: Pioneer Home, Grave, Billy the Kid and DNA." August 18, 2005. (**Has attachment of Gary Olson cover-up letter to her and implied internal cover-up. Also states that Sullivan paid for the exhumation**)

_____."To: Tim   Nelson;   Alan   Stephens.   Subject: Billy   the   Kid." September 8, 2005. (**"80% DNA match ..." The Doomsday Document**)

_____. "To Gary Olson. Subject: RE: the kid." October 17, 2005 (**Requesting any DNA results yet to him**)

Olson, Gary. "To Anne Winter. Subject: RE: the kid." October 17, 2005. (**Reporting on no DNA results yet to him**)

Winter, Anne. "To: Jeanine L'Ecuyer. Subject: FW: the kid." October 17, 2005. (**Reporting on no DNA results yet to Olson**)

JournalABQ@aol.com. "To: Gary Olson. Subject: re. John Miller." October 19, 2005. (**Reporter Rene Romo seeking information**)

Olson, Gary. "To: Anne Winter. Subject: FW: re. John Miller." October 20, 2005. (**Cover-up `planned for Romo. "I thought you and the Governor may want to know about this request"**)

Winter, Anne. "To: Tim Nelson; Alan Stephens. Subject: FW: re. John Miller." October 20, 2005. (**Cover-up plan for Romo presentation: "Remember there was the legal issue that they dug up two bodies."**)

_____. "To: Jeanine L'Ecuyer. Subject: FW: re. John Miller." October 25, 2005. (**Planning cover-up for media requests**)

Sederwall, Steven. "To: Barbara J. Miller; Steve McGregor; Rick Staub; Misty Rodarte; Emily Smith; Bob Boze Bell. Subject: in the Albuquerque Journal." November 6, 2005. (**Copy Romo article**)

Olson, Gary. "To Anne Winter, Mark Wilson. Subject: FW: in the Albuquerque Journal." November 7, 2005. (**Copy Romo article**)

Winter, Anne. "To: Jeanine L'Ecuyer; Tim Nelson; Alan Stephens. Subject: Billy the Kid. November 7, 2005. (**Reporting Gary Olson's cover-up in KPNX interview**)

Liptak, Adam. "Re. Follow-up on Billy the Kid Hoax Article." November 17, 2005.

Mnookin, Seth. "Re: Revised Proposal for Hoax Article." November 15, 2005.

_____. "Re: Kid Stuff." November 16, 2005.

Saar, Meghan. To Gale Cooper. "BTK Hoax Article." January 31, 2006.

Nolan, Frederick. "Response." May 22, 2006 (**Response of D. Ceribelli from the *New York Times* Executive Editor's Desk. Did not take article.**)

Sederwall, Steve. To confidential recipient. "Well we have the governor reaching out to the Arizona to stop this investigation." May 16, 2006.

Sams, Dale. Arizona Pioneers' Home Administrator. To Gale Cooper. Confirming approximate date of John Miller's birth as 1850. August 8, 2006.

Sederwall, Steven. To Jay Miller. "Subject: What is wrong? Can I help?" September 19, 2006. (**Exhibit 3 in IPRA response to me of October 11, 2006 from Sheriff Rick Virden through Lincoln County Attorney Alan Morel.**)

302

Miller, Jay. To Steven Sederwall. "Response: Subject: What is wrong? Can I help?" September 20, 2006. (**Exhibit 3 in IPRA response to me of October 11, 2006 from Sheriff Rick Virden through Lincoln County Attorney Alan Morel.**)

Sams, Dale. "Re: Statement." November 4, 2006. (**Statement in response to a letter using his name and addressed to Mr. Alan Morel, Lincoln County Attorney, and signed by Tom Sullivan and Steve Sederwall.**)

Nolan, Frederick. Re: Maxwell Family Questions. May 15, 2007. (**About dates of sale of buildings.**)

BLOGS

Andrews, Pat. Chairman GRIEF (Gambling Research Information & Education Foundation). Quotes blog on April 15, 2003 from "Dockside must be watched closely"/ No author given/*6.25.02/Indianapolis Star* an "Casino fined $2.26 million over allegations of prostitution" and Mike Smith/*7.30.02/Las Vegas Sun.* (**On R.D. Hubbard's corruption**)

No author. "Fraud Alleged at Cellmark, DNA Testing Firm. TalkLeft: The Politics of Crime. http://www.talkleft.com./new_archives/008809.html. November 18, 2004.

Sederwall, Steve. "The Wild is back in the West." April 24, 2006. (**Announcement of invitation with Sullivan to the Cannes Film Festival.**) http://www.truewestmagazine.com/weblog/blogger1.htm. (Bob Boze Bell Blog)

No Author. "AG won't investigate governor's hires." newmexicomatters.com: RichardsonWatch. December 19, 2006.

CHAT ROOM

Sederwall, Steve. To "Loretta." "Wild Goose Chase." May 4, 2007. http://disc.server.com/discussion.cgi?disc=167540;article=33266;title=Billy%20the %20Kid... (**Admitting that John Miller DNA could not match bench DNA**)

_____.   "Billyondabrain."   May   13,   2007. http://disc.server.com/discussion.cgi?disc=167540;article=33266;title=Billy%20the %20Kid... (**Claim that Arizona participated in Miller exhumation**)

TELEVISION PROGRAM

History Channel. "Investigating History: Billy the Kid." Week of April 24, 2004 and May 2, 2004.

BILLY THE KID CASE LEGAL DOCUMENTS (BY LOCATION)

CAPITAN, NEW MEXICO

Sederwall, Steve, "Mayor's Report, May 5, 2003." *Village of Capitan: Capitan Village Hall News.* Capitan, New Mexico.

ALBUQUERQUE, NEW MEXICO

"Response of Office of Medical Investigator to Petition to Exhume Remains of Catherine Antrim. In the Matter of Catherine Antrim. Case No. MS 2003-11 [sic]." January 9, 2004. Sixth Judicial Court, County of Grant, State of New Mexico. Signed: Ross E. Zumwalt, MD. (**This document refuses exhumation. Without an OMI permit it could not be done. Note that the Petitioners and Judge Quintero ignored it.**)

"Affidavit of Ross E. Zumwalt, MD. In the Matter of Catherine Antrim. Case No. MS 2003-11 Sixth Judicial Court, County of Grant, State of New Mexico. Signed: Ross E. Zumwalt, MD. ." January 9, 2004.

"Deposition of Debra Komar, Ph.D. In the Matter of Catherine Antrim. Case No. MS 2003-11." Sixth Judicial Court, County of Grant, State of New Mexico. Taken by Adam S. Baker, Attorney for Town of Silver City. Signed: Debra Komar, Ph.D. January 20, 2004.

LINCOLN COUNTY, NEW MEXICO

Sullivan, Tom. Lincoln County Sheriff. To Attorney Randall M. Harris. "Denial Letter." October 8, 2003. (**This IPRA denial for the Probable Cause Statement used the IPRA exception of ongoing law enforcement investigation**)

Sullivan, Tom. Sheriff, Lincoln County Sheriff's Office, and Steven M. Sederwall. Deputy Sheriff, Lincoln County Sheriff's Office. "Lincoln County Sheriff's Office, Lincoln County, New Mexico, Case: William H. Bonney, a.k.a. William Antrim, a.k.a. The Kid, a.k.a. Billy the Kid: An Investigation into the events of April 28, 1881 through July 14, 1881 – seventy-seven days of doubt." No Date. (**Possible rejected precursor to the Probable Cause Statement for Case # 2003-274. This document was part of the Lincoln County Sheriff's Department case file for 2003-274.**)

Sullivan, Tom. Sheriff Lincoln County, and Steve Sederwall, Deputy Sheriff, Lincoln County. "Lincoln County Sheriff's Department Case #2003-274, Probable Cause Statement." Filed in Lincoln County Sheriff's Department. Carrizozo, New Mexico. December 31, 2003.

No Author. "Contact List, William H. Bonney Case # 2003-274, Lincoln County Sheriff's Office & Investigators." No Date. Probably 2003 or 2004. (**This document was part of the Lincoln County Sheriff's Department Case file for 2003-274**)

Sederwall, Steven M. Lincoln County Sheriff's Deputy. "Lincoln County Sheriff's Department Supplemental Report, Case # 2003-274. Subject: Exhumation of John Miller." May 19, 2005.

Virden, R.E. Lincoln County Sheriff. To Jay Miller. "We are interested in the truth surrounding Billy the Kid and are continuing the investigation ..." November 28, 2005. (**Confirmation from Virden that continued the Billy the Kid case and deputized Sullivan and Sederwall for it.**)

Virden, R.E. Lincoln County Sheriff. To Hamilton, Texas, Mayor Roy Ramsey [sic]. "This letter will inform you that Tom Sullivan and Steve Sederwall are both commissioned deputies ..." No date, but around May 2007. (**Confirms Virden's participation in the attempt to exhume "Brushy Bill" Roberts**)

SILVER CITY, NEW MEXICO

Tippett, Sherry. Attorney. To Richard Gay, Assistant to the Chief of Staff, Governor Richardson's Office. "Memorandum, RE: Exhumation of Catherine Antrim." July 11, 2003. (**Tippett's secret communication with governor's office about Antrim exhumation, with misrepresentation of OMI position.**)

_____. To Steve Sederwall and Lincoln County Sheriff. "In the Matter of Catherine Antrim, Order." October 10, 2003 (mailing date). (**This is an unsigned order prepared by Attorney Tippett for the Antrim exhumation and claiming Medical Examiner [sic] participation.**)

_____. "Petition to Exhume Remains. In the Matter of Catherine Antrim. Case No. MS 03-011." Sixth Judicial Court, County of Grant, State of New Mexico. Signed: Sherry J. Tippett, Attorney for Petitioners. Filed October 3, 2003.

Kennedy, Paul J., Adam S. Baker, Thomas F. Stewart, Robert L. Scavron, Attorneys for Mayor Terry Fortenberry on Behalf of the Town of Silver City. "Response in Opposition to the Petition to Exhume Remains. In the Matter of Catherine Antrim. Case No. MS 03-011." Sixth Judicial Court, County of Grant, State of New Mexico. Filed October 31, 2003.

Tippett, Sherry J. Attorney for Petitioners. "State of New Mexico, County of Grant, Sixth Judicial District Court, In the Matter of Catherine Antrim, No. MS. 2003-11. Petitioner's Response in Opposition to the Town of Silver City's Motion to Intervene." (Unfiled) No Date.

Robins, Bill III and David Sandoval. Attorneys for Billy the Kid. "Billy the Kid's Unopposed Motion for Intervention and Request for Expedited Disposition. In the Matter of Catherine Antrim. Case No. MS 2003-11. Sixth Judicial Court, County of Grant, State of New Mexico." Filed November 26, 2003. (This is the first document in which Billy the Kid is claimed as a client. The petitioners, Sullivan, Sederwall, and Graves are omitted.)

Quintero, H.R. District Judge, Division 1. "Order. In the Matter of Catherine Antrim. Case No. MS 03-011." Sixth Judicial Court, County of Grant, State of New Mexico. Filed December 9, 2003. (This is a notice for rescheduling hearing from January 6, 2004 to January 27, 2004.)

Tippett, Sherry J. Attorney. To Mayor Steve Sederwall, Sheriff Tom Sullivan, Sheriff Gary Graves. "Attached is a copy of Judge Quintero's Order of December 9, 2003, ruling on our Hearing ..." December 17, 2003. (States surety that they will win the case on January 27, 2004; encourages the completion of the Probable Cause Statement; encloses her pre-printed senate proposal to back the case from Senator Benny Altamirano.)

Altamirano, Benny. State Senator. "Senate Memorial Number ____." (Prepared on December 17, 2003 by Attorney Sherry Tippett.) Undated.

Robins, Bill III and David Sandoval. Attorneys for Billy the Kid. "Billy the Kid's Pre-Hearing Brief." Case No. MS 2003-11. Sixth Judicial Court, County of Grant, State of New Mexico." Filed January 5, 2004. (This is the document linking pardon with exhumation - and cracking the Billy the Kid Case hoax as a "Brushy Bill" Roberts promotion.)

Quintero, H.R. District Judge, Division 1. "Order of Continuance. In the Matter of Catherine Antrim. Case No. MS 03-011." Filed January 23, 2004. Sixth Judicial Court, County of Grant, State of New Mexico. Filed January 23, 2004. (In this document the Court orders Petitioner's attorney, Sherry Tippett, as a sanction, to pay airfare for witness, Frederick Nolan.)

_____. "Decision and Order. In the Matter of Catherine Antrim. Case No. MS 03-011." Sixth Judicial Court, County of Grant, State of New Mexico. Filed April 2, 2004. (Document in which the judge permits the dead Billy the Kid to be the client in his court, and dismisses the case without prejudice with stipulation that DNA should be obtained from his grave before his mother's.)

FORT SUMNER, NEW MEXICO

"De Baca County Commissioners' Special Meeting September 25, 2003." Minutes. (Supported stand against exhumation.)

"Petition for the Exhumation of Billy the Kid's Remains. In the Matter of William H. Bonney, aka 'Billy the Kid.' Case No. CV-04-00005." Filed February 26, 2004. Tenth Judicial District, State of New Mexico, County of De Baca. Signed: Bill Robins III, David Sandoval, Mark Acuña; Attorneys for the Sheriff-Petitioners.

"Notice of Excusal. In the Matter of William H. Bonney, aka 'Billy the Kid.' Case No. CV-2004 [sic]-00005." Filed March 5, 2004. Tenth Judicial District, State of New Mexico, County of De Baca. Signed: Bill Robins III and David Sandoval; Attorneys for the Sheriff-Petitioners. (This is the Petitioners' removal of unbiased Judge Ricky Purcell from hearing the case.)

"Village of Fort Sumner's Unopposed Motion to Intervene. In the Matter of William H. Bonney, aka 'Billy the Kid.' Case No. CV-04-00005." Filed April 12, 2004. Tenth Judicial District, State of New Mexico, County of De Baca. Signed: Adam S. Baker and Herb Marsh, Jr. Attorneys for the Village of Fort Sumner.

"Response in Opposition to the Petitioners for the Exhumation of Billy the Kid's Remains. In the Matter of William H. Bonney, aka 'Billy the Kid.' Case No. CV-04-00005." Filed April 12, 2004. Tenth Judicial District, State of New Mexico, County of De Baca. Signed: Adam S. Baker and Herb Marsh, Jr. Attorneys for the Village of Fort Sumner.

"Village of Fort Sumner's Motion to Dismiss Against Petitioners Sullivan, Sederwall, and Graves for Lack of Standing. In the Matter of William H. Bonney, aka 'Billy the Kid.' Case No. CV-04-00005." Filed June 24, 2004. Tenth Judicial District, State of New Mexico, County of De Baca. Signed: Adam S. Baker and Herb Marsh, Jr. Attorneys for the Village of Fort Sumner.

"Notice of Hearing. In the Matter of William H. Bonney, aka 'Billy the Kid.' Case No. CV-04-00005." Filed July 6, 2004. Tenth Judicial District, State of New Mexico, County of De Baca. Signed for the Honorable Teddy L. Hartley.

"Petitioner's Response to the Village of Ft. Sumner's Motion to Dismiss. In the Matter of William H. Bonney, aka 'Billy the Kid.' Case No. CV-04-00005." Filed July 29, 2004. Tenth Judicial District, State of New Mexico, County of De Baca. Signed: Mark Anthony Acuña; Attorneys for the Petitioners Sullivan, Sederwall [sic] & Graves.

"Stipulation of Dismissal. In the Matter of William H. Bonney, aka 'Billy the Kid.' Case No. CV-04-00005." Filed August 23, 2004. Tenth Judicial District, State of New Mexico, County of De Baca. Signed: Bill Robins III, David Sandoval; Attorneys for the Billy the Kid; and Adam S. Baker and Herb Marsh, Jr., Attorneys for the Village of Fort Sumner. (**Dismissal was with prejudice**)

"In the Matter of De Baca County Sheriff Gary Graves. Petition for Order Allowing Recall Vote. Case No. CV-04-00019." Filed September 13, 2004. Tenth Judicial District Court, State of New Mexico, County of De Baca. (**Beginning of Recall of Sheriff Gary Graves**)

"In the Matter "Stipulation of Dismissal with Prejudice. In the Matter of William H. Bonney, aka 'Billy the Kid.' Case No. CV-04-00005." Filed September 24, 2004. Tenth Judicial District, State of New Mexico, County of De Baca. Signed: Mark Anthony Acuña, Attorneys for the Petitioners Sullivan, Sederwall & Graves (**Note the switch of clients**) and Adam S. Baker and Herb Marsh, Jr., Attorneys for the Village of Fort Sumner. (**Definitive victory against exhumation**)

PRESCOTT, ARIZONA

Fulginiti, Laura C. Ph.D., D-ABFA. Forensic Anthropologist. To Dale L. Tunnell, Ph.D. "RE: Exhumation, Pioneer Home Cemetery, Prescott, Arizona." June 2, 2005. (**Forensic report of the John Miller William Hudspeth exhumations**)

Cahall, Anna, Detective Prescott Police Department. "CASE REPORT 0600012767." April 5, 2006. 13;30:14. (**Concerning the John Miller exhumation**)

PAST ATTEMPT TO EXHUME WILLIAM H. BONNEY

"Motion to Intervene. In Re Application of Lois Telfer, Petitioner for the Removal of the Body of William H. Bonney, Deceased, From the Ft. Sumner Cemetery in Which He is Interred for Reinterment in the Lincoln, New Mexico, Cemetery. Case No. 3255." December 5, 1961. In the District Court of the Tenth Judicial District Within and For the County of De Baca. Signed: Victor C. Breen and John Humphrey, Jr., Attorneys for Louis A Bowdre. (**Louis Bowdre was the relative of Charles Bowdre whose grave is contiguous to William Bonney's.**)

"Decree." In Re Application of Lois Telfer, Petitioner for the Removal of the Body of William H. Bonney, Deceased, From the Ft. Sumner Cemetery in Which He is Interred for Reinterment in the Lincoln, New Mexico, Cemetery. Case No. 3255." April 6, 1962. In the District Court of the Tenth Judicial District Within and For the County of De Baca. Signed: E. T. Kinsley, District Judge. (**Petition for**

306

exhumation was denied on basis that Bonney's grave could not be located and the search would disturb Bowdre's remains. That precedent was ignored by the current Petitioners and their attorneys.)

OPEN RECORDS INVESTIGATIONS (CHRONOLOGICAL)

LETTERS BY AND TO JAY MILLER

Miller, Jay. To Steve Sederwall, Mayor of Capitan and Deputy Sheriff of Lincoln County. "FOIA/IPRA." May 13, 2004.
_____. To Village of Capitan Records Custodian. "I would like to inspect and copy the following documents of Steve Sederwall ..." May 13, 2004.
_____. To County Clerk of Lincoln County/Records Custodian, Lincoln County Courthouse. "Re: I would like to inspect the following documents of Tom Sullivan, elected Sheriff of Lincoln County." May 13, 2004.
_____. To County Clerk of DeBaca County/Records Custodian. "Freedom of Information Act Request: Inspect and copy records pertaining to Gary Graves, elected sheriff ..." May 13, 2004.
Morel, Alan P. Lincoln County Attorney. To Jay Miller. "RE: Freedom of Information Act Request dated May 13, 2004." May 19, 2004.
Grassie, Anna Gail. (For Village of Capitan and Mayor Steve Sederwall). To Jay Miller. "Reference: Freedom of Information Request from Jay Miller dated May 13, 2004." May 25, 2004.
Miller, Jay. To Michael Cerletti, Secretary, Department Tourism. "RE: FOIA/IPRA on Billy the Kid Case promulgators and Department of Tourism." May, 28, 2004.
_____. To Attorney Alan P. Morel. "Re: Response to your letter dated May 19, 2004 on behalf of the County Clerk of Lincoln County and Lincoln County Sheriff Tom Sullivan." June 1, 2004.
_____. To Mayor Steve Sederwall. "FOIA/IPRA on Steve Sederwall as Mayor of Capitan and Deputy Sheriff of Lincoln County." June 1, 2004.
Morel, Alan P. Lincoln County Attorney. To Jay Miller. "RE: Response to your letter dated May 19, 2004 on behalf of the County Clerk of Lincoln County and Lincoln County Sheriff Tom Sullivan. June 1, 2004.
Sederwall, Steven: Mayor. To Jay Miller. "I am in receipt of your letter dated June 1, 2004." June 3, 2004.
Morel, Alan P. Lincoln County Attorney. To Jay Miller. "RE: Freedom of Information Act Request June 1, 2004." June 4, 2004.
Cerletti, Mike (through Jon Hendry, Director of Marketing). To Jay Miller. "Reply to your freedom of information request." June 7, 2004. (**Denied participation of Tourism Department in Billy the Kid Case**)
Miller, Jay. To Lincoln County Attorney Alan Morel. "Copy all documents relevant to David Turk, historian for the U.S. Marshals Service ..." June 9, 2004.
_____. To Mayor of Capitan and Deputy Sheriff of Lincoln County Steve Sederwall. "Evade response by claiming that you were being addresses solely in your capacity as Mayor ..." June 9, 2004.
_____. To Sheriff Gary Graves and Nancy Sparks, De Baca County Clerk. "Freedom of Information Act Request: I would like to inspect any and all documents relevant to David Turk ..." June 9, 2004.
Sederwall, Steven M. To Jay Miller. "This office has no records ..." June 10, 2004.
Miller, Jay. To Mayor Steve Sederwall. "FOIA/IPRA on Steve Sederwall as Mayor of Capitan and Deputy Sheriff of Lincoln County." June 10, 2004.
_____. To Attorney General Patricia Madrid. "Re: Follow-up on FOIA/IPRA Request to Lincoln County Sheriff Tom Sullivan." June 14, 2004. (**This was stonewalled. No response ever came.**)

Sparks Nancy. (Clerk for Sheriff Gary Graves). To Jay Miller. "Re: FOIA/IPRA request for records of De Baca County Sheriff Gary Graves." June 14, 2004.

Miller, Jay. To Mayor of Capitan and Deputy Sheriff of Lincoln County Steve Sederwall. "Thank you for your prompt response to my letter of June 1, 2004 ... " June 21, 2004.

_____. To Attorney General Patricia Madrid. RE: Follow-up on FOIA/IPRA Requests to Steve Sederwall, Mayor of Capitan and Deputy Sheriff of Lincoln County." June 21, 2004.

_____. To Lincoln County Attorney Alan Morel. "I would like to inspect and copy any and all documents relevant to your client Tom Sullivan, Sheriff of Lincoln County with regard to a statement made by his attorney Sherry Tippett ..." June 23, 2004.

_____. To Mayor of Capitan and Deputy Sheriff of Lincoln County Steve Sederwall. "To inspect and copy all records relevant to your attorney, Sherry Tippett's, claims ..." June 23, 2004.

_____. To Michael Cerletti, Secretary Tourism. "Thanks for your response ..." June 23, 2004.

Morel, Alan P. Lincoln County Attorney. To Jay Miller. "RE: Freedom of Information Act Request/Inspection of Public Records Act Request dated June 23, 2004."

Lama, Albert J. Assistant Attorney General. To Jay Miller. "Concerning an alleged violation of the Inspection of Public Records Act by the Lincoln County, De Baca County, and Village of Capitan." June 24, 2004. **(This was sent to Assistant AG Mary Smith, who later covered-up for Sederwall.)**

Miller, Jay. To Attorney General Patricia Madrid. "Re: Follow-up on FOIA/IPRA Requests to Steve Sederwall, Mayor of Capitan and Deputy Sheriff of Lincoln County." June 21, 2004. **(This was information on the "maturing problem" not a complaint, but was used to close the case.)**

Graves, Gary W. De Baca County Sheriff. To Jay Miller. "I am writing in response to your request ..." June 22, 2004. **(Denies information on David Turk)**

Miller, Jay. To Sheriff Gary Graves. "Freedom of Information Act Request: Inspect and copy all records relevant to your attorney, Sherry Tippett ..." June 23, 2004.

_____. To Sheriff Gary Graves and Nancy Sparks. "Re: FOIA/IPRA request for records." June 25, 2004.

Graves, Gary W. De Baca County Sheriff. To Jay Miller. "I do not maintain requests for travel reimbursements ..." June 29, 2004. **(His clerk did send the records!)**

_____. To Jay Miller. "As per your FOIA/IPRA Request on June 23, 2004 ..." June 29, 2004. **(Denies records on Attorney Sherry Tippett.)**

_____. To Jay Miller. "I do not maintain or have any records in reference to Sherry Tippett ..." June 29, 2004.

Miller, Jay. To Attorney Alan Morel. "Re: Deputizing of Capitan Mayor Steve Sederwall as referenced in your letter dated June 4, 2004 on behalf of Lincoln County Sheriff Tom Sullivan." July 1, 2004.

Morel, Alan P. Attorney for Lincoln County. To Jay Miller. "Re: Deputizing of Capitan Mayor Steve Sederwall as referenced in your letter dated June 4, 2004 on behalf of Lincoln County Sheriff Tom Sullivan." July 1, 2004.

_____. To Jay Miller. "RE: Freedom of Information Act/Inspection of Public Records Act Request dated June 23, 2004." July 2, 2004.

Sparks, Nancy. De Baca County Clerk. "I have sent you everything I have on Sheriff Graves ..." July 2, 2004.

Prelo, Marc. Attorney for Village of Capitan. To Jay Miller. "RE: Village of Capitan/Freedom of Information Act - Inspection of Public Records Request. July 5, 2004. **(Response for Sederwall to Jay Miller)**

Miller, Jay. To Assistant AG Mary Smith. "Re: Response to your letter of June 24, 2004." July 8, 2004.

_____. To Sheriff Gary Graves. "Re: Follow-up on your responses to my prior FOIA/IPRA requests." July 8, 2004.

Morel, Alan P. Lincoln County Attorney. To Jay Miller. "RE: Freedom of Information Act Request dated July 1, 2004." July 9, 2004.

Smith, Mary H., Assistant Attorney General. To Jay Miller. "Re: Determination of Inspection of Public Records Act Complaint v Village of Capitan." August 3, 2004.

_____. To Jay Miller. "Re: Determination of Inspection of Public Records Act complaint v De Baca County." August 3, 2004.

Miller, Jay. To Sheriff Tom Sullivan. "Re: David Turk, Historian for the U.S. Marshals Service." August 5, 2004.

_____. To Office of General Counsel - FOIA REQUEST, Attn. Arleta Cunningham, U.S. Marshal's Service. "Re. David Turk, historian for U.S. Marshal's Service, FOIA on Sederwall/Sullivan/Graves/ Billy the Kid Case." August 5, 2004.

_____. To Assistant AG Mary Smith. "Re. Response to your letter of August 3, 2004 about determination of my IPRA complaint v Mayor of Capitan Steve Sederwall, who also represents himself as Deputy Sheriff of Lincoln County; and the Village of Capitan." August, 10, 2004.

Sullivan, Tom, Lincoln County Sheriff. "In response to your 'Inspection of Public Records Act" request dated August 5, 2004." August 18, 2004. (**Refuses IPRA records on David Turk based on ongoing criminal investigation**)

Morel, Alan P. Lincoln County Attorney. To Jay Miller. "In response to your "Information Act Request dated August 5, 2004." August 18, 2004.

Miller, Jay. To Deputy Attorney General Stuart Bluestone. "Re: Complaint and appeal for assistance with regard to non-compliance with FOIA/IPRA requests made to Capitan Mayor Steve Sederwall, who represents himself as Deputy Sheriff of Lincoln County and the Village Clerk of Capitan." August 28, 2004. (**No response**)

_____. To Deputy Attorney General Stuart Bluestone. "Re: Complaint and appeal for assistance with regard to non-compliance with FOIA/IPRA requests made to Lincoln County Sheriff Tom Sullivan and Lincoln County Clerk." September 4, 2004. (**No response**)

Smith Mary. Assistant Attorney General. To Jay Miller. "Re: Inspection of Public Records Act complaint v Steve Sederwall, Mayor of Capitan and Lincoln County Deputy Sheriff." May 17, 2005. (**Nine months later: Rejection of complaint**)

Bordley, William E. To Jay Miller. "Freedom of Information/Privacy Act Request No. 2004USMS7634, Subject: David Turk, Historian U.S. Marshals Service, FOIA on Sederwall/Sullivan/Graves/Billy the Kid Case." June 22, 2005. (**Note that this response to the Turk FOIA was a year later! It did contain Turk's taxpayer monies used.**)

Miller, Jay. To William E. Boardley, Associate General Counsel/FOIPA Officer, U.S. Marshal's Service. "Follow-up on your response titled Freedom of Information Act Request No. 2004USMS7634 Subject: David Turk, Historian U.S. Marshal's Service, FOIA on Sederwall/Sullivan/Graves/Billy the Kid Case." July 25, 2005.

DeZulovich, Mavis. FOI/PA Liaison, Office of Public Affairs. To Jay Miller. "This letter is in response to your Freedom of Information/Privacy Act Request No. 2004USMS7634 in reference to David Turk. August 24, 2005. (**States Turk is not Probable Cause Statement author, but references his pamphlet..**)

Virden, R.E. Lincoln County Sheriff. To Jay Miller. "We are interested in the truth surrounding Billy the Kid and are continuing the investigation ..." November 28, 2005. (**Confirmation from Virden that continued the Billy the Kid case and deputized Sullivan and Sederwall for it.**)

Miller, Jay. To Paul Hutton. "As a journalist following the Billy the Kid Case ..." February 6, 2006.

_____. To Attorney General Patricia Madrid. "Re: Follow-up on non-response by Attorney General to my September 4, 2004 Complaint and Appeal for assistance with regard to non-compliance by past Lincoln County Sheriff Tom Sullivan with my FOIA/IPRA Requests." March 20, 2006.

_____. To Paul Hutton. "Repeat of one sent to you on February 6, 2006, because I received no response to it." March 20, 2006.

_____. To Sheriff Rick Virden. "Inspection of Public Records Act/Freedom of Information Act request." March 27, 2006.

_____. To Attorney Marc Prelo. "Re: Follow-up on Freedom of Information Request response dated July 5, 2004." March 27, 2006. **(Requests information on his use of taxpayer money for Sederwall's Billy the Kid Case participation)**

Prelo, Marc Attorney. To Jay Miller. "RE: Village of Capitan/Freedom of Information Act – Inspection of Public Records Request." Match 31, 2006. **(Confirms his use of taxpayer money for Sederwall's Billy the Kid Case participation)**

Morel, Alan P. Lincoln County Attorney. To Jay Miller. "RE: Freedom of Information Act/Inspection of Public Records Act request dated March 27, 2006, to Lincoln County Sheriff Rick Virden. April 3, 2006.

_____. To Jay Miller. "Re: Follow-up on Freedom of Information Act Request Responses Dated May 19, 2004 and June 4, 2004." April 17, 2006. **(Confirms his use of taxpayer money for Sullivan's Billy the Kid Case participation)**

Miller, Jay. To Attorney General Patricia Madrid. "Re: Follow-up on FOIA/IPRA Request to Lincoln County Sheriff Tom Sullivan." May 6, 2006. **(This repeat of the June 14, 2004 IPRA complaint was stonewalled. No response ever.)**

_____. To Assistant Attorney General Mary Smith. "Re. Response to your letter of May 17, 2005 rejecting my IPRA complaint against then Mayor of Capitan Steve Sederwall, who also represented himself as Deputy Sheriff of Lincoln County." May 6, 2006. **(No response.)**

Sides, John D. Director, Investigative Division of Attorney General. "Re: Impersonating a Peace Officer File 5264." May 18, 2006. **(After 2 year stonewall, merely refers him to D.A. Scot Keys.)**

Miller, Jay. To Assistant Attorney General Mary Smith. "Re. Response to your letter of May 17, 2005 rejecting my IPRA complaint against then Mayor of Capitan Steve Sederwall, who also represented himself as Deputy Sheriff of Lincoln County." June 13, 2006. **(Repeat complaint with new information. No response.)**

_____. To Paul Hutton. "Re. Clarification of my letter to you dated March 20, 2006, and reframing of it as a FOIA/IPRA Request." June 13, 2006.

_____. To Attorney Mark Acuña. "Re. Follow-up on your legal participation in the New Mexico Billy the Kid Case and participation of the Jaffe Law Firm in the New Mexico Billy the Kid Case." June 22, 2006. **(No response.)**

_____. To Attorney General Patricia Madrid. "Re. FOIA/IPRA Request with regard to your relationship with Attorney Bill Robins III and/or his law firm Heard, Robins, Cloud, Lubel & Greenwood LLP." August 8, 2006.

_____. To Attorney Mark Acuña.. "Re. Follow-up on my unanswered letter of June 22, 2006 with regard to your legal participation in the New Mexico Billy the Kid Case and the participation of your Jaffe Law Firm in the New Mexico Billy the Kid Case." August 8, 2006. **(No response.)**

_____. To Mavis DeZulovich. FOIA/PA Liaison U.S. Department of Justice. "Re: Follow-up to your August 24, 2005 response to my Freedom of Information Act request No. 2004USMS7634 in reference to David Turk, Historian for the U.S. Marshals Service." August 8, 2006. **(Request for Turk's pamphlet)**

Kupfer, Elizabeth, Records Custodian. To Jay Miller. "Need additional time ..." August 14, 2006.

_____. To Attorney General Patricia Madrid. "RE: FOIA/IPRA request regarding Attorney Bill Robins III and/or his law firm Heard, Robins, Cloud, Lubel, and Greenwood." August 24, 2006.

Cedrick, Nikki. FOIA/PA Liaison U.S. Department of Justice. "Per your FOI request No. 2004USMS7634." August 31, 2006. **(Refuses to send copy of David Turk's pamphlet on Billy the Kid)**

310

Miller, Jay. To Attorney General Patricia Madrid. "Re: Second FOIA/IPRA Request with regard to documentation of financial relationship of Attorney General Patricia Madrid and/or her Office, and Attorney Bill Robins III and/or his law firm Heard, Robins, Cloud, Lubel, and Greenwood LLP." September 1, 2006.

_____. To Assistant Attorney General Mary Smith. "Re. Response to your letter of May 17, 2005 rejecting my IPRA complaint against then Mayor of Capitan Steve Sederwall, who also represented himself as Deputy Sheriff of Lincoln County." September 1, 2006. (No response)

_____. To Deputy Attorney General Stuart Bluestone. "Re: Follow-up on your recent telephone call to me about my current, repeated, FOIA/IPRA non-compliance complaints to Attorney General Patricia Madrid with regard to Tom Sullivan's and Steve Sederwall's participation in the Billy the Kid Case in their capacities as public officials." September 1, 2006. (No response)

Bordley, William E. Associate General Counsel/FOIPA Officer for U.S. Department of Justice. To Jay Miller. "Re: Freedom of Information/Privacy Act Request No. 2006USMS9782 Subject: Copy of Report Entitled *The U.S. Marshals Service and Billy the Kid.*" September 5, 2006. (Refuses to send copy of David Turk's pamphlet on Billy the Kid)

Kupfer, Elizabeth, Records Custodian. To Jay Miller. "Need additional time ..." September 6, 2006.

Miller, Jay. To Nikki Cedrick, FOIA/PA Liaison U.S. Department of Justice. "Re: Follow-up to your August 31, 2006 response to my Freedom of Information Act request No. 2004USMS7634 in Reference to David Turk, Historian for the U.S. Marshals Service; and request for clarification." September 11, 2006.

Smith, Glenn R., Deputy Attorney General and Elizabeth Kupfer, Custodian of Public Records. (For Attorney General Patricia Madrid). To Jay Miller." RE: Inspection of Public Records Request." September 20, 2006.

LETTERS BY AND TO GALE COOPER

Cooper, Gale. To Governor Bill Richardson and Records Custodian for FOIA/IPRA Requests. "Re: Freedom of Information Act (FOIA)/Inspection of Public Records Act (IPRA) request concerning participation of Governor Bill Richardson in the New Mexico Billy the Kid Case and related issues." September 22, 2006.

_____. To Governor Janet Napolitano. "Re: Freedom of Information Act (FOIA) request pertaining to the Prescott, Arizona exhumations of John Miller and William Hudspeth at the Arizona Pioneers' Home Cemetery on May 19, 2005." September 22, 2006.

_____. To Sheriff Rick Virden. "Re: Freedom of Information Act (FOIA)/New Mexico Inspection of Public Records Act (IPRA) request pertaining to Lincoln County Sheriff's Department Case # 2003-274 ("Billy the Kid Case") and to its May 19, 2005 Prescott Arizona exhumations of John Miller and William Hudspeth." September 22, 2006.

Morel, Alan P. Lincoln County Attorney. To Gale Cooper. "Re: Freedom of Information Act/Inspection of Public Records Act Request dated September 22, 2006, to Lincoln County Sheriff Rick Virden." September 29, 2006.

Maestas, Marcie. Records Custodian for Governor Bill Richardson. To Gale Cooper, M.D. "Received your request to inspect certain records ..." October 3, 2006.

Morel, Alan P. Lincoln County Attorney. To Gale Cooper. "RE: Freedom of Information Act (FOIA)/New Mexico Inspection of Public Records Act (IPRA) to Lincoln County Sheriff Ricky [sic] Virden and the Lincoln County Records Custodian, dated September 22, 2006." October 11, 2006.

Maestas, Marcie. Records Custodian for Governor Bill Richardson. To Gale Cooper, M.D. "Response to your Inspection of Public Records request received by our office on September 28, 2006 ..." October 13, 2006. (Denial of each item, but miscellaneous documents provided)

Michael R. Haener. Deputy Chief of Staff to Governor Janet Napolitano. "Enclosed records responsive to your request ..." November 13, 2006.

Cooper, Gale. To Governor Janet Napolitano. "Re: Repeated Freedom of Information Act (FOIA) request pertaining to the Prescott, Arizona exhumations of John Miller and William Hudspeth at the Arizona Pioneers' Home Cemetery on May 19, 2005." March 20, 2007. **(Repeated because of no response)**

_____. To Governor Janet Napolitano's Records Custodian. "Re: Repeat submission of incompletely answered Freedom of Information Act request dated September 22, 2006. March 21, 2007.

_____. To January Contreras, Policy Advisor for Health for Governor Janet Napolitano. "Re: Freedom of Information Request." June 29, 2007.

Shilo Mitchell, Deputy Press Secretary for Governor Janet Napolitano. To Gale Cooper, M.D. ""We have no responsive documents from your last request ..." August 2, 2007.

Cooper, Gale. To January Contreras, Policy Advisor for Health for Governor Janet Napolitano. "Re: Non- response to my Freedom of Information Act request dated June 29, 2007." August 10, 2007.

INVESTIGATIONS: DR. HENRY LEE; ORCHID CELLMARK LAB (CHRONOLOGICAL ORDER)

LETTERS BY AND TO JAY MILLER

Miller, Jay. To Dr. Henry Lee. "Re: Forensic consultation in the New Mexico Billy the Kid Case." March 27, 2006. **(Included all the articles with Lee's forensic claims)**

Lee, Henry, Dr. To Jay Miller. "In response to your letter dated March 27, 2006 ..." May 1, 2006. **(Says sent carpenter's bench forensic report to the Lincoln County Sheriff's Department directly)**

Miller, Jay. To Dr. Henry Lee. "Re: Follow-up on your letter of May 1, 2006 responding to my request of March 27, 2006 for information on your forensic consultation in the New Mexico Billy the Kid Case." June 15, 2006.

_____. To Dr. Henry Lee. "Re: Follow-up to my letter of June 15, 2006 with regard to your forensic consultation in the New Mexico Billy the Kid Case." August 8, 2006.

_____. To Dr. Rick Staub. "Re: The participation by you and Orchid Cellmark in the New Mexico Billy the Kid Case." August 8, 2006. **(No response)**

LETTERS BY AND TO GALE COOPER

Cooper, Gale. To Haskell Pitluck, AAFS Ethics Committee Chairman and members of the AAFS Ethics Committee. "Re: Formal Ethics Complaint against Dr. Henry Lee for his work as a forensic expert in Lincoln County, New Mexico, Sheriff's Department Case # 2003-274 ('the Billy the Kid Case')." October 2, 2006..

Cooper, Gale. To Haskell Pitluck, AAFS Ethics Committee Chairman. "Re: Follow-up on my October 2, 2006 complaint on Dr. Henry Lee to the Ethics Committee of the American Academy of Forensic Sciences." March 5, 2007.

_____. To Dr. Bruce Goldberger. President AAFS. "Re: Informing of non-action to date on my American Academy of Forensic Sciences Ethics Committee complaint filed October 2, 2006 against Dr. Henry Lee." April 10, 2007.

Goldberger, Bruce. Dr. and President AAFS. To Gale Cooper. (via fax) "I have received the complaint today ..." April 12,, 2007.

_____. To Gale Cooper. (via fax) "You should receive a letter from Mr. Pitluck in the coming week or two ..." May 4, 2007.

Pitluck, Haskell M. AAFS Ethics Committee Chairman. To Gale Cooper, M.D. "Ethics Committee has completed its investigation ..." May 9, 2007. **(Denial of any** ethical violation by Dr. Lee based solely on his report to Lincoln County Sheriff's Department. Date of report given as February 5, 2005.)

Cooper, Gale. To Haskell Pitluck, AAFS Ethics Committee Chairman. "Re: Follow-up on the May 9, 2007 AAFS response to my October 2, 2006 Ethics Complaint on Dr. Henry Lee. May 30, 2007.

_____. To Dr. Bruce Goldberger. President AAFS. "Re: Informing you about the need for clarification in the May 9, 2007 AAFS Ethics Committee response to my AAFS Ethics and Conduct Complaint of October 2, 2006 against Dr. Henry Lee." May 30, 2007.

Pitluck, Haskell M. AAFS Ethics Committee Chairman. To Gale Cooper, M.D. "Ethics Committee has completed its investigation ..." June 2, 2007. (Denial of any responsibility by Dr. Lee for "actions or statements of others.")

Cooper, Gale. To Rene Romo. *Albuquerque Journal*. "Re: Attributions made by you in your August 2, 2004 *Albuquerque Journal* article titled 'Forensic Expert on Billy's Case: Questions Remain on Outlaws Fate.'" June 19, 2007.

_____. To Haskell Pitluck, AAFS Ethics Committee Chairman. "Re: Requested clarification of your responses of May 9, 2007 and June 2, 2007 to my October 2, 2006 AAFS Ethics Complaint against Dr. Henry Lee." June 19, 2007.

_____. To Den Slaney. Albuquerque Museum of Art and History. "Re: Information request for Dreamscape Desperado exhibit." June 29, 2007. (Documentation for carpenter's bench blood claim requested)

Pitluck, Haskell M. AAFS Ethics Committee Chairman. To Gale Cooper, M.D. "Ethics Committee has completed its investigation ..." July 6, 2007.

Cooper, Gale. To Albuquerque Museum of Art and History Director Cathy Wright. "Re: Information request concerning past Dreamscape Desperado exhibit." July 30, 2007. (Concerning their labeling of the carpenter's bench as having blood according to Dr. Henry Lee)

Slaney, Deborah. Curator of History at the Albuquerque Museum of Art and History. To Gale Cooper. "Re: Information request concerning past Dreamscape Desperado exhibit." August 6, 2007. (Claim that Paul Hutton, not Dr. Lee, made the bench blood statement)

Walz, Kent. Editor-in-Chief *Albuquerque Journal*. To Gale Cooper. "Response to your letter concerning Rene Romo's story of August 2, 2004." August 13, 2007.

VIRDEN ET AL IPRA VIOLATION CASE (CHRONOLOGICAL ORDER)

Cheves, Philip W. Barnett Law Firm. To Sheriff Rick Virden. "Re: Request for Inspection of Public Records." April 24, 2007.

Morel, Alan P., Lincoln County Attorney. To Barnett Law Firm. "Re: Freedom of Information Act/Inspection of Public Records Act Request Dated April 24, 2007." April 27, 2007.

Cheves, Philip W. Barnett Law Firm. To Sheriff Rick Virden. "Re: Request for Inspection of Public Records." May 9, 2007.

_____. To Alan P. Morel, Esquire. "Re: Request for Inspection of Public Records." May 9, 2007.

Morel, Alan P., Lincoln County Attorney. To Barnett Law Firm. "RE: Freedom of Information Act/Inspection of Public Records Act Request to Sheriff Rick Virden Dated May 9, 2007." May 11, 2007.

_____.. To Barnett Law Firm. "RE: Freedom of Information Act/Inspection of Public Records Act Request to Alan P. Morel, Esq., Dated May 9, 2007." May 14, 2007.

Cheves, Philip W. Barnett Law Firm. To Alan P. Morel, Esquire. "Re: Request for Inspection of Public Records." June 8, 2007.

Morel, Alan P., Lincoln County Attorney. Thomas Stewart, Lincoln County Manager, and Rick Virden, Lincoln County Sheriff. To Tom Sullivan and Steve Sederwall. "Re: Request for Inspection of Public Records." June 21, 2007.

Sederwall, Steven M. and Thomas T. Sullivan. To Rick Virden, Lincoln County Sheriff. "Memorandum. Subject: Billy the Kid Investigation." June 21, 2007.

Morel, Alan P. Lincoln County Attorney. To Barnett Law Firm. "RE: Freedom of Information Act/Inspection of Public Records Act Request to Alan Morel, Esq., Dated June 8, 2007." June 22, 2007.

"Verified Complaint for Declaratory Judgment Ordering Production of Certain Records and Information. Cause No. D1329-CV-07-1364." Thirteenth Judicial District Court, State of New Mexico, County of Sandoval." Attorneys Mickey Barnett, Phil Cheves, and David Garcia for Plaintiffs Gale Cooper and De Baca County News. Filed October 15, 2007.

"Verified First Amended Complaint for Declaratory Judgment Ordering Production of Certain Records and Information. Cause No. D1329-CV-07-1364." Thirteenth Judicial District Court, State of New Mexico, County of Sandoval." Attorneys Mickey Barnett, Phil Cheves, and David Garcia for Plaintiffs Gale Cooper and De Baca County News. Filed November 1, 2007.

Zimitski, Dewayne. Process server for Steve Sederwall and Tom Sullivan. "Affidavit of DeWayne Zimitski for Cause No. D 1329 CV 2007-01364." December 27, 2007.

Cooper, Gale. To Attorney General Gary King. "Re: Informing about an IPRA violation case: Sandoval County Thirteenth Judicial District Cause No. D1329-CV2007-1364." January 22, 2008.

_____. To Attorney Leonard DeLayo for FOG. "Re: Sandoval County Thirteenth Judicial District Court Cause No. D 1329 CV2007-1364; an IPRA violation case." January 22, 2008.

"Motion to Dismiss Based on Improper Venue and Failure to State a Claim. Cause No. D1329-CV-07-1364." Thirteenth Judicial District Court, State of New Mexico, County of Sandoval. Filed March 5, 2008. Attorney H. Nicole Werkmeister for Defendant Rick Virden.

Brown, Kevin M. Attorney for defendants Sullivan and Sederwall. To Barnett Law Form. "Thomas T. Sullivan's Responses to Request for Production of Documents, No. D. 1329-Cv-2007-01364." March 17, 2008.

_____l. To Barnett Law Form. "Steven M. Sederwall's Responses to Request for Production of Documents, No. D. 1329-Cv-2007-01364." March 17, 2008.

"Plaintiffs' Response to the Motion of Defendant Rick Virden to Dismiss For Improper Venue and Failure to State Claim." Cause No. D1329-CV-07-1364." Thirteenth Judicial District Court, State of New Mexico, County of Sandoval. Attorneys Mickey Barnett and David Garcia for Plaintiffs Gale Cooper and De Baca County News. Filed March 24, 2008.

Shandler, Zachary. (For Attorney General Gary King). To Gale Cooper M.D. "RE: Gale Cooper and De Baca County News vs. Lincoln County et al., Cause No. D1329-CV2007-1364." April 3, 2008.

Stinnett, Scot. To Gale Cooper. (via e-mail). "IPRA Case Updates." August 12, 2008.

Sullivan, Thomas T. "Deposition for State of New Mexico County of Sandoval Thirteenth Judicial District No. D 1329-CV-2007-01364 Gale Cooper and De Baca County News, Plaintiffs, vs. Rick Virden, Lincoln County Sheriff and Custodian of Records of the Lincoln County Sheriff; and Steven M. Sederwall, Former Lincoln County Sheriff [sic]; and Thomas T. Sullivan, former Lincoln County Sheriff and former Lincoln County Deputy Sheriff, Defendants." Taken by Mickey D. Barnett, Attorney for the Plaintiff." August 18, 2008.

Sederwall, Steven M. "Deposition for State of New Mexico County of Sandoval Thirteenth Judicial District No. D 1329-CV-2007-01364 Gale Cooper and De Baca County News, Plaintiffs, vs. Rick Virden, Lincoln County Sheriff and Custodian of Records of the Lincoln County Sheriff; and Steven M. Sederwall, Former Lincoln County Sheriff [sic]; and Thomas T. Sullivan, former Lincoln County Sheriff and former Lincoln County Deputy Sheriff , Defendants." Taken by Mickey D. Barnett, Attorney for the Plaintiff." August 18, 2008.

Barnett, Mickey. Attorney. To Gale Cooper. (via e-mail). "FOG is in." August 22, 2008.

Virden, Rick. "Deposition for State of New Mexico County of Sandoval Thirteenth Judicial District No. D 1329-CV-2007-01364 Gale Cooper and De Baca County News, Plaintiffs, vs. Rick Virden, Lincoln County Sheriff and Custodian of Records of the Lincoln County Sheriff; and Steven M. Sederwall, Former Lincoln County Deputy Sheriff; and Thomas T. Sullivan, former Lincoln County Sheriff and former Lincoln County Deputy Sheriff, Defendants." Taken by David A. Garcia, Attorney for the Plaintiffs." August 18, 2008.

Werkmeister, Nicole. Attorney. To Attorney Mickey D. Barnett. "Re" Gale Cooper, et al, v. Rick Virden, et al. Thirteenth Judicial District Court Cause No. D1329-CV-2007-01364." September 3, 2008. (**Virden turn-over of Sheriff's Department file for Case # 2003-274 – expurgated and minus any forensic documents**)

Rogers, Patrick J. Attorney. "Docs for editing. To: Mickey Barnett; David A. Garcia." (via e-mail). Monday, September 22, 2008. (Forwarded to Gale Cooper on September 25, 2008.)

Cooper, Gale. From Attorney David Garcia. (via e-mail). "Re: FW: Docs for editing." September 25, 2008.

_____. "Subj. IPRA Case Communication for Review. To Attorneys Barnett and Garcia and Scot Stinnett." (via e-mail). September 28, 2008.

_____. To Attorney Leonard DeLayo. "Fwd: Response regarding IPRA Case." September 29, 2008.

Rogers, Patrick. Forwarded from Scot Stinnett. (via e-mail). "No Subject." September 30, 2008.

_____. "Re: Second Response To Your FOG Proposal." To Gale Cooper. (via e-mail) October 1, 2008 4:40:27 AM..

Barnett, Mickey D. Attorney. "Re: Sullivan Sederwall Depositions. To Gale Cooper." (via e-mail). October 1, 2008.

Brown, Kevin M. Attorney. "Re: Cooper v. Lincoln County, et al. No. D-1329-CV-07-1364. To Patrick J. Rogers." October 16, 2008.

Cooper, Gale. To Attorney Pat Rogers. "Re: Response documents forwarded to me by e-mail on October 20, 2008 concerning NMFOG's actions in relation to my IPRA case No. D-1329-CV-1364." October 27, 2008.

Rogers, Patrick J. Attorney. Letter of withdrawal as the FOG attorney pertaining to my IPRA case. November 10, 2008.

Cooper, Gale. "Re: My response to your letter of October 16, 2008 to Attorney Pat Rogers, and my dissociation from the referenced Foundation For Open Government communications. To Attorney Kevin Brown." November 17, 2008.

Threet, Martin E. Attorney and Attorney A. Blair Dunn." Plaintiffs' Motion for Summary Judgment. Gale Cooper and De Baca County News, a New Mexico Corporation, Plaintiffs, vs. Lincoln County and Rick Virden, Lincoln County Sheriff and Custodian of Records; and Steven M. Sederwall, Former Lincoln County Deputy Sheriff; and Thomas T. Sullivan, Former Lincoln County Sheriff and Former Lincoln County Deputy Sheriff, Defendants. No. D-1329-CV-07-1364." County of Sandoval , Thirteenth Judicial District Court. July 31, 2009.

Werkmeister, H. Nicole. Attorney. Defendant Rick Virden's Response to Plaintiff's [sic] Motion for Summary Judgment and Cross-Motion for Summary Judgment. Gale Cooper and De Baca County News, a New Mexico Corporation, Plaintiffs, vs. Lincoln County and Rick Virden, Lincoln County Sheriff and Custodian of Records; and Steven M. Sederwall, Former Lincoln County Deputy Sheriff; and Thomas T. Sullivan, Former Lincoln County Sheriff and Former Lincoln County Deputy Sheriff, Defendants. No. D-1329-CV-07-1364." County of Sandoval , Thirteenth Judicial District Court. August 29, 2009.

Brown, Kevin. Attorney. "Defendants Sederwall and Sullivan's Response to Motion for Summary Judgment. Gale Cooper and De Baca County News, a New Mexico Corporation, Plaintiffs, vs. Lincoln County and Rick Virden, Lincoln County Sheriff and Custodian of Records; and Steven M. Sederwall, Former Lincoln

County Deputy Sheriff; and Thomas T. Sullivan, Former Lincoln County Sheriff and Former Lincoln County Deputy Sheriff, Defendants. No. D-1329-CV-07-1364." County of Sandoval , Thirteenth Judicial District Court. September 2, 2009.

Threet, Martin E. Attorney and Attorney A. Blair Dunn. "Plaintiffs' Reply and Motion to Exceed Page Limit For Exhibits. Gale Cooper and De Baca County News, a New Mexico Corporation, Plaintiffs, vs. Lincoln County and Rick Virden, Lincoln County Sheriff and Custodian of Records; and Steven M. Sederwall, Former Lincoln County Deputy Sheriff; and Thomas T. Sullivan, Former Lincoln County Sheriff and Former Lincoln County Deputy Sheriff, Defendants. No. D-1329-CV-07-1364." County of Sandoval, Thirteenth Judicial District Court. September 29, 2009.

Motion for Summary Judgment Hearing. "Transcript of Proceedings. Gale Cooper and De Baca County News, a New Mexico Corporation, Plaintiffs, vs. Lincoln County and Rick Virden, Lincoln County Sheriff and Custodian of Records; and Steven M. Sederwall, Former Lincoln County Deputy Sheriff; and Thomas T. Sullivan, Former Lincoln County Sheriff and Former Lincoln County Deputy Sheriff, Defendants. No. D-1329-CV-07-1364." County of Sandoval , Thirteenth Judicial District Court. November 20, 2009. **(Motion for Summary Judgment granted)**

Eichwald, George P. Judge. "Summary Judgment. Gale Cooper and De Baca County News, a New Mexico Corporation, Plaintiffs, vs. Lincoln County and Rick Virden, Lincoln County Sheriff and Custodian of Records; and Steven M. Sederwall, Former Lincoln County Deputy Sheriff; and Thomas T. Sullivan, Former Lincoln County Sheriff and Former Lincoln County Deputy Sheriff, Defendants. No. D-1329-CV-07-1364." January, 2010.

Threet, Martin E. Attorney and Attorney A. Blair Dunn. Motion for Summary Judgment Documents. Gale Cooper and De Baca County News, a New Mexico Corporation, Plaintiffs, vs. Lincoln County and Rick Virden, Lincoln County Sheriff and Custodian of Records; and Steven M. Sederwall, Former Lincoln County Deputy Sheriff; and Thomas T. Sullivan, Former Lincoln County Sheriff and Former Lincoln County Deputy Sheriff, Defendants. No. D-1329-CV-07-1364." County of Sandoval , Thirteenth Judicial District Court. January, 2010.

ARTICLES (CHRONOLOGICAL ORDER)

Smith, Gene. "The National Police Gazette." *American Heritage Magazine.* October, 1972. Volume 23. Issue 6. **(Reference for debunking David Turk's "Report")**

Reed, Ollie. "Board approves Hubbard license." *Albuquerque Tribune.* December 4, 2002. Page 1, A1.

Virden, R.E. Lincoln County Undersheriff. Documentation letter. "I participated in the investigative reconstruction ..." April 28, 2003. (Documents his **participation in Case # 2003-274.**)

Clark, Guy C., Executive Director of New Mexico Coalition Against Gambling. " 'Dollar Bill' Richardson." *Albuquerque Journal Op-Ed.* December 16, 2002.

Janofsky, Michael. "122 Years Later, the Lawmen Are Still Chasing Billy the Kid." *The New York Times.* June 5, 2003. Vol. CLII, No. 52,505. Pages 1 and A31. **(First national announcement of Billy the Kid Case)**

No Author. "Lincoln County deputy sheriff sends his own letter to governor." *Silver City Daily Press.* June 25, 2003. Pages 1, 13.

DellaFlora, Anthony. "State Not Kidding Around: Governor won't mind if probe of the notorious 19th century N.M. outlaw boosts tourism." *Albuquerque Journal.* June 11, 2003. No. 162. Pages 1 and A1. **(First big New Mexico announcement of Billy the Kid Case)**

Bommersbach, Jana. "Digging Up Billy: If Pat Garrett didn't kill the Kid, who's buried in his grave?" *True West.* August/September 2003. Volume 50. Issue 7. P. 42-45.

Bommersbach, Jana. "From Shovels to DNA: The inside story of digging up Billy." *True West*. October/November, 2003. Volume 50. Issue 7. Pages 42-45.

Editors, W.C. Jameson, and Leon Metz. "Was Brushy Bill Really Billy the Kid? Experts face off over new evidence." *True West*. November/December, 2003.Volume 50. Issue 10. Pages 32-33.

Murphy, Mary Alice. "Billy the Kid 'Hires' a Lawyer." *Silver City Daily Press Internet Edition*.http://www.thedailypress.com/NewsFolder/11.17.2.html November 17, 2003.

Fecteau, Loie. "No Kidding: Governor Taps Lawyer For Billy." *Albuquerque Journal*. November 19, 2003. Page 1, A6.

No Author. "Lawyer Appointed to Represent Dead Outlaw." November 19, 2003. *AP*, Silver City. http://www.krqe.com/expanded.asp?RECORD_KEY[Content} = ID&ID%Content%5D

No Author. "Lawmakers Consider Posthumous Pardon for Billy the Kid." *abqtrib.com News*. November 21, 2003.

Boyle, Alan. "Billy the Kid's DNA Sparks Legal Showdown: Sheriffs and mayors face off over digging up remains from the Old West." *msnbc.com*. November 21, 2003.

Romo, Rene. "Kid's Mom May Stay Buried: Silver City wins round to block exhumation for outlaw's DNA." *Albuquerque Journal*. December 9, 2003. Section D3.

Janna Bommersbach. "Breaking Out More Shovels: Fort Sumner's Sheriff Gary Graves commits to digging up Billy the Kid's Grave." *True West*. January/February, 2004. Volume 51. Issue 1. Pages 46-47.

Benke, Richard. "N.M. Re-Opens Case of Billy the Kid." AP Associated Press. Yahoo! News. January 13, 2004.

Miller, Jay. "Digging Up the Latest on Billy the Kid." *Las Cruces Sun-News*. February 3, 2004.

Gonzales. Carolyn. "Hutton writes wild frontier stories for History Channel." *University of New Mexico Campus News*. February 16, 2004. Volume 39. No. 12.

Miller, Jay. "The Billy the Kid Code." *Las Cruces Sun-News*. March 29, 2004.

Nathanson, Rick. "Grave Doubts: 'Investigating History' series tries to clear up the mysteries surrounding Billy the Kid." *Albuquerque Journal Weekly TV Guide: Entertainer*. April 24, 2004. Pages 3, 5.

Garrett, Wm. F. "Letters to the Editor." *De Baca County News*. Page 4. May 6, 2004.

Murphy, Mary Alice and Melissa St. Aude. "Sederwall, Sullivan uninvited to ball." *Silver City Daily Press Internet Edition*. June 10, 2004.

Hill, Levi. "Billy the Kid Stirring Up Dust in Silver City." *Las Cruces Sun-News*. June 12, 2004. Section 5A. Pages 1, A2.

No Author. "Attorney Refuses Judge's statements concerning exhumation." *thedailypress.com*. June 15, 2004. (**Attorney Tippett misrepresents OMI**)

Richardson, Bill. "Verbatim: I have to decide whether to pardon him. But not right away – after the investigation, after the state gets more publicity." *Time*. June 21, 2004. Vol. 163. No. 25. Page 17.

Romo, Rene. "Back off on Billy, Gov. Asked: Silver City says inquiry into death of Kid would harm state tourism. *Albuquerque Journal*. June 23, 2004. Section B-1, B-5.

No Author. "Lincoln county deputy sheriff sends his own letter to governor." *Silver City Daily Press*. June 25, 2004. Pages 1, 13. (**Letter from Steve Sederwall**)

No Author. "Editorials: New Racing Schedule Tramples Horseman." *Albuquerque Journal*. June 26, 2004.

Miller, Jay. "Inside the Capitol. Bizarre case of Billy the Kid." *Roswell Daily Record*. July 2, 2004. Page A4.

Romo, Rene. "Forensic Expert on Billy's Case: Questions Remain on Outlaw's Fate." *Albuquerque Journal*. August 2, 2004. Page 1.

No Author. "Forensic expert joins Billy the Kid inquiry in New Mexico." *AP SignOnSanDiego.com*. August 2, 2004.

Miller, Jay. "Inside the Capitol. Sheriffs slippery on Billy the Kid Case." *Roswell Daily Record*. August 9, 2004. Page A4.

Cherry, Doris. "Forensics 101 for 'Billy'." *Lincoln County News*. August 12, 2004. Pages 2, 10.

Miller, Jay. "Inside the Capitol. Expert questions Kid probe." *Roswell Daily Record*. August 20, 2004. Page A4.

_____. "Inside the Capitol. Hat dance on probe funding." *Roswell Daily Record*. September 1, 2004.Page A4.

_____. "Inside the Capitol. Three sheriffs push Kid Case." *Roswell Daily Record*. September 5, 2004. Page A4.

_____. "Inside the Capitol. Sheriffs hoax is world-class." *Roswell Daily Record*. September 8, 2004. Page A4.

_____. "Inside the Capitol. Kid gets day in court Sept. 27." *Roswell Daily Record*. September 12, 2004. Page A4.

_____. "Inside the Capitol. Kid probe making us think." *Roswell Daily Record*. September 13, 2004. Page A4.

Stinnett, Scot. "De Baca County Citizens' Committee Files Petition for Recall of Sheriff Gary Graves." *De Baca County News*. September 14, 2004.

Miller, Jay. "Inside the Capitol. Who is Attorney Bill Robins?" *Roswell Daily Record*. September 15, 2004. Page A4.

Green, Keith. "Mountain Asides: Billy's restless bones are stirred up once again. *RuidosoNews.com*. September 16, 2004.

Miller, Jay. "Inside the Capitol. Kid Case: David fights Goliath." *Roswell Daily Record*. September 17, 2004. Page A4.

_____. "Inside the Capitol. Many reasons to dig up Kid." *Roswell Daily Record*. September 19, 2004. Page A4.

_____. "Inside the Capitol. Nothing to worry about." *Roswell Daily Record*. September 20, 2004. Page A4.

Stallings, Dianne. "Showdown in the County Seat." *RuidosoNews.com* September 21, 2004. (**Commissioner Leo Martinez's meeting**)

Miller, Jay. "Inside the Capitol. Who speaks for Pat Garrett?" *Roswell Daily Record*. September 22, 2004. Page A4.

Stallings, Dianne. "Showdown in the County Seat: shouting match erupts at County Commissioners meeting Tuesday over investigation of Billy the Kid." *Ruidoso News*. September 22, 2004.

Cherry, Doris. "Lincoln County 'War' Heats Up Over 'Billy: Capitan Mayor Tracks His Kind of '---' To County Commission Meeting. Tells Jay Miller where to go: wonders why commissioner has his panties in a wad." *Lincoln County News*. September 23, 2003. Vol. 99. No. 38. Pages 1-3.

Miller, Jay. "Inside the Capitol. Is there a new Santa Fe Ring?" *Roswell Daily Record*. September 24, 2004. Page A4.

Stinnett, Scott. "Rest in Peace, Billy! Exhumation case dismissed." *De Baca County News*. September 30, 2004. Vol. 104. No. 2. Pages 1, 5, 6.

Miller, Jay. "Inside the Capitol. Fort Sumner celebrates win." *Roswell Daily Record*. October 1, 2004. Page A4.

Jana Bommersbach. "Kid Exhumation Nixed: Billy and his mom to rest in peace. *True West*. January/February 2005. Volume 52. Issue 1. Pages 68-69.

Massey, Barry. "Casinos, contracting lawyers fund Madrid." The New Mexican. http://www.freenewmexican.com/news/13746.html May 14, 2005.

Roosevelt, Margot. "Bill Richardson: The Presidential Contender." *Time*. August 22, 2005. Vol. 166. No. 8. Page 50. (**Identifying him as likely leak in Wen Ho Lee case**)

Stinnett, Scott. "Judge rules Graves recall can proceed: Parker finds probable cause after two-day hearing." *De Baca County News*. August 25, 2005. Vol. 104. No. 49. Pages 1, 4, 10. (**The Recall Hearing of Sheriff Gary Graves**)

_____. "Testimony paints Graves as 'above the law': Recall probable cause hearing emotional, contentious." *De Baca County News*. September 1, 2005. Vol. 104. No. 50. Pages 1, 5, 6, 8, 9, 10.

Auslander, Jason. "N.M. state treasurers indicted in kickback scheme, thousands taken." *New Mexican*. September 16, 2005.

Carter, Julie. "Follow the Blood: In the Billy the Kid Case, Miller Exhumed." *RuidosoNews.com*. October 6, 2005.

Sullivan, Tom. "Letters: Your Opinion." *RuidosoNews.com*. October 21, 2005. (**Sullivan letter to the editor: "Why are they so afraid of the truth?"**)

Carter, Julie. "Billy the Kid in Prescott? *New Mexico Stockman*. November, 2005. Pages 38, 39, 76.

Romo, Rene. "Billy the Kid Probe May Yield New Twist. *Albuquerque Journal*. *ABQ Journal.com*. November 6, 2005.

No Author. "after a big fundraiser by his pal, casino owner. R.D. Hubbard..." "The Journal Op-ed Page." *Albuquerque Journal*. December 12, 2005.

Struckman, Robert. "Bitterroot man hopes to uncover truth about Billy the Kid." (Misshttp://www.helenair.com/articles/2006/03/13/montana/a05031306_01.txt (Missoulian) March 13, 2006.

Dodder, Joanna. "Officials could face charges for digging up alleged Billy the Kid." *The Daily Courier of Prescott Arizona*. April 12, 2006.

Banks, Leo W. "The New Billy the Kid? The mad search for the bones of an American outlaw icon has come to Arizona." *Tucson Weekly*. http://www.tucsonweekly.com/gbase/Currents/Content?oid=oid:81013 April 13, 2006.

Carter, Julie. "Digging up bones, Arizona may protest Miller exhumation." jcarter@tularosa.net. April 19, 2006.

Carter, Julie. "Culture Shock: The cowboys and the Kid go to France." jcarter@tulerosa.net. May 5, 2006.

Shafer, Mark. "N.M. pair may face charges in grave case." May 13, 2006. markshafer @ArizonaRepublic.com. http://www.azcentral.com/arizonarepublic/local/articles/0513billythekid0513.html

Myers, Amanda Lee. "New Mexicans Dig Up Trouble in Arizona." *Albuquerque Journal, New Mexico and the West*. May 14, 2006. Page B4. (**Appeared in gulfnews.com**)

_____. "Billy the Kid Still 'Wanted.' " May 16, 2006. gulfnews.com. http://archive.gulfnews.com/articles/06/05/16/10040234.html.

No author. "Festival de Cannes, May 17-28, 2006. Requiem for Billy the Kid." http://www.festival-cannes.fr/films/fiche_film.php?langue=4355535. (**Cannes Film Festival synopsis**)

McCarthy, Todd. "Requiem for Billy the Kid." May 21, 2006. Variety.com. http://www.variety.com/review/VE1117930570?categoryid=2220&cs=1&nid=2562.

McCoy, Dave. "L 'Ouest Américain." May 25, 2006. MSN Movies. http://movies.msn.com/movies/canneso6/dispatch8.

Bennett, Ray. "Requiem for Billy the Kid." TheHollywoodReporter.com. May 26, 2006. (**Best demonstration of the hoax damage to history**)

Smith, Emily C. "What an honor for two of New Mexico's finest citizens ...." Letter to the Editor. June 2, 2006. *RuidosoNews.com*. http://ruidosonews.com/apps/pbcs.dll/article?AID=/20060602/OPINION03/6060203 42/101 (**Advertising the hoaxers as heroes**)

_____. "The cowboys are back in town, film in six months." jcarter@tulerosa.net. June 9, 2006.

Valdez, Jannay. "Digging Up the Truth About Billy." *RuidosoNews.com*. http://ruidosonews.com/apps/pbcs.dll./article?AID=/2006069/OPINION03/6060903 51/101... June 9, 2006.

Dodder, Joanna. "Back at Rest: Bones of Billy the Kid return to Prescott." *The Daily Courier*. July 9, 2006. http://prescottdailycourier.com/print.asp?ArticleID=40353&Section ID=1&SubSectionID=1

Daniels, Bruce. "O Fair New Mexico." July 14, 2006. ABQNewsSeeker (from ABQjournal.com).http://www.adqjournal.com/abqnews/index.php?option=com_cont ent&task=view d=117...

No Author. AP. "PRESCOTT, Ariz. - Prosecutors won't seek charges against two men who exhumed the remains of a man who claimed to be the outlaw Billy the Kid." AOL News. October 23, 2006.

_____. AP. "Billy the Kid Case Dropped." *Albuquerque Journal. Metro.* D3. October 24, 2006.

_____. AP. "Men Who Exhumed Billy the Kid Won't Be Charged." October 24, 2006. *New York Sun.* http://www.nysun.com/article/42176.

_____. AP. "Arizona: No Charges Sought for Exhuming Remains." *New York Times.* A-26. October 24, 2006. http://www.nytimes.com/2006/10/24/us/24brfs-002.html?r=1&oref=slogin.

No Author. Forged Check Article with check photo. *Ruidoso News.* November 25, 2006. Page 1.

Cameron, Carl. "New Mexico Gov. Bill Richardson says He's Running for President in 2008." FoxNews.com. December 7, 2006.

Martínez, Tony and Alison. "Better Days Ahead for New Mexico Highlands University?" *The Hispanic Outlook in Higher Education.* December 4, 2006.

Goddard, Terry. "Guest Opinion: Public officials not above law. *Arizona Star.* January 5, 2007.

Geissler, Jeff. "Richardson to explore presidential bid. New Mexico Democrat hopes to become nation's first Hispanic president. AP. January 19, 2007.

Turk, David S. "Billy the Kid and the U.S. Marshals Service." *Wild West.* February 2007. Volume 19. Number 5. Pages 34 – 41. **(Link of David Turk and Probable Cause Statement)**

Cole, Thomas J. "Govzilla 24/7: As Governor, Bill Richardson Has Pushed an Aggressive Agenda and is Wildly Popular - But Critics Grumble That He's a Power-hungry, Self-aggrandizing Bully." *The Sunday Journal (Albuquerque Journal).* February 11, 2007. No. 42. Pages A1, A10-A14.

Crowley, Candy. "Richardson Pitch: Regular guy with extraordinary résumé." CNN Washington Bureau. March 14, 2007.

Jason Strykowski. "A Tale of Two Governors ... And one Kid." *True West.* May, 2007. Vol. 54. Issue 5. Page 64.

_____. AP. "Billy the Kid Exhumation a Possibility." *Roswell Daily Record.* May 2, 2007.

Carter, Julie. "Brushy Bill targeted for DNA testing; Billy the Kid workbench goes on display." *Ruidoso News.* May 3, 2007.

_____. AP. "Manhunt for Real Billy the Kid Goes On: Deputy hopes DNA will finally reveal outlaw's true identity." *Albuquerque Journal.* May 4, 2007. B3.

Zorosec, Thomas. "DNA could solve mystery of Billy the Kid." Chron.com - Houston Chronicle. May 5, 2007.

Carter, Julie. AP. "Texas town denies request to exhume Billy the Kid claimant." *Houston Chronicle.* May 11, 2007.

_____. "Evidence Hidden in Spector Trial." BBC Internet News. May 24, 2007. **(Dr. Henry Lee alleged as destroying evidence)**

_____. AP. "Famed experts credibility takes a hit at Spector trial." CNN.com law center. May 25, 2007. **(Dr. Henry Lee allegedly destroyed evidence)**

Barry, John. "Lax and Lazy at Los Alamos: Officials at nuclear weapons laboratory, already struggling to calm concerns over security lapses, now have two more breaches to explain." newsweek.com. June 25, 2007.

Cole, Thomas J. "Tycoon Backs Gov. All the Way: Hobbs businessman has helped raise millions, but he's had his share of controversy." *Albuquerque Journal.* July 8, 2007. No. 189. A1, A7, A8.

Turk, David S. "Billy the Kid and the U.S. Marshals Service." *Wild West.* February, 2007. Vol. 19. No. 5. pp. 34-39.

Cole, Thomas J. "Cope Makes Most of His Millions in Oil, Gas." *Albuquerque Journal.* July 8, 2007.

Nagourney, Adam and Jeff Zeleny. "First a Tense Talk With Clinton, Then Richardson Backs Obama." NYTIMES.com. March 22, 2008.

Weisman, Jonathan. "A Coveted Endorsement. Richardson Throws Support to Obama." Washingtompost.com. March 22, 2008.

Stallings, Dianne. "Billy the Kid case straps county for insurance." *RuidosoNews.com.* August 13, 2008.

Carter, Julie. "Lincoln County deputies resign commissions for Kid case." *Ruidosonews.com.* August 16, 2007. **(Sederwall quote that case was both public and private at the same time!)**

Romo, Rene. "Seeking the Kid, Minus Badges. Deputies Resign to Hunt for Billy." *Albuquerque Journal.* August 18, 2007. No. 230. pp. 1-2.

Brunt, Charles D. "Suit Targets Investigation Into Billy the Kid's Death. *Albuquerque Journal.* August 28, 2008. **(FOG joins as parallel Virden et al IPRA case)**

Concerned Citizens of Lincoln County. "Should Lincoln County Have Grave Concerns Over A Person Like Steve Sederwall Running for Sheriff? *Lincoln County News.* October 16, 2008. p. 6.

Braun, Martin Z. and William Selway. "Grand Jury Probes Richardson Donor's New Mexico Financing Fee." bloombergnews.com. December 15, 2008.

Dunn, Geoffrey. "Richardson's Lies Have Finally Caught Up With Him." December 15, 2008. huffingtonpost.com. December 15, 2008.

Pickler, Nedra. "Richardson withdraws bid to be commerce secretary." breitbart.com. January 4, 2009.

No Author. "Bill Richardson bows out of commerce secretary job." CNN.com. January 4, 2009.

No Author. "Bill Richardson Withdraws Nomination as Commerce Secretary." FOXNews.com. January 4, 2009.

Ridgeway, James. "Why Did Obama's Transition Team Ignore Bill Richardson's Long History of Dubious Dealings?" motherjones.com. January 4, 2009.

Stephanopolous, George. "George's Bottom Line: Impossible for Obama to Keep Richardson." abcnews.com. January 4, 2009.

Pickler, Nedra. "Richardson withdrawals name. 'Pay-to-play' probe won't be completed by Cabinet hearings." *Albuquerque Journal.* January 5, 2008. No. 5. p. 3B.

Auslander, Jason. "Police work to dispel hit-run rumors." sfnewmexican.com. January 9, 2009. **(Rumor of Richardson fleeing crime scene)**

Sher, Lauren and Susan Aasen. "Whistleblower in Blago Case: Corruption 'Never Ceased to Amaze Me.' " abcNews.go.com. January 9, 2009.

Dendahl, John. "Exclusive: Leaving Emperor Bill's Realm - Years of Buyer's Remorse Lie Ahead." January 12, 2009. familysecuritymatters.org. (Also printed as Dendahl, John (Former gubernatorial candidate). "Leaving Emperor Bill's realm - and the corruption of New Mexico. January 15, 2009. *Ruidosonews.com.*)

Lowy, Joan. "69 computers missing from nuclear weapons lab: 69 computers missing from Los Alamos nuclear weapons lab, including 13 stolen last year." newsweek.com. February 11, 2009.

Barr, Andy. "Bill Richardson Tarnished by Scandal." Politico.com. February 9, 2009.

ACKNOWLEDGMENTS

This roster of appreciation also includes some contributing sources from my Billy Bonney novel, *Joy of the Birds*, and my non-fictions: *MegaHoax: The Strange Plot to Exhume Billy the Kid and Become President* and *Billy the Kid's Writings, Words, and Wit*. Responsibility for errors is my own. Overriding is my appreciation of William Bonney himself, whose cause, courage, brilliance, and joie de vivre are my inspiration.

Historical bedrock came from books by Frederick Nolan on Billy the Kid, the Lincoln County War, and John Henry Tunstall. As valuable was Leon Metz's Pat Garrett biography and Jerry Weddle's book on Billy Bonney's adolescence.

National Archive specialists were Clarence Lyons, Wayne DeCesar, and Fred Romanski at the Civilian Records Branch; Dr. Milt Gustafson at the Civilian Records Branch Classification; Janice Wiggins at the Justice Department; Joseph Schwarz at the Department of Interior; Michael Sampson at the Secret Service Library Counterfeit Division; and Mike Meir at the Department of War, Old Military and Civil Branch.

Libraries and archivists assisting were the Las Cruces, New Mexico State University Library's Archives and Special Collection's Herman Weisner Collection with processing archivist Charles Stanford; the University of New Mexico Library's Southwestern Collections' Catron Papers; the Roswell, Chavez County Historical Center for Southeast New Mexico with curator Elvis Flemming; Midland, Texas Nita Stewart Haley Memorial Library with archivist Jim Bradshaw; the Santa Fe, New Mexico Fray Angélico Chávez Historical Library with archivist Tomas Jaehn; the Canyon, Texas Panhandle-Plains Historical Museum with archivist Warren Stricker; Ken Earle from the State of New Mexico Office of Cultural Affairs Historic Preservation Division; past New Mexico State Historian Estevan Rael-Galvez and current State Historian Rick Hendricks at the Office of the New Mexico State Historian; Susan Berry of the Silver City Museum and Library; and President Rutherford B. Hayes's Memorial Library in Fremont, Ohio with curator Nan Card.

Specific to collections with William Bonney's writings were the Indiana Historical Society's Lew Wallace Collection in Indianapolis with Doug Clanin, retired Chief Editor of the Lew Wallace Collections; Paul Brockman, Director of Manuscript and Visual Collections; Suzanne Hahn, Director of Reference Services; Susan Sutton, Coordinator Visual Reference Services; Susan Rogers, Paper Conservator; David Turk, technical photographer; and Steve Haller, Senior Director Collections and Library.

Spencerian penmanship was discussed with Mott Media; David Sull; and the Iowa, Ames Historical Society's curators, Dennis Wendell and Sarah Vouthilak.

Antique New Mexico newspaper archivists and experts who assisted were New Mexico Highland University's Cathleen Kroll for the Las Vegas *Daily Optic* and Las Vegas *Gazette*; Dennis Daily and Austin Hoover of the Rio Grande Historical Collections at the New Mexico State University Library at Las Cruces; Marilyn Fletcher at the Center For Southwestern Research at the University of New Mexico Library in Albuquerque; Jim Bowers of the *New Mexico Optic*; and Michael E. Pitel, retired Heritage Tourism Development Program Officer for the New Mexico Tourism Department and current President of TravelSource New Mexico.

For the pretender believers and modern Billy the Kid Case hoaxers, thanks for the laughs.

For my secret "team" helping to fight the Billy the Kid Case hoax, I appreciate your dedication to truth, and I honor my promise to keep requested names confidential. Special thanks goes to brave journalist, Jay Miller, reporting in his "Inside the Capitol;" and to my attorneys willing to fight Santa Fe Ring-style corruption in modern courts.

Computer graphics were done by Bobbi Jo MacElroy and Samantha Morris.

Encouragement for my writings came from my mother, Dr. Rose Cooper and her sister, Attorney Ann Kaplan.

INDEX

149, 159-164, 166-168, 170, 179, 187-188, 197-198, 204, 216, 218-222, 225, 233, 235, 237, 239-240, 242, 246-247, 251-252, 259, 262-263; **Billy the Kid**: 3, 5-6, 9-11, 28, 34, 37, 47, 50-51, 55-59, 61-62, 64, 66-69, 73-74, 81-82, 84, 88, 91-94, 96-97, 102-105, 109, 112, 114-116, 122-124, 126-139, 142-143, 147-154, 156-158, 161-180, 183-188, 197-204, 209-210, 215-216, 222, 225-227, 238-239, 242, 246, 249-253, 255-256, 258-262, 265-269; **history**: 9-34; **speaking for self**: 37-49; **deposition to Frank Warner Angel**: 19, 38, 41-45, 73-74, 76-77, 99, 108, 190; **Hoyt bill of sale**: 23, 38, 41, 75, 83; **Billy-Dolan peace meeting**: 23; **pardon deal by Lew Wallace**: 9, 24-25, 27, 29, 38, 40, 45, 49, 75, 77, 79, 119-120, 182, 184-185; **sham arrest and sham escape**: 24, 26, 40, 75, 109, 121, 191, 217; **Lew Wallace interview**: 75; **1879 Grand Jury testimony**: 24-25, 27, 38, 78, 182, 191, 216-217; **lost testimony transcript**: 49-50; **Dudley Court of Inquiry testimony**: 45-49, 74, 77-78, 92, 120; **pardon deal by Secret Service**: 79-80; **letters of**: 28-29, 38-40, 74-75, 92, 109, 115, 182; **reward for capture and killing**: 24, 28, 64, 110, 119, 179, 182-184, 225, 233, 243; **newspaper interviews**: 75-76; **Coroner's Jury Report**: 74, 76, 111-112, 179, 184, 198, 222, 232, 234-236, 242, 244; Spanish version: 112; English translation: 232-233; **tintype of**: 38, 74, 76, 94-95, 98, 103, 126, 128-129, 193, 199, 206; **butcher knife holding**: 32,

155, 231; **exhumation attempt 1961-1962**: 252; **vigil for corpse (see carpenter's shop vigil)**
Booth, John Wilkes - 63, 267
Bosque Grande - 23, 98
Bosque Redondo - 14
Bowdre, Charles "Charlie" - 12, 14, 18-19, 22, 26, 28-29, 33, 102, 109, 121, 162, 199, 218-219, 263; **exhumation attempts by modern hoaxers**: 132-136, 166-175, 185, 187, 197, 247-248; APPENDIX: 2 - 251-269
Bowdre, Manuela - 22, 162, 199
Bowlin, Joe - 93, 242
Bowlin, Marlyn - 242
Boykin, Syd - 150
Brady, Nadine - 150-151
Brady, William - 16-20, 23, 25, 29, 44, 58, 80, 94-96, 99-100, 106-108, 111, 118, 120-121, 140, 150, 170, 181, 183, 190-191, 200, 214, 259
Brewer, Richard "Dick" - 18-19, 42-45, 82, 107-108, 118
Briscoe, Joe - 13
Bristol, Warren - 17, 25, 29-30, 117, 140
British Ambassador - 19
Brown, Henry - 29, 43, 121
"Brushy Bill" Roberts - (see Oliver P. Roberts)
Buckboard Days - 82
Buffalo Bill Cody's Wild West Show - 92, 124
Buffalo Gap, Texas - 97, 114, 116, 188
burning building (see McSween house)
Burns, Walter Noble – 73, 87, 92, 126, 216
butcher knife (see William H. Bonney)
Cahill, Frank "Windy" - 13, 18-19, 31, 98, 116, 139, 189
Campbell, Billy - 23-25, 40, 49, 109, 182, 217

CPSIA information can be obtained at www.ICGtesting.com
Printed in the USA
BVOW08s1030190416

444756BV00001B/50/P